Every Wrong Direction

Every Wrong Direction

•••••••••••••••••••••••••

An Emigré's Memoir

DAN BURT

Rutgers University Press

New Brunswick, Camden, and Newark, New Jersey

Library of Congress Cataloging-in-Publication Data

Names: Burt, Dan M., 1942– author.
Title: Every wrong direction : an emigré's memoir / Dan Burt.
Description: New Brunswick : Rutgers University Press, [2022] | Includes bibliographical
references and index.
Identifiers: LCCN 2022009351 | ISBN 9781978830141 (cloth) | ISBN 9781978830158 (epub) |
ISBN 9781978830165 (pdf)
Subjects: LCSH: Burt, Dan M., 1942– | Poets, English—21st century—Biography. | South
Philadelphia (Philadelphia, Pa.)—Biography. | Americans—Great Britain—Biography. |
United States—Social conditions—20th century.
Classification: LCC PR6102.U778 Z46 2022 | DDC 821/.92 [B]—dc23/eng/20220425LC
record available at https://lccn.loc.gov/2022009351

∞ The paper used in this publication meets the requirements of the American National Standard for Information Sciences—Permanence of Paper for Printed Library Materials, ANSI
Z39.48-1992.

www.rutgersuniversitypress.org

Manufactured in the United States of America

To my daughter, Hannah

Contents

Author's Note

At twelve, I took a first step outside my ancestral streets in Philadelphia's poorer neighborhoods to work as a butcher boy in a North Jersey farmer's market. Ten years later, I left those streets for Cambridge, England, and three decades later, quit America for good. This is my recollection of that span, the childhood, youth, and labors that made me an emigré.

The stories in this book are true, every one of them, as best I remember them. All persons are, or were, actual individuals and businesses and not composites. No lilies have been gilded. Only some names and identifying details have been changed to protect their privacy.

Every Wrong Direction

He's a poet, he's a picker,
He's a prophet, he's a pusher,
He's a pilgrim and a preacher and a problem when he's stoned,
He's a walkin' contradiction, partly truth and partly fiction,
Takin' every wrong direction on his lonely way back home.
—Kris Kristofferson, *The Pilgrim*

Part I

Certain Windows

● ● ● ● ● ● ● ● ● ● ● ●

THE SPUR
You think it horrible that lust and rage
Should dance attention upon my old age;
They were not such a plague when I was
    young;
What else have I to spur me into song?[1]

W. B. YEATS, *New Poems*

We trail no clouds of glory when we come. We trail blood, a cord that must be cut, and a postpartum mess, which mixes with places, people, and stories to frame the house of childhood. We dwell in that house forever.

In time, there will be others, bigger, smaller, better, worse. But how we see the world, how much shelter, warmth, food we think we need, whether the outer dark appears benign or deadly, depends on what we saw from

---

[1] All lines and poems quoted can be found online at poetryfoundation.org, poemhunter .com, and poetrynook.com, as well as otherline poetry sources.

certain windows in that house. We may burn, rebuild, repaint, or raze it, but its memories fade least; as dementia settles in, first things are the last to go.

Childhood ended when I turned twelve and began working in a butcher shop on Fridays after school till midnight and all day Saturdays from 7 a.m. to 6 p.m. or, as we said in winter, "from can't see to can't see"—dark when you go to work, dark when you leave. By sixteen, I was working thirty hours a week or more during the school year, fifty to sixty hours in the summers. "Certain Windows" recalls my world before I left to study at Cambridge: places, people, and tales from childhood and youth.

1. Ancestral Houses
Fourth and Daly

Joe Burt, my father, was born in Boston in 1916, almost nine months to the day after his mother landed there from a shtetl near Kiev. She brought with her Eva, her firstborn, and Bernie, her second. Presumably my grandfather Louis, whom we called Zaida ("ai" as in "pay") or Pop, was pleased to see my grandmother Rose, or Mom, even though she was generally regarded as a *chaleria* (shrew).

Zaida had been dragooned into the Russian army a little before the outbreak of World War I. Russia levied a quota of Jewish men for the army from each shtetl, and these men invariably came from the poorest *shtetla-chim* (shtetl dwellers). Zaida deserted at the earliest opportunity (which was certainly not unusual), made his way to Boston, and sent for Mom.

Mom and Pop moved the family in 1917 to a small row (terraced) house at Fourth and Daly in South Philadelphia, the neighborhood where my father grew up, worked, and married. Pop was a carpenter, Mom a seamstress, both socialists at least, if not Communists. Mom was an organizer for the International Ladies' Garment Workers' Union (ILGWU), which seems in character. Yiddish was the household tongue, my father's first, though Pop spoke and read Russian and English fluently. Mom managed Russian well, but English took more effort.

The family's daily newspaper was *Forverts* (Forward), printed in Yiddish. *Forverts* published lists of those killed in pogroms when they occurred. Ukrainian Cossacks allied themselves with the Bolsheviks and used the Russian civil war as an excuse to continue the pogroms that had been a fact of Jewish life in the Pale from the 1880s. Pop was hanging from a trolley car strap on his way home from work in 1920 when he read the names of his family among the dead, all eighteen of them: father, mother, sisters, brothers, their children. He had become an orphan. He never went to *schul* (synagogue) again.

A few years later, he learned how they were killed when some of Mom's family, who had hidden during the raid, emigrated to America. I heard the story from him when I was ten, at Christmas 1952. I came home singing "Silent Night," newly learned in my local public elementary school. I couldn't stop singing it and went caroling up the back steps from the alley into our kitchen, where Pop—putty colored, in his midsixties, and dying of cancer—was making what turned out to be his last visit. Zaida had cause to dislike gentile sacred songs, though I didn't know it. He croaked, *Danila, shah stil (Danny, shut up!)*, and I answered, "No, why should I?" His face flushed with all the life left in him, and he grabbed me by the neck and started choking me. My father pulled him off, pinioned his arms, and when his rage had passed, led me to the kitchen table where Zaida sat at the head and told me this story:

The Jews had warning of a raid. Zaida's father, my great-grandfather, was pious and reputed to be a *melamed*, a learned though poor Orthodox Jew. As such, he was prized and protected by the community. Pop's in-laws urged him to take his family and hide with them in their shelter below the street. Great-grandfather refused. He said, so I was told, *God will protect us*.

The Cossacks rousted them from their house and forced everyone to strip. They raped the women while the men watched. Done, they shot the women, then the children, and, last, the men. They murdered all eighteen of them, my every paternal forebear excepting Pop, who went on to die an atheist, as did my father.

* * *

My grandparents' house at Fourth and Daly was a three-up, three-down house in a very narrow street. Cars were parked on the side of the street opposite their house, leaving just enough room for a small car to pass. Big-finned 1950s Caddies, had anyone owned one, would have had to straddle the pavement to get through. The front door stood two feet from the side-walk at the top of three marble steps, with dips worn in their middle from eighty years of footsteps and repeated scrubbings. It opened onto a minus-cule vestibule off a living room, after which came dining room and kitchen, all three no more than twelve by fourteen feet. There was a four-foot-wide wooden stoop past the back door, two steps above a small concrete yard where clothes hung out to dry and children could play. A six-foot-high wooden fence enclosed the yard.

Nothing hung on the walls: there were no bookcases, no books. There was no Victrola record player. But there was a large console three-band radio, which could receive shortwave broadcasts from Europe. The house was always spotless, sparsely furnished, lifeless. Two low rectangles projected from either party wall to separate the living from dining room; on each end of these little walls stood two decorative white wooden Doric columns pretending to hold the ceiling up and give a touch of class to what was in fact a clean brick shotgun shack.

We did not visit Fourth and Daly frequently. My mother was never keen to go, perhaps because she learned too little Yiddish after she married my father to make conversation easily or perhaps because Mom had refused to speak to her until after I was born. (My maternal grandmother had been Italian; hence my mother was a gentile according to Jewish law.) But while Zaida was alive, we always went for seder dinner on the first night of Pesach (Passover), the Jewish holiday commemorating the Exodus from Egypt. That tale had some heft when I was old enough to grasp it, a few years after the fall of Nazi Germany.

A year or two before Zaida died, my brother and I, aged six and eight, were dropped off at the house early on Passover, to watch him and Mom prepare the Passover meal. Boredom soon set in, and Zaida led us out to the back stoop, where he produced two blocks of grainy pine and proceeded to carve two dreidels, the square-sided spinning top that Jewish children have played with for centuries. With a hard pencil, he inscribed a letter in Hebrew on each of the dreidel's four faces—the traditional *shin*, *gimmel*, *hay*, and *nun*—and explained how each letter determined the player's fate once the dreidel was spun. If the dreidel came to rest with the *shin* side uppermost, the spinner had to put in the pot all the nuts, pennies, and so on they were playing with; if the topside letter was *gimmel*, they took all the counters in the pot; if on *hay*, half; and if on *nun*, zero. Then he counted twenty hazelnuts apiece into our hands and set us gambling on the stoop while he went inside to help Mom.

Three things always happened at the Passover dinner. Someone spilled the wine on Mom's white-lace tablecloth, producing a scramble for cold water and lemon juice; there was a fight during which Zaida had to restrain my father; and Zaida lingered over the wicked son's role in answering the Four

The dreidel Pop carved for Danny seventy years ago

Questions. The Questions are the raison d'être for the seder, a religious service-cum-dinner to celebrate and teach the story of the Jews' deliverance from Egypt. Shortly after the service begins, the youngest boy must ask, *Why is this night different from all others?* and the leader of the seder will retell the story of the Exodus, the repeated experience of our wandering tribe's history.

Though Zaida wasn't a believer, he was an ethnic realist who wanted his grandchildren to understand that Jewish blood is a perfume that attracts murderers, a pheromone no soap can wash away. So he dwelt on the role of the second son, the wicked one, who asks, *What does this service mean to you?* implying that he is different, that he can be what he wants, that the seder and his blood's history mean nothing to him. The answer ordained for this son is *It is because of what the Lord did for me, not for you*—meaning, had you been there, you'd have been left to be killed.

Today, the dreidel Zaida made for me lies on my desk in Cambridge, as it has lain on other desks in other cities, other countries, down the years. I don't know what happened to the one he made for my brother, who was cremated, a Christian, in San Francisco in 2005.

* * *

At Fourth and Daly, my father—Joe everywhere else—was always Yossela, Joey. He was a thin, short man, five feet five, with intense blue eyes, dark skin, and thick black hair. He could have passed for an Argentinian tango dancer or a Mafia hit man; perhaps the latter image had attracted my mother to him. Broad thick shoulders, large hands, and well-muscled legs perfectly suited the featherweight semipro boxer he became.

Lust and rage beset his every age until he died in 1995. His fists rose at the slightest provocation against all comers and sometimes against me. Bullies and every form of authority were his favored targets. A local teenager who had been tormenting him when he was ten was struck from behind with a lead pipe one winter night. When he came to in the hospital several hours and sixteen stitches later, he could recall only that he was passing the Borts' house when something hit him. He gave little Joey no more trouble.

Joe hated bullies all his life. One Sunday driving home from the store, he saw two bigger boys beating a smaller boy beside the SKF ball bearing factory. He hit the brakes, leapt out, and knocked down both older boys, then waited till the victim took off.

The Depression scarred him. He was twelve when it began. There was little work for carpenters, and for a time, Yossela stood on a street corner hawking apples with Zaida. But the family needed more money, so at thirteen, he left school without completing eighth grade and found work in a butcher shop on Fourth Street, a mile north of Fourth and Daly. His older sister and both brothers, older and younger, all finished high school. My father regretted his lack of formal education, because he thought it denied him the chance to make more money.

Yossela spent part of his first paycheck on a new pair of shoes. Zaida beat him when he turned over that first week's earnings minus the cost of the shoes. The legend was that his father's belt struck him so hard, there were bloodstains from his ass on the ceiling.

Jewish boys undergo two rituals: circumcision at birth, about which they remember nothing, and at thirteen, Bar Mitzvah, when they are called on a Saturday morning to read a passage from the Torah before the congregation as part of a rite admitting them to Jewish manhood. A celebration follows, however small, for family and friends. My father left *schul* immediately after his Bar Mitzvah, changed his clothes, and went straight to work, Saturday being the busiest business day of the retail week.

Ninth and Race

Prostitution, gambling, fencing, contract murder, loan-sharking, political corruption, and crime of every sort were the daily trade in Philadelphia's Tenderloin, the oldest part of town. The Kevitch family ruled this stew for half a century, from Prohibition to the rise of Atlantic City. My mother was a Kevitch.

Not all Jewish boys become doctors, lawyers, violinists, and Nobelists; some sons of immigrants from the Pale became criminals, often as part of or in cahoots with Italian crime families. A recent history calls them "tough Jews": men like Meyer Lansky and Bugsy Siegel, who organized and ran Murder Incorporated for Lucky Luciano in the '20s and '30s, and Arnold Rothstein, better known as Meyer Wolfsheim in *The Great Gatsby*, who fixed the 1919 baseball World Series. The Kevitch family were tough Jews.

Their headquarters during the day was Milt's Bar and Grill at Ninth and Race, the heart of the Tenderloin, two miles north of Fourth and Daly. At night, one or more male clan members supervised the family's "after-hours club" a few blocks away. We called Milt's Bar "the Taproom" and the after-hours club "the Club."

The Taproom stood alone between two vacant lots carpeted with broken bricks and brown beer-bottle shards. Bums, beggars, prostitutes, and stray cats and dogs populated the surrounding streets; the smell of cat and human piss was always detectable, mixed with smoke from cigarette and cigar butts smoldering on the pavement. Milt's was a rectangular two-story building, sixty feet long and eighteen feet wide. It fronted on the cobbles of Ninth Street and, through the back door, onto a cobbled alley. Both front and back doors were steel; the back door was never locked. The front window was a glass block, set in the Taproom's brown-brick facade like a glass eye in an old soldier's face. It could stop a fairly large caliber bullet, and the wan light filtering through it brightened only the first few feet of the bar, the rest of which was too dark to make out faces.

More warehouse than pub, the Taproom served no food and little liquor. It was dank and smelled of stale beer, with too few customers to dispel either. I never saw more than a rummy or two drinking, or in the evenings, perhaps a few sailors and a whore. The bar, with maybe a dozen stools, ran from the front door for a school bus's length toward the rear. Three plain iron tables stood near the back door with two iron chairs each. One of these tables had a large colorful Wurlitzer jukebox beside it that only played when a Kevitch—Abe, Big Milt, Meyer, or Albert—sat there to talk with someone. On those occasions, one had to wonder how the two men heard one another and why their table was placed so close to the Wurlitzer it drowned them out.

I never visited the Club, which began life as a "speakeasy" during Prohibition. My mother's father, Milton or Big Milt (to distinguish him from his nephew Little Milt), and his brother Abe owned the Club and a nearby illegal still. "G-men"—federal Treasury agents—raided the still one day, razed it, and dumped its barrels of illegal alcohol in the gutters of the Tenderloin. Abe and Big Milt stood in the crowd as their hooch went down the drain and cheered the G-men on, as upright citizens should. The Kevitch family owned the Club for years after Big Milt and Abe died.

Big Milt was a Republican state legislator elected consistently for decades to represent the Tenderloin ward, which continued to vote 90 percent Republican for many years after the rest of the city went Democratic. It moved into the Democratic camp by a similar 90 percent margin after the Kevitch family struck a deal with the Democratic leadership in the early 1950s. I had little contact with Big Milt, a distant figure who drove a black Lincoln Continental his state salary could not have paid for. He did not like my name and preferred to call me Donald. One birthday present from him of a child's camp chair had "Donald" stenciled across its canvas back. He handled what might politely be called "governmental relations" for the family and died in the Club one night, aged sixty-seven, of a massive lung hemorrhage brought on by tuberculosis.

His brother Abe headed the Kevitch family and ran the "corporation," the family loan-sharking business, along with the numbers bank, gambling, fencing, prostitution, and protection. When I got into trouble with the police as a teenager, Uncle Abe told me what to say to the judge at my hearing and what the judge would do, then sat in the back of the courtroom as the judge gave me a second chance and I walked without a record. Abe sat on a folding canvas chair in front of the Taproom in good weather with a cigar in his mouth. Men came up to him from time to time to talk, and sometimes they would go inside to the table beside the jukebox and talk while the music played. Inclement days and winters found him behind the bar. All serious family matters were referred to Abe until he retired, when Meyer, the elder of his two sons, took over.

Meyer always greeted me with *Hello, Shit Ass* when my mother took us to the Taproom for a visit. In good weather, he sat on the same chair outside the bar his father had occupied and had the same conversations beside the jukebox. But unlike Abe, he did not live in the Tenderloin, his Italian wife wore minks and diamonds, and his son Benny attended a city university before becoming a meat jobber with lucrative routes that dwindled after his father died. Also unlike Abe, Meyer traveled, to Cuba before Castro, Las Vegas, and in the 1970s, Atlantic City.

My father began playing in a local poker game and, on his first two visits, won rather a lot of money. The men running the game knew he was married to Meyer's cousin. They complained to Meyer that they could not continue to let Joe win, and Meyer told my father not to play there again. The game was fixed. Joe ignored him. At his next session, they cleaned him out.

Meyer had a surprising reach. Joe briefly owned a meat business with a partner, Marty. It did well for eighteen months, the partners quarreled bitterly, and Joe bought Marty out. A year later, agents from the Internal Revenue Service (IRS) criminal division began investigating my father's affairs to discover whether he had been evading taxes by not reporting cash sales, which he and many other owners of cash businesses in the '50s certainly had done. The agents were getting closer, and jail loomed.

Joe spoke to Meyer, who told him, several days later, "Joe, it'll cost $10,000," a large sum then and one Joe couldn't raise. Meyer suggested he ask his ex-partner to pay half since the IRS audit covered the partnership years. Marty told my father, "I'll give it to you when you need it for bread for your kids." Joe reported this to Meyer, but the price remained $10,000. Joe put a second mortgage on our house, which Abe cosigned. He paid Meyer, and three days later, the IRS agent called and said, "Mr. Burt, I don't know who you know, and I don't know how you did it, but I've had a call from the IRS National Office in Washington, DC, ordering me to close this case in one week."

A year later, the IRS criminal investigators returned, this time to audit Marty. Nothing Marty's tax lawyers could do put them off. He begged Joe to ask Meyer for help. But this time, Meyer said there was nothing he could do. Marty endured a long trial that ended in a hung jury. Before the IRS could retry him, he dropped dead of a heart attack; he was forty-six.

My mother's brother, Albert, was a taciturn man. He lived with his wife, Babe (née Marian D'Orazio), and their four girls in a row home at Twenty-Fourth and Snyder in South Philadelphia's Italian neighborhood. He had no son. Babe was a great beauty, hence the nickname that she still bore proudly at ninety-two, and her daughters were beautiful as well. From the street, their house looked like any other working-class row home in the neighborhood, but inside, it brimmed with toys, televisions, clothes, and delicacies; the daughters were pampered and much envied. Education for Uncle Al, Aunt Babe, and their daughters stopped with South Philly High. They attended neither church nor synagogue. There were no books on their tables or art on their walls except a mural of a bucolic Chinese landscape in their living room.

* * *

Uncle Al was a detective on the Vice Squad, the Philadelphia police department's special unit charged with reducing prostitution, gambling, loan-sharking, fencing, protection, and other rackets. The opportunities for corruption were many; some said the Vice Squad's function was to protect vice. Clarence Ferguson was the head of the Vice Squad. Babe's sister was Ferguson's wife.

We went to visit Uncle Al's house one Sunday when I was ten. A week before, Billy Meade, the boss of the Republican machine in Philadelphia, had been shot and nearly killed in the Club. He was drinking in the early hours at his accustomed spot at the bar when someone shot him with a silenced pistol shoved through the inspection grill in the door when it was slid aside in answer to a knock. The shooter was short, he stood on a milk crate to fire through the grill, and he must have known Meade could be found in the Club in the wee hours of Sunday morning and where along the bar he customarily stood.

Billy Meade and Big Milt, Uncle Al's father, were on the outs at the time, and Meade had done something that caused Big Milt real trouble. Uncle Al was just five feet five, had ample experience with and access to firearms, and would have known Meade frequented the Club. I watched the police take Uncle Al from his house that morning and confiscate a large chest containing his sword and gun collection. He was tried but not convicted because the weapon used was never found, and Babe said he had been making love to her in their marriage bed when the shooting occurred. No one else was accused of the attempted murder, and when Meade recovered, he made peace with Big Milt. They both died of natural causes.

Some years later, Uncle Al was again involved in a shooting. This time, there was no question that he was the shooter. He had stopped for a traffic light in a rough neighborhood on the way home from work. Four young

Black men approached his car. According to Al, they intended to carjack him.

I never saw Uncle Al without his gun, a .38 police revolver he wore in a holster on his belt. When he drove, he always unholstered the gun and laid it on the seat beside him. One of the men tried to open the driver's door, and Uncle Al grabbed his gun from the seat and shot through the window, seriously wounding him. The other three fled, and Al chased them, firing as he went. He brought down a second, and the other two were picked up by the police a short time later.

The papers were full of pictures of the car's shattered windows, the two Black casualties, and the White off-duty detective who had shot them. The police department commended him for bravery. I never saw Uncle Al angry; crossed, he stared at you coolly with diamond-blue eyes and, sooner or later, inevitably evened the score and more.

All the Kevitch men of my grandfather's and mother's generation had mistresses and did not disguise the fact. Their wives and all the mistresses were gentiles, excepting Abe's wife, Annie. Uncle Al had a passion for Italian women and consorted openly with his Italian mistress for the last twenty-five years of his life. Divorce was not unheard of in the family, but Al died married to Babe.

One of Uncle Al's daughters described her father by saying, *He collected*. The things he collected included antique swords, guns, watches, and jewelry; delinquent principal and interest on extortionate loans the family "corporation" made; protection money from shopkeepers, pimps, madams, numbers writers, gambling dens, thieves, and racketeers; and gifts from the Philadelphia branch of the Gambino Mafia family run by Angelo "the Gentle Don" Bruno. Joe and Uncle Al died within months of each other, and at Joe's funeral, Babe proudly told me how Al would make the more difficult collections, say from a gambler who refused to pay his debts. He would cradle his .38 in the flat of his hand and curl his thumb through the trigger guard to hold it in place, so it became a second palm. Then he'd slap the delinquent hard in the head with his blue steel palm. His collection record was quite good.

Angelo Bruno and Uncle Al were close for years, until Bruno was killed in 1980 at the age of sixty-nine by a shotgun blast to the back of his head. Albert had protected him and his lieutenants from arrest. In exchange, Bruno contributed to Uncle Al's collections. Uncle Al often told his daughters what a wonderful, decent, kind man Bruno was and that he did not allow his family to deal in drugs. The Albert Kevitch family held the don in high regard.

Babe adored her husband, and my four cousins adored their father. They were grateful for the luxurious lives he gave them and proud of the fear he inspired. No one bullied them. Babe called the four girls together before they went to school the day the newspapers broke the story of Al's arrest on suspicion of shooting Billy Meade and told them if anyone asked whether the Al Kevitch suspected of the shooting was their father, they should hold their heads up and answer yes.

* * *

My mother, Louise Kevitch, Albert's younger sister, was born to Milton and Anita Kevitch (née Anita Maria Pellegrino), a block or two from the Taproom in 1917. Nine months later, my maternal grandmother, Anita, a Catholic, died in the 1918 flu epidemic; her children, Louise and Albert, were taken in by their Italian immigrant grandmother, who lived nearby. She raised Louise from the age of two until thirteen in an apartment over her candy store, its profits more from writing numbers than selling sweets. Louise was thirteen when her grandmother died; she lived with Uncle Abe and Aunt Annie in their large house across the street from the Taproom from then until, at twenty-one, she married my father.

Louise graduated from William Penn High School in central Philadelphia, wore white gloves out and about and shopping in the downtown department stores, went to the beauty parlor once a week and had a "girl," a Black maid, three days a week to clean and iron, a luxury that Joe could ill afford. She did not help him in the store. She spoke reverentially of her brother, Al, and his role as a detective on the Vice Squad; of Big Milt, who worked in Harrisburg; and of Uncle Abe and the family "corporation," which would help us should we need it. Meyer was Lancelot to her, though we never quite knew why. Louise constantly invoked the principle of "family" as a mystic bond to be honored with frequent visits to the Taproom and the Kevitches. Joe did all he could to keep us from their ambit. It was a child-rearing battle he won, but not decisively. Louise kept trying to force us closer to her family; they fought about it for fifty-three years.

My mother never *bentsch licht* (lit Sabbath candles) or went to schul, except on the high holidays, Rosh Hashanah and Yom Kippur. She never told us her mother and grandmother were both Italian. When Babe revealed the secret to me, Louise didn't speak to her for months. We never knew her father had married another Gentile shortly after her mother (Anita) died, and fathered aunts and uncles we never met. She never mentioned Big Milt's mistress, Catherine, who was with him at his death. She never explained how four families—Abe and Annie's, Meyer's, his brother Milton's first and second ones—lived well on earnings of what appeared to be a failing bar and after-hours club in the red-light district. Why her brother was so important if he was only a detective, how his family lived so well on a detective's salary—these were never explained. She did not tell us her mink coat was a gift from her brother or how he came by it. Any questions about what Uncle Al or Meyer actually did, any suggestion that any Kevitch male was less than a gentleman, infuriated her, brought slaps or punishment, and went unanswered. We learned about the Kevitches from observation, from what they told us, and from the papers.

2. Childhood Houses
716 South Fourth

My parents' marriage was a bare-knuckle fight to the death. The early rounds were fought at 716 South Fourth Street, roughly equidistant from Fourth and Daly and Ninth and Race, where I lived from a few days after my birth in 1942 till I was nearly five. I watched the next fifteen rounds from a seat at 5141 Whitaker Avenue in the Feltonville section of North Philadelphia, where we moved in 1947. The match continued after I left.

Joe and Louise were introduced through mutual friends at a "clubhouse" in South Philadelphia that he and other bachelor friends rented to drink, throw parties, and take their girlfriends to "make out." Respectable lower-middle-class girls in the late 1930s did not allow themselves to be "picked up," nor did they copulate till married and then not often. Louise and her girlfriends lived in the Tenderloin, which made their virtue suspect even as it conferred allure. But there was no question that Louise Kevitch, Al's sister and Big Milt's daughter, took her maidenhead intact to the wedding sheets: a gynecologist had to remove it surgically after my parents tried and failed for several days to consummate their marriage. This difficulty was a harbinger of my mother's enduring distaste for sex.

She was an attractive woman at twenty when they met and, shortly thereafter, married: five feet, slim, brown eyes, with good breasts and fine legs, long soft brown hair, and the hauteur of someone with roots to hide, who sniffed at anything or anyone not quite comme il faut. But Louise was unacceptable to Grandmother Rose Bort because she was not Jewish, if not for other reasons. Louise would not consider converting. Rose did not attend their wedding.

* * *

The waves of Ashkenazim from the Pale who came to Philadelphia from the 1880s through the early 1920s settled near Fourth Street in South Philadelphia. Louise—or Lou, as my father called her—went to live with her husband above Joe's Meat Market, the "Store," at 716, in the heart of the cobbled South Fourth Street shopping district. Their home was the top two floors of a three-story, forty-five-by-fourteen-foot brown-brick late-Victorian building with a coal furnace. The ground or "first" floor was the Store. A refrigerated meat case extended some twenty feet from the front display window, also refrigerated, to a small area holding basic dry goods: black-eyed peas, lima beans, rice, Bond bread, Carnation canned milk, Campbell soups, tea, Maxwell House ground coffee in airtight tin cans, and sugar. The next fifteen feet contained a small cutting room, the "back room," with two butcher blocks, hot and cold water taps, and a fifty-gallon galvanized iron drum for washing platters. Behind the cutting room was a ten-by-twelve-foot walk-in icebox, where rumps and rounds of beef, pork loins, frying chickens, and smoked meats waited to be cut up and put on sale in the window or the case. A decoratively stamped tin ceiling ran from the front door to the icebox. I came to live two floors above Joe's Meat Market three days after I was born.

The Store's front door was almost entirely plate glass, so that customers could see we were open if the door was closed, but, to avoid missing a sale, it almost never was. A screen door was hung in summer to keep out flies. Inside, just opposite the meat case, was a trapdoor that opened on rickety steps down to the coal bin and furnace in the cellar. The cellar also held fifty-pound sacks of rice, cartons of sugar, and other goods, along with the rats and roaches that fed on them. You had to tend the furnace once in the middle of the night or the fire would go out. If that happened, it was hard to rekindle.

Behind the case ran the counter on which meat was wrapped, chopped, cut, or piled while serving a customer. Bags in sizes that held from two to twenty-five pounds were stacked beneath the counter in vertical piles divided by wooden dowels. Midway down the counter was the register, which only my father was allowed to open. On a nail under the register hung a loaded .38 caliber revolver and a blackjack on a leather strap; a baseball bat leaned against the back wall by the cosh. All three were used at one time or another.

Three scales trisected the top of the refrigerated case. One-pound cardboard boxes of lard for sale were stacked two feet high on either side of the weighing pans, making it impossible to see the meat being weighed on them. The butcher slid a box of lard onto the scale as he placed the meat on it and stood back in a "Look, Ma, no hands" pose so the customer could see him. Slabs of fat back, salt pork, and bacon also stood in piles on enameled platters atop the case. Toward the end of the day in summer, beads of grease dripped from these piles onto the platters. Flies were everywhere, more in summer than winter, but always there.

Out the door to the left was a poultry shop where chickens, ducks, and turkeys in cages squawked, honked, and gobbled, and the stink of rotten eggs and ammonia from fowl shit mixed with sawdust drifted onto the street. These birds were awaiting death and let every passerby know it. To the right was a yarn shop and, next to it on the corner, the fish store. The odor of rotting fish heads, tails, scales, and blood rose from a garbage can beneath the filleting block, stronger on busier days than slow. Carp milled in galvanized tubs, finning and thrashing until Mr. Segal, the fishmonger, thrust his hand among them and snatched the one the customer pointed to. A brief commotion as he yanked it from the tub, then with his left arm, he held it still on the chopping block while his right hand severed the head and tail with one blow each. Mr. Segal's right arm, the one that held the machete-sized beheading knife, was much thicker than his left, the result of dispatching fish Monday through Saturday. My father's right arm and shoulder were similarly muscled from cutting meat.

Pushcarts lined the curbs for blocks like huge wheelbarrows, their rear two spoke wheels four feet in diameter, the front wheel a third that, with long shafts extending from the barrow, as if for horses. During business hours, the carts rested on their smaller front wheels with the shafts angled skyward. They clogged the street so that there was just enough room for a single file of cars or a trolley to pass, and fouled the curb with the smell of rotting tomatoes, cabbage leaves, and onions. In winter, rusty fifty-five-gallon oil drums stood between some of the pushcarts with trash fires burning in them all day. The pushcart vendors stood around them for warmth until a customer appeared.

Mr. Drucker—a tall, thin, kindly-looking man—sold fruit and vegetables from his pushcart in front of the yarn store. He smiled at me and

Fourth Street south of Bainbridge, looking north toward the Store

asked, "*Nu, Danela?*" (What's up, Danny?), as I toddled by. He was there Monday to Saturday, no matter how hot or cold, and always wore a cloth flatcap. He could have been a peddler in Lvov. At night, Mr. Drucker closed up shop by levering onto the cart's shafts so that his weight brought the front wheels off the cobbles as his feet hit the ground and the cart balanced on its two large wheels. Then with a heave, he swung it from the curb, negotiated the trolley tracks, and slowly pushed it round the corner and down three blocks to the pushcart garage, where he locked it up for the night. The pushcarts, with their high wooden sides, steel-rimmed wooden wheels, and goods, were heavy and didn't roll well. Moving them was a job for a horse, but Mr. Drucker had no horse.

* * *

Fourth Street was declining as a Jewish shopping district when my father bought the Store in 1940. Jewish immigration from the Pale had been choked off in the 1920s by the new U.S. quota system and the diminishing anti-Semitism that accompanied the first stages of Bolshevism in Russia. The first Jewish generation born in Philadelphia prospered and promptly moved to better neighborhoods in Northeast and West Philadelphia. Poor Blacks from the southern states took their places, and with them came poverty, different foods, more alcohol, different violence, different street crime and prejudice. Rye bread, pickles, herring, and corned beef gave way to hominy grits, collard greens, catfish, and chitlins; the odor of garlic and cumin replaced by the barbecue tang of wood smoke mixed with pig fat. At

New Year's, Joe's Meats had wooden barrels four feet high and three wide with mounds of smoked hog jaws for sale, bristles and teeth still intact. This ghoulish food, roasted for hours with black-eyed peas and collard greens, was the traditional New Year's turkey for southern field hands and was supposed to bring luck.

There was a bar across the street about two hundred feet north of the Store, at the corner of Fourth and Bainbridge. Payday was Friday. Friday and Saturday nights, the sirens would wail their way to that bar; sometimes screams or shots were heard. Knife fights and back-alley crap games that ended in violence were common. Many customers on Saturday and Sunday mornings were hung over, and it was not unusual for the men to sport freshly bandaged hands and heads. Joe sometimes ate lunch at Pearl's, a small luncheonette around the corner from the Store. One Sunday, we were sitting on stools at Pearl's counter eating lunch when a young Black man said something, which led him, his companion, and Joe to walk outside and square up. The tough pulled a nine-inch switchblade. Joe crouched, called him a *n----- motherfucker*, and beat him bloody.

Joe's Meat Market would have failed ten years earlier than it did but for the coming of war. The U.S. Navy Yard at the foot of Broad Street, four miles southeast of William Penn's hat, was working three shifts a day when the Japanese attacked Pearl Harbor on December 7, 1941. Local woolen mills, machine shops, and foundries soon followed suit. They drew laborers, many of them Black, to the city; any capable man or woman in South Philadelphia who wanted steady work at good wages had it, including some of my relatives. And these workers bought their meat at Joe's. For the first time, my father was making more than a living.

The U.S. government rationed meats and staples like coffee and sugar, which spawned a black market. It created a federal agency, the Office of Price Administration (OPA), with inspectors to police the ration system and prevent profiteering; this drove black-market prices higher. Joe struck a deal with a black-market slaughterhouse to assure his supply of meat. He fetched it from the slaughterer's at night in a Chevy panel truck and unloaded it himself. Word got around that you could always get plenty of pork chops and roasts at Joe's without ration coupons.

Whitey—an OPA inspector in his fifties, nearly six feet tall, fat and officious—walked into the Store one Saturday morning when it was packed with customers come to buy meat without ration coupons. If a customer asked the price per pound of a cut, the butcher called out *Next!* and she left meatless, business too good to humor a troublemaker. Whitey asked to see the ration coupons for what was being sold.

*   *   *

South Philadelphia's ghettos—Jewish, Italian, Irish, Black—produced many good semipro boxers, and Joe was one of them. At twenty-nine, he was fast, with an eastern European peasant's arms and shoulders thickened from butchering; he could take a punch. He had little respect for authority, a Depression-era fear of anything that threatened his living, and an uncontrollable temper. Joe asked Whitey to come back on Monday when the weekend rush was over. Whitey asked again. Joe came from behind the counter, faced him, and told him to come back another day. Whitey started to shut the front door, saying he would order the Store closed if Joe didn't show him the coupons. Joe knocked him through the front door's plate glass.

The Kevitch family lawyer defended Joe at his trial, which Uncle Abe attended to see justice done. When Whitey was called to the stand, he rose, looked at Uncle Abe, and said, *Abe, if my dead mother got up from her grave and begged, I wouldn't lift a finger to help that kid of yours*, then testified as damningly as he could. My father did not go to jail. He paid a modest fine; business went on as usual.

Joe began to teach his wife to drive shortly after they married. Those days, trolley cars ran frequently along the steel tracks in front of 716 South Fourth. The prewar family coupé had a manual clutch and gearshift, which Louise found difficult to master. She began to pull away from the curb one Sunday afternoon, my father in the passenger seat instructing, and stalled on the tracks. She flooded the carburetor trying to restart the car, while a trolley car, bell clanging, stopped inches from the coupé's back bumper. The starter turned the engine over futilely while the conductor continued to ring his bell. After a minute, he leaned from his window and cursed Louise, her sex, her intelligence, and her parents. The passenger door flew open, and Joe ran to the trolley car, prized open the front double doors, dragged the conductor from the car, and knocked him out. The conductor lay on the cobbles, not moving. My father walked back to the car, got behind the wheel, started it, and drove away.

A few days before Christmas 1946, Joe won $250 in a crap game and blew it all on two sets of O-Gauge Lionel model electric trains, passenger and freight, for my brother and me. Lionel did not manufacture model trains during the war, and the first postwar sets were in short supply and dear. The freight set's six-wheel driver workhorse steam engine pulled a coal tender and silver Sunoco oil tanker, an orange boxcar with the Baby Ruth logo, an operating black flatbed log car, and a caboose. A sleek ten-wheel Pennsylvania Railroad passenger steam engine with tender rocketed three passenger cars and a club car around the layout, their windows lit by a bulb inside each car. Both engines puffed fake smoke when a white pellet dropped down their smokestacks and melted on the hot headlight bulbs below. The whistle diaphragm was located in the tenders and activated by a button on a controller clipped to the track. Pressing a button on a remote-control track would trigger a plunger below the log car to tip the floor of the car up and dump the three logs it carried. Accessories included a gateman with a swinging lantern, which popped out of his gatehouse when a train rolled over a nearby contact; a half dozen streetlights; and a transformer to run it all. Joe and a buddy sat on the floor in the front room above the Store that Christmas morning, assembling the track and wiring the controllers. He ran those trains around whistling and smoking all Christmas day and every Christmas after until I was twelve. My father had few toys as a child and no trains. Sixty-five years later, I still run them around at Christmas.

Early in 1946, slicing abdominal pains doubled Joe up, and doctors diagnosed acute Crohn's disease, or rotting guts—the consequence of Jewish genes, bad boyhood diet, and heavy smoking—shortly after I turned three. He left the hospital six months later, a surviving experiment in radical intestinal resectioning, eighty-five pounds, short-gutted, and permanently diarrheic. His bowels plagued him for the rest of his life: diarrhea irritated his anus, and for years, he drove sitting on an inflatable child's plastic swim ring; there was talk of a colostomy as he trudged from doctor to doctor, seeking relief. His groans and diarrhea-browned toilet bowls were a fixture in our house. Into my teens, I was afraid he might die at any minute.

The famous surgeon who removed much of his rotted tripe in the pioneering operation that saved his life ordered him to convalesce and find a hobby. He went to Florida with Louise for his first-ever vacation and there, as a form of therapy, began to fish from a Miami pier. By the time he returned from Florida, he had his hobby. A diversion became a passion, then an obsession, and finally a calling; he died a charter-boat captain on the Jersey coast. But his bowels and stomach tortured him the remaining forty-nine years of his life; he developed stomach cancer at eighty, which would have killed him had a heart attack not carried him off first.

5141 Whitaker Avenue

Stacks of twenty-, fifty-, and one-hundred-dollar bills with rubber bands around them, the four-year fruits of war, covered the kitchen table on V-J Day, August 15, 1945, waiting to be hidden in a bank's safe-deposit box. One year later, Joe returned from convalescing in Florida, thirty-two years old, with his newfound passion for saltwater sportfishing, an even chance he would die young, and memories of signs at southern hotels saying, *No Jews or dogs allowed*. It was the worst possible time to buy a house: demand penned by the war, servicemen returning with GI loans, and a wartime dearth of construction combined to inflate prices. But for the first time in my father's life, a pigmy front lawn, grassy side plot in a private alleyway between the next row of two-story houses, garage, basement with oak floors, and a six-foot mahogany bar with three leather stools were his if he wanted them. Joe took some stacks from the safe-deposit box and bought an end-of-row house in Feltonville, a working- and lower-middle-class neighborhood in North Philadelphia to which we moved a few months before my fifth birthday. The house was never worth as much as it was that spring of 1947, and my parents lost most of their investment in real terms when they sold it forty years later.

Joe often visited the box over the next eight years. War work dwindled, and with it went Fourth Street's shoppers. Each month, my parents spent more than the Store took in. Joe's innards continued to rot, his money worries worsened, Louise grew fat, and bickering turned into screaming matches with fists slamming tables and smashed plates. But Joe's visits to the *shvitz*—the local steam baths—each Monday of the year and fishing trips each Tuesday, March through mid-December, continued, as did Louise's help, her weekly beauty-parlor visits, and the family's annual two weeks at the shore, whether Atlantic City or Long Beach Island. They borrowed money for emergencies and took the last cash stack from the box when I was twelve.

My parents used my fifth birthday to display their new house to the Burts and Kevitches. (When Uncle Bernie changed his name after the war from Jewish-sounding Bort to a Waspier Burt to help his career as a lingerie buyer for a downtown department store, Joe followed suit.) The Burt family war hero, Uncle Moishe, showed up. So did his Kevitch counterpart, Uncle Milton. Both had served in the Pacific, Milton as a military policeman, Moishe as a paratrooper. Milton brought home a Japanese rifle and malaria; Moishe, a chest of medals, a metal right arm, leg, and chrome-claw hand, and addiction to morphine. He had charged and destroyed an enemy machine-gun nest on Guadalcanal to earn medals, prostheses, pensions, and federal benefits. Handsome, still dashing, Uncle Moishe married five times before he died, a successful chicken farmer, in Texas.

I met him for the first time that birthday and quickly told him about my Japanese rifle, which he asked to see. We went down to our basement, and when I showed it to him, he picked it up with hand and claw, made me promise not to tell anyone, then taught me how to make a bayonet thrust. I saw him once more a few years later at Fourth and Daly when Joe would have beat him unconscious had my grandparents not managed to drag him away. Moishe, the youngest of their four children and Mom's favorite, had persuaded them to mortgage their house to fund a business deal. The deal, if there was a deal, went south, leaving Mom and Pop with a mortgage they couldn't pay, Pop dying, and no other assets to speak of. We went to their house for my father to discuss what was to be done, but when he saw Moishe, he lost his temper and punched him. I never saw or heard from Moishe again; he did not attend either of his parents' funerals nor my father's. He had numerous children, my first cousins, whom I have never met and whose names I have never known.

The new house in Feltonville had a "breakfast room," where we ate at a table for six, separated by a half wall from a small kitchen, the last of five modest rooms on the first floor. Joe sat at the head of the table on the two or three nights a week when he was home early enough for us to eat as a family. If he was not present, his chair stayed empty, as did the large red plush armchair with thick feather-stuffed cushions in the living room. We were forbidden to sit in it after the cushions were plumped for his return from work.

There was no art, no pictures on the walls, no musical instruments. Volumes of the Reader's Digest Condensed Book Club and a set of *Encyclopedia Britannica* and *The Naked and the Dead* stood on four shelves in the basement. Our periodicals were *Reader's Digest*, *Life*, *Look*, *Vogue*, and *Salt Water Sportsman*. A television rested on the living room's "wall-to-wall" carpet. There was a large prewar 78 Victrola-cum-radio with an amber-colored tuning face on a shelf in the basement above a small stack of "swing" and "big band" records from the 1940s, one of which contained Al Jolson singing "Anniversary Waltz." The first two lines Jolson sang go "Oh how we danced on the night we were wed / We vowed our true love though a word wasn't said," which Joe rendered in a loud baritone as *Oh how we danced on the night we were wed / I needed a wife like a hole in the head*. Linoleum covered the breakfast room and kitchen floors.

The door slammed behind him when Joe came home and called out, *Lou, is dinner ready?* They did not greet each other, nor touch. I never saw them kiss. If dinner was late, a fight would start. On five out of six work nights, Joe came home too late to eat with us and had dinner alone, reading the paper. At breakfast, he would go over yesterday's receipts and lists of provisions to be picked up at the wholesalers. When the family ate together, he talked to his sons rather than his wife. If he spoke to her at the table, it was about how bad business had been that day or week or month. After dinner, he flopped in his chair to read the paper, smoke a cigarette, and doze. He went to bed around 10 p.m.

Louise did not go with him. She sat watching television in the living room or in the kitchen talking on the telephone, drinking coffee, smoking, and doodling on scraps of paper and newspaper margins. After half an hour, he would call, *Lou, Lou, come to bed*. Most mornings, I found her asleep on the couch in the living room. They shared a bedroom, but she rarely slept there when he was in the bed. He was consistently unfaithful to her all their wedded life, either with whores or girlfriends. She set her brother to catch him in one suspected affair that worried her more than most. A scene followed: she presented the evidence in front of us children. He began to pack, she kept berating him, dishes flew, he raised his fist, and she threatened to call Uncle Al. Joe didn't hit her, then or ever. In time, their marriage decayed into indifference. His excuse for not leaving was "you kids;" hers was "how would I support myself" and "what would people say?" The day began with screams and shouts. Our house had one bathroom with tiled floor, a single sink, shower, and tub for the four of us, and a basement water closet. We had a washing machine and later a dryer, but clean clothes often shirked the climb from the basement laundry room to the bedrooms. Mornings were a scramble to empty bowels and bladders, find clean underwear and socks, and get to work or school; the house rang with cries of *Lou, where's my shorts?* or *Mom, I need socks*. Yesterday's dinner dishes tilted at odd angles in a yellow rubber-coated drying rack by the kitchen sink, where unwashed pots with congealed rice or potatoes were piled.

Pop died in 1954, and Mom turned her *kvetching* (corrosive whining) on her children and their wives. She always worried about money—though between her social security checks and her children's help, she had more than enough—and used a "limited" phone service. This allowed her two free calls a day for a nominal fee. She husbanded her free calls for "emergencies" and signaled with two rings when she wanted family to call her. Her signals became a *ukase* (a decree with the force of law), ignored at your peril. Almost every evening before Joe came home, while Louise struggled with supper, Mom signaled. Apparently bearing two sons, time, and an old widow's loneliness had cleansed the *shiksa* (gentile woman) from Louise's blood. If she didn't ring back immediately, Mom would use one of her emergency calls to complain to Joe when he came home from work. Dinner was never on time; asked when it would be ready, Louise snapped, *When I say so*. We ate hostage to the signal. Mom died at ninety-nine and lived alone until her death.

* * *

The neighborhood was about 60 percent gentile and 40 percent Jewish when we moved there, but the Jews were leaving for the suburbs. It was 70 percent gentile by the time I was twelve, and today it's a Hispanic section of Philadelphia's inner city. The Catholic kids mostly went to Saint Ambrose parochial school on Roosevelt Boulevard. Saint Ambrose was attached to a large Catholic church in the next block west from our synagogue. Fights with the Saint Ambrosians were a staple of Jewish high holy days. It was generally accepted that the gentile boys, the *shkutzim*, were tougher than the Jewish, with a few exceptions.

Non-Catholics attended Creighton Elementary, the local public primary school, teaching grades kindergarten through eight. It was a five-story ocher brick building set on a third of a city block. An adjoining concrete schoolyard and a gravel playing field occupied the rest. Six-foot-high pointy iron palings set three inches apart formed a palisade from the school's north facade around the cement schoolyard and gravel ball field to the building's south facade. There were heavy steel-mesh grills painted off-white on the ground-level windows. It looked like a prison. The gates were locked from 4 p.m. to 7:30 a.m. the next morning. There was an assembly hall where, every morning, we said a prayer, pledged the flag, and heard a reading from the Bible, mostly from the New Testament; an oak-floored gym half again the size of a basketball court, with several vaulting horses, sweat-gray tattered tumbling mats, rings, ceiling-high climbing ropes, and basketball hoops at either end; a woodshop where sixth-, seventh-, and eighth-grade boys learned to handle the tools they would need for adult jobs and made zip guns; and a home ec (home economics) room with stoves, refrigerators, and sewing machines where girls learned the skills of their sex. Thanksgiving, Christmas, and Easter were the big holidays, with paper turkeys, crèches, dyed eggs, bunnies, and baskets in profusion. Few Old Creightonians went to college.

Our neighborhood was eight blocks long and four blocks deep, bounded on the north by the Boulevard, east by railroad tracks, south by a creek where we trapped tadpoles, and west by the Boulevard again. It supported eleven mom-and-pop stores on eleven corners: two groceries, two kosher butchers, two candy stores, a corner drugstore, barbershop, beauty parlor, shoe repair, and Polan's, a luncheonette. The Northeastern U.S. headquarters of catalog retailer Sears and Roebuck—with a two-square-block, three-story department store attached—was four blocks away across the Boulevard. The department store entrance housed a popcorn machine and a clerk selling large bags of it for fifteen cents. A baseball, knife, or deflated football or basketball fitted neatly below the popcorn at the bottom of one of these bags, and the advent of spring and fall found groups of boys wandering the sporting goods aisles, munching popcorn and looking out for store detectives.

We played on Whitaker Avenue's wide asphalt street, a six-blocks-long dead end. There were no parks or playgrounds. Boys played stickball with a cut-off broom handle for a bat and a hollow rubber ball two and a quarter inches in diameter; half-ball with the same bat but with the ball cut in half and inverted so it looked like a deep saucer, which dipped, curved, and floated unpredictably when properly pitched; and hose ball, again with the same broom-handled bats, and four-inch hose lengths cut from rubber garden hoses. Sensible neighbors kept their brooms and hoses inside from Easter until the players had stolen enough for the coming season. The street game from September till Christmas was rough-touch American football. Participants left these games cut and bruised from slamming into parked cars and curbs, sometimes with sprains, occasionally with a broken bone. The parked cars did not fare well either. There was a stop sign where a side street from the Boulevard intersected Whitaker Avenue. Joe drove down that street every day coming home from work but never stopped. The neighbors cursed him.

Competition from the national food chains (A&P and Food Fair), along with the Jewish exodus, slowly throttled the local stores, except for Polan's, where the Jewish *gonifs* (thieves) hung out. Every Monday night between seven and eight, they gathered to settle the weekend's gambling debts. Accounts were squared when "Fats," a 350-pound man in his late thirties, and his two bodyguards drove off in his white Cadillac convertible. One afternoon, drink-fueled insults—kike and sheeny—from mourners at an Irish wake a few doors along from Polan's led to shoving, a hey rube, and brawl, followed by police and ambulances. The guys who hung out at Polan's were not sissies, and the grade school boys there, eating hamburgers and fries, looked up to them.

* * *

Joe worked five and a half days a week, fishing and schvitz his only recreations. The Store was open every day except for national holidays like Christmas and Easter Sunday, and he had only one helper. He was too tired or worried to talk much when he came home from work; he never encouraged his sons to become butchers. During our two-week holiday at the shore in August, he arrived from Philadelphia late on Sunday night, spent Monday afternoon with us on the beach, and returned to Philadelphia after fishing Tuesday. The one vacation he took was a fishing trip to Cape Hatteras, North Carolina, for channel bass, five years after his convalescence, with me along.

Hatteras is ten hours southeast by car and ferry from Philadelphia. We arrived at a motel near Ocracoke Inlet, North Carolina, at two in the morning in the middle of a nor'easter. It was still blowing hard four hours later when we woke to seas too rough to fish. A grand old wooden resort hotel, just opening for the season, was recommended for breakfast. There was one table in use in the otherwise closed dining room. We were seated with another party of breakfasting fishermen from Philadelphia at the long table; Joe knew one of them. A tall, courtly, white-haired Black waiter was serving. He took our order, and ham, bacon, and eggs arrived with large sides of hominy grits: a ground-maize porridge served slathered in butter, and a staple of southern breakfasts.

North Carolina had been a slave state and a linchpin of the Confederacy. Segregation—de jure and de facto—was the iron rule in 1952, two years before the U.S. Supreme Court ruled that segregated schooling was illegal. The Klan was large and powerful; there were separate toilets, washrooms, restaurants, water fountains, and motels for Blacks and Whites; and Blacks rode at the back of the bus. Jews were not popular either.

The other party finished before us, and one of them called to the waiter, *Boy! Boy! Cum y'ere!* in an ersatz, mocking, field hand's patois from *Gone with the Wind.* The waiter approached. *Yes, sir, can I help you?* The man replied, *Boy, dem's was rail fahn grits. Why's, dey's de bestest grits ah evah did have! Could ah's have's some more of dem dere grits?* The waiter said, *I'm glad you liked them, sir. I'll check with the kitchen.* The bigot sat down, smirking, and the waiter headed for the kitchen. My father rose, plate in hand, before the waiter had taken two steps, walked round, and scraped his grits onto the man's plate, saying, *Here, you want some more grits?* Joe stood over him while the man ate the grits; the waiter looked on from the side of the room.

*   *   *

Joe did only two things religiously: he fished each Tuesday from March till mid-December, and he went to schvitz on Mondays. He saw his aging mother once or twice a month when her nagging made him feel guilty; visited his brother-in-law with the family at Christmas; met cousins-in-law if there was a problem or at a crap game; went to a movie, dinner, or family celebration three or four times a year with his wife; and worked the rest of the time. His stomach troubles had stopped his serious drinking in 1947, and he generally whored discreetly.

The schvitz, the Camac Baths, was a three-story, half-a-block-square building, built almost to the curb on Camac Street, an alley eight minutes' walk southeast from City Hall. A clerk stood behind a desk in the small foyer in front of rows of steel lockboxes with keys on elastic wristbands hanging from their little doors, behind which steel trays a foot long with two-inch-high sides rested in cubbyholes. The clerk handed Joe a tray for valuables as he signed in. Joe always carried a wad of cash two or three inches thick, which he placed with his wallet and Timex in the tray, then watched the clerk lock it in its cubbyhole. The clerk handed him the key to the lockbox, a bedsheet, and paper bath shoes, and Joe went through another door on his right into the locker room.

The locker room, a well-lit forty-foot-square space smelling of liniment and disinfectant, had a tiled floor and several hundred sheet-metal hanging lockers arranged in facing rows of thirty, with benches between. There was a barbershop, shoeshine stand, cafeteria, and sunroom for tanning. Bathers undressed, draped the sheet over themselves like togas, shouted, *Locker!* for an attendant to lock up their clothes, and shuffled through another door and down a staircase to the baths. Along the far perimeter of the basement that housed the baths were two twelve-by-eighteen-foot white-tiled hot rooms behind a plate glass door; towel-draped deck chairs lined their walls. The temperature in one was 125 degrees; in the other, 150 degrees Fahrenheit. A ten-by-ten-foot steam room reeking of pine adjoined the cooler hot room. Marble benches lined its walls, and there was a cold shower in the corner for bathers to cool down, so as to prolong the time they could bear the steam.

At the other end of the baths was the *platza* (traditional Russian massage) room where the platza man—naked except for a black canvas loincloth, cold water coursing down him from a hose stuffed under a floppy canvas hat he wore—scrubbed bathers down with soapy brushes fashioned from eucalyptus leaves. Joe always took a platza. He would lie on the highest of the room's three oak racks with a canvas hat fished from a bucket of cold water on his head and Willie, the platza man, six feet one and a good 230 pounds, looming over him. Willie controlled the heat from a lever under the second level of benches; each time he depressed it, the room got hotter. Joe viewed a platza as a contest between him and Willie to see who would quit first. Willie had the advantage of standing in the cold-water shower from the hose under his hat and could give platzas for hours. He would bear down on bathers with the brush—massaging, washing, and cooking them at the same time. Every three or four minutes, he would ratchet up the heat and, once in a while, take the hose from under his hat and sprinkle their most tender parts, like the backs of calves, with cold water. Joe outlasted anyone else taking a platza when he took his; once, even Willie wilted.

Finished, Willie helped bathers down from the platza bench and into the stall immediately outside for a cold shower. He handed favorites a shot of bourbon from a pint bottle secreted in the platza room, and then they went for their sheet wrap. Twelve or so deck chairs stood along rails forming a twelve-by-twelve-foot square between the platza and hot rooms. An attendant covered a deck chair with towels and a sheet, and bathers reclined in it. He laid towels across their chests, legs, and arms, swathed heads and necks in more towels, then wrapped the sheet around them like tinfoil around a roast. There they lay, sweating and dozing or talking to other shrouded men.

The Camac Baths transplanted to America an Eastern European ritual from the Pale. Camac's midcentury habitués were mostly men who did heavy labor, frequently out of doors—butchers, fishmongers, and poultry men; pushcart men who sold clothes, fruit, and vegetables; knife grinders; rag-and-bone men; sheet-metal workers; carpenters like Zaida; plumbers and painters; and the panoply of working-class trades from the shtetls—aging immigrants and their first-generation sons. They came to Camac to get the fat, grease, gristle, and grime out of their skins and the cold out of their bones in winter. The older men spoke Yiddish and English, as did my father, changing from one to the other midsentence; the younger men talked in English. Imprecations and curses were almost always in Yiddish. The second generation moved away, and Camac closed in the late eighties.

Aaron Wildavsky was a butcher nearly six and a half foot tall with hawser arms, bollard legs, and a surprisingly mild disposition. One day after a platza, while he and Joe lay near each other wrapped in sheets, Joe got into an argument with him about why eastern Europe's Jews went so meekly to their deaths. Aaron's mother tongue was Yiddish, and he slipped into it more and more often as he tried to counter Joe's contempt. He kept saying, *Yossel, Yossel, du fa'shtaisht nisht, du fa'shtaisht nisht* (*Joe, Joe, you don't understand*), and told him the ruses, reasons, and overwhelming force the Nazis used. When Aaron rose to shower and loosed his sheets, I noticed faded black numbers on his upper-left forearm. At the time, I thought my father had been cruel; now I think he was scared.

Newsboys hawked the evening dailies between lanes of traffic on the Boulevard when Joe drove home from work or schvitz, and he always tried to time the lights so he could buy a paper. In winter or when it rained, he always bought a paper from them, even if the lights were green.

3. No Expectations

Though nothing fixes at conception what we will become, or where end—criminal or saint, inner-city shotgun shack or seaside mansion—statistics show that most finish where they start. A boy born in Hell's Kitchen will likely have a harder life, ending in a harder place, than one born the same day on Manhattan's Upper East Side. In my case, the smart money was on ending as ex-con rather than saint and on mean streets, not East Egg.

That bet looked safe through my high school years. A passage from Rocky Balboa's South Philadelphia to West End London, from inner-city state schools and Catholic commuter college to Cambridge and Yale, was unthinkable. John Deans, a reedy, gentle, intellectual boy, had the gym locker above mine in high school; we were not friends. He went on to an Ivy League university; I, to a local commuter college. Six years later, we met again, on the steps of Yale Law School. I was enrolling; Deans was in his third and final year. *My God! Dan Burt! What are you doing here?*

Toddler

World War II was ten months old when I was born in Jefferson Hospital, ten blocks from the Store. Two steel trolley tracks trisected the cobbled street outside the Store into nearly equal thirds; trolleys kept them shiny, rolling down them day and night, bells clanging to shove pedestrians and pushcart vendors from their path. The nearest trees were six blocks north, plonked down along the curbs of Spruce and Pine Street; the nearest park, Washington Square, a twenty-minute pram ride northwest.

The Store stood at a refugee crossroads, where the last shtetl immigrants traded with Black migrants from the Jim Crow South. Its smells, sounds, and faces lingered from my infancy: dust rising from sixty-pound sacks of sawdust hauled from the cellar; woodsmoke and burning-fat tang from fatback piled atop a refrigerated display case; and sickly sweet, moleskin-color Carnation condensed milk, oozing from a leaky can on a shelf at the dry goods end of the Store, beyond the cold cases, make me sniff. A miasma of squashed pears, bananas, grapes; rotted onions, carrots, apples; dung and piss (horse, dog, cat); and smoke from cigarettes and oil drums burning trash to warm the street vendors in winter swirl above the gutters. Mr. Segal's corner store reeked of fish. Smells of cumin from rye breads, of garlic and onions from wooden buckets of pickles in brine, and of coarse-crushed peppercorns coating corned beef and pastrami puffed onto the street from Famous's Delicatessen, an institution then, as now, with the creak and slap of its screen door as customers come and go.

The sounds of Yiddish, English, and southern Black patois mingled in the streets from 8 a.m. to 6 p.m. business hours. Pushcart vendors—part of the last Jewish wave from the Pale before the 1924 U.S. Immigration Control Act kettled their kinsmen in eastern Europe—sold fruit, vegetables, and secondhand clothing to passers-by and spoke Yiddish and its bastard Yinglish among themselves. These greeners learned English sufficiently to trade—*Zo, lady, you vant szum apfels?*—adapting traits from their mother tongue; their hard g and k and softer ch and sh, heard in infancy, left me better able to hear German and Hebrew than French.

Behind plate-glass storefronts across the pavement from the pushcarts, first-generation storekeepers spoke Yiddish to parents but English to customers in the flat, nasal *The Irishman* accent of South Philadelphia, full of reverberant hard "ng's," "o's" turned "uh's" and "er's" turned "ah's," as in *muthah fuhkah*. Hello was a question—*Nu?* or *Whadda yuh know?*—in Yiddish or English; goodbye a hope—*Zei gezint*—or prediction, *See yuh läduh*.

The mostly Black customers contributed the sibilant, slow drawl of Stephen Foster's darkies to this cacophony. Field hands fleeing the South, drawn by war work in Philadelphia's Navy Yard and factories, were crammed in the oldest, poorest housing in North and South Philly slums. Their deferential *Yas suh; Ah wants dat one* and *be* for *is*, as in *He be cum'n soon* or *Danny, doan be doin dat*, were the only soft sounds on the street. I thought all Black people spoke like that until I left Philadelphia for England in 1964; today, you have to visit backwoods Mississippi or the red clay hills of Georgia to hear that dialect.

* * *

The faces I recall are Mary's, Willy's, and Mr. Drucker's. Mary was our daily, nearly six feet tall, a middle-aged, big-breasted mammy from the Deep South. She dressed, fed, and pushed me in my stroller to Washington Square or walked behind me as I wobbled up and down Fourth Street. She smiled a lot and called me Danny; there was nothing harsh or frightening in her large face and slow, comforting movements.

We called Willy, Mary's brother, Big Willy. He stood six feet five. Almost a doorway wide, he had a hand that could palm a basketball upside down, and worked beside my father in the butcher shop. He'd driven a Jeep at Anzio for an army officer, seen action, and had the Jeep blown out from under him. Shrapnel buried in his back and shoulders plagued him in winter. Big Willy had the equable temperament of a large man with few natural enemies; only the foolhardy would want to fight someone his size.

His face was broad, like his sister's, and he moved with her languid grace; years later, in Saudi Arabia, I worked with a Sudanese lawyer, Abdul Salam al Omari, who looked and moved like him. Willy's curse was alcohol; at least one Monday morning a month, he would not appear at 8 a.m. when the Store opened, and my father would send Mary to Willy's house, or his girlfriend's, to roust him out.

Our apartment over the Store did not have its own entrance; we had to go up or down a staircase at the back and then pass through the Store to leave or enter. *Mawnin*, or *Aftuhnoon, Lil Joe*, Willy would say when I appeared with Mary for an outing. If there were no customers and he was at a task that could be put by, he would bend down and ask, *Hey, Lil Joe, wunnuh go for a ride?* then swing me seven-and-a-half feet into the air and seat me on his shoulders, walk out through the front door—bending to clear the lintel—and parade up and down the street.

During the day, Mr. Drucker's pushcart stood canted forward on its small front wheel like a chicken pecking corn, twenty feet south of the Store. Mr. Drucker stood on the curb before it, chanting the day's bargains at passers-by. Almost six feet tall, no more than 160 pounds, his stubbled cheeks were sunk, and his gabardine cloth cap, the Jewish pushcart vendor's hallmark summer and winter, grayed and encrusted from weather, car exhaust, and fruit-grimed hands.

He never failed to hail me, even if he was with a customer. To him I was always Danila, never Little Joe, or *kleyne Yusselle* (*little Joey*), as I was to most of the Black help and other merchants, like Mr. Velushin, whose pushcart was next in line to the south. I never learned where Mr. Drucker came from, though most local pushcart men came from the Russian portion of the Pale around Kiev, where my father's family had lived and been murdered. Years later, staring at pictures of Shoah survivors in striped rags before their bunk racks, Mr. Drucker rose before me, skeletal rather than gaunt, and I guessed why he might have been so sad and gentle.

My father's face is less distinct than Mary's, Willy's, or Mr. Drucker's; he is more of a presence. I don't see him as short, though he was. His hands and feet move fast. He shouts at Willy, at customers; treads heavily; does not move out of people's way; tears rather than lifts the cellar trapdoor to fetch sacks of rice or stoke the furnace; yanks the front door open when he leaves and slams it behind him; and cleaves pork chops from loins like they were Cossack heads. He stares, not looks at people, as if they have done him wrong or are about to.

I liked it when people called me Little Joe, though I was not naturally his double. In a picture, aged three, in winter—thick woolen coat, leggings, wool mittens, peaked cap, a toy drum slung from my right shoulder, left thumb near my mouth though not in it—I stand alone, straight-backed, insolent, indifferent to the camera.

Danny Burt on Fourth Street in 1945, one shop south of the Store

I remember nothing of my mother from toddlerhood; not face, nor voice, nor hands, nor scent. No incident comes to mind: a void. But if a lover raises her hand to caress me unexpectedly, I flinch.

Framework

Parents have favorites. They parcel out attention, instruction, and affection unequally to their children, based on order of birth, sex, looks, a child's strength or weakness or force of personality, and parents' narcissism and aspirations. Isaac favored Esau, his firstborn, the hunter. Isaac's wife, Rebecca, doted on Jacob, her second, who lingered in their tents. She prompted and plotted with him to steal Esau's birthright. Cheated, Esau

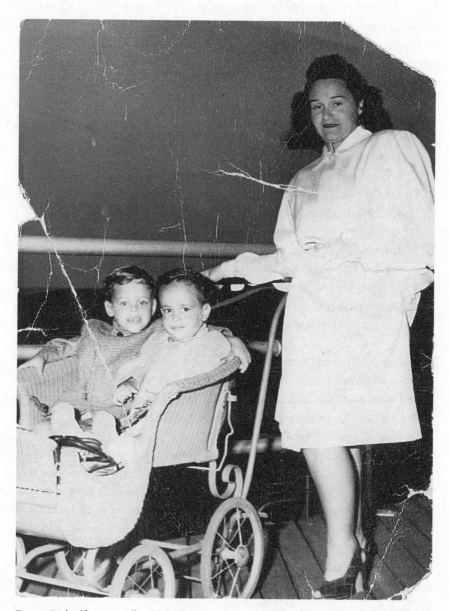

Danny, Ricky (foreground), and their mother on the Atlantic City Boardwalk circa 1948

left to form his own tribe, and when Jacob met Esau again, years later, Jacob feared for his life. I was my father's Esau, my brother my mother's Jacob: it is not an uncommon story.

Jungle ethics were our family's touchstone, and I was steeped in them. Along with "Baa Baa Black Sheep" and "Twinkle Twinkle Little Star," I was rocked to sleep with

Taffy was a Welshman, Taffy was a thief,
Taffy went to Daddy's store and stole a piece of beef.
Daddy went to Taffy's house, Taffy wasn't home;
Taffy came to Daddy's store and stole a marrow bone.
Daddy went to Taffy's house, Taffy was in bed.
Daddy took the marrow bone and bashed in Taffy's head.

Fourth and Bainbridge was not thick with Welshmen, and my parents were notably free of prejudices. Neither was a student of British folklore, and I have no idea where they heard this rhyme, or if one passed it to the other. All its elements appealed: family threat, courage, violence, and effective, vigilante justice. It was their favorite, and it became mine.

* * *

I was an undersized, nearsighted child; horses were a blur from a car's length away until kindergarten, when the defect was discovered and corrected with glasses. I went speechless till past the age of three, learned to read early, and had a library of superhero, war, and cowboy comics by five. Fears came naturally; fighting was instilled.

From five onward, I feared my father's rage. His ungovernable temper loosed, he struck with belt, fist, brass knuckles, cosh, gaff, pipe, whatever came to hand, until spent. When the Teamsters Union, a rough bunch, picketed his store in Pennsauken while they were trying to unionize it, I watched him after breakfast prepare to deliver the meat himself: a loaded .38 in a paper bag for the seat beside him, cosh and brass knuckles for jacket pockets, and a baseball bat for the floor. When he turned into the Mart and made for the picket line, he saw Jack, one of his countermen, walking the picket, and tried to run him down.

He beat me with a strap when I was small, for talking back, disobedience, breaking a lamp, and staining the carpet, and with his fists when I was older for intractability and for hitting my brother. Two beatings stand out. On a hot, sticky, late Sunday summer afternoon in 1948, I was reading a comic on the first-floor landing of our house, three feet from the foot-stool for his armchair. Half an hour earlier, he'd come home from the Store, eaten, and flopped in his chair to smoke a cigarette, read the Sunday papers, and nap. Out of smokes, he commanded, *Danny, go get me a pack of Luckys.* I didn't want to stop reading, and his cold command rankled. *No.*

What did you say?

No! Get 'em yourself.

He exploded from his chair, dragged me screaming upstairs, and threw me on my bed. *You gonna get me my cigarettes?*

No!

How about now! And he began to lash my arse with his belt. My mother ran into the bedroom and tried to stop him. She grabbed his arm, but he shook her off. She screamed in English, *Joe, Joe, stop it, you'll kill him!* then in the scraps of his mother tongue she knew, *Yussel, Yussel, Genug! Genug!* (*Joe! Joe! Enough, enough!*). But he flailed away until his rage cooled. Red-rumped and sore, I carried the quarter he forced into my hand to Much-nick's, a corner candy store open till nine, to fetch a pack of Luckys.

The whaling left more than welts; his savagery felt senseless, given the scale of provocation, and it undermined the patriarchal reverence I'd been taught. A few years later, after another beating, all reverence collapsed. He came home, found me hitting my brother, and, without asking why, knocked me four feet across the living room with his first punch.

* * *

The childhood fear that endured was want. It was a groundless terror. I never wanted; we were never poor. True, business dwindled with the war's end; as local factories and the Navy Yard cut back, customers moved to where there was more work. From 1946 to 1954, the family spent more than my father earned each year, until his war profits were exhausted and the Store on the brink of failure. But he rented a concession in a farmers market and, in time, did well enough to fish three days a week; he retired and became a full-time charter captain at sixty.

Yet the fear that we might be homeless or jobless or shamed hung over me like a guillotine, too high to see distinctly, but there, waiting just ahead, honed and ready to sever my neck with a casual pull on the *déclic* (blade trigger). The Depression's hardships crippled my father, and he spoke of them often: wearing his brother's hand-me-downs, leaving school at thirteen to work, selling apples on street corners with his father. He pul-sated with worry every day—even when business was good—the ghost of hard times pursuing him even at sea, where, to the last, each day he'd tally the season's fishing trips already sailed to tell if he was breaking even. I absorbed his dread, glimmering, irrational, marrow deep.

Tales, hearsay, examples, and training taught me to fight. Dinnertimes and fishing trips were filled with stories of vengeance, brawling, pride, and violence, my father hero of them all: mauling this or that anti-Semite, telling that cheap boss to *Take this job and shove it!*, yanking rude conductors from their trolley cars. All had the same point: *Son, this world is rough / And if a man's gonna make it / He's gotta be tough.*[2]

I saw him threaten, curse, double men up with a right hook to their guts. I watched him short-weight customers, stand unflinching while Holmes—the charter captain who taught him to fish—cut gang hooks from his cheek when a cast went awry. I watched and cowered when he crashed his fist to the table, he and my mother screaming and cursing each other, throwing plates to the floor.

Boxing lessons complemented the tales. I was four when he first showed me how to make a fist, crouch, raise and bend my right arm to protect my face and belly, while I carried my left just below my left breast, tensed to deliver a haymaker; how to bob, weave, dance out of range, jab, roll with a punch, and shift my weight to put it behind a hook. He would kneel, raise his fists and arms to protect his face and torso, and taunt me to hit him; it was futile. His adult reach, weight, and sixteen-inch biceps were impregnable. He flicked each sally off, harder and harder, stinging one side of my face, then the other with one palm while he slapped my fist aside with the other, knocking me down, all the while yelling, *C'mon, c'mon! Hit me! Get inside; hit me, hit me*, until, frustrated, enraged, and tearful, I charged.

My father repeated these lessons till I was nine or ten. Sometimes I got inside the walls of his arms and hit him as hard as I could with my little boy's fists. I would have killed him. But I never learned to box well; small boys, shortsighted and slight, make poor Muhammad Alis. But I did learn to hit first, rush bigger opponents, and pick up whatever came to hand as a weapon if, as usually seemed the case, I was outweighed or outclassed. Rage sank into my cells. When I charged and fought, the true target of fist, club, or writ was my father.

---

[2] "A Boy Named Sue," song written by Shel Silverstein and recorded by Johnny Cash for the album *At San Quentin*, 1969.

My mother reinforced his teachings. The gentile boys in our neighborhood bullied the Jews. A few months after we moved to Whitaker Avenue, a gang of five fixed on me. Their ringleader was Tommy Mann, six months older and three inches taller than me. I ran into the house whenever I saw him coming, and in time, my mother noticed it. When I told her why I'd come in, she told me to go fight him. I whimpered that he was bigger than me; his friends would jump me. Her left hand took my right arm and dragged me down the back steps to the alley, where Tommy and friends loitered; her right hand carried a broom. *Fight him!* She warned his buddies she'd club them with the broom if they interfered, then prodded me toward Tommy with its bristles till we fought.

* * *

Several years ago, my high school class organized a fiftieth reunion. On the back of a form letter encouraging alumni to attend, the organizer wrote a note saying his daughter had married the son of David Gold, a boy I'd played and fought with sixty years earlier. David asked to be remembered, saying although we often fought, he thought we were friends in the end.

He was the local druggist's eldest son, a half year younger than me. Big for his age, fat, he was a local princeling because his father was a professional and wore a starched white doctor's tunic while serving malteds at his drugstore soda fountain. One day when I was nine, David and six of his retainers lined up across the end of our alley and made for my brother, me, and Warren Sofian, a local boy playing with us. The gang began yelling, tossing garbage as they came; a serious beating loomed. I worried about my brother, seven at the time, too small for the fight ahead. Warren had a large metal cap pistol in a holster at his waist. I grabbed the pistol, grasped it by the barrel so the butt turned billy club, and rushed at David. I hit him as hard as I could in the face, above his left eye; he screamed and fell bleeding. It took stitches to close the wound, but the fight was over. I don't recall reasoning that taking out the ringleader would stop the assault, nor thinking what might happen if it didn't.

Our neighborhood was not a war zone. I played the street ball games of U.S. inner-city row-home neighborhoods, after school and on weekends; played Monopoly on rainy days; went to the movies on Saturdays to eat popcorn and watch cartoons until, at twelve, I began working weekends. We trick-or-treated on Halloween, lit firecrackers on the Fourth of July, had newspaper routes, roller-skated down pavement and street, and ice-skated at a rink on the other side of the city. The family ate Chinese on

Sunday nights and visited relatives. I read an illustrated Greek myths, and a children's history of western heroes—Davy Crockett at the Alamo, Daniel Boone—till their hardcovers crumpled; read *Reader's Digest* and *Time* in the bathroom and scoured *Salt Water Sportsman* every month.

Nevertheless, fear and ambition dominated childhood. Suspicion, aggression, and violence at home, at school, and in the streets galvanized my small bones, my weak eyes, and what intelligence I had to precipitate my fledgling character. I eyed adults warily as if they might beat me, kids as if they might hurl a rock. Strangers, the slightest challenge, triggered my fight-or-flight reflex. I developed a volcanic temper and spent years trying to discipline it, questioned authority and often disobeyed it, formed no deep or lasting friendships, and did not trust.

Victories bought my father's favor, weakness my mother's scorn. Hunger for the first and shame from the second nurtured ambition. *Come you home a hero / Or come not home at all* seeped into my bones long before I read Housman or heard of Spartan mothers or watched Tony Soprano's mother, Livia, order him hit. I studied my father's faults to extirpate them in myself and marked the worst beatings for when I might even the score. At thirteen, no one called me *Little Joe*.

Grade School

Creighton Elementary was an inner-city school for the children of truckers, machinists, clerks, and a few small tradesmen; the only ones I knew whose parents were professionals were the Gold boys. Perhaps a third of its pupils were Jewish. Almost all its graduates finished their education at Olney, the local public high school, which they left at eighteen for the army, trades, or minor white-collar jobs. The girls got married and were soon pregnant, or the other way around. Two boys out of sixty from my eighth-grade class went to Central High, Philadelphia's magnet school for bright boys.

I'd had little experience of other children when we moved to North Philadelphia in 1947 and, a few months later, entered kindergarten. I was reading by then and paid no attention to threshold alphabet or reading lessons. Next year, in first grade, my printing slanted the wrong way because I was left-handed. The rote-learning arithmetic bored me; no one could explain why 1 + 1 must equal 2, and I had trouble with it. Games were problematic; no one wanted on his team a diminutive batter who wore Coke-bottle glasses, and I disliked team sports. When boys yelled, *Hey, four-eyes!* I'd hit them, which made me a discipline problem.

* * *

The first-grade teacher, Mrs. Grey, was a kindly woman who helped me through the year. Her second-grade successor, Miss Fitzmaurice, was a hatchet-faced, fifty-year-old Calvinist in brimstone-hued tweed suits and starched white blouses with a reputation for breaking mavericks. She wore thin-rimmed silver glasses that hung a few inches above her modest breasts from a gold-link chain or perched like pince-nez on her nose and had a voice that made me think of rat claws scratching glass.

I could not please Miss Fitzmaurice: my sums were wrong, my times tables faulty, and I never knew where we were when the class read *Dick and Jane*. Worst of all, I tried to use my left hand to write when she began to teach us script. My p's and q's slanted left when she insisted that they lean right; hung on the wall for a parents' day, they boldly ran *à rebours*, and Miss Fitzmaurice was not having a little Huysmans in her second grade. Seven years old, in 1949, I met my nemesis.

She broadcast my mistakes to the class, gave me extra homework, kept me in at recess, stood me for a half hour in the cloakroom for inattention or arithmetic errors, and, worst of all, for writing with my left hand, she branded me intractable and sent me to the principal for discipline. I tried to satisfy her and cried over my homework regularly. Report card days twice a semester inscribed my shame; columns of blue Us (for unsatisfactory) opposite arithmetic, reading, penmanship, gym, drawing, neatness, cooperation—all leaning in the right direction in Miss Fitzmaurice's flawless hand—filled the piece of folded cardboard I reluctantly carried home. My parents did not question her judgment on parents' night when they came to discuss my performance.

My right hand was shaping cursive script slanted right rather than left by the time the school year ended, but it looked more like a Cy Twombly charcoal than a legible hand. Miss Fitzmaurice pinned a note to my sweater to take home several weeks before our last report card was due. It said I would not be promoted to the third grade with the rest of the second graders, was to be sent to a special school for slow learners, and would have to repeat second grade. This social shame my parents could not accept.

A few mornings later, instead of the yellow bus to school, I boarded the R bus to Frankfurt with my mother, then the El, an elevated train that ran on rails thirty feet above the street for several miles before descending under Center City Philadelphia. We climbed the steps from the subway at Broad and Walnut and walked several blocks down Walnut Street to an imposing, five-story brownstone divided into apartments with eight doorbells beside brass plaques. We waited in one of the apartments until a gentleman in his fifties—gold-rimmed glasses, waistcoat with gold fob chain slung across, thinning hair, avuncular demeanor—opened a frosted glass-panel door from an inner room, walked over to us, and surprised me by smiling, asking my name, telling me his, and putting me at ease. He asked my mother if she would mind waiting while he and I went into his office to play some games. We entered his office, and he closed the door. I was in a large room, a desk piled with papers, book-lined walls, and a leather couch near a low table with three child-sized chairs around it. We talked awhile. I told him about school, what I loved and loathed, then we played some games, and I solved some puzzles he gave me.

My mother, twisted handkerchief in hand, rose when I emerged; she left me rifling through pictures in old copies of *Life* while she went into the inner room. Twenty minutes or so later, she came out, tearful, an envelope in hand, and we left to board the subway home. She walked me to school next day, met with the principal and Miss Fitzmaurice, and gave them the letter. Creighton promoted me to the third grade with the rest of my class. Years later, I learned that this kindly man was a child psychologist, our games were IQ tests, and he did not think I was retarded. If there is a hell, I will surely go there, but skippingly, so long as Miss Fitzmaurice is there, too, in the eighth circle along with Caiaphas and other Pharisees.

* * *

School dread diminished after I left Miss Fitzmaurice's class. But while there were fewer "U's," when the baby boomer flood swamped state schools four years later and they coped by ordering the best students to skip a half year, I was not among them.

I have only three Creighton memories from the subsequent six years there: learning to make zip guns in Shop, suspension for emulating characters in *Blackboard Jungle*, and Charlene Cores. The curriculum included mandatory vocational classes for both sexes in grades seven and eight, our last two years before high school. Girls went to home ec and learned to sew, bake, and clean; boys to Shop, where they used handsaws, hammers, and screwdrivers to waste white pine and shellac making footstools, bookracks, and pencil trays. Our one memorable product was extracurricular.

A few classmates were older, confirmed delinquents, who had done time in reform schools. One day in eighth-grade shop, one of these boys taught us to make a zip gun. You draw a butt with, say, a six-inch barrel on a length of two by four, cut the shape out, then fashion it into the semblance of a wooden gun with a coping saw, file, and sandpaper. Next, you rout a channel half an inch deep the length of the barrel, place a six-inch length of copper tubing in it, and tape the tube tightly to the barrel with duct tape. A small screw is sharpened and punched through a thick rubber band, the band stretched across the end of the tube and nailed to the butt for a firing pin, so when the screw is stretched and released, its sharp end slams a sixteenth of an inch into the tube.

You're in business: place a .22 caliber shell in the butt end of the tube, draw the rubber band, and hope for the best. Zip guns were often more dangerous to the user than the target, the round exploding in the tube and spraying its user with copper shrapnel. But at close range, five to ten feet, and if all went well, a zip gun could kill. Teenagers used them in gang fights in the 1950s, when guns were less ubiquitous than they are now and drug trafficking hadn't enriched gang members; prisoners still use them.

* * *

Rebellion is a hallmark of puberty, and puberty struck hard at twelve. One weekday in late spring, 1955, Irv Cossrow and I cut school and went to see a new movie, *Blackboard Jungle*. Sociologists mark the film's release as the start of the American youth revolt that peaked in the 1960s. Its theme music, Bill Haley's "Rock around the Clock," became our teen anthem. We imagined ourselves *Blackboard Jungle*'s bored, dangerous, juvenile delinquents in an inner-city school, good at heart and unfairly charged with threatening our teacher. We, not Sidney Poitier, charged the villain with the pointy end of a flagpole; we could be cool like Vic Morrow. The movie caused riots in some cities, and the Eisenhower administration refused to approve it as the U.S. entry at Cannes. Irv and I pushed out through the movie house's glass doors that afternoon, blinking in the sunlight and singing, *One, two, three o'clock, four o'clock rock / Five, six, seven . . . / We're gonna rock, around, the clock tonight* as loud as we could: we were transfigured.

A year before this metamorphosis, the Cossrows had arrived in our neighborhood from the Bronx. Irv's father, Nate, a failed Manhattan furrier, bought the corner grocery store across the street from our house. He and his wife, Gertrude, whom we named Dirty Girty, kept store from

7 a.m. to 7 p.m.; in ten years, it failed too. Nate was thin, worn, and avuncular. Gertrude, a half foot taller, fifty pounds heavier, a cigarette dangling from her lower lip—its ash threatening to thicken the pans of coleslaw or barrels of pickles—did the heavy lifting in the shop. You could imagine Dirty Girty repairing Russian tanks at Stalingrad, immovable under a Nazi barrage.

Suki, Irv's five-years-older sister, was thin but big breasted, medium height, with high cheekbones, long blond hair—which never seemed clean—pale, northern Russian skin like all the Cossrows, and full lips. She aped Brigitte Bardot and was the subject of much salacious speculation.

It's difficult for a newcomer to fit into a neighborhood at twelve, Irv's age when the family moved to Philadelphia. Twelve- and thirteen-year-olds are naturally clannish, their customs and rituals mysterious to an interloper, who is particularly vulnerable to exclusion if he or his family looks and behaves differently from the locals. Irv was preternaturally tall and gangling, nearly six feet; more sophisticated than us, having grown up in the Bronx; had parents we mocked, especially his mother; and generally thought, or pretended to think, of himself as a superior being. Nature and chance seemed stacked against him; he committed suicide before he was thirty.

Irv and I, outsiders both, were friends for a few years; high schools parted us, and that metamorphic movie afternoon was the friendship's high point. We decided to buy black motorcycle boots, jeans, turtlenecks, and leather jackets, and to wear this gangster garb to school to announce our coming-of-age. Irv suggested we cap our outfits with black berets and call ourselves The Black Pierres. The suggestion must have been his, because at the time, I might have been able to find France on a globe, but no more. Next day, we marched into our seventh-grade classroom, proclaimed our new identities to teacher and classmates, and were suspended minutes later.

My parents did not harangue or punish me for this suspension nor those that punctuated my high school years. They had no concern for education as a process or end in itself, only for its possible social and commercial consequences. My mother coveted the prestige that would accrue from having a college graduate son but counted on my brother to provide it. He did not disappoint her. When Creighton "skipped" the five brightest children in grades five, six, and seven to relieve overcrowding, he was one of his grade's five.

My father's fundamental values trumped the lip service he paid to education. For him, education's purpose was to make money. He told me often

I should *Get an education, 'cause they can't take that from you*, but did nothing to encourage my studies. I had little will to swot lessons after working thirty-odd hours, Thursdays through Sundays, in his butcher shop. He had little regard for teachers and none for intellectuals. He respected charter captains, like Holmes, and boxers; he was proud I broke rules and got into trouble—it was what real boys did. If that meant poor school performance, so be it. There was more than a tinge of the sociopath in Joe.

Butcher Shops

Butcher shops, Central High, the sea, and girls schooled my late childhood and adolescence, school as such the least important.

The Store

Mort Tannenbaum, a tall, porky, buttoned-up, gray-suited man, carrying a large black briefcase, made weekly house calls on small businessmen like my father, whose accountant he was. Monday nights at 7 p.m. they sat side by side at the dining-room table, so close their knees touched, examining black columns on pale-blue-lined graph paper that autopsied the Store's prior week's performance, often totaled in red ink at the bottom right. He was a meek angel of death.

Joe would call Louise to the dining room after Mort's visitations and show her the papers he had left. Her face would fall, then their voices; they'd talk of cutting expenses or another trip to the safe-deposit box for the residue of the war profits. Then Joe binned the papers. He continued to fish once a week at least; Louise missed no beauty appointments and kept her daily on. But I understood the Store was in trouble, and my duty was to help.

Old enough for a paper route, I began delivering the *Evening Bulletin* after school and on weekends. And from the spring of 1952, my father shanghaied me on Sundays to wash platters, sweep, and do odd jobs if his regular cleaning man was absent. He paid me twenty-five cents an hour, and my mother did not object. I was nine and a half.

We left at 7:30 a.m. in his brown 1947 ex–Philip Morris delivery van. It had no passenger seat; I sat in the middle of a spare tire on the floorboards where the passenger seat should have been and held on to the doorframe to keep from sliding as we bounced over cobbles and slewed in trolley tracks down Fifth Street toward the Store. Big Willy dressed me in a clean apron and butcher's coat, the hems hiked and cuffs rolled to fit my four-foot frame, and by 8:30 a.m., more swaddled than clothed, I was washing platters.

The washtub was a fifty-gallon stainless steel can set over a drain below a spigot in the right-hand corner of the tiny cutting room at the rear of the Store. Beside the tub were two chopping blocks, stacked with dozens of yard-long, greasy, blood-congealed platters, weighing fifteen to twenty pounds, their enamel chipped from years of use. Opposite, by the back door, clumps of soiled greens soaked in two ten-gallon tin buckets that had once held chitterlings. Greens were platter-length grooved steel rods, holding three-inch tall, bunched green rubber strips no thicker than a matchbook; they were inserted between platters to suggest freshness.

I stood on an upturned Coke case beside the tub, filled it two-thirds full with the hottest water I could bear, immersed six or seven platters one at a time, added two cups of strong soap powder and a half glass of ammonia, and washed: scrubbed the platter's top half with a stiff bristle brush, turned it end for end, washed the bottom half, then balanced it on the tub rim below the spigot and rinsed. The last greens and platters lay drying on the block just before lunch.

After lunch, I raked the cellar floor; shoveled spilled rice, beans, burst cans, and rat shit into a garbage can; and sprinkled fresh sawdust, terrified a rat would jump me from behind a sack or carton. Then I swept and sprinkled the Store's floor, restocked the bags below the back counter, and with the help of a stepladder, the dry goods shelves in front, before washing the outside of the display-case windows with ammonia and clean rag.

Done most Sundays before closing time, I stood behind the counter, watching my father wait trade, bag orders, and make change. Some of the women, as well as the men, were hungover or still drunk after Saturday night. Joe's thumb, hidden below the countertop, held down the paper under the meat he was weighing; his pencil paused as he added a column of prices incorrectly in his favor, bantering with the customers while he robbed them. Sometimes he had me carry a large bag around the counter to a customer rather than lifting it over the countertop to them himself, while he made change for a ten rather than the twenty he'd been given. They'd say, *Thank yuh, L'll Joe*. Some tipped me a nickel or dime, and I would drop my head, red-faced, mute, avoiding their eyes; they thought me shy.

The Pennsauken Merchandise Mart

Pennsauken

Childhood's venues changed at twelve and a half, when I went to work in the Pennsauken Merchandise Mart, a windowless farmers market on forty level acres in New Jersey, five minutes across the Delaware River from Philadelphia. Joe bought a half interest in a butcher shop there after he closed his failing Fourth Street store. To save money, he put me to work in the cutting room and on the counter selling lunch meat. The partnership ruptured within two years, leaving my father in possession.

The Mart was a one-story, flat-roofed yellow cinder block coffin, floating in an open sea of asphalt where one thousand cars could park. Five blocks long, two boxcars wide, it took more than ten minutes to walk one of its two aisles end to end. Customers, almost all of whom were working class or poor, entered through one of the eight steel double doors evenly spaced down its two long sides, or the double glass doors at either end. It had no windows or skylights; once inside, whether it was night or day, fair or foul became a mystery, except when hail or heavy rain thrummed on the sheet-metal roof. You could see heat rise in waves from the asphalt parking lot, the Mart shimmer when the temperature hit one hundred degrees in summer, and feel the tar suck your shoes down as you walked across the melting parking lot. But you could not see, or smell, or hear childhood any longer.

The Mart's two uncarpeted concrete aisles, each a car-length wide, were stained with grime from patrons' work boots and plimsolls. There was neither air conditioning nor insulation. Six-foot-long fluorescent lights, two to a pod, hung ten feet from the floor and ran almost unbroken down both sides of the Mart's two aisles, tinting trade and tradesmen slightly green. A PA system blared country music (Hank Williams, Gentleman Jim Reeves, Patsy Cline, and Ernest Tubbs), '50s rock (Elvis, the Shirelles, Chuck Berry), and pop (Peggy Lee's "How Much Is That Doggy in the Window?" and Pat Boone singing "Love Letters in the Sand") from opening till closing time except on Christmas, when Alvin and the Chipmunks squeaked, "Here Comes Santa Claus"; Bing Crosby crooned "White Christmas"; and various groups and solos wailed the traditional religious songs in an endless loop.

Along the gray aisles, stalls crowded with folding tables were piled with boxes of seconds: Levis, Keds, socks, underpants, panties, bras, sweaters, skirts, wash-and-wear white shirts, clip-on ties, and caps. Lunch counters sold Philly steak sandwiches, hot dogs, burgers, French fries, kielbasa on buns, Coke, coffee, ice cream, and water ice; sweet stands vended soft pretzels, plain and candied popcorn, cotton candy, candy apples, jawbreakers, Hershey bars, chocolate kisses, and candy of every description. Other stalls offered axes, bowie knives, shotguns, rifles, hunting bows, work boots, and foul-weather gear; reject bowls, plates, cutlery, pots, and pans; light fishing tackle, toys, bicycles, strollers, belts, coats, tropical fish, pets, and pet supplies, the staples of the working poor.

Wednesday nights at 6 p.m., the Mart awoke to chains rattling up through eyebolts. Merchants opened locks, raised chain-link shutters, and bedded down at ten to their jangling descants. Open forty-two of the next ninety-six hours—twelve hours Friday, fourteen hours Saturdays—it accommodated the rhythm of the working man's week; not a destination shopping center, it attracted no rubberneckers.

I worked there fifty weeks a year for the next eight years. Fridays 4 p.m. to midnight and Saturdays 8 a.m. to 6 p.m. stretched to Thursday nights through Sundays by the time I was sixteen, with the exception of one three-month interlude. My last working day at Pennsauken was the Sunday before Christmas, 1963.

The three-month hiatus occurred a year into my hitch, coinciding with the hiring of a new cashier. She was the only woman employee; a fetching woman in her midthirties with long black colleen hair, blue eyes, and long thin legs, she lightened the atmosphere in the place. My father began to take pains with his appearance, curse less, and take longer lunch breaks. A few weeks after she entered the cashier's booth, my presence seemed less essential; I was given occasional Friday nights off and sent home early some Saturdays. Longer hours resumed when Uncle Al, my mother's detective brother, produced proof of dalliance, and the cashier was fired.

* * *

Pennsauken Meats had two parts: the back room—hidden from customers, where meat and poultry were received, prepared, and stored—and the counter, a line of white enameled refrigerated cases, where the meat and poultry were displayed and sold. The back room was the store's industrial heart, a windowless, eighteen-by-thirty-foot rectangle with three walk-in iceboxes, chopping blocks, cutting tables, slicers, grinder, band saws, and washtubs. Knives, cleavers, slicers, and saw blades were all that gleamed there. An automatic slicer the size of a V8 car engine; a meat grinder with a throat as large as a man's forearm; and a Hobart band saw, seven feet tall with a one-hundred-ten-inch circular blade, a half inch wide and three teeth to the inch—these growled, screamed, and whirred all day long. The back room sounded like a machine shop.

You could hear rats—we called them freezer rats—scuttle away when you opened the door to the large walk-in freezer opposite the back room. They gnawed through a foot of concrete foundation and three-inch plywood floor to nibble frozen turkeys stored for the holidays. We shaved the chewed areas with the band saw to remove the teeth marks before the turkeys went on sale. When we made sausage, you could smell the rancid grease from the green pork trimmings that comprised it as well as the sage mixed with sodium nitrite to turn the trimmings pink again.

Frankie—the deli man—sliced lunch meats; helped make hamburger and sausage; cut up frying chickens for sale as breasts, legs, wings, and giblets; and generally cleaned. I was his understudy. Lean, five foot nine, Black, about twenty-five, he had developed his heavily muscled body in the prison where he had spent two years before coming to work at Pennsauken Meats. He straightened and pomaded his hair, wore a do-rag after the fashion of gang members, was a professional-level checkers and Ping-Pong player—also courtesy of the penitentiary—and a rough trade's gentle teacher.

We sold nearly a one-third ton of sliced lunch meats between 5 p.m. Friday and 11 p.m. Saturday, all of it sliced by Frankie and me. He showed me

how to set the slicer's blade for slice thickness. Each item had its own setting: cut too fine, the meat or cheese broke up; too thick and it made poor
sandwiches. Either way, it wouldn't sell. Frankie taught me to slice faster by
darting my hand under the slicer's stacking arm on its upswing and whisk-
ing a lunch meat pile from the slicer tray while the slicer ran, so it didn't
stop till a whole baloney or ham was sliced. The slicer ran from 8 a.m. to
10 p.m. Fridays, Saturdays 8 a.m. to 8 p.m. Clean, set, slice, platter, store in
the deli box; clean, set, slice . . . over and over, twelve hours a day.

I learned to push hamburger and sausage while standing on a rickety
stool above the grinder tray, feeding scraps into its maw so they emerged
smoothly from the forcing plate into the hands of the butcher below me.
Frankie taught me to cut and platter the frying chickens that came buried
in congealed ice inside flimsy, thin-slatted pine crates, each weighing north
of sixty pounds, bound with stapled hanger wire. Grasp a chicken's legs;
drag it from the ice; sever the legs, wings, and back from the breast; nick
the breastbone so the breast spreads easily; then pile the parts separately
for plattering. Within weeks, it took no more than ninety seconds from
the time I plunged my hand into the ice until the severed parts joined their
proper piles.

Chickens are dirty birds, their frozen tombs no cleaner. The ice's jagged
edges pricked fingers and wrist as you jammed your hand in to extract a
chicken; the fowl's sharp shank spurs jabbed your palm as you tightened
your grip to pull it out. No one wore gloves; none were offered. I was slicing lunch meats one Saturday a few hours after segmenting fryers when a
lump began to form in my armpit and my temperature began to rise. I told
one of the butchers cutting pork chops at his block across the room, and
he came over, took my arm, turned it palm up, and pointed to a red line
running up the vein from my wrist to armpit: blood poisoning. Frankie
drove me in the truck to the emergency room, where I gave my name,
age (thirteen and a half), and address; received a shot; and went back to
work. The telltale line, the swelling and fever, reappeared a few months
later, again a few hours after cutting up chickens. I took a taxi to the hospital, asked the driver to wait, and returned to work after the injection.
This process repeated itself once or twice each year while I worked at
Pennsauken. Gloves would have reduced the risk but slowed the dismem-
bering. It was faster and cheaper to risk occasional septicemia and a quick
visit to the hospital than take seconds more per chicken. When we were
busiest, breaks were few and short: piss outside against the wall between

the back-room door and walk-in freezer; fifteen minutes for hamburger, fries, and coffee at the lunch counter next door; and perhaps thirty minutes' break in a twelve-hour Saturday. I was wolfing a burger at the lunch counter one Saturday just before noon, some months into my apprenticeship, in a gory apron and butcher's coat. A prim, school-marmish older woman stopped for a coffee, noticed me, and asked, *How old are you, young man?*

Thirteen.

Do you work at that butcher's next door?

Yes, ma'am.

You shouldn't be working there!

She downed her coffee, stepped up to our meat counter, and asked for the manager. I heard her tell my father it was illegal to employ a boy my age in a butcher shop and that she was going to report him. If she did, no one did anything about it.

* * *

Pennsauken's counter—ten cases, each four feet high and three feet wide, packed with sixteen kinds of thinly sliced deli, cuts of beef, veal and pork, chickens, turkeys, hamburger, and sausage—ran the length of two buses down the Mart's north aisle. I was taught to work it a few months after starting in the back room: how to stand, greet shoppers, weigh, bag, make change, and read a scale. Each cut's price per pound fronted every platter in the case, but when the counterman weighed an item, the scale showed the customer only the weight, though the counterman could see weight and cost in the magnifying window on his side of the scale. The customer knew the correct cost of what was weighed only if (1) the weight equaled the per-pound posted price, (2) you told her, or (3) she could multiply and divide fractions handily. Few could.

My father taught me to steal after I learned to read scales. He told me we advertised lower prices than the chain stores to compete, and at those prices, we might well lose money or, at best, break even. To make a profit, we had to add 5 percent to every sale. Then he showed me how.

We eschewed the crude methods he'd used in the Store: holding down the scale paper, sliding boxes of lard onto weighing pans, shortchanging. At Pennsauken Meats, we cheated customers by exploiting their difficulty with fractions. The trick was to avoid even weight. Boiled ham was eighty-nine cents a pound—five and a half cents an ounce, that is; if asked for a pound, you laid enough on the scale so that, even after removing a few slices, more than a pound remained. *A little over OK?* You asked the customer, and if so, you charged for a pound and three ounces ($1.05 with rounding), not the pound and two ounces ($.99) the scale showed.

Where odd-weight opportunities were lacking, you estimated the bill as you began toting, calculated 5 percent, and added that amount to the total. Sometimes you used both methods. If caught using either, you apologized, corrected the bill, and fixed the customer's face in mind, in case she shopped there again. Most walked away unaware they'd been cheated.

Every week I stole from every customer I could steal from, and mostly got away with it. Few expected a boy to fleece them. I chattered so as to ingratiate and distract and studied their clothes, faces, and conversations to guess those brighter or more alert and harder to cheat. A fair few became regulars and trusted me. From them, I stole 10 percent to keep my average up. Almost all were working-class women in shabby clothes and thin coats in winter with poor teeth and squalling infants or puling toddlers, faces smeared with chocolate or lollipops, tugging their mother's skirts.

I flushed with shame, not embarrassment, whenever I was caught, once or twice a week, making hard lots harder. I was ashamed each time I cheated, and I waited on tens of thousands in those eight years on the counter. The sense of guilt stayed with me. Ever since, when an affair begins, I rehearse the "5 percents" with my new lover.

THIEF

Dad taught me to steal when I turned 12.
In white apron over butcher's coat
hiked up a foot to clear the sawdust floor,
pencil stub on trussing twine
dangling from a buttonhole,
boyhood snatched and left behind,
I was hammered into a counterman.
    "Smile, say 'Help you ma'am?,'
give her odd weight
(even's too easy to calculate)
and add 5 percent to every sale,
or the Chains will eat our lunch."
Long ago I forgave his lies
that made me a thief so he could buy
a Jersey skiff, flash a two-inch roll,

and Mondays after schvitz visit his trull.
But the customers don't pardon me:
should grandee, politician, College Fellow praise
service I've rendered, building raised,
once more across the counter shoppers stand
empty bags in outstretched hands,
Blondie, with her seven ragged kids,
street sweepers, dailies, handymen,
discount coupons crumpled in their fists,
the working or redundant poor
I stole from weekly at his store,
stare, point, till I turn aside,
crimson, drop my eyes, and they convert
laudation that should shrive me into dirt.[3]

Central High

Central High School sits like the Acropolis on a hill at Ogontz and Olney Avenues, in the Logan section of North Philadelphia. For 175 years, superior secondary schoolers citywide have gone there to prepare for the colleges they will nearly all attend; it offers no vocational courses, no carpentry or plumbing, no bricklaying. Famous alumni are legion: Thomas Eakins, Daniel and Simon Guggenheim, Alexander Woolcott, Louis Kahn, Albert Barnes, Noam Chomsky, Bill Cosby, and more. Alone among U.S. public high schools, it may confer an academic degree, the BA. But I knew none of this in 1956. Olney was my neighborhood high school, which almost all Creightonians attended. Olney graduates were unlikely to go to college, and Olney was where I was headed until puppy love took a hand.

* * *

We call lust love at thirteen. Charlene Cores—a slight, blue-eyed, black-haired girl—lived four long blocks away across Roosevelt Boulevard, the eight-lane highway bisecting our neighborhood. She was probably in my class from first grade, but I didn't notice her till puberty sharpened my sight. Charlene, however, would have been happy had I remained blind: Valentines, Christmas cards, home runs smashed in half-ball as she

[3] Dan Burt, *Salvage at Twilight* (Manchester: Carcanet, 2019).

passed by, and devotion confessed to her friends had no more effect on her than did moping past her house at night or dating her best friend, Sonia Steinberg, to induce jealousy. But perhaps she would admire me if I went to Central, and admiration morph to more?

All I knew about Central was it did not take all comers. You had to apply: boys with higher IQ scores had a right to enroll; those with lower scores had to pass an entrance exam. I had done well in the ubiquitous mid-1950s American IQ tests; perhaps I wouldn't have to take the exam and likely fail. No grade school teacher said, "Try Central"; my parents objected: too far away; you're no student; nobody you know is going. Charlene failed to swoon when told that Central might have me, but I persevered, too young to understand that pheromones remain indifferent to test scores and determination.

*   *   *

I climbed the hill toward Central's three embossed, twelve-foot high, steel-fronted doors the Thursday after Labor Day, September 7, 1956. Charlene went to Olney. Central did not impress her, nor I it. An hour after my first day there had begun, I shuffled back home down the hill, suspended within minutes of arriving. Charlene never spoke to me again, not even at our grade school class reunion in 1986, when she ignored me as she had done thirty years before.

Behind Central's front doors, the main hall ran the length of half a football field to the South Lawn, where at lunch break in good weather, we dawdled, sneaked cigarettes, and occasionally fought. That first day, the hall's sixteen-foot ceilings and marble walls bearing portraits of past school presidents and notable alumni cowed me. Signs labeled "Orientation" and older boys with armbands herded us up four flights to the top-floor lunchroom, which served four hundred at a time; it could have been an army mess hall. Rows of yard-wide, three-inch-thick, rectangular oak-top dining tables—drawn up in serried ranks like soldiers on parade—flanked the stainless steel serving counters. Each table sat forty boys, twenty a side, on round oak stool tops bolted to curved steel arms, hinged to the table's central support; diners swung the seats out to sit, and back when they rose. We found a table posted with the first letter of our last name, sat, and waited for orientation to begin.

Most of the boys knew what to expect. They lived in middle- and upper-middle-class homes—80 percent of them Jewish—in Oak Lane, Oxford

Circle, Mount Airy, Wynnefield, and Society Hill—Philadelphia's better parts. Second-generation Central boys whose fathers had gone to college were not unusual. They came in cliques from gleaming junior high schools, where they had spent grades six, seven, and eight preparing for Central, with a view to college. They were ambitious, superior, self-confident, elite, and they disdained outsiders.

Elmer Field, Central's president ("principal" in lesser schools) called, *Boys, boys,* welcomed us to ninth grade, and began explaining how to find our homerooms, where each morning, we would meet before class for roll-taking and administrative matters. I turned to the boy on my left and asked, *What's a homeroom?* Two seats to my right across the table, a boy guffawed. *Hey, look at that shmuck; he doesn't even know what a homeroom is!* I flushed, sprang across the table, and knocked him off his stool. We were quickly parted, and I was sent, not for the last time, to Mr. Christman—vice principal and disciplinarian—who suspended me.

My parents didn't punish me. My father would have done the same, and he was quietly proud. My mother's clan would have done worse. And my parents no longer had a lash to hand: I was too big to beat (I might hit back), had little free time to dock (school, homework, and butcher shop took almost all of it), no allowance to halt (I earned my spending money), and my father wouldn't forfeit cheap, trusted labor that allowed him to fish a second or third day each week.

* * *

Central forbade us to break bounds—leave school grounds—for lunch; we had to buy it in the cafeteria or "brown-bag" it from home. But school food was execrable, brown-bagging a nuisance and "square." There were hamburgers and hot dogs, Cokes and malted milks at the luncheonettes a short sprint past the school monitors up Olney Avenue, where our lit cigarettes smoldered on the steel rims of pinball machines pinging and flashing away, and fumes from the grease and oil in which your order fried made your mouth water. Mr. Christman suspended me a third time that year, not for fighting or cutting class, but for breaking bounds. He insisted this time that my father, rather than just my mother, come to school to reinstate me.

We filed into his office for our audience: swarthy, thick-armed ghetto butcher; fair-skinned, white-gloved housewife, fattened from a third child in her late-fertile years; pint-sized, slouching ninth grader. John D. Christman unfolded himself from behind his desk to receive us in a dark-gray three-piece suit with a gold watch fob showing what might have been a dangling Phi Beta Kappa key slung across his undistended stomach, his thin white hair combed straight back and trimmed short of a white collar—six inches taller than my five-foot-five father and every inch a WASP. We sat before him in a row while he chastised me.

He rehashed the rule against breaking bounds and reminded me this was not the first time I'd been caught. He explained the rule's reasons and intoned the consequences for flaunting it. *Now, give me your word you won't leave school grounds again during lunch period.*

No! School food stinks. He turned to my father, said, *You see, Mr. Burt, what we're up against,* and waited for his reply. *Well, how bad is the school food?* I suffered more suspensions during my Central years, but my father was not requested to attend another reinstatement.

* * *

Classwork was no more palatable than school lunches. We studied set subjects in the ninth grade—English, algebra, Latin, history, science, social studies, and art—and were graded twice a year at the end of each semester. If you failed Latin 1A in the fall semester, you had to repeat and pass it in the spring, then take Latin 1B at summer school to stay with your class. You could end up attending school twelve months a year during your four high school years—if you failed consistently—and in my first two years, that was what I did, flunking two subjects the first year, one the second. But with electives, one teacher's interest, and a girl, came better grades; the last two years, I avoided summer school.

John Mulloy taught European history at Central during the day, and at La Salle College, a Christian Brothers institution, three nights a week. He was a first, or at most, second-generation Irish American, five feet ten or so with tortoiseshell oval glasses above crooked yellow teeth and a purple-pocked face—so gaunt he might have landed from Famine Galway. Catholicism enveloped and sustained him; he had six children, an ash cross on his forehead every Wednesday at the start of Lent, and he regarded Chartres, Aquinas, and monasticism as the consummation of European history. Mr. Mulloy, humble before his God, was a countercultural figure amid Central's striving Jewish majority.

Average sophomores at Central chose one elective in tenth grade; members of the advanced class, the top 10 percent, could choose two. Modern European history interested my father; he followed international news in the local press and on national radio and TV and read historical novels from the Reader's Digest Condensed Book Club, articles on foreign affairs, and history in *Reader's Digest*, *Life*, and *Time*. He argued about prewar Europe with immigrant acquaintances at schvitz and with his sons, when they began to learn about such things in their grade school *Weekly Reader*. I chose modern European history as my tenth-grade elective and studied it in a class of mostly advanced students whose second-choice elective it was.

The boys besieged Mr. Mulloy from the outset, and he was often outmatched. He knew more, of course, but they were smarter, with quicker minds. Virtues he claimed for what they believed were the Dark Ages were inconsistent with what they'd been taught, and medieval achievements of a culture that brought their forebears pogroms and, at its end, the Inquisition, were always going to be a hard sell. Many in the class were headed for careers in science, medicine, or law. Their rationalist faith held revealed religion in teenage contempt. A few were bullies.

Michael Kirsch, their ringleader, for example: fifteen, in the advanced class, Mulloy's height, and sporting vestigial baby fat, smart clothes, and popularity. He wore the black wool bomber jacket of a Jewish Greek-letter fraternity to class each day: gold-piped sleeves, cuffs, waistband, gold collar, and gold AZA in Roman letters across its front, Mike in cursive on the back. From his second-row seat by the windows, opposite the door, Mike Kirsch raised his hand in Mr. Mulloy's face every day to argue and quibble for his peers' amusement, waste time, and try the patience of John Mulloy. No one took the teacher's side.

I sat in the back, silent, ignored, where the rear and door-side walls met, ten rows diagonally behind and to the right of Kirsch. Modern European history intrigued me: my paternal grandmother, still hale and vicious, had lived part of it; I knew men who'd been in the camps. Like me, Mulloy was a Central outsider, though for different reasons. His Catholic, spiritual critique of American materialism and exceptionalism focused my anger. I wanted to hear what he had to say; I wanted Kirsch to shut up.

Had I hit Kirsch in class, I would have been expelled rather than suspended, and by the class's end, the fury had always passed. Some three weeks into term, seething with frustration, I spoke up on Mulloy's side during an inane argument and, to my surprise, silenced Kirsch. As I left class, Mulloy told me to come to his office during lunch period. There, he praised my argument and me for speaking up, asked where I lived, what school I'd come from, and invited me to drop by again to talk. I was suspicious—no teacher had shown interest in me before. But if the Temple veil was not rent, that lunchtime, there was at least a small tear.

4. The Blue Guitars

> The man replied, "Things as they are
> Are changed upon the blue guitar"
>
> **WALLACE STEVENS**, "The Man with the
> Blue Guitar"

John Mulloy

Mr. Mulloy's refuge was on Central's second floor, above the doors to the South Lawn: a narrow rectangle, three doorways wide, squeezed by books shelved floor to ceiling down east and west walls. A standard-issue, yellowed oak office desk stood before the south window at the far end. Two chairs faced the desk, and behind the desk sat Mr. Mulloy, back to the window, facing the door five yards away. It was a good defensive position.

His invitation offered an alternative to disruption, cutting class, and mooching about with hunched shoulders looking for an excuse to fight. But what would we talk about? I paid more attention in his class, read the textbook, and thought about both. If a question went unanswered or unasked in class, I'd stop by to talk about it. By academic year's end, we were talking in his office half an hour each week.

Words worked no miracles; I failed another course that year and went to summer school again, but for one subject, not two. After our conversations began, I still fought, cut classes and school, but less. We talked more the next year, when he did not teach me, and often twice a week in my senior year. History and politics were not our only subjects. I told him about Pennsauken, girls, drag racing, and what had grown to be loathing for classmates and their superciliousness. He listened, countered Madison Avenue and Engine Charlie Wilson with Maritain and Huizinga, Levittown with Notre Dame.

John F. Kennedy began his run for the Democratic presidential nomination in New Hampshire in January 1960, the beginning of my last term at Central. The country wondered whether a Catholic could be elected president in Protestant America. Mr. Mulloy recalled Catholic Al Smith's loss to

Hoover in 1928 and pondered whether the country had changed. For the first time, I saw bigotry's scars on a man not Black or Jewish. When JFK won the primary in West Virginia, a southern Baptist stronghold, Mulloy walked taller into his classes.

Life magazine ran a feature on Kennedy's Hyannis and Harvard—photos of gray shingle cottages on Cape Cod beaches, sailboats, blue blazers and white ducks, grand-columned Widener library, red-and-gold-leaved Yard, and redbrick student dorms called houses, named for the Brahmin dead. My mentor told me what little he knew about this Olympus that he had not tried to scale, and an unknown world became my lodestar. Mr. Mulloy believed in the American dream and in education as its ladder; he just wanted Catholics on it.

Our conversations ended when I left Central, before JFK won the election on the back of Chicago corpses resurrected to vote—before the Cuban missile crisis, Sam Giancana, Judith Exner, Frick and Frack in the White House pool when Jackie was out of town; before assassination clawed the gilt from Camelot. I made no friends at Central, rejected its ethos, returned to no reunions. But I remembered John Mulloy, who opened the borders of my mind. When I returned to Philadelphia from Cambridge and Yale, a decade later, I looked him up to thank him.

The Sea

> Sixty miles due east of Philadelphia lay another country: Barnegat Light and the sea.

Captain J Burt

Long Beach Island is an eighteen-mile sandspit facing the Atlantic Ocean, which Barnegat Bay splits from the New Jersey Pine Barrens. The narrow island is pancake flat except for a sand dune spine one story high down its entire length, a few hundred feet back from the surf; the ocean cut it in two at least three times in the last century during spring nor'easters. It has clean beaches for vacationers and the best fishing in Jersey out of Barnegat Light. Joe fished its bays, inlets, and offshore waters from the time I was four and a half.

The sea is a perilous place. I went down to it for the first time in late spring 1947. My father and I, plus a nurse for him, *just in case*, boarded a charter boat at Beach Haven to fish for flounder. A charter boat, booked in advance, fishes for whatever the party wants, unlike the much cheaper head boats that take all comers at so much a head to fish for what's advertised. We were catching flounder when the captain told us to reel in and made for a distress flare from a U-Drive garvey drifting half a mile away.

Tyros could rent small boats like garveys to run themselves—U-Drives—for the day. The driveshaft came out the back end of an engine box mounted on deck amidships and down through the deck to form a small triangle covered by a wooden housing. Nothing covered this garvey's driveshaft: when the engine was running, the shaft and propeller coupling rotated unprotected above the deck. One of the men aboard her had caught his trouser cuff in the turning coupling, shredding his leg from ankle to knee. There was blood everywhere—I saw the man's shinbone white through his flesh before my father bundled me away—and he was screaming. Our nurse bandaged his tatters, gave him a shot of morphine from a first aid kit, and we waited for the coastguard.

Holmes Russell ran parties on his garvey in 1947 to fish for striped bass and bluefish inshore. He was a North Carolinian from a hillbilly family, wiry, white-haired, and missing three fingertips—two from his left, one from his right hand. Sun and salt water had tanned his skin almost to leather. Holmes—or "Russ," as Joe called him—grew up on the waters around Oregon Inlet, ran a still in the North Carolina Blue Ridge Mountains during Prohibition, and delivered white lightning liquor (moonshine) to the towns below. He could fix anything, built his own thirty-six-foot fishing boat named the *Jolly Roger*—as well as his house at Barnegat Light—and was reputed to be the best inshore skipper on the Jersey coast. He used the garvey to catch grass shrimp for bait in summer and to clam in winter. The garvey was battleship gray; on a rainy December afternoon, bent over its side, jamming a pair of long-handled clamming tongs into the Barnegat mud flats, both he and it seemed wraiths.

HOMAGE FOR A WATERMAN
  (i.m. Holmes Russell)

He jams clam tongs down three feet
and fetches bottom, pulls them so wide

he's spread-eagled over the bay,
scissors back, heaves till knuckles meet,
and hoists the bales over the side,
squinting for little necks or oysters,
a black stick figure in oil-skins
pile driving in November sleet.[4]

Joe began chartering with Holmes when he still fished from the garvey. Striped bass are a prized inshore game fish: wily, hard fighting, and weighing up to eighty pounds, their white, dry flesh is especially good to eat. Holmes knew more about them and how to catch them than anyone else. They wintered in brackish creeks that feed Barnegat Bay, and in the spring, schools of three to five pounders, schoolies, headed down the bay and out the Inlet to feed on sand eels offshore and migrate north. Bigger fish haunted the jetties and bars of the Barnegat Inlet from spring through late fall; if you wanted big bass, it was the Inlet you fished to catch them.

The shoals, which stud the east coast's inlets south of Cape Cod, make the inlets treacherous gauntlets in an onshore wind: Barnegat Inlet is one of the worst. A tiara of sandbars rings it from north to south, and sandbar pendants choke its approaches. Dutch settlers named it *Barendegat*, inlet of the breakers, in 1614, for the seas that rear meerschaum-white and break over its bars in the calmest weather. The Inlet is impassable when strong easterly winds pile seas on its bars. There is always a boom and roar of waves breaking; close up, it sounds like rushing trains. Lines from "The Charge of the Light Brigade" come to mind as you round the Barnegat Lighthouse and head east toward the breaking seas:

Cannon to right of them,
Cannon to left of them,
Cannon in front of them
Volly'd and thunder'd.

For nearly 150 years, men tried to tame the Inlet. The Army Corps of Engineers built two gray granite boulder jetties in the early 1900s from

[4] Dan Burt, *Salvage at Twilight*.

the Inlet's north and south shores, like a half-mile-long rock funnel, to channel water from bay to ocean and stop the north tip of Long Beach Island from eroding. The Corps had no more success than Canute; the bars continued to grow, shrink, and shift, and the island's sands washed away. The Corps beefed them up with more rocks every fifteen years or so, to no avail. The U.S. Life-Saving Service opened station number seventeen at the Light around 1872; the coastguard has a well-manned station there to this day. A thirty-five-foot coastguard lifeboat, double-ended like a great white canoe with a wheelhouse in its middle, always lay in the Inlet in rough weather to rescue boats in trouble. She had two powerful engines and could roll through 360 degrees, right herself, and stay on station. Nevertheless, one or two boats got into trouble in the Inlet every year, and one or more men were lost. Few amateurs used the Barnegat Inlet in the 1950s.

I was six my first time in the Inlet. Joe had chartered Captain Jack Sylvester's twenty-eight-foot skiff to troll for blues offshore. The mate was Sylvester's twelve-year-old son, Barty. A storm had passed offshore a few days earlier, and big swells were running. They made up into breaking seas higher than the skiff's cabin top when they fetched up on the bars. The coastguard lifeboat rolled wildly on station at the inshore edge of the north bar. Sylvester had a drinking problem and may not have been quite clearheaded enough that morning to realize it was not a good day to take a twenty-eight-foot skiff through the Inlet, or perhaps he was desperate for his hire. We were a third of the way out of the Inlet and taking big seas on the bow every few minutes by the time he decided to quit, but turning back was dangerous. Barty went below and came up with life jackets: big, bulky yellow prewar canvas vests with cork blocks sewn in pockets for flotation. Joe helped me into mine and tied it tight. The critical moment would come when Sylvester tried to go about, and we would be sideways to the waves rather than with our nose into them. If a sea caught us broadside, we could capsize.

Joe cut an eight-foot length of rope and tied one end around his waist and the other around my left ankle. As Sylvester prepared to put the wheel over, my father looked at me and said, *Whatever happens, don't let go of the rope.* He had beat me, he had yelled at me, but he had never told me to do anything the way he told me to hold on to that rope. We came about in the trough of a sea and, pitching and rolling, scuttled safely back through the Inlet. That was Joe's last trip with Sylvester, who left Barnegat and his

Danny, age seven or eight, with two bluefish on a dock in Forked River

family not long afterward. Holmes married Sylvester's ex-wife, and Barty became his stepson and the *Jolly Roger*'s mate.

*　*　*

The favored ways to catch stripers, requiring the most skill and with the greatest chance of catching a large one, were to chum the jetties or cast the bars. Inch-and-a-half-long grass shrimp with shells the color of the sandy bottom on which they lived made the Barnegat jetties a buffet for stripers. Holmes would anchor within ten feet of their rocks so that a rivulet of chum, four or five grass shrimp sprinkled from a live-bait box every few minutes, trickled down the jetty from the boat. Light lines with two shrimp impaled on little black hooks floated along with the chum. There is an art to chumming: Holmes explained it to Joe the first time they anchored on the jetty—how to bait the hook, strip the line, what the trick was—then stood beside him and started catching bass. After baiting, stripping, and going fishless for an hour while Holmes caught bass after bass, Joe asked him to explain again. Homes said, *I showed you once; watch me.* Joe never asked again; he fished next to Holmes for a year and a half before he caught his first bass. Most men can remember when, where, and with whom they caught theirs; I was eleven, chumming on the inside of the north jetty with Holmes.

*   *   *

It was a fair fight between angler and striper on the jetties: one had tackle, skill, a boat; the other, strength, sea, and rocks. Big bass head for the open sea when they're hooked. You can't stop them with light chumming tackle, and a fish much over twenty pounds runs until it tires of fighting the rod tip and reel drag. Joe and Holmes were chumming inside the south jetty in the garvey at high tide in early spring when Joe hooked a bass he couldn't slow, a fish more powerful than any he'd hooked before. It steamed across the jetty, bound for Ireland, and would shortly either strip the reel or cut the line on the jetty's barnacles. Joe hollered, *Russ, I can't hold him*, and Holmes yelled back, *Hold on!* Net boats had caught some very large bass offshore a few days before, and Holmes had visions of a light tackle world record. He started the engine, severed the anchor line, and eyed the seas washing over the jetty. He picked a big one, gunned the garvey toward the rocks, cleared them, and chased that bass into the open sea with Joe in the bow, rod tip high, reeling when the bass paused. Ninety minutes later, they were nearly two miles out at sea when Holmes gaffed the striper. Not a record, but not many pounds shy.

The *Jolly Roger* lay in the wash of six-to-eight-foot-high seas breaking across the north bar one fall afternoon, her party casting with light spinning tackle for bass. Joe hooked one too strong to turn that headed for deep water beyond the bar. The only chance to land it was to follow it through the breakers into deep water. Holmes reversed the engine and backed down across the bar. The cockpit swamped, but Holmes kept going. When Joe stood beside the sixty-pound bass for photographs that evening, someone asked him why he was wet almost to his armpits.

Holmes rarely cast off more than half an hour past sunrise; if one of the party was late, he didn't fish with Russ that day. Barnegat Light was a ninety-minute drive from Whitaker Avenue down a two-lane highway, so Joe often left before 4 a.m. One morning, he overslept and, when he started his new 1954 Chrysler Windsor, had less than an hour before the *Jolly Roger* sailed. A state trooper fell in behind him as he accelerated east from the last circle down Route 72. Joe saw the flashing light, heard the siren, and held the hammer down. The chase continued at a steady 100–115 miles an hour—as fast as that Chrysler went—for 30 miles down 72, across the causeway, onto the island, and north to the dock where Holmes had the engine running and all but one mooring line untied. Joe screeched into the parking lot, and the trooper roared in behind. Joe leaped from the

Joe with two big striped bass caught from Holmes's garvey, circa 1948

car, ran the few feet to the boat, jumped aboard, and Holmes cast off. They had a good day. Two state police cruisers and four troopers were waiting on the dock to arrest Joe when the *Jolly Roger* backed into her slip that afternoon.

Heavy black rubber bags filled with iced fluke, stripers, and weakfish in spring and fall and blues, tuna, and stripers in summer rode home with Joe from the Tuesday fishing trips. Neighbors watched his car roll up our alley and hoped he'd had a good day. They came with newspaper under their arms to ask if he had fish for them. He dumped the catch—ice, blood, and melt on the cement by our back drain—hosed it down, and gave away what we didn't need, often most of what lay on the ground. He washed, rinsed, and left the bags to dry in the garage until the next Monday night, when he loaded the car again with rods, reels, and tackle for the predawn drive to Barnegat Light. The alley smelled of fish on Wednesday mornings, and local trash cans brimmed with fish heads, tails, and scales wrapped in old newspapers.

Holmes and Joe fished together for ten years. After Holmes built the *Jolly Roger* and overfishing had decimated bass stocks, they abandoned the jetties for offshore: the Barnegat Ridge, twenty miles northeast, to catch blues on spinning tackle till hands were too tired to turn the reel cranks, and the ocean beyond for tuna weighing up to 100 pounds, Mako sharks of 150 pounds, and a white marlin or two. But the *Jolly Roger* was slow, and Holmes's forte was not blue-water work beyond the ridge, where charts, parallel rulers, compasses, and protractors were needed; he never was quite comfortable farther offshore than dead reckoning could take him. It was long before the days of GPS, and Holmes's reading was a little uncertain. Joe had learned almost all that Holmes had to teach him about the sea and fishing.

* * *

Ducks and geese rose quacking and honking out of the bay's salt marshes at daybreak as the charter boats headed for the Inlet. Ribbons of them streaked the skies, heading north in spring and south in fall. Clouds of gulls wheeled above the bars and beyond the breakers off the beaches and dived on fleeing baitfish. The sun rose like a new penny from the sea's edge as we'd head offshore; helmsmen squinted into it to avoid flotsam and keep their course. It died rose red and blinded them again when they were heading home. White caps formed when the wind rose above ten knots and the sea backs glowed mint green. Beyond the sixty-fathom line, the green of the ocean took on a magnolia tint. At sea, there were no vomiting drunks, no aprons with dried rust-brown pork blood, no customers demanding cuts from the front of the case, no cops on the take, no rats behind rice sacks, no registers, and no pushcart men and boys huddled around oil drum trash fires waiting for trade. There were no Jews remembering pogroms, no hit men, no bullies. Barnegat Light was Joe's Blessed Isles, and he fell in love with the sea.

After a few years, fishing one day a week was too little; Joe began to fish Wednesdays as well and muse on the long predawn drives to the dock about buying a boat and becoming a charter captain. Holmes was hardly encouraging, and other charter men told him he had too much to learn before he could handle a boat in the Inlet and fish the waters offshore and that he was too choleric to make a skipper. He bought a twenty-five-foot single-engine MayCraft early one summer in the mid-1950s, named her *Dan-Rick* after his two sons in the order of their birth, and a week later, took her tuna fishing. He was forty miles off when the prevailing southwesterly built to twenty miles an hour from ten, as it will on a summer afternoon, and what had been a following sea became a head sea when he came about for home. The course back was almost dead into the wind and a five-foot sea: it was four hours going and eight coming back. He took more water over the bow than he ever did again and was soaked through when he reached the dock, shaken, aware the *Dan-Rick* would not serve his purpose.

Seamen say that thirty feet and over, it's the skipper, not the boat, that counts. The MayCraft was gone within days, replaced by a thirty-foot Pacemaker with twin ninety-five horsepower Chrysler engines, carvel planked and soft chinned. She rolled but didn't pound and made her way featly through a head sea. It's supposedly bad luck to change your boat's name; he christened the Pacemaker *Dan-Rick*, and so she remained when his third and final child, a daughter, was born. His third boat and then his last were *Dan-Rick*s too.

Joe took friends fishing on *Dan-Rick* for a few years with me as mate and began to study for a charter captain's license to take people fishing for hire. He was known as Captain Joe when he died forty years later, in 1995, the only Jewish charter captain on the Jersey coast. Some said he was as good as was Holmes in his prime, but I had been gone too long to attest to that. We buried him in his fishing clothes, Capt. J Burt in blue-thread script stitched across the right breast pocket of his short-sleeved khaki shirt, *Dan-Rick* across the left.

* * *

We fetched the second *Dan-Rick* from the Pacemaker yard at Forked River on a gray, windy late summer's morning. Thirty-five minutes later, we were leaving the channel opposite the Barnegat Lighthouse when Joe decided to try her in a sea and headed east toward the south jetty rather than west to our dock. A palisade of breaking seas stretched in a concave arc from jetty to jetty beyond the Inlet's mouth, like a shark's jaw. The coastguard lifeboat rolled on the north bar; there were no boats offshore. Two boat lengths off the rocks and halfway up the south jetty, it was clear that it was too rough to leave the Inlet. Joe put the wheel over to port to come about, but nothing happened. He twirled the wheel to starboard, but she did not answer. We had lost our steering in the inshore approach to the Barnegat Inlet in a twenty-five miles per hour northeast wind, and wind and waves were pushing us rapidly toward the south jetty's rocks. Joe grabbed the ship-to-shore's handset and tuned the dial to the distress channel. I heard the first and, so far, only *Mayday! Mayday! Mayday!* from a vessel I was aboard. The Barnegat Light Coastguard Station answered and told us to anchor up and wait for the rescue boat; it was already underway. I went forward, untied the anchors, and threw and set them both.

The coastguard towed us to the station where a young coastguard came aboard and helped us fix the steering. The *Dan-Rick* left the station at about 1 p.m.; we'd been there an hour. The wind had strengthened; rain squalls blew through from time to time, hiding the salt marsh sedge the gusts bent almost double. Joe sat on the bridge in the wind and rain, and when we reached the channel a hundred yards or so from the station, he turned northeast toward the Inlet rather than southwest toward our dock and berth. We rounded the lighthouse into the Inlet's approaches and picked up speed, heading seaward. I called up, *Hey, Dad, where you going?* No answer. He was hunched stiff over the wheel, right hand on the twin throttles, long-billed fishing cap pulled low over his crew cut to keep out the rain and occasional spray. Twelve-foot waves built and crashed in the channel as we slammed past the tower at the end of the south jetty.

Breaking seas in the Inlet come in sets. Captains hold their boats just short of where they break, backing down if necessary (reversing to let the seas break in front of you) and counting seas, waiting for a lull. When the last sea breaks, the water beyond is white with foam but flat for half the length of a soccer pitch, and a boat can cross where the waves make up before the first sea in the next set builds. The *Dan-Rick* was new and fast for her day. Joe shouted from the bridge, *Hold on!* and jammed the throttles all the way forward when a last sea broke. We skittered across a white foam tabletop through brown spots churned from the sandbar four or five feet below, swerved right toward the south bar to avoid a sea making up, took a small wave bow on, and burst into the white-capped open ocean. Joe sat silent on the bridge.

We circled north outside the bars and reached the north jetty about halfway down from the tower at its seaward end. The north bar is shallower than the others, the seas steeper but not so wide, more dangerous if you're caught but with narrower seas to catch you. In a blow, the professionals always went in the north side. They'd sneak up alongside the north jetty—almost to the tower, keeping as close to the rocks as possible—wait for a lull, turn their bow into the bar, and head across the mouth of the Inlet. When the next sea made up, they turned right, got on its back, and rode it like a surfboard shoreward toward the south jetty. Timed right, they were inside the bar safe home when it broke; too fast and they overran the sea and pitchpoled; too slow and the following sea pooped them. Once committed, you cannot stop. A coastguard in a life jacket watched through binoculars from the lifeboat as Joe began his run. He turned into the bar, opened her up, caught the next rising sea, and rode its back across the shoal till it collapsed well down the south jetty.

I climbed the ladder to the bridge and sat beside him for the short run to the dock. He throttled back near the marina, so our wake did not disturb the boats tied there. I had started down the ladder from the bridge to handle the bowlines when he said, without looking at me, *You know, Danny, if I hadn't done that, I'd have never fished again.*

Mate

I fished with my father sporadically during the years he chartered Holmes; it would have been unfair to impose an extra rod too often on the other men who shared the party's cost, even if held by a boy. My line tangled with theirs as easily as would a man's; I jockeyed for the best place along the gunwale, had to be given room fighting a fish, and by twelve could claim a man's share when the catch was divvied. But from 1955, when my father bought the first *Dan-Rick*, through the '63 season—before I broke my neck—I mated for him twice a week when school was out, barring days lost to summer school.

Few vehicles shared Route 70 East with us at 4 a.m., when we headed for Barnegat, though truckers and fishermen patronized the all-night diner at the third traffic circle, where we stopped for breakfast. Suburban sprawl and strip malls had not yet gnawed the villages, truck farms, and dairies dotting the first twenty-five miles from Pennsauken, a few miles east of Philadelphia across the Tacony-Palmyra Bridge to the start of the Jersey Pine Barrens. The Barrens didn't stop then, as they do now, at a palisade of summer cottages ten miles west of Long Beach Island but loomed for thirty uncurving miles on either side of Route 72's two concrete lanes, from the fourth traffic circle to Barnegat Bay.

No road lamps, farm lights, or clearings relieved the darkness through the Barrens to the sea. Colonial settlers' crops had struggled in the sandy, acidic soil; early industries—bog iron, logging—failed; in the twentieth century, the forest reclaimed it. Stubby, inflammable pitch pines crowded the road, renewed in the frequent fires summer lightning storms ignited. Roadkill included snakes—even timber rattlers—raccoons, deer, squirrels, turtles, feral cats, and dogs. Burning rubber stink, thickening the air and clinging to the car, tolled a skunk's knell.

The Pine Barrens is a primeval land, where men don't belong. They occupy a quarter of New Jersey's territory, and the absence of humans in so large an area, so close to major cities—New York and Philadelphia—combined with its impenetrability, the dialect, and alleged backwardness of the few Pineys living on its outskirts, nourished tales of ghosts and ghastly murders, in the same fashion as do Louisiana's bayous. The Barrens are a popular place for mafiosi to dispose of problems. I hunched my shoulders and scrunched down when we started through them and peered northeast for dawn's loom.

The *Dan-Rick* lay tied fore and aft, plus secured by two spring lines amidships, at the Barnegat Light Yacht Basin, which never berthed a yacht. An acrid mix of creosote-coated pilings, salt-stained teak, dried fish blood, vegetation, and discarded fish entrails rotting on mud flats charged the air around her. A few young charter and commercial skippers had mortgaged themselves at midcentury to build this working marina on Barnegat Bay's tidal fringe, two water miles from the Inlet, to free themselves from high dockage fees and low catch prices at their mainland docks and shorten their forty-five minutes' run to and from the sea; founders and locals called this dock "The Independent."

It had two sides: south for commercial fishermen like draggers and net boats, north for charter boats. The commercial dock inscribed a capital *E* on its back and the charter dock a backward capital *E*, its three arms parallel to the shore. The best charter men, including the Independent's founders, tied up along the charter dock's front row. Part-time charter boats and a few commercialmen under forty feet rocked in their slips along the middle and outer arms, bows to shore. *Dan-Rick*, the sole amateur's boat among the thirty-five in the basin, lay five slips in from the channel end of the outer arm, farthest from the pros.

A one-story, flat-roofed, cinder block building the size of a boxing ring and painted white, squatted on the parking lot's tarmac, six steps from the front slips; one half housed a walk-in icebox, the other a tackle shop. Front slips were handiest to bait-house and tarmac for loading ice, bait, and fishing parties in the morning, and for disgorging catch and fishermen to fish bags and cars in the afternoon; tourists hungering for a day's deep-sea fishing prowled them to select their hire; founders and their boats—Louie Puskas (who owned the *Gracee*), Johnny Larsen (*Miss Barnegat Light*), Charlie Eberle (*Doris May*)—sailed from them for the rest of their lives, as do their grandsons sixty years later. A half hour before sunup, we pulled into the parking lot and joined them.

* * *

Skippers—pro and tyro—turned cheeks from side to side to feel the wind, sniffed for rain, and tapped the bait-house barometer for any augury of afternoon thunderstorms as soon as they stood dockside in the dawn. Weather forecasts were subjunctive in the 1950s, before satellites, high-resolution infrared cameras, computers, and GPS combined to foretell the hourly weather precisely, days in advance, for a few-square-mile patch. Nowadays, fast, twenty-four-foot fiberglass open outboard skiffs safely chase tuna one hundred miles off; in 1955, they dared not leave the Inlet.

Skippers stood by the boats in clumps of twos and threes—waiting for parties, or in the tackle shop replacing gear lost the day before—and swapped information about how they'd done or where they might try that day. They were taciturn men, fourth- and fifth-generation Americans with Scotch Irish (Russell, Montgomery), Polish (Puskas, Kubell), and German (Eberle) surnames; light skinned, excepting arms and faces leathered by sun, sea, and wind; and flat-bellied, ectomorphic bodies from physical labor and staying upright on rolling small boat decks. They spoke quietly, with a slight bluegrass Carolinian drawl, curses limited to damn and shit; shouting was reserved for warnings. Talk mattered little. The catch thrown on the dock for sluicing measured captains at the end of every day. Salesmanship, clever arguments, threats, and fits were equally irrelevant: if you were skunked—returned fishless—you had failed. You could not cheat the fish or con the sea.

They were Christians, not a Jew among them. Whatever persecution, famine, or dream may have driven their forebears west was too far back for recall. Their ambition for their sons was to fish home waters; for their daughters, to marry and have kids. Doctors and lawyers did not impress them. The beau monde was beyond their ken. None had a passport nor wanted one. They were not materialistic, and wealth did not awe them. They had a reserved contempt for yachties and weekend boatmen. Barnegat Light, the Inlet, and the sea were Philadelphia's, Central's, and Pennsauken's contrapositive; the Independent's skippers were my father's antitype. I wanted their world to be mine and to be one of them.

The *Jolly Roger* lay on the first row, directly in front of the bait house, befitting its skipper's reputation. The only fault I ever heard my caustic, cynical father find with Holmes was that blue-water sorties, beyond the ridge's outer edge, were not his long suit. Holmes Russell was my first skipper.

I was Danny, or Danny Boy, to him when I first fished aboard the *Jolly Roger*, mostly Danny after I was nine; it was just Boy if I'd done something wrong or dangerous. He taught me the rudiments of deep-sea fishing and some refinements: how to tie fishing knots in thread-line and monofilament; how to twist leader wire in a double helix so the twists lock, to bring the gaff up under a fish to impale it; how to jig for weakfish, cast for stripers, chum blues, troll tuna. I remember those lessons. But neither my fishing skills nor the rush of fighting sport fish was his enduring legacy.

Danny, always keep one hand for the boat. Remember, one hand for the boat were the first two sentences Holmes spoke to me, the first time he helped me board the *Jolly Roger*. Then he illustrated what he meant by ostentatiously grasping the gunwale as he walked forward toward the cabin. I was seven then, and I reflexively grip a fixed part of any boat I board, seventy years later; *Keep one hand for the boat* are my first words to novices who sail with me.

From the time Holmes jumped down onto the *Jolly Roger*'s deck in the predawn dark till he left her fast in the late afternoon, he watched: where and how we stowed gear, ice, bait, and food for the trip; the rods and rigs we'd use; where seas made up and how many were in a set as we headed out the Inlet past the south jetty's rocks. He checked engine temperature, oil pressure, tachometer gauges, and compass headings while making for the ridge; observed birds working nearby and circling far off; gauged our swing if we anchored, our speed when drifting, and which way the chum streamed after he ladled it into the sea; scanned the chum slick for stalking shark fins; and weighed the wind making up after noon. Rolling home, he glanced down from time to time at the mate cleaning the catch in the stern and the dozing fishermen behind him; nothing at sea was alien to Holmes, nothing ignored. When we were about to cross one of the Inlet's sandbars, Holmes always turned from where he sat at the wheel on the flying bridge and scanned the cockpit for loose gear, bait, or a careless angler a big sea might toss from the boat. In good weather he warned us to hold on; in rough to move from cockpit to the wheelhouse below the bridge.

* * *

I was eleven the day I caught my first bass. We'd been shrimping the outside of the south jetty on the flood tide for several hours, without success, and were crossing the Inlet to try the inside of the north, half a mile away, as the tide began to turn. Six-foot seas were breaking on the bar we had to run to get there, and the *Jolly Roger* was not a fast boat; we would take one or more. My father sat beside Holmes on the bridge; I sat on a chair in the cockpit. Holmes looked back and down and said, *Danny, get up in the wheelhouse and hold on*, as he turned the bow northwest to face the bar three hundred feet away and increased speed. A few minutes later, we reached the bar's southern edge, breasted a small wave, lifted, slammed down, and kept going. We drove through one more—slightly larger—ran another boat length, then suddenly, Holmes throttled all the way back. A wave to starboard as high as the cabin top blew the bow skyward and tossed us violently onto our port side until the gunwale lay even with the water. The Coke cooler flew off the bridge and crashed ten feet down onto the cockpit's stern. It would have killed the man it hit, had one been in the cockpit.

I was staring out the wheelhouse window at the oncoming seas, frightened by their size, hiss, and rumble as they began to break, when the cooler hit the stern behind me. The report, the sound of deck splintering, startled me; fear turned to terror. I started aft, grabbed the rail of the ladder to the bridge, and looked up to see Holmes glancing at the stern, checking for damage. He noticed me and read my eyes: *It's OK, Danny* was all he said in his slow cadence, his normal pitch, then turned back to the oncoming waves. The engine revved, we pounded through one more small sea, and we were across, curving west to anchor halfway down the north jetty. A decade later, when I first read Shakespeare describe a king-dispelling fear, I saw Holmes looking down from the bridge:

> there is no note
> How dread an army hath enrounded him;
> Nor doth he dedicate one jot of colour
> Unto the weary and all-watchèd night;
> But freshly looks . . .
> That every wretch, pining and pale before,
> Beholding him, plucks comfort from his looks . . .
> —*Henry V*, Act IV, Prologue

Half an hour after we anchored up, I was seasick for the first and last time in my life, panic's aftereffect as much as the seas rolling under us while we chummed. When I straightened from spewing over the leeward rail, Holmes told me to drink some Coke to dispel the tinny taste of vomit and settle my stomach. Then I tried to follow his instructions on how to strip six-pound test monofilament line from my reel, so the grass shrimp impaled on my hook looked natural drifting toward the rocks. Shortly after noon, I hooked and landed my bass.

For my father, the Atlantic was an opponent, never finally floored: he contended with it every day he sailed. For Holmes, it was a homeland; there he lived, fishing—kinned with waves, sky, and the *Jolly Roger*'s planking. Long dead, he comes to mind often.

* * *

The sunrise drill when we reached the dock changed when my father bought the *Dan-Rick*, and I became his mate. At dawn, a mate readies his boat. First, he opens the engine hatches to air the bilges; in the 1950s, boats under forty feet had gas engines, not the high-powered diesels of today, and every skipper had seen or heard of a boat blowing up and burning when a starter spark exploded gasoline fumes in its bilges. Next, he stows lunches, strips covers from deck and flying bridge, hauls cushions from cabins for folding chairs if the party is going bluefishing, or wrestles fighting chairs from dock to deck sockets if the quarry is tuna; lifts rods from cabin-top racks and lays them forward on deck below the gunwales to be placed in rod holders after clearing the slip; and sets out hooks, leaders, lures, and feathers. Last, he collects and stows ice, chum, bait; settles the party; and casts off.

When the car stopped on the Independent's tarmac before daylight, I scooped sweaters, jackets, and lunch from the back seat and walked to the *Dan-Rick*, where seaboots, fishing knife and scabbard, pliers and holder, and foul weather gear lived. Aboard, I went through my checklist and, last, lifted the engine's ignition switches so Joe could fire them up. The party wedged themselves in chairs or on a bunk below for the two-and-a-half-hour haul to the ridge; I cast off, and we headed east-southeast toward the Inlet and the sea.

On a typical bluefishing trip, I sloshed seawater onto the chum defrosting under the starboard gunwale to help it soften as we ran; tied nine-inch-long wire leaders—black barrel-swivel on one end, six-foot O'Shaughnessy stainless steel hook on the other—to thirty-pound test monofilament on the boat rods; then turned to cutting the butterfish we'd use for bait. I unhooked the fish box where it sat against the stern, dragged it to the center of the cockpit, and swung it parallel to the keel, leaving stern and both gunwales free for fishing. Old boning knife in hand, honed almost to stiletto, and legs spread to roll with the seas, I braced myself against the side of the fish box, used its lid as a cutting board, and began slicing half-frozen blue tourmaline-colored butterfish into chunks—three or four per fish depending on size. Heads and tails went onto the chum cans to sweeten their gruel, the rest into the bait bucket in the fish box, wedged against a block of ice to keep the chunks from softening. The boat's pitching and rolling heightened the chance of slicing off a fingertip—Holmes was missing two from his left hand and one from the right—and butcher-shop training was no bad thing.

I would climb the ladder to the bridge about ninety minutes into the trip, tell my father all was ready, and take the wheel. He'd go below to check the preparations, *kibitz* (banter) with the party, rest, eat the chicken his wife had prepared for him, and talk on the ship-to-shore radio to the other skippers about where they were headed and, if any were already fishing, how they were doing. We would go fishing between 7:30 and 8:00 a.m., depending on how long it took to find a spot.

For the next five hours, I baited hooks; untangled lines; gaffed or swung fish aboard and unhooked them; cut more bait; brought the anglers Cokes, beer, and lunch from the cooler; flushed the deck with buckets of seawater before chum and fish blood could dry; tied on new hooks and leaders when fish broke off. I said almost nothing, after the fashion of my models, the charter captains and their mates. Those were the days before factory ships followed pelagic species like bluefish and tuna to and from their summer feeding grounds; before species like striped bass were netted almost to extinction; before countries increased their offshore national boundaries, enforced catch limits against foreign and domestic fleets, and regulated local fishermen's catches. Today, a charter boat is limited to ten bluefish per boat, and catch-and-release is the rule. But when I was a mate, the ridge teemed with them July through mid-October, ten fish per man was a small catch, and twenty to thirty was not uncommon if the party was competent. I often threw between seven hundred and one thousand pounds of gutted bluefish onto the dock when we returned, and fishermen, asked by onlookers how they had done that day, would answer, *We slaughtered 'em*.

When the action heated up, there was no time to gaff fish. Reach down over the side of the boat; guide the line and thrashing fifteen-pound bluefish toward you with thumb and forefinger; with your free hand, grasp the wire leader below the swivel, just above the fish's jaws; and swing it aboard. Thrust the fingers of one hand under and into the gills, spread them to force the mouth open, and with the other, work the hook loose, lift the fish by the gills, and dump it into the fish box.

Bluefish jaws can crack walnuts, their teeth glass-shard sharp, like small man-eating sharks; they could and did sever digits from the unwary. Gloves made it difficult to feel the swivel and grasp the leader at the right spot. Gloved hands were clumsy trying to work a hook loose, especially if a fish had swallowed the bait when it struck, and it was hooked deep in its cartilaginous throat. The best mates worked barehanded. The leader wire sliced palms and fingers, and gill spines pierced fingertips. Seawater cauterized and annealed the cuts. Hands burned at the day's end, heading home.

* * *

We reeled in and headed for the beach when the fish box was full or overflowing, or the last of the chum ladled over the side. I leaned out and down over the gunwale as we ran to skim buckets of water for swilling deck and rods. Dip the bucket too deep and the sudden weight as it filled, added to the boat's forward momentum, could jerk your arm from its socket. The trick was to swing the bucket down to skim the surface of the waves as the boat sliced through them so your swing carried the bucket clear of the water as it filled. I sluiced deck and rods, stored them forward in the wheelhouse for freshwater washing when we tied up, and set to cleaning the catch.

Bluefish rot quickly and must be gutted as soon as possible. Shirtless, feet wide apart, boning knife again in hand, I grasped the top fish in the box by the tail, lifted it clear, and laid it on the upturned fish box lid. I stuck the knife an inch or two into the fish's anus, slit it belly to throat, grasped the entrails in the abdominal cavity with my other hand, severed them from gorge and rectum, and tossed the gutted fish on the deck astern. The entrails I threw to the terns and sea gulls loitering for an effortless dinner just above the waves, a boat's length behind in our wake. In time, it took less than a minute to gut a fish; within an hour or so, I'd done them all, depending on catch size, rinsed them with seawater, tossed them back in the fish box, closed its lid, swabbed box and deck, and squared away the wheelhouse. There was generally a sixty-to-ninety-minute run left to the dock.

My father kept tabs on my progress from the bridge. *Danny, ya done?* I nodded. *Geh me a Coke and come up here.* I climbed the ladder to the bridge, handed him the Coke, and swung into the starboard seat. We rolled on through the southwesterly chop. He finished the Coke and, without looking at me, said, *Here, take 'er home.* I stood up, leaned forward against the bridge coaming, and grasped the wheel while he edged across behind me and started down the ladder to the deck. There was nothing said. Then he'd pause and clutch my right shoulder firmly for a moment before lowering his torso from the bridge, and like the *Dan-Rick*, the decks were cleared. Staring west into the sun at the waves on the port quarter, course home 300 to 305 degrees—the Furies, cursings, beatings, and butcher shop vanished like blood and bluefish entrails through the scuppers earlier that day.

TRADE

Barnegat Inlet is a gauntlet
in the sea, where waves break on sand
bars that pen a bay. An unquiet
place, lethal when easterlies stand
the long swells up to lumber

white capped across the shoals
then crumble in a khaki welter
of seaweed, mud and spray that rolls
west through the cleft Atlantic coast.
Chartermen say little on the docks
at dawn, standing by for parties,
for mates to ready boats—pull chocks,
dog ports and stow necessities,
bait, ice, and beer—for copper gleam
to port ahead, gulls working gore
from schools of sand eel stripers glean,
or terns on bluefins hours offshore,
the world shrunk to a compass rose.
After noon the wind comes up, skippers
go topside, shout Reel in! and head
for home; crews gut the catch, scuppers
clog with viscera, decks turn red
till seawater sluices them teak
again, and sunburned weekend
warriors, beers wedged, peaked,
doze and in daydreams pretend
they're heroes home from the sea.

Lines secured, the anglers leave
for row homes, showers, bowling club;
but by slips boatmen remain, reeve
rod guides, observe the weather, rub
penetrant on rusted pliers,
and pause—to watch sedge sway on flats,
geese rise honking from wetland choirs,
the sun decline, a whirl of gnats
and the Light flick on at Barnegat.[5]

[5] Dan Burt, *We Look Like This* (Manchester: Carcanet, 2012).

The Barnegat Light

Girls

In the beginning, they were just cunts. A boy's role was to lay a girl as soon as he could, and then as many as possible; a girl's role, to snare the potential best provider. Sex was the coin she paid for security—something endured. The butchers I worked with, the neighborhood boys, asked, *What'd ya get?* when you came back from a date, not *What was she like?* or *Did you have fun?*

A woman's place in 1958 was in the home—baking cookies, making dinner, having babies, and standing by her man. My parents' marriage typified the barter basis, and 1950s middle-class American cultural organs—television, *Life, Look, Reader's Digest*—reinforced it. The pill was two years off, Simone de Beauvoir just a name, and Germaine Greer in university.

I learned about sex when puberty kicked in, around twelve—from *Esquire*, from forbidden *Playboys*, from the embellished exploits of older boys, from pornographic pictures slipped from hand to hand in a far corner of the schoolyard. In eighth grade, our coed classes split twice a week into boys and girls sections for forty-five-minute personal hygiene classes—dubbed sex ed—where red-faced gym teachers explained clinical photos of mature male and female sex organs and their workings. Sex went unmentioned in mixed company, and lovemaking, as opposed to *Wham, bam, thank you, Ma'am*, was a pastime neither parents, family, nor the men I worked with ever spoke of.

Pennsauken completed my sex education. Butchering coarsens a man; the enveloping blood, cold, steel, cutting, chopping, and rotting strips life of its grace. Everything is raw, crude, brutal: pale-orange blood-flecked marrow, splintered pork loins, and tubs of calves' livers marinating in bloody swill, sweating salt back and kielbasa. My coworkers, excepting my father, were all under fifty; only one had reached his midforties, and they talked constantly about sex. Women were cunt, snatch, poontang, pussy, gash, slit, slot, twat, fucks, bangs, tits, boobs, knockers, rockers, headlights, pairs, racks, mountains, bazooms. Their view of cunnilingus was *Once you get past the smell, you got it licked* and of rape, *A woman can run faster with her skirt up than a man with his pants down.* My father was coarsest of the lot. I spent more time with these men than with high school classmates; their view of the female became mine.

A boy had few opportunities before the sexual revolution and the women's movement to mix with girls in daily circumstances, especially if he attended a single-sex secondary school. Nice girls stayed home on school nights, Sundays through Thursdays. A teenage date, butcher-boy style, was no place to learn what girls were like. Dates were highly stylized, a Kabuki play whose purpose was sexual satisfaction: malted, pizza, or hamburger; protestation of passion; then movies, car, or other dark place to French kiss, cop a feel, and, one prayed, more. Central boys could develop more rounded views of girls at mixers with Central's sister school, the Girls' High, and at parties, dances, football games, or at social events at the local synagogue. Mixers happened after school on Fridays; parties and dances on Friday nights; football games on Saturday afternoons; and synagogue events on Sunday afternoons, times when I couldn't attend.

I worked Fridays after school until the Mart closed at 11 p.m. It was generally past midnight when we locked up, and the butchers made for the bowling alley across from the south end of the Mart for a beer. Sometimes I went with them, hoisted myself onto a barstool and, short legs swinging two feet from the floor, gulped the beer they cajoled the bartender to serve a minor eight years underage. I was rarely in bed before 1:15 a.m. on Saturday mornings, woke five to six hours later to ride to work with my father at 7:30 a.m., and left work between five and six p.m. Every other Sunday, often two out of three, was a workday. I never learned to do more than shuffle through a slow dance, and—with one exception—I was twenty-two before I spent an evening à deux with a young woman where sex was not the aim.

Jill Rubinson stood in a corner of the den—slightly to the left of the fireplace—before a wall of books in her parents' split-level, suburban house, on a third of an acre of grass, in a costly, postwar subdivision in Lower Merion. As you turned onto the tract's entrance road, on the right-hand verge, a sign atop a seven-foot-high steel pole warned, *No Commercial Vehicles Allowed*. Her living room could have swallowed three of mine; as you entered, it was anchored on the left by a second ceramic fireplace, on the right by a grand piano; opposite the front door, another wall of books. The levels were unsplit in the homes I knew, the walls bookless, no hearths, no dens. Their lawns were small green chin whiskers, two bricks' length narrower than the houses they bearded, no deeper than the setback from the pavement, and normally fifteen feet. Backyards, if any, were paved. I had never been in a house that was too far from the neighbors to hear them quarrel, and I had never seen a girl like Jill.

She had a gamine air: just five feet tall, thin, flat chested, with a tiny bump on the dorsum of her nose a fingertip's width below the bridge; head large for her body, high forehead and cheekbones; skin Celtic fair; no Gisele Bündchen, then, but come-hither cute. Sapphire-blue eyes, her strongest feature, confirmed that maternal German Jewish genes had vanquished her father's inheritance from the southern Pale. Her hair, pulled back in a short, bouncy ponytail, suited the clothes below: bobby socks, plaid wrap skirt, cotton shirt—all in shades of purple—the skirt's sides clamped shut just below the left thigh with a six-inch, decorative, brass-plated safety pin. Her taut body fit the cheerleader she was. But her airs, clothes, cheerleading, and no doubt padded bra were protective teenage coloration; she was her superior suburban public high school's best student, soon to be class vale-dictorian, who would graduate Phi Beta Kappa from Cornell and take her PhD in English literature from Harvard. Though the den was filled with noisy teenagers flirting, twisting, shouting in clumps and couples, she stood alone—inviolable, above us all—as if on an altar, a cleared space around her in the gaggle, a Jewish virgin princess sceptered by right.

Academic ineptitude threw us together, mine not hers. I had begun pall-ing around with boys from Overbrook High, met in summer school during my second remedial summer. Their neighborhood was Overbrook Park, a small, lower-middle-class Jewish neighborhood of postwar row homes a ten-minute walk from Jill's house across City Line Avenue—in effect, the other side of the tracks. Her fifteen-year-old suburban girlfriends were experimenting with social and academic inferiors and persuaded Jill to host a rare Saturday-night party for them. I joined the five Overbrook boys who turned up; none of us knew Jill or had been to her house.

Ezio Pinza, an operatic bass of the period, was singing "Some Enchanted Evening," a popular song from *South Pacific*, on a 45 rpm record player when I walked the three steps down to the den. I misheard its first lines, *Some enchanted evening / You may see a stranger* as *One enchanted evening / You will meet a stranger*, thought this was that evening, and have misre-membered those lines ever since. I stared across the room, met her eyes, and was felled, *bouleversé*, Michael Corleone's first sighting of Apollonia across a Sicilian field. Jill was somewhat less affected.

We dated for three months before she tired of me: six or seven times for two or three hours on Saturday nights between March and May 1959; two Sunday afternoons, one of which she was housebound nursing a cold; and penultimately, my junior prom. I would have called her every night and talked till the conversion of the Jews, spent every Saturday night with her—and Sundays when I wasn't working—had the choice been mine. But it was not. Her father forbade her to date me more than once every other week or speak to me by phone more than once every other night for more than ten to fifteen minutes. There was not world enough and time.

Our dates were simple: pizzas and Cokes at Alfredo's on City Line Avenue, three blocks from her house (and the only romantic place I knew), and the occasional corned beef sandwich and soda at Murray's, a mile north on City Line Avenue, with sometimes a movie first. Booths for couples lined Alfredo's walls. Tables for four and six stood in the middle of the room. White-and-red-checked tablecloths were set with white cloth napkins and empty Chianti bottles with candles in them, their necks thickened with dribbled white candle wax. We always sat in a booth, cocooned from other diners, Jill facing the door. Each booth had a jukebox terminal, on which I selected the *Warsaw Concerto* and Tchaikovsky's First Piano Concerto or *Swan Lake*, the only classical pieces I could identify. I never chose pop or country, genres I knew well. Food, music, movies—all were excuses to stare into her blue eyes and talk.

We had little in common: no mutual friends, different schools—hers wealthy, WASP, suburban, coed; mine mostly Jewish, urban, magnet, single sex. Her forebears had settled—and then left—the same South Philadelphia cobbled streets as my father's people but a generation earlier. She heard no Yiddish at home, played classical piano, frequented the Philadelphia Academy of Music, the museums, and the main branch of the Philadelphia Free Library. Summers were spent at overnight camp in the Poconos. She had traveled, read the right books, and knew she would attend an Ivy League college as her parents had done.

Chopping blocks, hind quarters, steels, grinders, cleavers, freezer rats; drag racing, pool rooms, gang fights, suspensions, truancy; docks, jetties, feathers, chum, gaffs, seas over the bow—and sex—were alien to her. She was curious about all but the last, and I talked about them all, honoring the exception. One Sunday, desperate to see her, I drove to her house in my father's meat truck, stared at the sign at the subdivision's entrance—*No Commercial Vehicles Allowed*—and parked, like a thief, two blocks away, walking the rest of the way to her front door. She insisted on going for a ride in the truck, but I remember that sign telling me I did not belong there.

Harold and Louise, Jill's parents, had graduated from the University of Pennsylvania, one of America's eight Ivy League universities. Harold held an MBA from Penn's Wharton Business School, esteemed Harvard's equal. He and his brother inherited a large department store from their father, in the Amish country of southwestern Pennsylvania, an hour from Jill's house. Louise painted porcelain and was always flawlessly dressed, often in fine wool suits no mother I knew wore. They had a maid Mondays through Fridays, who cooked and served dinner.

Mr. Rubinson answered the door when I called for Jill. He never said hello, simply called out, "Your date's here." He never said good-bye. To Mr. Rubinson, I was nameless. I was not offered water or soda, invited to lunch or dinner, or asked about my family or myself. On our last date but one, my junior prom, Jill descended from her bedroom in a billowing lavender dress, perfumed, her hair piled high and tight on her head à la Audrey Hepburn; her parents took no pictures.

Graduation photograph from class yearbook of Jill Rubinson, class valedictorian, Lower Merion High School, 1961

Mr. Rubinson's silent parental disdain was new to me: not a physical threat such as a punch or knife could counter. I was properly dressed, on best behavior, worshipped his daughter, and drove my father's white late-model Oldsmobile to fetch her. But none of that mattered. My offense was who I was, who my parents were, where I lived, how my father made his living, how little we had. Years before, on a fishing trip with my father to North Carolina, near midnight on a classic dark and stormy night, I wandered down the deck of the Kiptopeke Beach ferry, transporting us across the mouth of Chesapeake Bay to Virginia's eastern shore, looking for a men's room. I saw a Black man symbol on a door and reached to pull it open when a hand the size of a pancake skillet materialized out of the downpour and clamped my right shoulder. The white six footer to which it was attached drawled, *Y'all can't go in there, Boy. Why? Cuz das fuh niggahs.* I looked at him, bewildered; aged ten, I knew the word, as I did kike, sheeny, dago, mick, goy, shiksa. But what did a man's race have to do with where he could piss? Seven years later, I understood; to Mr. Rubinson I was a n----.

He had nothing to fear; I had no thought of soiling his daughter. Always presentable, billingsgate in abeyance, I never laid fingers on more than her forearm, except once on the small of her back during the slow dance I shuffled through in her den the night we met. We did not park to make out; I never fumbled with her clothes. Our tongues did not touch the few times we kissed. We stopped only once at a lover's lane, that prom night, where Jill fell asleep in the crook of my white sports-coated right arm, while Ken Klee and Mary, the couple with whom we had doubled, petted furiously in the back. I gazed down at Jill for almost an hour, entranced, till it was time to drive her home. There was no need of a sword between us to keep her chaste. Jill was not a person but a myth I breathed to life.

I failed no more courses after my sojourn chez Jill and understood that her father would not be the last adult to greet me silently if I did not go to college. But courtly love and shame would not have driven me as they did, unconjoined to indignation. Incandescence that indignation spawned still fired me when, by the remotest chance, Jill and I met again fifty years later.

Fool Me Once

Any boy might have felt a moment's envy on the way home from his Friday night's work, passing boys he knew coming from dances and parties. But mine dissipated quickly, until I was seventeen. Others might have remarked their family's late model, expensive car; father's twin-screw sport fishing boat; mother and siblings' month-long August seashore holidays—and might have questioned the tales of hard times and illness told to justify their working hours. Until the summer before my seventeenth birthday, I did not. My parents' second son, Ricky, two years my junior, approached fifteen never having held a job. He was hale and several inches taller than me. My father gave him a weekly allowance for carfare, school lunches, books, movies, treats, and pocket money; my mother supplemented it as needed. Now Joe said it was time for Ricky to work. Louise objected, but I thought it a necessity, and my father would prevail. My brother joined me in the back room and on the counter in the summer of 1959.

Louise dropped him off at the Mart one late June Saturday morning. He put on a butcher's coat and apron and was set to washing platters. He washed them so slowly the butchers stopped him and did it themselves. On the counter he stared past approaching customers or shuffled to serve them. Even sweeping the floor seemed beyond him. Handed a broom and shown where to sweep, he meandered across the floor, shifting sawdust and scraps from place to place to no effect. I watched the sawdust flakes spiral behind him and settle back where they had been.

And nothing happened: no beating, no punishment. His mother fetched him home at 10 a.m., two hours into his second—and last—Saturday's labor as a butcher. His allowance continued; he drove the car, never the truck. He went from Central to Gettysburg College, a respected, expensive, residential liberal arts school in southwestern Pennsylvania. Its tuition was three times that of my Philadelphia commuter college, and Joe had warned him not to apply. He enrolled there in the autumn of 1962 after Louise, unbeknown to her husband, wrote the check for his first year's fees and board.

* * *

My brother's ability to refuse without consequence even to sweep a floor was an epiphany. Nine months earlier, sixteen and issued a driving license, it seemed axiomatic I would use my savings to buy a car. But title could not pass to a minor; a parent had to sign, and my father refused. Appeal to my mother would have been futile; by then, warfare between us was open, mean, and continuous. After the epiphany of the broom, I toughened up.

My father was driving a year-old, white, two-door '98 Oldsmobile that summer. Its four hundred horsepower engine, four-barrel carburetor, and gearing made it a blur accelerating from zero to sixty miles per hour. I was allowed to drive it on Saturday nights. Si Hannan, a local tough who hung out at the R&W, drove his father's 1957 gunmetal-gray Olds Super Rocket '88—lighter than ours with trips, three two-barrel carburetors on the manifold; Si's car, at least on paper, was faster.

I pulled up at the R&W around 12:30 a.m. one Sunday morning after a date. Si and others began arguing whose car was faster, and within moments, his friends had put up one hundred dollars, equal to eight hundred dollars today. I matched it, and we headed for the dead end at the bottom of Whitaker Avenue to find out who was right.

During the day, Whitaker Avenue was a residential street six blocks long, four lanes wide from dead-end beginning to its intersection with Roosevelt Boulevard; after midnight, it was a drag strip, my house a block before the finish line. We lined up side by side near the dead end, put a friend as observer in the front seat of our competitor's car—Irv Cossrow in Si's, Harvey Webb in mine—then the juvenile shadow standing between the loom of our headlights raised his hand. We stood our cars up, revved the motors with them in gear while applying maximum pressure on the power brakes, which lifted their rears, and watched for the shadow hand to drop. The key to drag racing is to get off the line at maximum speed without burning too much rubber; a slower car can beat a faster one if the faster car spins its rear wheels for seconds because its driver applies too much power leaving the line; cooler drivers win, even in slower cars.

Eight hundred horsepower of revving engines carries a long way on a city street in the middle of the night. My father, home from Pennsauken a half hour earlier, left his cornflakes and went outside to see the racers pass. I got off the line with a perfect chirp of tires; the other driver spun his wheels. I was two car lengths ahead by the first one hundred feet, pedal to the metal, headed for the finish at the cross street a half block past my house. We roared past my father at over ninety miles per hour, front bumpers almost in line, but even eight hundred screaming horses and five rocketing tons of high-grade steel and chrome could not drown his curses as we passed; he had recognized his car.

There was no sense going home. The observers settled bets, switched cars, and I took off with Irv to roam Northeast Philadelphia streets and West Jersey highways until dawn, when I would have to go home to shower and change for work at 8 a.m. I walked through our front door six hours later. Joe was hunched over his breakfast cereal. *Danny!* I walked toward the breakfast room and stopped just shy of a swing's length from the patriarch in his chair at the head of the table and stood and waited. Without looking up, he asked, *D'yuh win?*

Yeah. Five heartbeats, then, *If I catch you racing my car again, I'll beat you to death*. We both knew I would race his car until I had my own and that beating me to death might be more of a chore at seventeen than it had been when I was five. He had lost all moral authority the morning he allowed my brother to funk work.

On October 1, 1959, my seventeenth birthday, Joe signed for a red 1959 MGA 1600 Roadster, my first car. I wanted a hot rod, but he thought mixing a rod's speed with my temperament too dangerous. When Albert's eldest, Anita, had dropped by a month earlier in her husband's MG, my father had asked to drive it. He disappeared up the Boulevard and returned ten minutes later, confident it was tame enough, to say I could buy one. An MG wasn't what I wanted, but any car meant freedom.

* * *

My father paid me a third of a man's wage when I went to work for him; then, after a few years, half. I complained about not receiving equal pay for equal work. Mobile now, complaints ceased. *Pay me what you pay the other men, or I'll get another job*. He raised my pay.

College was no certainty when the time came to apply in my high school senior year. My grades, with two exceptions, were average or worse; only one teacher would recommend me. But a butcher's nasty, brutish, short working life; the increasingly uncertain prospects in the meat business; and the contumely of my betters scotched all thoughts of butchering. I fantasized about becoming a charter captain, but that remained a romantic velleity. The charter men's days were numbered, swamped by ninety-foot, multimillion-dollar gas-turbine head boats, carrying seventy-five fishermen a trip at so much per head. The sea would remain a mistress, not a wife.

College applications required Scholastic Aptitude Test (SAT) scores as well as high school grades. I took the SAT on Saturday, October 10, 1959, and fared better than expected, one score so high it seemed anomalous. But a high test score was a feather in the balance against twelve years' dismal grades and bad behavior. My choices were few. A residential college was too expensive. Temple University—though local, cheap, and likely to accept me—was vast with maybe twenty thousand students, undistinguished, and filled with Central's strivers' lesser kin.

Mr. Mulloy suggested that he approach La Salle, a Christian Brothers college where he taught nights, on my behalf. It admitted me a week later. My parents objected that it was Catholic—almost all the faculty, all department heads, the administration, and 98 percent of the students—and its academic standing at best no better than Temple's. I ignored them. Run by an order founded in late-seventeenth-century France to educate working-class boys, its day program was small and inexpensive; an unusual destination for Central grads, La Salle College was the best I could do.

* * *

Zaida had known more about America when he fled the Russian army than I did about La Salle when it accepted me. He'd heard glowing tales from relatives and landsmen, read about New York *Yekkes* (upper-class German Jews) in the Yiddish press, and was not the first to leave his Dnieper shtetl for *das goldene land*. My knowledge of the church came from books and Mr. Mulloy; of Catholics, from gangs and neighborhood fights. I'd never been in a church, and my putative Catholic relatives were no more than names. No ancestor of mine had gone to college.

I met my first religious the day I visited La Salle. The black-cassocked brothers floating across its small concrete campus were aliens: quiet celibates who smiled politely as they passed, cheeks occasionally roseate from drink, robes swishing a thumb's width off the ground. La Salle sent no summer reading list with its admissions letter, no orientation tips, no dates to meet alumni. No one said expect this, do that, prepare. But I did not want to repeat my first day's homeroom gaffe at Central, four years before.

From newspapers and TV and from my mother's reverential tone when she said X or Y went to college, I had learned to couple college and high culture, which at the time meant classical music to me. My mother would hint that an aunt Femi, supposedly an opera singer, had sung at the Philadelphia Academy of Music and taught voice at the Curtis Institute, though we never met Femi, heard her speak or sing, had any communication from her, or were sure if she existed. Neither opera nor any other classical music was heard in our house. Jill played Chopin on the grand piano in her living room, but not for me. My car radio was locked on WIBG, Philadelphia's premier rock 'n' roll station, and Joe Niagra, its nationally known disc jockey.

Two months before starting La Salle, I changed stations; WFLN, 95.7 on the FM dial, was Philadelphia's classical music station and mine from late June 1960. For six weeks, I tuned in, bored and uncomprehending, to the unknown—sonatas, concertos, symphonies, fantasias, tone poems, plainsong, madrigals, arias—while yearning for the Platters wailing "The Great Pretender." But the dial stayed put.

On an August Saturday just before 10 a.m., I waited in the truck on Levick Street at the intersection with Frankford Avenue for the light to change, heading for Callowhill Street's packing houses to fetch hindquarters and pork loins. August in Philadelphia is like June in Dhahran; the humid inner-city air smothered me in my soiled butcher's coat. The crossroad was cacophonous and rank: trolley cars snapping and sparking on their overhead wires; trucks and cars rumbling north and south on Frankford Avenue; a newsboy's Inquirer! *Get'cha mornin'* Inquirer!; a distant, wailing siren; diesel particulates spewed from a route R bus by the curb; a sidewalk hot dog stand adding the stink of frying onions and sauerkraut. Behind me in the cab, greenhead flies buzzed, scratching dried blood on the dirty brown butcher's paper carpeting the floor of the truck; on the dashboard, the radio played the usual unintelligible but cultured noise.

I popped the clutch as the light changed and rattled off to get ahead of the R bus's exhaust when, from the radio, three repeated piano notes stood proud of the odor and din—*da da da, da da da, da da da*—the opening triplets of Beethoven's Piano Sonata Opus 14, the *Moonlight Sonata*, though I didn't know it then. Something had clicked, and for the first time, I understood the relationship of one note to the next in a classical piece and could hear it. I marked every note of its dying fall, almost a lament, and began to comprehend. I did not know it was a famous piece, that it drew on an Albinoni Adagio and the commendatore's death scene in *Don Giovanni*, nor was I familiar with its familiar name. All I knew was that the Mart receded from one piano keystroke to the next, swept away on a purifying tide of notes. The next Monday, I bought my first stereo system and my first LP, with Rudolf Serkin playing the *Moonlight Sonata* on one side, the *Appassionata* on the other. That record's midnight-blue sleeve—an image of moonlit ruins—is clear in my mind's eye, fifty-two years later.

La Salle's entering freshmen, short haired, beardless, and polite, lined up in College Hall in early September to register. Most wore ties, coats, and wool slacks or chinos. There were no jeans—ripped or whole—no sneakers, T-shirts, shorts, armbands, hammer-and-sickle or peace-sign buttons, no logos of any kind. Cigarette smoke filled the corridor; no one smoked a pipe. It was a few years too early for the sweet/acrid smell of pot in the air, and few of the young men would have recognized it. La Salle was an all-male, inner-city, workingman's commuter college. There were one or two Blacks. It was 1960, but the swinging '60s never came to La Salle.

Freshmen had no electives; they chose either science or humanities, which determined whether their courses included math, chemistry, and physics—or history, sociology, and economics. Everyone took biology, freshman composition, two years of a foreign language, and religion (for Catholics) or Thomist philosophy for the heathens. ROTC, the American army's Reserve Officer Training Corps, was compulsory for the first two years. Twice a week, we donned heavy-wool uniforms to straggle around the athletic field in imprecise formations and smash thumbs trying to work an M1 rifle's spring bolt. Some students, paid for by Uncle Sam, would stay in ROTC for four years, graduate in 1964 as second lieutenants, and head off to Vietnam as forward artillery observers, service quite likely to get them killed.

La Salle was a poor college, almost bankrupt in the early 1930s and again during the war. Three large buildings anchored the campus; the five-story, gray-brick College Hall (administrative offices and classrooms); the student union; and the new, whitewashed, precast concrete science building. They formed a scalene triangle, at whose incenter stood two parallel brown-brick, rectangular, barrack-like halls, two stories high and three bus lengths long. The one closest to the science building housed the English faculty.

Mr. Cunningham—a small, balding layman in his early thirties—taught us freshman composition in a first-floor classroom of the English hall, from 10 to 11 a.m., Mondays, Wednesdays, and Fridays. We read and discussed short stories, a novel or two, a few poems, and a Shakespeare play (perhaps *Julius Caesar*), and we wrote short essays as directed. Freshman comp was an American college course devised, in part, to hone students' writing skills; even Ivy League universities required it. I had written what was demanded at Central and got by but had made no attempts at fiction or poetry or diary keeping.

At the close of Mr. Cunningham's first class, he asked us to write 750 words on someone we knew and hand them in that coming Friday; his only instructions were as to the essay's length and form: in ink or typed; on standard 8.5-by-11-inch paper; folded in half lengthwise; our name, his name, and class (English 101) in the middle of the outer sheet's right-hand fold. I wrote about Holmes Russell clamming the tidal flats of Barnegat Bay from his garvey in a gray November drizzle. My father had pointed him out to me one day in the early 1950s, when we were crossing the causeway from Long Beach Island to the mainland, and the image stuck. As I wrote, I imagined standing beside Holmes in the piercing salt cold, stomach muscles knotted, straining to close a clam digger. The image of him clamming in the cold remains clear seventy years on.

Dennis Cunningham hurried into class through the door to our right a few seconds past ten the following Monday, plopped a bundle of folded essays on the pale oak table near the window, and took a breath. Almost bouncing with excitement, he began to praise one of the essays, halted, then opened the top paper on the stack and began to read. He was into the second paragraph when I lowered my head. He finished, looked around the room: *Mr. Burt? Here.* He handed me my paper with a nod of approval, then gave the others theirs.

I had put my back into that first college week: attended all my classes, completed all assignments, read the articles for sociology and history on reserve at the library. The Holmes essay had not come easy; it was the product of drafts and blotted lines, a process new to me. There would be no more chances if I failed. Mr. Cunningham's enthusiasm convinced me what La Salle required I could do. On that proof, rather than self-belief, I've built.

A week earlier, college had meant trade school to me, leading to a degree and white-collar job. Not any longer; nothing had satisfied me so intensely as producing those two pages. Mr. Cunningham beckoned as we were leaving class, told me his office hours, and asked me to stop by. When I did, he encouraged me to write for *The Collegian*, the student newspaper, and perhaps the quarterly literary magazine. A few weeks later, *The Collegian* published my first editorial.

* * *

La Salle students with consistently high grades qualified for the dean's list, which conferred the privilege of skipping class. I was on the list by the end of my first term, and I used the freedom to read at the direction of Bob Smith, a thirty-year-old English literature professor at La Salle and PhD candidate at the University of Pennsylvania. We met when I took his survey course, "Chaucer through Eliot," in the fall of my sophomore year and fell in lasting love with English poetry. He began suggesting books—poetry, fiction, criticism, history of ideas—then spent hours discussing and arguing about them with me in his office or in an Irish bar a few blocks away. For two and a half years, Bob labored to remedy my literary and cultural lacks.

He played Henry Higgins, and by my senior year, I no longer sounded like Tony Soprano when I was sober. Drunk or furious, I revert to type. Bob would have remained a friend had he not suffered severe, irreversible brain damage in the car wreck in which I broke my neck. My poetry chapbook *Certain Windows* is dedicated to him.

Sophomore year, I began struggling to write poetry while continuing to contribute sporadically to *The Collegian*. La Salle's literary journal published two of my haikus. Shortly after they appeared, Claude Koch, an English professor and poet in the English faculty, greeted me as we were passing in the English faculty's hall and asked what I'd like to do when I graduated.

Write.

Do you have anything to say?

I knew instantly I did not.

For the next forty-three years, I made notes and drafted poems but kept them to myself.

Six years ago, I asked a typographer to design a font for a stele I was erecting on land I own and, at his request, sent him the sonnet intended for it. After reading it, he asked, *Do you have more?*

A few.

May I show them to Michael Schmidt, PN Review's *editor? I design their covers.* Had he not done so, I doubt I would have published more than those two college haikus.

* * *

The reception of the Holmes essay and my college life went unmentioned to my parents. My first two and a half years in college, I studied and slept at home only during the shank of the week; my last year and a half, I moved out completely. College life—reading, studying, writing, talking—occurred either on campus, at local bars, or at my teenage girlfriend's house in Overbrook Park, where, from the time I entered La Salle, I ate, read, wrote, fornicated, and was made welcome.

A gaggle of shrieking teenyboppers filed through the City Line Avenue bowling alley's doors and started down its steps as I swaggered up them on a dateless Saturday night in January 1960. Prominent in the rank of parked cars opposite was my shiny, now-customized and hopped-up MG. One of the girls was short, thin, heavily made-up, around seventeen years old, I guessed, and the prettiest of the lot. Her name was Sharon Guard.

I hadn't seen Sharon or her friends before, nor had my two companions from Overbrook High. Our three heads turned as one. Her short skirt left a long clear run for her fishnet stockings, and prominent breasts parted her car coat. I stared—big black hair, pale skin, Norman nose, white teeth in bondage to braces. I tried a pickup line, she parried, and in five minutes, she was sitting beside me in the passenger seat of my roadster while we took a joyride around her neighborhood. Two months shy of fourteen, she'd be jailbait for another two years, but she jumped in my car with the brio of the older girl she looked.

We dated frequently in the following months. She was ambitious, aggressive, capable, and above all, determined; she became superintendent of a Dallas, Texas, school district as an adult. Our phone calls were unlimited: she had a generous curfew, and her mother was eager for us to go steady. It was not an untumultuous romance; I was certainly unbesotted. We broke up every five weeks or so. I dated other girls, but she remained my default squeeze. At dawn after my high school senior prom, we lay grappling on the sofa in her living room when she said suddenly, *Tell me you love me, and things will be different.* Two things were certain: my glands ached for things to be different, and I did not love this fourteen-year-old girl. I didn't exclaim, *I love you*, and rip off her bodice; I thought about what to say, wrestled with my answer. Then I lied, and things were different, not completely at a stroke but soon enough to satisfy me.

Sharon covered her school notebooks with my name. She changed how she spelled hers to conform to how I pronounced it; for decades after we disentangled, she continued to spell it "Shairon" rather than Sharon as in the Bible and on her birth certificate. Her hair, teased and heaped when we'd met, now hung long and straight just above her shoulders; her makeup lightened; she frequented Lord & Taylor; and she became an emblem of the Ivy League, coed look I favored, a precursor to Ali MacGraw in *Love Story* a decade later. But unlike prepill coeds, she never had a headache, and she quickly mastered sophisticated sex.

Dorothy "Dot" Guard promoted her daughter's desires; what Sharon wanted, Dot helped her get. A poor cook but master of takeout, Dot ministered to my penchant for hamburgers and fries from Bassin's; corned beef, potato salad, and sour tomatoes from Murray's; pizza from Alfredo's; and Chinese from the Mandarin Kitchen on Sundays after work. All were available on demand. Her son, Melvin, slept in his mother's bed so that I could sleep in his room. Dot knew that her daughter and I were sexual partners;

once, through the basement window, she glimpsed us double backed but turned a blind eye.

Jack Guard, Sharon's father, sold newspapers and wrote numbers from a sidewalk kiosk at Fifteenth and Market Streets in Center City Philadelphia, a block from the statue of William Penn atop City Hall. The racket allowed his family to live in the lower-middle-class neighborhood of Overbrook Park. Jack left for work before 5 a.m. each morning and went to bed by 8 p.m. Dot had the stronger personality and dominated the family. If Jack objected to the drama playing out in his house, he never said so to me.

My father warned me more than once on our predawn drives to the *Dan-Rick* that an early marriage was inevitable. He crudely adduced Sampson, *one hair on a woman's cunt is more powerful than the strongest man on earth*, and painted Sharon as a succubus, her mother as coconspirator. But a quiet place to study with calm meals, feminine affection, and testosterone all shouted him down.

Sharon was sixteen and a half and five months gone when she told me she was pregnant. It was early October of my junior year, just after I turned twenty, and the leaves were red and gold, still crisp, crackling when you trod them. Pennsylvania's autumn swan song was never so vibrant again. She had been radiant that summer, sweet sixteen, an hourglass in a scarlet one-piece swimsuit; now we knew why. Morning sickness vexed her, but she said nothing; no one noticed. We told our parents. They assumed we would marry.

I refused. After a halfhearted effort to change my mind, my father defended my decision. My mother's view had no weight. It was too late for an abortion; the baby would have to be given away. Her parents were not opposed; Dot was more fearful of local gossip should her daughter be tarred as an unwed mother. The sticking point was Sharon.

My father's first meeting with Sharon was to persuade her to surrender her unborn. They clashed as equals in the living room of our house. Joe's logic, persuasion, inveigling, threats, shouting, and promises of a bright, child-free future for the two of us changed nothing. She left him astonished at her fortitude and determination to keep the child. In the end, she did not give her babe away.

A few weeks later, she began to show and moved into a home for unwed mothers ten minutes' drive from her house. The understanding was that she would offer the baby for adoption; the sop was that we would then marry—an uncertainty with the child gone. But the home had a telephone, and once a day, Sharon called. She wrote every day as well. I took her calls, read the letters: their unvarying themes were loneliness, fear, and betrayal; they demanded my assurance that if she gave up the baby for adoption, I would marry her. Her tears provoked mine; each reassurance compromised me. One night, six weeks into her stay, trying to prepare for class, I blacked out. When I came to, I called Sharon and told her I would pick her up the next day and drive south to a state where we could marry without parental consent.

Early evening the next day, in a cheap motel outside Elkton, Maryland, Sharon's water broke. An ambulance took her to the local hospital while I followed in my car. Two months premature, after long labor, she gave birth to a tiny girl. The preemie died in an incubator, unnamed, a few hours later. I had seen it; Sharon had not. I authorized its disposal, told Sharon her newborn baby was dead, and married her two days later, an hour after she left the hospital. *Dele iniquitatem meam* (erase my sins).

We stitched up our lives and education: Sharon returned to Overbrook High's eleventh grade, half a year behind her class, and went on the pill; I rented a cheap apartment for us in an iffy neighborhood, apologized to professors for late papers but did not explain, and worked longer hours at the Mart. Law school loomed, though I'd never met a lawyer. Neither politics nor law enthralled me; what workings I'd seen of both were venal and corrupt. Stocks, bonds, property, trusts, multinational business, and finance—meaningless constructs in economics textbooks.

Words alone are certain good was what I knew then[6]. In the small, still place where faith hides from reality, I still believe that. Marvell, Wordsworth, Yeats, Eliot, Auden I read, reread, and remembered. Brooks, Warren, Ciardi, Blackmur guided me. I took my sense of form from Americans: Ransom, Lowell, Stevens, Sissman. But I had no academic calling; I lacked the faith in people, reason, and the human capacity to change that a teacher needs; and academic disputes, journals, publish or perish left my pulse unquickened. The social requirements for advancement in an American university's English department would have been beyond me.

Most of all, I was afraid: of the Depression-era poverty that my father and the butcher shop drip-fed into my blood; of the penumbral gentile world that might take every stick and loaf without reason, warning, or

---

[6] Yeats, "The Song of the Happy Shepherd," online at poetryfoundation.org.

recourse; of the relegation my lack of pedigree foretold. Fear trumped love. It almost always does. La Salle's English faculty pressed me to pursue a PhD in English—but lawyering, the default choice for American liberal arts graduates, was mine.

* * *

There was no faculty lounge in the English hall. Two professors shared each faculty office, and there, they and fellow English teachers would gather to swig soft drinks, sip tea brewed on a hot plate, argue about literature, and pass the bruit of the day. My last two years, I usurped a corner in Bob Smith's office and took part in these conversations. There, a few days after the Kennedy assassination in late November 1963, four faculty were battering me with arguments for graduate school rather than law school. A newcomer asked, *Have you thought about going to Oxford or Cambridge?*

John Eldergill, an Englishman on a year's teaching exchange between La Salle and a minor English public school, had been up at Downing College, Cambridge, and studied under F. R. Leavis. My world was bounded by two Philadelphia neighborhoods and Barnegat Light; I had read of Oxford and Cambridge, but attending them was inconceivable. Eldergill asked if I had written anything that might be publishable. I thought of an essay I'd done on Eliot. He suggested I send it, with recommendations and a personal letter, to Balliol College, Oxford, and to Trinity and St. John's Colleges, Cambridge. *Who do I send them to?—Senior Tutor, Balliol College, Oxford, and Trinity and St. John's Colleges, Cambridge.*

Over the next two weeks, I assembled the ersatz applications, and a day or two after December 8, 1963, mailed them to England, one each addressed to "The Senior Tutor" at the colleges he named; no street addresses, their salutations "Dear Sir." I mentioned no wife, having left Sharon, intending to divorce.

After dinner on December 26, Boxing Day in Britain, I leave in my roadster with Bob Smith for the Modern Language Association Convention in Chicago, a third of a continent west, to get a better sense of what graduate work in English will mean if I decide against law school. We stop just beyond Pittsburgh for coffee, and I take another antihistamine to quell the symptoms of a cold. Snow begins to fall lightly. An hour later, shortly after midnight on the Ohio turnpike near Ravenna, I doze off at the wheel.

The lights of a sanding truck startle me awake perhaps twenty feet from its tailgate. I yank the wheel left to avoid hitting it; the car jackknifes and slides toward the medial ditch. I spin the wheel hard to the right but can't get traction. We run off the road and begin to flip. As the rear end rises, I think, *Well, here it goes. I've had mine.* The roadster flips end for end, and my head slams the ground; there is no roll bar. I come to in the wreck, death rattling in my unconscious passenger's throat, and I cannot move nor even wiggle my fingers.

I waver in and out of consciousness, am dragged from the wreck, and open my eyes again on a gurney in an ambulance, my teacher's rasping gurgle the only human sound. I keep asking, *Am I going to die?* until the attendant says, *No, no; why keep asking?* and I reply, *Because I don't want to make a fuss if I am.*

For eight days, I lay comatose in a small rural hospital in Ravenna, Ohio, waking only once, briefly. My father was by the bed. Ashamed of my paralysis, I screamed, *Go away! Get out of here! Leave me alone!* He left.

They took me for X-rays when I emerged from the coma. I was paralyzed from the neck down; below my chin, only my left little toe was sensate. Whiplash, they thought. Orderlies tried to lift me into a wheelchair to go to radiology; pain knocked me out. When I came to, the orderlies wrapped a towel around my neck to stop it lolling and asked if I could bear the pain. *Yes.* I was rolled off, blacking out intermittently until the X-rays were done.

I woke at dawn to a nurse and orderly packing sandbags around me under the direction of the local neurosurgeon. My neck was broken; the fifth and sixth cervical vertebrae had mashed the seventh and crushed, but not cut, the spinal cord. The surgeon told me that he planned to fuse my neck: take a bit of bone from the hip, insert it between the crushed cervical discs, and pin the lot together. *What happens if your hand slips?* I asked for a second opinion.

The doctors decided to try Crutchfield traction first, to see whether the vertebrae might heal themselves. Orderlies bolted a triangular steel armature with a pulley at its apex to the head of the bed, eighteen inches beyond and three inches above my head. One shaved my skull, and the neurosurgeon drilled two holes toward the rear of its crown. He augured in two stainless steel eye screws, threaded two filaments of fine stainless steel wire—each five feet long—through each screw eye, wound them around the eyes like guylines around tent pegs, then twisted them tightly around each other to form a braided wire queue. Last, the surgeon draped the queue's running end over the armature's pulley, passed it through the eye of a large hook, and wrapped it around to secure it. The orderlies placed bricks under the two forward legs of the bed frame, so it sloped at a twenty-degree angle from head to foot, and suspended weights from the hook now dangling below the pulley.

Crutchfield traction is a medical rack with gravity the Torquemada: the weight of your body drags you down the inclined bed, while the weights dangling from the pulley haul your head up toward the armature. Weights are added or subtracted from the hook until the opposing pulls balance, relieving pressure on the neck. The crushed vertebrae unclench the spinal cord, return to their proper position, and heal, as broken bones do, if you're lucky. But as the tug of war between head and feet pulls rope, neck muscles and cervical vertebrae part, their creeping, remorseless separation builds the pain, akin to what women endure in childbirth. The first forty-eight hours were the worst.

I was awake, unmedicated, silent, pinioned to this machine. The pain from separating bone and muscle began to build when they hung the weights on the wire. I called for my first shot of painkiller—allowed every four hours—was injected with morphine, and slept. But that first evening, the wings of morphine could not carry me away for long; my eyes snapped open in the darkness with two hours left before I could call for my next dose.

Pastor William McCabe—Pastor Bill—a large, gentle Lutheran minister, made a daily round of seriously ill patients. That first evening, he visited me. He stood by the bed for an hour while I confessed all I was ashamed of, said how talking to him helped shunt the pain aside, how grateful I was—though an atheist then and now—to have him standing there. Finally, he said he'd promised to visit a woman dying of cancer one floor above. A few minutes later, they gave me a second shot.

The pain dwindled after a few days. Worried about addiction, I weaned myself from the morphine. Pastor Bill appeared less regularly, for shorter visits. Three months later, a nurse buckled me in a stainless steel brace from hips to chin, gently raised me from my bed to grasp a medical walker, and shuffled beside me as I began relearning how to walk. When my father came to take me back to Philadelphia, I did not mention Pastor Bill.

And we did not talk about Bob Smith. They wheeled him in to see me the day before he left the hospital, while more than six weeks in Crutchfield traction still lay before me. No one would tell me how badly damaged his brain was or if it was permanent. But the friend and mentor who came to say goodbye spoke haltingly and simply, like a Down syndrome sufferer. It was the last time we met or spoke. La Salle gave him a job as a janitor at the college after it became clear he could never teach again. More than half a century has not lessened the guilt I felt when they wheeled him away.

We flew to Philadelphia and drove to my parents' house for dinner. My mother and Sharon, with whom I had reconciled while I lay knitting, had dinner waiting. At the table, my father, seated to my left in his customary place at the head, asked me to pass the thick, green-glass quart bottle of Canada Dry Ginger Ale that served for our champagne. I could not lift it. He blenched: his strength could do nothing for me now.

Two hours later, I labored up the stairs in the middle of the afternoon to a furnished first-floor flat Sharon had rented in a poor section of Germantown, ten minutes by car from La Salle. The phone rang as we entered; I hobbled over and managed to lift the receiver. My mother said, *Danny, there's a letter here from England.*

Who's it from? I don't know anybody in England.

J. A. Crook, Tutor.

Open it up. She began to read:

St John's College, Cambridge
25th March 1964

Dear Mr Burt,
The College Admissions Committee instructs me to say that it has agreed
to offer you a place here to read for the B.A. Degree in English, beginning in
October this year. I am sorry this answer has been long in coming, and I hope
it is not too late.

Yours sincerely,
J A Crook, Tutor

It was not too late.

5. Shadow Maker

Here I sit, an old man in a grand house on a cliff above the North Atlantic, ruminating on failure. It's nothing new.

Half a century ago, in January 1965, when a concatenation of flukes sent me to St. John's College, Cambridge, to study English, I began to keep a notebook. An early entry acknowledges the shadow beside me now: *I am still dogged by that feeling of failure, of lack of effort, and of ignorance, which chases my spirit into the gutter with dirty rainwater.*[7]

Feeling a bit manqué, eh? asked John Crook, the Tutor who had admitted me to St. John's twenty-five years before, as we talked in his set about what I'd done since *going down* (graduating). A decade later, I wrote of *my fear, push come to shove / I am no good at what I love* in "Manqué," a poem about writing.[8] A few months ago in a poem titled "Imposter Syndrome," I reported, *my familiar hissing / "You have no business in this place . . . / you're a wannabe from a trading floor,"* during a recent stay at a research institute.[9]

I have less cause than most to dwell on bars uncleared, races lost, nests fouled, love denied. Yet nothing—wealth, honors, love, a compliment on a poem—shoos the shadow away for long. Experience argues it will attend all my years to come. You cannot lose your shadow, though many try.

I hewed to my father as a boy and craved, if not his love, a word he never used, at least his respect. I mimicked his walk, cursing indifference to pain, rage, misogyny, and contempt for society in general. At home, I fought with my mother, hit my brother, and raised hell in the neighborhood. I swore like a trooper by nine, smoked, broke windows, was a petty thief. Years before I was old enough to have a driver's license, before I could simultaneously reach the pedals and see over the steering wheel, I'd steal his truck and careen around the neighborhood with pals. By twelve, I hung out at the corner luncheonette, gambling on the pinball machine with gonifs (Yiddish for thief or scoundrel) twenty years my senior.

Schools from kindergarten through high school punished me for fighting, inattention, and general bolshiness. I regularly failed courses and had to make them up in summer school. Education's use, if one it had, was to

---

[7] Author's notebook (Blue Cover), January 19, 1965.
[8] Dan Burt, "Manqué," in *We Look Like This* (Manchester: Carcanet, 2012).
[9] Dan Burt, "Imposter Syndrome," in the Institute Letter, Institute for Advanced Studies, Spring 2017, https://www.ias.edu/ideas/2017/burt-imposter-syndrome.

make a living; teachers were contemptible; bright kids butts. Schools, neighbors, family fingered me for failure.

My father left my social sins unpunished. He might beat me for talking back, not springing from his armchair when he came home, for fetching cigarettes or whatever else he wanted too slowly, or for hitting my brother, but not for neighborhood misadventures or poor scholarship. Complaining about work, funking a fight, losing a fish at the gaff earned curse or cuff; a bad report card, school suspensions, neighbors or police complaining about windows smashed, kids hit, or threats made did not.

But pride in a scapegrace is not paternal love. Early on, I dimly apprehended that he saw me, like all males, as a competitor. For Isaac's blessing, I would have to prove the better man.

I studied his passions—fighting, sex, speeding, the sea—and made them mine; studied his faults—raging temper, panacean fists, scant schooling, future-fear, sentimentality—and struggled to avoid them. Shortly before my twenty-fifth birthday—by when I had sailed the Atlantic on a thirty-nine-foot boat, married and divorced, graduated from Cambridge, and was about to enter Yale Law School—he bestowed his accolade: *Danny, you're harder than me.* But I was still unworthy.

My father had been a semipro boxer; he prized brute force and violence above all else. The time never came when he could not have "taken" me in a street fight. At seventy—on his second pacemaker and obese; me forty, in superior health, able to press my weight and running seven miles a day—he would have pulped me. Though childhood enemies wear scars I gave them, I was never a boy named Sue.[10]

We met last twenty-five years ago, a few months before he died, aged eighty. The coastguard had revoked his charter captain's license a year earlier. He was in pajamas and bathrobe when I walked into the apartment he shared with my mother to introduce him to the last of the four women I would marry. A long, thin tube clipped to his nose leashed the oxygen tank that trailed him.

Ya still can't put my arm down was his greeting. He forced me to sit opposite him at the dining room table, planted his elbow on its top, raised

[10] "A Boy Named Sue," song written by Shel Silverstein and recorded by Johnny Cash for the album *At San Quentin*, 1969.

his forearm, hand open to clasp mine, and made me try, a scene from *The Old Man and the Sea*. This octogenarian, who needed canned air to breathe, a pacemaker (his third) for heartbeat, who would be dead in three months, slowly forced my right arm flat. His life depended on beating me, as it always had; the outcome was never in doubt. Esau didn't curse Isaac; I could not want him dead.

Part II

Credentials

• • • • • • • • • • • • •

1. The Offer

On a warm May evening more than half a century ago in Overbrook Park, Philadelphia, in a cinema watching a British rom-com titled *Bachelor of Hearts*, I first saw the Backs of St. John's College, Cambridge. I knew nothing about John's, or Cambridge, and of England only what poets, historians, and filmmakers told. But two months earlier, John's had offered me a place to read English, beginning with the Michaelmas term that fall, and I instantly accepted.

My preference had been an Ivy League law school, not English at Cambridge. Though my father, his parents, and siblings were little schooled, they were certainly Jewish. Jews had been doctors and lawyers for centuries. Tribal lore had it that if you could obtain an "education," you should aim to join their ranks. As a boy, the only professions I heard mentioned, reverently, were medicine and law, in that order.

No tribeswoman or man of mine spoke of advertising, investment banking, stockbroking, management consulting. If there were Jewish bankers in Philadelphia, no one I knew would have known them. Electoral politics, beyond ward heeling, were for the goyim (gentiles). My mother's family's criminal enterprises were unappealing. A PhD, a writer? Inconceivable. I could quibble well, and school essays came easy, so career choices defaulted to law or the butcher shop.

My last year in high school, 1960, I came to political consciousness. JFK was running for president. The glossies filled with him waving to crowds, smiling his wide white-toothed smile, pillbox-hatted Jackie beside him; striding the Hyannis white sand beaches in white ducks, wind tousling his hair; and the image of him I recalled best, in oiled Jersey sweater, big sunglasses, hand on the tiller of a white-sailed catboat on Buzzards Bay. Campaign biographies, interviews, magazine features, a popular song, hymned the brilliance, charm, and courage of the photogenic second Catholic to run for the U.S. presidency. Camelot had come again.

Stories about JFK, his brothers, and their entourage often mentioned their patrician schooling. *Primus inter pares* was Harvard, forge of poets (Frost, Eliot, Stevens), philosophers (Santayana, James), presidents (both Adams, Teddy, and Franklin Roosevelt). Harvard, it seemed, was where the faery dust that brought American success fell thickest, and Harvard became my Canaan.

I applied there and to Yale, Chicago, Columbia, and Penn law schools in October 1963. I knew no more about law school and lawyers than about Cambridge or the Ivy League. No one at La Salle could tell me what my chances were, nor could anyone else I knew. But aged twenty-one, Ozymandian, I believed next fall, I'd stride to class over gold and scarlet leaves in Harvard Yard.

As I lay immobilized in the hospital, Harvard rejected me. Within days, Yale and Columbia did the same. Chicago offered a place but no scholarship; Penn offered both. Barred from Canaan, I accepted Penn; the letters to Oxbridge had slipped my mind.

Now admitted to Cambridge, I reasoned its degree might open Harvard's gates. Penn and Chicago had found me fit. Perhaps poor pedigree, not performance or prospects, had made me a Harvard reject? Top of the class at La Salle is not top at, say, Columbia. Whatever else Cambridge might offer, and I had no idea what that might be, I believed the world recognized its imprimatur. So franked, surely Harvard would have me. Sammy Glick's progenitors were mine as well, and there was more than a little Sammy in me.[1]

---

[1] Budd Schulberg, *What Makes Sammy Run* (New York: Random House, 1941).

Adventure as well as calculation dictated Cambridge. I had traveled scarcely farther than forty miles offshore of the Barnegat Ridge; now, I'd see England and Europe, compete against an international field, plumb the depths of my arrogance, acquire a gentleman's veneer to hide the skulking butcher boy.

Above all, it was a romantic shot in the dark. In fantasies, I was Rick Blaine from *Casablanca*, driving Ilsa Lund down the Champs-Élysées; *Young Lochinvar* come out of the west; *Le Grand Meaulnes*,[2] a.k.a. Danny Burt, MA Cantab; Danny Burt, MA Cantab, running into the open arms of the girl from Lower Merion I'd met five years before, rich father behind her smiling at me as he never had the few months we dated. A poker player as a teen, I knew the paltry odds on drawing to an inside straight, say 8 percent, yet almost always drew to it.

My father was furious. Why put off for two years a career and making money, to study something useless in England? There was hardly shame in attending Penn on a scholarship. If I spurned it now, what chance I would do better later, or they'd have me back? How would I pay tuition and board at Cambridge?

Calculation, adventure, and romance swamped practicalities. Paternal authority could not break my stride; it had withered long before, beginning one classic dark and stormy March night.

* * *

We were four males in a '52 Chevy hurtling through heavy rain in the dark toward Hampton Roads and the ferry from Kiptopeke Beach, Virginia, that crossed it, three fishing buddies from South Philly—Joe Axlerod, early fifties, fat, owner of a car repair shop; Lou Brood, thirtyish, lean, maybe gay, partner in a family fabric shop; the demon driver, my father, Joe; and me, an eleven-year-old on his first trip far from home. We were headed for Oregon Inlet off the southern tip of Bodie Island on North Carolina's Outer Banks to fish for channel bass, a bottom-feeding, guppy-shaped, immensely powerful game fish that runs to ninety pounds or more.

We were late leaving Philadelphia, 250 miles north of the Kiptopeke ferry crossing. If we missed the 10 p.m. ferry, the night's last, we'd lose one of our three fishing days before the men had to return to their shops. By the time we cleared the city, it was 7 p.m.; we had three hours left to drive

---

[2] Alain Fournier, *Le Grand Meaulnes* (Paris: Émile-Paul Frères, 1913).

240 miles, meaning we'd have to average eighty miles per hour. The highway skirted towns and suburbs when we'd have to slow; to keep our average, we'd have to do one hundred miles per hour for long stretches, almost our brown '52 Chevy's top end. Joe held the hammer down.

I could feel the car hydroplane when it hit a puddle or headed downhill under sheets of rain. Axlerod, riding shotgun,[3] asked my father to slow down. Joe ignored him. Brood, in the back seat behind Axlerod, did the same. Joe ignored him. After perhaps ten minutes' pleading, Axlerod switched to Yiddish. *Yossel, deyn kind iz mit aundz. Ir viln tsu teytn in aoykh?* (*Joe, your kid is with us. You want to kill him too?*) My father barked, *Shut the fuck up! I'm not gonna lose a day's fishing!* and tore on.

I observed the drama, silent in the back seat, understood Axlerod and Brood were scared, and their fear infected me. Why wouldn't my father slow down?

The deckhands raised the stern door behind us seconds after we rolled onto the ferry. As we climbed from car to passenger deck for the crossing, I thought about the risk my father had taken; our lives, my life, for a day's fishing. We'd caught the ferry, but was it worth it? Had what he'd done made sense? Doubt which that ride spawned metastasized. I began to observe my father skeptically, to question what he did in the house, butcher shop, at sea, his rages, the stories he told. By the time I was sixteen, my faith in him was dead.

We reached our motel near the Inlet around midnight, but it didn't matter. The storm we drove through to get there left seas too rough to fish the next day.

2. John's

On a warm late September day in 1964, I stood beside the river Cam on the Backs of St. John's College, Cambridge, staring northeast across a lawn at the neo-Gothic cloister of New Court and its wedding cake tower beyond, a sandstone-tracery cupola alight in the sinking sun.

---

[3] *Riding shotgun* derives from the position of the guard with a shotgun sitting to the right of stagecoach drivers in Westerns and refers to the passenger sitting on the right front seat of a car across from the driver.

The Backs looking toward New Court, St. John's College

Minutes earlier, I'd told a porter in the Main Gate Porter's Lodge I was a new student, visiting the college for the first time, and wished to look around. He asked my name, checked a list, said, *Of course, Sir*, and then suggested a route through the courts.

No one had called me *Sir* before. Henceforth, I'd be *Sir* or *Mr. Burt* to the porters, *Dan* to fellow students. It seemed, for an instant, *Danny Burt* was dead, but only for an instant. The presence of the seventeen-year-old American girl beside me, my wife, resurrected him.

Eighteen months earlier, in a rural Maryland registry office two days after the fruit of our teenage lust was prematurely born and died, I said *I do* to Shairon (*sic*) Guard before a Justice of the Peace, and nine months later, left her. My letters to Oxbridge had not mentioned the marriage because we were separated and divorcing when I wrote them.

It was two weeks after I posted those letters that I broke my neck. Shairon appeared at my hospital bedside to care for me, unbidden, soon after I was placed in traction. She hoped to reconcile. Paralyzed from the neck down; four hundred miles from home; unable to hold a book, feed myself, pee or shit unaided; continually rolled and rubbed to avoid bedsores; drugged with Demerol at night to cut the pain so I could sleep; and scheduled to stay that way for months even if I began to mend, I was grateful and weak and used her again as I had for the preceding three years when she—and her parents' house—offered a bolt-hole with benefits, a refuge from family and work, a place to study, eat, fuck. I understood each time she stood by my hospital bed and fed me, read to me, fellated me, and kissed me good-bye until next morning, she believed she earned a chit. From the first our match was based on exchange. But I was too weak to reject her care and lie alone dependent on nurses, too broken to bogart my IOUs.

When John's opened its gates to me, I asked her to stay behind in America. She refused. Seven days a week, January through March 1963, she'd stood by my invalid's bed; helped resettle me when I left the hospital; cared for me while I convalesced. Her hand held the moral high cards. Now she stood beside me on the bank of the River Cam, evidence of debt, bond, and a high school girl *Danny Burt* had used to get here.

Merton Hall is a small manor house within the college grounds behind New Court, added in the sixteenth century to the twelfth-century School of Pythagoras. The College had offered me rooms there so I could "live in," immersed in college life, rather than in digs (rented rooms) a bike's ride away. They rescinded that offer when I arrived with a wife; there was no room within the College walls, then or now, for the wives of married men. Forty-three years passed before the College offered me rooms again.

There was no orientation week, introductory lectures, tours of college or the university when I *went up* (matriculated); just tea or sherry with the senior tutor for thirty minutes, then a meeting with my supervisor at which he assigned the subject of my first essay, due a week later. Almost all new students came fully prepped from elite public (i.e., private, fee-paying) or grammar schools, academically superior, the public school boys socially superior as well. These young men—for the College was all male, as was most of the University—knew about gowns, Hall, bulldogs,[4] and supervision, the hour a week every week of term you spent tête-à-tête with your supervisor, discussing your weekly essay.

Married, American, older than the other first years, I was bound nevertheless by the same few rules in the same way as everyone else: dine in Hall, attend supervisions, be examined at the year's end, and go gowned to supervisions, lectures, Hall, and in the evening, on the streets. I'd bought a secondhand gown from Buttress & Co on the corner of John's Street,

---

[4] The *bulldogs* were University proctors who walked the streets of Cambridge at night, assuring that undergraduates wore gowns as required, were in their colleges by curfew, and refrained from mayhem, disorder, and rape. They were a relic of earlier centuries, when we young gentlemen warred with the townies and disported ourselves as the nobility we often were.

Hall today, looking toward High Table from the entrance

opposite Chapel Court's gates, the day after I arrived; had my senior tutor tea; been assigned my first essay. Showtime.

At 7:30 p.m. on the first evening of the Michaelmas term,[5] I crowded with the other undergraduates through the ancient wooden doors at the south end of Hall, a four-and-a-half-centuries-old rectangular room with a two-story-high, vaulted hammer-beam ceiling, where the dons and students dined. Carved wooden paneling, twelve feet high, lined all four walls, except where stained glass windows in oriels along the east wall admitted late spring and summer twilight. Rows of refectory tables an arm-and-a-half-length wide with benches that sat twenty student diners, ten a side, stood along the west and east walls. A third row, equally long, ran down the center of Hall, creating two aisles perpendicular to a step-high dais.

The dais filled the hall's north end, from west wall to east, at a right angle to the student tables. On it, two more tables, known collectively as High Table—set with College plate, white and red wine goblets, silver water cups and pitchers, and chairs for fifty—spanned. Here dined the dons, before and above us.

[5] The Michaelmas Term begins in October, the first of the three terms of the Cambridge academic year.

Portraits of dead College worthies—Wordsworth, Bishop John Fisher (Lady Margaret Beaufort's confessor), Wilberforce, Castlereagh, Prior—hung above us down the length of the room. A Renaissance painting of a kneeling lady at her devotions, Lady Margaret herself—the College founder and grandmother of Henry VIII—hung above and behind High Table, lest the dons forget to whom they owed their victuals, and we our prospects.

Awed, I followed two other newbies to a table on Hall's east side and prepared to sit down facing the wall. But no one sat. Once the students had filed in and stood by their tables, a door on the west wall near High Table opened, and the dons in their long black gowns—led by the Master in scarlet—processed from left to right onto the dais and down High Table, passing in front of us like the British dreadnoughts in 1916 "crossing the T" of the German battle line at Jutland. A bell rang when the last don stood behind his chair. We fell silent. John Crook, tutor and noted classicist, commenced the Latin grace: *Oculi omnium in te sperant, Domine* (*The eyes of all wait upon you, Lord*).

I lifted my eyes heavenward in what I hoped was a suitably respectful pose for an atheist Jew from a family of atheist Jews and criminals and saw the full-length portrait of Wordsworth directly above me, eyes lowered as if to judge me. In that spot of time, terror struck: my legs trembled, bowels loosened, breath came hard. Soon, I would be unmasked as an unprepared, inferior, colonial poseur. I'd been beaten by my father, declared retarded in second grade, poisoned by chicken bones at thirteen; at twenty, I'd waited for an ambulance to rush my sixteen-year-old girlfriend to the hospital from a cheap motel room in the Maryland boonies, where she'd gone into premature labor while we were eloping; swung knives, hammers, and chains in fights; been through breaking seas twelve feet high in a small Jersey skiff; flipped an Austin Healey Mk III at speed, lain eight days in a coma, and awoke a quadriplegic; but this was my first panic.

Something small and soft struck the nape of my neck. I turned and saw a student at the center table behind me, miming apologies for his misdirected bread ball. Pulse slowed, breath returned. Even had their brains been large as cannonballs with the manners of the Sun King's court, these black-gowned lordlings standing silently for grace were my doubles, my brothers.

* * *

Cambridge exposed fools in the nicest of places. Stupidity was denuded among the world's best-tended, charming, romantic lawns, riverbanks, and studies. An understated question, diffident comment, private word pointing out misquotation or wrong fact, comment ignored, or subject changed delicately unmasked fraud and presumption. Sometimes it wasn't until hours after being fatally skewered that I flushed, realizing how dumb I'd been. A Cambridge college is a poor venue for parading in the emperor's new clothes.

Completed in 1831, St. John's neo-Gothic New Court is laid out in the classic E pattern of an Elizabethan manor house. Hugh Sykes Davies (Hugh as we called him out of his hearing, Mr. Davies within it), St. John's Director of Studies in English, had rooms in New Court's Staircase I, on the first floor of the E's west wing. His set overlooked the Cam and the Backs to the east, south, and west through large mullioned windows, and was a College jewel. Beyond its oriel window seat, April through October, undergraduates and tourists punted sunward in the late afternoon, under the Bridge of Sighs, past Clare Bridge, King's College Chapel, and on to Grantchester, while undergraduates—a lucky few with girlfriends in those pre-coed days—played croquet, lazed on the Backs, or read in the Scholars' Garden. December through March, the westering winter sunlight—laid almost horizontal by the declining winter sun—kindled Hugh's study and the Wren Library across the Cam, as red-kneed choirboys in shorts and crimson-lined cloaks scurried to Evensong on the gravel path below. For me, chez Mr. Davies, the clock on Grantchester Church still stood at *ten to three*, and there was *honey still for tea*.

I knocked on Hugh's door for my first supervision at the beginning of my second full week at College. *Come in*, came a tenor command. Inside, a short, pot-bellied, impish-looking fifty-five-year-old man and two gowned second-year undergraduates sat waiting at a large table in the study.

Hugh had assigned "symbolism in modern British poetry" for my debut essay, a topic with which I was familiar. I'd dipped into Symons; sampled Baudelaire, Rimbaud, Mallarmé in *en face* editions; read Yeats, Eliot, bits of Pound; knew what the Yellow Book was and European history from 1875 through the Great War before I sailed for England. I beavered away for a week, refreshed my recollection of the style and times, read commentators and poets, and, by my essay's Friday due date, produced a fifteen-page paper.

Mr. Davies had it in front of him as I sat down. He welcomed me, introduced the two students invited, I later realized, to show me how supervisions were done, then picked up my essay. *Interesting Burt, very interesting.* I'd hoped for more but was too callow to appreciate how damning *very interesting* was. *Now let me see... Tell me, what exactly is a "symbol"?*

Through all my reading, labor, thousands of words too many, it was the unconsidered question. For a second time in eight days, my bowels loosened. It was, of course, the right question, the foundational interrogatory, and we both knew—Hugh and I—that it was new to me. I had read all the books, but not thought critically about what I'd read. I hadn't learned to ask foundational questions at college in America. Working-class American Catholic colleges are not known for critical or subversive thinking, and at mine, La Salle, I was consumed with cramming what I should have learned in secondary school as well as the college coursework. Some say Cambridge's only purpose is to teach you to ask two questions: *What does it mean?* and *How do you know?* The lesson had begun.

Hugh Sykes Davies was a surrealist, poet, novelist, and English literature scholar as well as a much-married, Marxist, eccentric individualist and member of the '30s *God That Failed* (a 1949 book of essays) generation. He came up to John's in the mid-1920s, earned a starred first with viva in the then new English Tripos, and was appointed a University Lecturer and Fellow of the College. There he remained till his death, a Johnian to the marrow.

*   *   *

His circle included famous intellectuals, critics, writers, artists, and spies: Wittgenstein, Russell, Keynes; T. S. Eliot among the older, Thom Gunn among the young British poets; Burgess and Maclean among the spies. A Wordsworthian, fisherman, and devotee of Isaac Walton, he wore a black pin-striped suit, tie, and waistcoat unbuttoned at the bottom to allow his pronounced potbelly to accommodate dining, the ensemble flecked with ash from the mottled meerschaum calabash he drew on ceaselessly, lit or cold.

The son of a clergyman, he lugged his Marxist hod with him from Yorkshire. No place in England was more hospitable than 1930s Cambridge to all shades of red, especially to young academic highfliers. Hugh shared a flat with Guy Burgess, one of the Cambridge five, and Roy Pascal at The Lodge on Chesterton Lane, known as the "Red House" in deference to its residents' politics. Hugh was long rumored to be "the fifth man" of the 1930s Cambridge Russian spy ring until Anthony Blunt was unmasked in the 1960s.

The Apostles, founded in 1820, is the premier Cambridge intellectual society. It has twelve current members, all undergraduates, their identities secret. When an Apostle *goes down* (graduates), those still *up* choose a new member from among the brightest undergraduates of the university. Hugh had been an Apostle, as were, for example, before and after him, Tennyson, G. E. Moore, Russell, Rupert Brooke, E. M. Forster, Wittgenstein, Keynes, Jonathan Miller, and Amartya Sen.

Anecdotes about him were rife. He wed his first wife, the poet Kathleen Raine, when he was twenty-two and divorced her shortly thereafter. He's said to have borrowed a bike within minutes of finding her making love to someone else and pedaled sixty miles through the night to London to file the divorce papers. One of his four wives he married twice, the second time so she'd receive his pension when he died.

An inveterate showman, he announced at the start of a lecture he gave on psychotropic drugs and literature that he'd just taken mescal to prime himself for it. For a poetry reading, he tape-recorded what he was to read while accompanying himself on the accordion, hid the recorder beneath the lectern before the reading began, and halfway through, laid the accordion aside, closed his mouth, and started the recorder with a hidden button. The audience was gobsmacked—instrument laid by, reader mum, words and music continuing. A don who heard him that night forty years ago talks about it still.

Hugh's pedagogy contained a strong iconoclastic streak. He surprised, unsettled, upset, and provoked you to examine the common as well as the exotic and sophisticated. *I try to do something different every day*, he said once, *even if it's walking a different way to the Sidgwick Site* (lecture halls).

His supervisions were like conversations with a slightly Socratic uncle. He didn't preach or lecture and, all but once, gave no ex-cathedra advice. He questioned, observed, told anecdotes. A supervision on moral seriousness in art and its pretensions, he pointed by telling an anecdote about a famous French literary scholar attending a Proust conference at Cambridge. Hugh invited him to Hall, and after dinner, they toured the college library. The Frenchman was bored. Hugh asked if he wished to see the college cellars, and hearing *Certainement!*, down they went to the caves. The Gaul appraised the stock and, engaged at last, enthused, *Quelle jolie bibliotheque vous avez ici (What a delightful library you've got)!*

T. S. Eliot wrote what was published as "Choruses from *The Rock*" for the religious pageant *The Rock*, first performed in 1934 to raise funds for building London churches. During a supervision on the place of Eliot's later poetry in his oeuvre, Hugh mentioned he'd gone with Eliot to *The*

Rock's premiere, during which Eliot had leaned over and whispered, *You know, Hugh, I'm not sure I believe some of this stuff myself.*

Hugh was mostly a pacifist, though he fervently supported the Republican side in Spain. He would have fought there had he not been sent to a TB clinic in the late 1930s. He never visited the United States. His left-wing, antiwar politics did not sit well with America's anti-Communist, exceptionalist imperialism, especially as the Vietnam war ramped up. One day, he explained the root of his distaste succinctly and tactfully, given my then nationality, by likening America to a brontosaurus, whose thoughtless sweep of its tail destroys half a forest without realizing what it's done. Nevertheless, he enjoyed American poets like Dickinson, Frost, and Bishop, and it was he who kindled my love of Lowell and Ransom.

* * *

As Director of Studies, Hugh chose six or seven students each year to read the English Tripos at John's. Among them, he included a *wild card* (his term), an applicant to whom the customary entrance requirements would have denied a place but whom, for whatever reason, Hugh thought worth a try. I was his 1964 wild card.

I didn't know when I entered John's if I would have to study two years or three for a degree. Graduates of affiliated universities like Harvard, Yale, Columbia, Princeton, and Stanford could do it in two. La Salle College in Philadelphia was not among them. I took ship understanding John's would watch me for a term and then would recommend to the university whether to allow me to take my degree in two years.

In mid-September 1964, in the third-class lounge of the SS *Rotterdam*—one day out of New York, bound for Southampton—were three superior young American males. They had come top of their undergraduate class at Columbia a few months earlier, their reward a two-year Kellet Scholarship to Oxbridge to study for an honors BA. One was deep in a chess match with an elderly *Mitteleuropean*, the other two watching. The chess player was Richard Epstein, a tall, gawky New Yorker going up to Oxford, the two others to Cambridge. They were the first Ivy League graduates of my age I'd met.

The Cambridge-bound Kellets and I fell into conversation. When I complimented their comrade's play, they said of the three he was the star, best at whatever he did. Epstein won the match, rose, spoke briefly in German with his opponent, then turned to where we were standing. *Boy, you looked pretty good*, I said, extending my hand. *I could have been a grandmaster, but it wasn't worth my time*, he replied and strode off, no introduction, no handshake. I met a number like him a few years later at Yale Law School.

* * *

I entered Hugh's set for my second term's first supervision on a cold, sunny January afternoon in 1965. *Come in, Burt, come in. Sit down. I have some news for you. The University considered the matter, and I'm happy to tell you that last week, the University Senate awarded La Salle affiliated status; you can take your degree in two years.* So now there were six affiliated institutions—Harvard, Yale, Columbia, Princeton, Stanford, and La Salle College.

Hugh leaned forward, removed the bowl from his calabash, knocked its dottle into an ashtray, paused . . .

Dan, I may call you Dan, mayn't I?

Yes.

You work very hard, don't you?

Yes.

Well, you know, you didn't come here to learn anything. You came to get an education. Why don't you take it a bit easy? Do you like cinema?

No one before had said *work less*, or distinguished learning from education. Until then, life had one end—win; only the object differed: fight, drag race, girl, degree, law school, money. I'd read Jaeger[6] at La Salle, at least struggled through it, but paideia remained a faint, distant siren. Now there was a chance to remove the wax and attend her song. I did, was beguiled, and succumbed to three passions: for art, in almost all forms; *custom and ceremony* (Yeats's rubric) that orders and dignifies the everyday; and sailing. They are passions still.

* * *

Kettle's Yard was a living work of art in 1964. Jim Ede—a Tate curator in the '20s and '30s—who championed Nicholson, Brancusi, Wallis, and more, moved to Cambridge in 1956. There, he melded three tumble-down, ancient cottages across the street from John's, known as Kettle's Yard, into one, painted the walls white, left the blond oak floors bare, filled it with the simplest furniture—stones and sea glass gathered on St. Ives' seashore and his collection of modern art—and lived there for thirteen years. Tuesdays,

[6] Werner Jaeger, *Paideia: The Ideals of Greek Culture* (Oxford: Oxford University Press, 1986).

Wednesdays, and Thursdays, he opened it to students, and I visited often, as did many others, including Nick Serota, progenitor of Tate Modern. Kettle's Yard was a house with art in it where an elderly couple lived, when I dallied there, not a museum. From it, I took my idea of what a living space should be.

Once a week or more, I spent midafternoon there, staring at paintings and sculptures, talking to Jim, and daydreaming in a small white room under the eaves in the northwest corner of the house, the only furniture a daybed opposite a west-facing window. On a supporting wall that bifurcated the entrance to that room hung a large Ben Nicholson—precise rectangles, arcs, circles in dun brown, gray, and white straining for sublimity; on the floor across from the daybed, a small bronze Gaudier-Brzeska bird swallowed a fish; on the bed itself, a striped, rough wool Connemara throw. Either side of the winter solstice, the sun slipped almost horizontally through the window, swamped the daybed and wall behind, and made the space—for an hour or two—a rare warm place in winter Cambridge. I sat mesmerized on the daybed, watching dust motes jig in the sunbeams, while the dying light drew a shadow over Gaudier's hungry bird. It was my first experience of *luxe, calme et volupté*. In my brown studies, those vivid motes still dance.

Alfred Wallis was an unschooled, retired harbor pilot in the early 1930s, living alone in a one-room cottage in St Ives. Poor and bereft after his wife died, to pass the time, he began painting ships in harbors and at sea—the world he knew—with leftover boat paint on cardboard. The vitality and presence of his paintings, found in the very best *Naïfs*, are unique for their threatening, cold, ice-gray seas and silver spindrift tops, so real you'd turn up your collar while you gazed at them. Ben Nicholson stumbled upon him painting outside his cottage and brought him to Jim Ede's attention. Nicholson and others gave Wallis brushes, paint, and boards on which to put it; Jim brought the works to London to sell and bought many himself; his Wallis collection is unparalleled.

A closet at Kettle's Yard was crammed with paintings there was no room to display. You could borrow one at the beginning of term, on the promise to return it at term's end. All came back, intact. Each term, a Wallis hung by my desk. One hangs in my London library today, purchased from Christie's half a century later.

* * *

Henri Gaudier-Brzeska might have become France's greatest modern sculptor had he not been killed early in World War I, and the small oeuvre he left impeded recognition. Jim owned a trove of his works, championed him, and wrote his biography, *Savage Messiah*. In December 1964, Jim was advising Paris's Musée d'Art Moderne on a forthcoming major Gaudier-Brzeska exhibition, to include a replica of his atelier. But he had not seen the exhibition space, and old age made travel a trial (there was no "Chunnel" then). When he learned I was about to spend two weeks in Paris trying to improve my French, Jim asked if I would visit the space in the museum proposed for the exhibition and give him my impressions to supplement the floor plans he'd been sent. I agreed. He wrote a note introducing me and my mission and told me to present it to the *Directeur Général* of the Louvre when I reached Paris.

On a raw December morning, wide-eyed, awed, and deferential, I entered the Louvre's administrative offices. It was my first time in France, first visit to an art museum anywhere. I handed Jim's letter to an official and was escorted immediately down long, dim, high-ceilinged sixteenth-century corridors into the *Directeur Général's* grand suite. He greeted me warmly as *un ami de Monsieur Ede*, said a few words in French I couldn't understand, then pulled a slip of headed paper from his drawer, scrawled a few words, put it in an envelope, and told me to present it at the *Moderne's* ticket desk. Outside, I opened it and read, in French simple enough even for me:

Madame, Monsieur

Laissez passer M. Dan Burt, a tous les musées de France.

[s] Directeur Général, Louvre

A free pass to every museum in France.

Mornings in Paris, I'd walk from my *pension* down the right bank of the Seine to the Moderne, present my pass, and wander there for an hour or two. After a few mornings, the guard recognized me and waved me through. A massive reclining bronze Maillol nude at the entrance stays with me, as do the Légers, and above all, the sense of being an initiate, not visitor, loose in a great store of art.

Forty-five years later, I sat in the *Directeur Général's* office again; only the *Directeur* had changed. This time, the gift was in my power—Cy Twombly's planned painting of the *Salle de Bronze's* ceiling, which I was negotiating, in English, on behalf of the benefactor paying for it.

* * *

John's had few rules but many customs and ceremonies. Some occurred daily: the snaking line of choirboys walking to chapel through the courts for Evensong; Evensong itself, the choir in red with white surplices, Master, Fellows, students, and visitors in the pews; the dons' daily evening procession to High Table; the Latin grace before we sat to eat; gowns worn to supervisions, Hall, and on the town's streets after dark. Some were regular but less frequent: Wine Circle in the Senior Common Room, where dons assembled two or three times a week after dinner for port or scotch; weekly supervisions; flags at half-mast on the death of a Fellow; subfusc funerals and memorial services; Council meetings; May Balls (annual); and College feasts for dons and guests, or dons alone, with engraved invitations that told whether dress was black tie or white and whether invitees could wear their decorations.

A diurnal round of university and college life underpinned these rituals. Cycling to lectures on cobbled streets amid throngs of other cyclists gowned as I was; afternoon tea and scones; drinks in the buttery before Hall; chess, and coffee after; visits to Kettle's Yard; twilight punts on the Cam; films, concerts, theatre, and the occasional evening lecture by someone famous socialized and civilized our time.

No one cursed you or threatened to beat your brains out; no taunts of *kike, jew-boy, dago, faggot, n-----, shkutz* trailed anyone; no one carried a knife. Shouts of *motherfucker, cocksucker, cunt-lapper* did not sound in the College courts or festoon arguments. Young men in evening dress striding to dinners, croquet players on the Backs evidenced long-settled, civilized customs. For the first time since I was twelve and a half years old, I did not spend the fag end of my week in a butcher shop, cutting and selling meat to the working poor.

These rituals and practices composed the daily college fabric, some practiced from John's founding five hundred years before. They enveloped you, whether you were part of them or not. Though undreamt of on the curbs of Philadelphia, or behind the counter in Pennsauken, none struck me as strange, but the sense of almost belonging in an ancient, ordered community did.

My world till then had been mutable, alien, hostile, and hard. Experience filtered through tales of immigration and pogroms: Pop's[7] of Cossacks

---

[7] See p. 16, above.

murdering his family; Dad's litanies of vengeance he wrought as boy and man on anti-Semitic goys. Household objects and language highlighted our foreign roots: *Forverts*,[8] the Yiddish newspaper in Hebrew type on Pop's armchair; the Yiddish my father spoke with his parents when we visited them. Local life reinforced family tales: kids taunting me with Jew-baiting slurs, fights with gentiles who shared our neighborhood. Economics 101, I learned through Depression stories of my thirteen-year-old father selling apples on street corners; his failed first two stores; parents' money worries; the butcher shop I worked in and customers cheated there. The cops I bribed as a teenager, the judge my great-uncle fixed so I could avoid a criminal record; my uncle's trial for attempted murder; the rackets my mother's family ran; the local elections they rigged, were my civics course.

America itself bred a sense of instability with its faith in change—moving on, the frontier, starting over, its palliating myth of success—that anyone can "make it," that one of humankind's three inalienable rights is *the pursuit of Happiness*,[9] not happiness itself but chasing it. I learned you could count on no one, or thing: people, law, promises, contracts, kindness, or love. Breath meant flux and risk, the only constant the sea, and fishing it, until I went up to John's.

I pined for three things American once the excitement and novelty of my first Michaelmas term at Cambridge subsided: the sea off Barnegat, warmth, and popcorn. Popcorn was inessential, the sea and warmth not.

* * *

For eighteen years, from four years old to twenty-two, I'd gone down to the sea with my father to fish, the last nine as his mate after he earned his charter captain's license. I could twist leader wire on a hook so it held a 250-pound marlin, gut and dress fish, gaff a tuna, shoot or drown a shark, set an anchor in 120 feet of water and raise it, chum bluefish and stripers, jig weakfish, spot breaking fish a half mile off, pilot a thirty-two-foot skiff to and from the canyons one hundred miles offshore by dead reckoning, run the Barnegat Inlet in bad weather. The sea was predictable, unforgiving, and fair; only competence mattered. It's the only part of childhood and youth I recall fondly. St. John's is some eighty miles due west of the North

---

[8] See p. 14, above.
[9] Declaration of Independence, 1776.

Sea. No smell of salt, rotting fish, and eelgrass rises off the Cam; there are no tarred bulkheads on its banks, no gulls diving on bait and fish entrails. When you reach the sea from Cambridge, there are no laconic charter men trading broken sentences on where to fish that day, no parade of thirty-five-to-fifty-foot wooden Jersey skiffs heading out in a long procession at five knots to Inlet and ocean beyond, no charter boats to mate on. I missed it all and did not hide my pining.

Peter Reid, a College friend from Bangor, Northern Ireland, where he'd sailed since childhood, suggested I join the Cambridge University Cruising Club (CCC). I did and was introduced to English euphemism. The CCC did not cruise. It sailed fourteen-foot dinghies on the Roswell Pits, an eight-hectare flooded gravel pit a few miles from Ely, forty minutes' drive away. There were no waves, no gulls, often no wind. Worst of all, the dinghies had no motors.

Sailing was a mystery to me when I went with Peter to join the CCC. There were no sailboats at Barnegat Light in the 1960s, nor are there many today. Local marinas did not cater for sail. Barnegat Bay is shoal, a brackish pond between a barrier island (Long Beach Island) and the Jersey Pine Barrens, its channels shallow, narrow, and twisting, not a fit place for even centerboard craft. Sailboats there had—and still have—at best, difficult ocean access from Barnegat Bay. The Inlet was a dangerous place, ringed by sandbars, the channel through it often shoaling up, and was used almost exclusively by commercial fishermen—trawlers, draggers, lobstermen—and charter men. My father was the only amateur at our dock, and he aspired to a charter license, in time earned. Above all, sailing was a Brahmin sport fifty years ago; to a large extent, it still is.

There were no Brahmins at Barnegat Light, only rough, weathered men who wrung a living from the waters below their skiffs. They taught me how to handle a boat, and how to fish. But going to sea under power teaches little about wind's subtleties. You learn the quadrants it comes from, what its strength and direction do to sea surface and inlet, what species bite in white water and what in glassy, but not about the slight wind shifts sailors heed. Sport fishing in powerboats can train you to read weather, develop sea legs, stay in the boat in rough weather and calm, dock no matter the wind—in short, seamanship, but not how to sail.

Sailing is all about the wind. A thousand days spent on the ocean in small fishing boats from the age of five had left me supremely unqualified to sail a fourteen-foot dinghy around a Cambridgeshire gravel pit. I could not *feel* the wind on my face and adjust sails or tiller to compensate. In light air, I'd often sit in *irons*, bow head-on to wisps of breeze, sails flapping, unable to make them draw. The principle of lift, by which air flowing over a curved surface—like wings of a plane, or leeside of a sail—draws the wing shapes and hence vessels they're attached to forward. Lift is the reason why planes remain airborne and boats can sail to weather, meaning at an acute angle to the direction the wind is coming from. For many years, it remained a mystery to me. How to sheet out (widen the angle of the sail to the wind) when a puff hit, not to sheet in too tightly in light air, to gybe[10] when the wind at your back is strongest—all the counterintuitive mysteries true sailors divine as children—are not quite second nature yet, though I've sailed for over half a century.

Comfort as well as competence eluded me. Bundled in waterproof surplus Royal Navy parka, fur hood over my head, long johns, two pairs of socks, seaboots, and impermeable gloves, I still sat shivering in my little dinghy for hours in the mist that rose off Roswell Pits from November through March. The racing rules bored me; though I've raced for fifty years, I've learned only three. In a half century at the helm of racing dinghies and keelboats, in perhaps two thousand races, I've won five.

But despite ignorance, cold, and incompetence, sailing bewitched me. Moving silently through the water—no propeller thudding, no engine screaming, sails trimmed optimally for peak speed—the harmony of sheet, tiller, wind, water, and craft, drew me ineluctably back to that miserable little inland gravel pit. I've sailed ever since.

* * *

Cambridge in winter is an academic tundra; it's quipped that there's nothing between St. John's and the North Pole but the spire of Ely Cathedral. Arctic air blown south across the North Sea mixes with vapors off dank East Anglian fens to brew a penetrating miasma, a gas that scrapes the throat and chills the marrow. I had never been so cold as in my first term at Cambridge, and have not been since.

John's was not centrally heated, nor my flat, nor much of England in 1964. There were few showers, and the temperature of the air in the few there were, in New Court bogs, was the same as the air outside. Colds and flus were a constant.

---

[10] Turn the boat from port to starboard when the wind is at its stern.

Brightly colored striped college scarves blossom in Cambridge like winter roses when the season cools in late October. Initially, I thought them an affectation—or at least a symbol I'd not earned the right to wear—until after almost two terms I realized they were a practicality to ward off colds, bought one, and wore it from November to May whenever I went out. Scarves have ever since formed part of my winter wardrobe, rendered an overcoat unnecessary, and kept colds at bay. The college scarf I bought fifty-three years ago—its navy field trisected with two sets of two thin red stripes for John's, bracketing a narrow light-blue stripe for Cambridge—lives in my college set's bottom dresser drawer or wrapped around my neck in cold weather when I go about in Cambridge.

No central heating meant fireplaces heated rooms or small gas fires where a fireplace would be. Gas was expensive, so you turned off the jet when you left a room, relighting it with a twist of the gas valve and a match when you returned. Huddled around the gas fire, reading Dickens or George Eliot in late afternoon or evening, you could imagine yourself a Victorian. Often, you nodded off, the air stuffy because you blocked all possible draughts, and sat as close as possible to the gas fire, there being so little of it. In this way, I set myself alight.

I wrote few letters home, but those I did—at least first term—must have moaned about the cold, for one dismal, gray November afternoon halfway through my first Michaelmas term, I received an unexpected parcel at college from Philadelphia, containing two fur-lined moccasin slippers. I sped to our flat for a test run—shut sitting room door, lit gas fire, dragged footstool close to it, propped feet, splayed blanket across legs and torso, burrowed in to struggle with Racine's *Phaedra* in French, and fell asleep. Smoke, stench of burning leather, and hot toes woke me to darkness and new fur-lined slippers smoldering on my feet at footstool's end. After that, I looked like any other Cambridge undergraduate in winter: college scarf, heavy sweater, cavalry twill or corduroy trousers, and at home, thick socks, sometimes two pairs.

* * *

Cambridge undergraduate life centered on your college, where you ate, slept, played sports, socialized, and were tutored. My cervical vertebrae had healed as well as they ever would and did not crimp me. Friends and acquaintances were mostly other college members, the majority reading what you were. The first year, mine were Johnians with one exception.

Geoffrey Couttson introduced himself while I was trying to buy a coke at the Sidgwick Site buttery. A red-and-white Coke cooler, four by four by four feet like a Judd cube, ubiquitous in U.S. luncheonettes and candy stores, stood just inside the buttery door. It looked like an American Coke machine—same size, color, cursive lettering—but wasn't. The lid on U.S. Coke coolers opened to allow you to remove a bottle after you inserted a coin in a slot on its front. The lid on the buttery's cooler did not; its sides were smooth, and there was no place to insert coins, more vault than soda machine. The only breaks in its surface were two ports, one on the top, the other halfway down the side facing me. I stared at it; ran my hands over the top and flanks; looked for a coin slot, for instructions; thought about kicking it open South Philadelphia style, à la Colonel Bat Guano demolishing the vending machine in *Doctor Strangelove*; and after five minutes, turned to slink away, Coke-less, too ashamed of my ignorance to ask for help.

May I help? The Samaritan was a thin, neatly dressed young man in cavalry twills; collared shirt; cravat; sharp, high cheekboned face; thin tortoiseshell glasses; light-brown hair; tenor voice with a posh accent. An Englishman would have marked him as from a leading public school and been right. He led me to the salesclerk, asked for a Coke, and in exchange for nine pence, was handed a room-temperature bottle of it. He returned to the machine, lowered the bottle into the top port, and a cold Coke burped from the lower.

I thanked him and tried to reimburse him for the soda. He refused, but asked if he could join me; I could hardly say no. We sat talking at a Buttery table for half an hour. He, too, was reading English, guessed I was American (trousers too short to be British) before he heard me speak or watched me fumbling with the Coke dispenser, had visited the United States on his gap year, liked the land and people. He said he *collected* Americans and asked me to join him at his college for dinner. We fixed a date a few days hence. When he left, I had a vague sense of having been picked up.

Homosexuals were "faggots" and "queers" in mid-twentieth-century working-class Philadelphia, ridiculed, loathed, and feared. I'd never knowingly met one but had the standard prejudices. That gays existed could hardly be denied at a male Christian Brothers college like La Salle, but that someone you knew—a teacher, a cassocked Brother wafting across the concrete campus—might be a practicing homosexual was never discussed;

hinted at, sniggered at perhaps, but always something shameful, certainly nothing a "real man" would do or have anything to do with.

Geoffrey had hinted he might be gay, and though I was not attracted to my smooth Etonian savior, I had wondered what a homosexual experience might be like. When the subject of homosexuals arose as I sipped my Coke, I said I was not one but willing if not quite eager to experiment with how sex with a man felt. I didn't emphasize how intellectual rather than physical was my curiosity or reflect on the absence of homoerotic urges in my till-then steadfastly heterosexual life. I led him on.

I dined at his college as agreed. Afterward, he invited me to his room for coffee and port. I did not demur but should have; what for me might be a clinical sexual experiment, for my host was a hunger. We sipped coffee and port in his bedsit for an hour and a half, me in the one chair, he on the bed.

Cambridge colleges had parietal hours in 1965; guests had to leave hosts' rooms by 10:30 p.m. on weeknights. Came the witching hour, I rose to leave. Geoffrey rose as well, walked a step or two toward me:

Dan, you don't have to leave.

Where would I sleep?

You can sleep here.

Where?

With me.

Oh, Geoffrey, don't be silly!

My exclamation was reflexive—the fact rather than the idea of spending a night in bed with a man a visceral impossibility. Physiology throttled curiosity and left me ashamed. I'd toyed with this boy to indulge intellectual curiosity. My homophobia vanished that night, as did my host, whom I never met again.

* * *

Of the three students at College who were more than familiar faces, one was there only a year. Avi Kishon was an Israeli educated in London, scion of a refugee who fled Romania for Palestine to escape Hitler, discovered a technique for concentrating citrus juice so it could be stored at room temperature, and made a fortune. A putative heir to this wealth, Avi was the only student I knew who could afford luxuries like chocolate liqueurs, port, and good dinners out; posh doesn't equal rich.

He was eighteen, some five feet eight or nine, pudgy with what looked like baby fat, dark skinned with an extremely heavy beard, visibly Semitic, and the only Jew I knew at College, though there were surely more.

Smiling, generous to acquaintances who enjoyed at every chance the delicacies he offered with coffee in his set after Hall, he was a fearsome Ping-Pong player. We played thrice weekly at least; I never won a game.

Avi invited me to dinner at the Turk's Head, a chain restaurant that passed for upscale in mid-1960s Cambridge. Hall food was dismal; I passed up no dinner invitation. We ordered starters and mains, and then the waiter asked if we wanted wine. Avi looked questioningly at me, and I nodded yes, though the only wine I'd ever had was a drop or two of sickly sweet Manischewitz from the kiddush cup at Passover. There'd been no bottle of wine on any table I'd sat at.

Avi chose a claret, which I seconded knowingly. The waiter returned with the chosen bottle, uncorked it, and poured a bit in my glass, having forgotten who ordered it. He stood over me, and stood, and stood. I was about to ask him what he wanted when Avi gently said, *Dan, he's waiting for you to taste it*, then picked up the glass, swirled it a few times, and introduced me to wine. Avi's soft voice saying, *Dan, he's waiting for you to taste it*, sometimes comes to mind when a waiter hovers beside my table while I taste the wine.

Avi proved the least fortunate of us. His passion, and gift, was for languages; he spoke and read a number. But his father insisted he become a lawyer, so Avi came to Cambridge to read law, was miserable, did no work, failed his first-year exams, and was *sent down* (expelled). I did not see him again, and the occasional letter from him soon ceased. Google told me a few moments ago, he died in 2009, is buried in Israel, and that the English on his headstone reads *He touched the hearts of all who knew him*. I raise my glass.

* * *

Sligo was deserted in March 1965 when I walked into Drumcliff churchyard to visit Yeats's grave. The last stanza of "Under Ben Bulben" describes the scene:

> Under bare Ben Bulben's head,
> In Drumcliff churchyard Yeats is laid.
> An ancestor was rector there
> Long years ago, a church stands near,
> By the road an ancient cross.
> No marble, no conventional phrase;
> On limestone quarried near the spot

By his command these words are cut:
Cast a cold eye
On life, on death.
Horseman, pass by!
               Under Ben Bulben, Yeats.

When I looked up from those lines on the limestone tombstone, there rose Ben Bulben in the middle distance, bare, isolated.

This was my first gravesite pilgrimage, but not my last, to Sligo churchyard. Each time after, a woman has been with me, each of whom I later married. *Cast a cold eye* is engraved on the back of my wristwatch case. I will make one more visit to Drumcliff Churchyard, alone, before I die, even though Yeats's bones don't there lie but at Roquebrune on the Riviera.

* * *

Peter Reid had driven us to Sligo on Saturday from his family home in Bangor, where his family owned a lace factory. Peter was the Johnian I knew best, a first-year English student, socialist, atheist, provincial, the first in his family to attend university. We shared a passion for Yeats, atheism, the sea, and had a bit of straw behind our ears, though from very different haystacks.

The Reids were prosperous, proper, Northern Irish Protestants; except for Peter, they were Orange to the core. He told me little about them when he invited me for the weekend, except to beware maiden aunt Selena, who lived with them. He didn't say why.

An old matron sat alone, enthroned on a couch before the sitting room windows, as I crept past on my way for a Sunday morning run. Peter and I had been pub-crawling the night before, and though after ten, he was still snoring. She beckoned me to her in reply to my *Good Morning*.

Have you been to church this morning?

No.

You're not a Catholic, are you?

No.

They're no good, you know . . . began her anti-Catholic diatribe. Hate gushed from the crone: Catholics were stupid, lazy, dirty, sneaky, thievish, promiscuous, genetically inferior, greedy, liars; there was no failing not theirs and no calumny they'd not commit. Then she introduced herself as Peter's aunt Selena. Shocked, I excused myself and went running.

Bigotry was familiar to me, but its targets were Blacks and Jews in my experience. I'd not heard anyone espouse anti-Catholic slanders. Irish and Italian Catholics in the half-Catholic neighborhood we moved to when I was five were dangerous boyhood enemies, feared and hence respected. I'd read about anti-Catholicism in America after Irish immigrants fleeing the Famine poured into America in the nineteenth century, especially in Boston, New York, and Philadelphia. But this was a March morning in 1965; John Kennedy was a global martyr; Grace Kelly, a famous actress and daughter of a multimillionaire Irish American contractor and Olympic gold medalist barred from rowing at Henley because he started life as a bricklayer, was the fairy-tale Princess Grace of Monaco. Aunt Selena introduced me to the experience of sectarian and class hate.

A few hours later, I unintentionally offended her, as well as all Peter's family seated with her at the dinner table. After grace, the Reid clan tucked into their Sunday lamb joint and mint jelly, wine, spuds, and made polite conversation. How did I find college, and England? Was I enjoying myself? They and the claret put me at my ease.

Talk turned to Prince Charles, who'd recently gone up to Trinity. Relaxed, insensitive to the Six Counties' fraught politics, Peter's family for the nonce indistinguishable from Peter, I mentioned Charles was seen from time to time around Cambridge and looked like Alfred E. Neuman, the idiot *Mad Magazine* satirical character whose smiling face and jug ears grinned foolishly from its covers beneath his trademark thought bubble: *What, me worry?* an American sophisticate's symbol for stupidity, a butt. Only Peter knew the reference and signaled me to stop before I explained it to the company. I missed his cue and jauntily explained not only the reference but that *tout* Cambridge—or at least my small acquaintance of smug, leftish undergraduates—thought Charles a fool.

Talk stopped, then Peter's father intoned that Windsors were held in high esteem in his house. The conversation did not include me when it resumed. Till that moment, I had a sketchy, academic knowledge of the Battle of the Boyne, Orangemen, marching season, fife and drum bands gleaned from desultory reading about Yeats and his world. After it, I could see the tabernacle where British rule and royal family rest in Ulster Protestant hearts.

* * *

One November evening during my first term, in a packed Cambridge lecture hall, I witnessed another cankered heart spew hatred. F. R. Leavis was a controversial Cambridge literary critic, read wherever English literature was studied. Superficially, he was Cambridge through and through: born and raised there, a product of a minor Cambridge public school, up at Emanuel College after World War I, a lecturer at the University from 1927, in time Reader, till he retired in 1964. But his father had been *in trade*, his wife a Jewess; this background magnified real or imagined slights and scarred him.

He pronounced sanctifying or damning literary favorites or hates. He made disciples, who laid about wherever they landed after going down, preaching the high seriousness and moral value of Leavis's favored writers—poets T. S. Eliot, Yeats, and Pound; novelists Austen, Eliot, James, and Lawrence. Some thought him a cultist, others a scold. But all I knew of him when Peter Reid suggested we attend his lecture was what I'd read in his early literary criticism.

It was standing room only in Lady Mitchell Hall. At 7 p.m., a small avian figure, thin, wispy white hair, beaked nose, sunken cheeks, and an angry mien, took the stage. What Leavis's subject was, I don't recall, because he spent the evening vilifying a younger rival, Raymond Williams, a prominent Cambridge Marxist literary and cultural critic. Williams's reputation was waxing, Leavis's waning. Peers and students loved Williams; Leavis was widely loathed. But Williams would have had to have been a serial ax-murdering pedophile to merit the vitriol Leavis lavished on him. *That man has a twisted soul*, Peter said as we left the hall.

Acid envy and spite didn't animate my boyhood; no one in my neighborhood had so much more than the rest of us to inspire it. There was time for vengeance but no leisure for spite. Making a living, or preparing to make one, left little chance to brood on real or imagined slights till their venom embittered the psyche. Moreover, in the Cambridge idyll, Leavis's meanness seemed incongruous, where it wouldn't have in business or politics. That evening should have warned me how common envy is, but it was two decades more before I understood how many quietly mutter their versions of Robert Browning's "Soliloquy of the Spanish Cloister" and act on it when they can.

* * *

My sister found my John's entering year class picture among our mother's possessions after she died and sent it to me with a cover note saying she could pick me out because of my shoes. All but one of thirty-five pairs of feet visible in the photo's front rank are shod in dark Oxfords. The

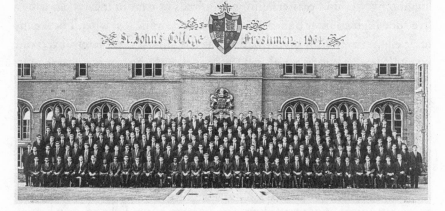

St. John's first-year class, 1964, Dan Burt front row, sixth from right, the only student in gray rather than black shoes

out-of-step undergraduate wore gray Hush Puppies, an inexpensive, somewhat clumsy slip-on loafer popular with young mid-1960s American college men. Told to wear gown, jacket, and tie but uninstructed on footwear, I ignorantly, innocently, and uniquely got it wrong.

No one remarked on my shoes nor other gaucheries I surely committed. British courtesy, and tolerance of eccentricity, left my social gaffes unmarked; belief in British cultural superiority, summed up in Macmillan's *These Americans represent the new Roman empire and we Britons, like the Greeks of old, must teach them how to make it go* excused them. It took me a year, and brush with an exception to English gentility, to begin to appreciate when I was being patronized, ridiculed, or snubbed.

The exception was Mark Yeoman, a first-year English literature student and budding hater. He was a little Yorkshireman, less than five feet, four inches tall, jet-black curly hair, dark skin with working-class roots. Perhaps frame, hue, class, provinciality, or some combination of them bred hostility in him early on to compensate for his outsider status. Whatever its etiology, from the first, he aimed his spite and sarcasm at outsiders and misfits. One morning at the end of my first year, he targeted me.

Students often moved rooms at the end of summer term. Mark, Peter Reid, Chris Evans, and I gathered early one June morning to help John Titmus, reading English like us, migrate from New Court to First. His belongings included a heavy trunk that two of the others were carrying. After we paused for breath, I picked it up alone and lugged it across the Bridge of Sighs. Humping hindquarters, cutting up frying chickens and lunch meats, lugging sixty-pound platters, lifting hundreds of bags of meat a day over a five-foot-high counter builds muscle. The tone mine lost when I broke my neck eighteen months before had recovered almost completely. Everyone knew I'd been a butcher, and, as I walked off with the trunk, saw one of its plusses. Impressed, someone said so, to which Mark added, *Well, Dan, I guess you've found your "métier."*

I knew métier meant trade, or calling, but took a few seconds to understand I'd been politely called a stevedore, an insult in the circumstances. Before my fists could clench, the others rounded on him and demanded he apologize. It was the first time anyone had come to my defense. A quarter century later, in a Manhattan conference room, I had a similar experience; again, my knight errant was a Brit. Taught from five to fight my own battles, I neither expected nor solicited defenders; in America, I found none.

* * *

Country music in all its forms played from the minute the Pennsauken Mart opened till the second it closed, every open day, fifty-two weeks a year. Osmotically, over the nine years I worked in the Mart, that sound became part of me. But unless, as at work, I had no choice, I stopped listening to it the summer before I entered La Salle and would not have admitted to having heard it by the time I walked through John's main gate.

The cords of Elvis's "Heartbreak Hotel" played on an electric guitar were the last thing I expected to hear when I knocked at Tim Horsler's Third Court set. Tim, a first year like me, had invited me for coffee when we became acquainted in Hall a few days earlier. He began asking me about country music as his door closed behind me. Did I know it; like it; been to Nashville; seen Leadbelly, Elvis, or other country stars perform? Did I realize how much rock 'n' roll owed to blues and country, the Beatles to Buddy Holly?

American GIs from the south and west carried country music to Britain and Europe along with their M1s and tanks in World War II. It caught on there but shorn of hillbilly and Black associations that led America's elite to scorn it. Europeans of all stripes and Cambridge undergraduates from Britain's leading public schools, like Tim's Haberdashers' Aske's, felt no need to apologize for enjoying it. Tim's enthusiasm restored mine for a genre I knew well but had learned to be ashamed of. I've listened to country on Saturday mornings ever since, wherever I was, to remind me who I am.

* * *

No bombs fell on New York or Washington in World War II; America had no Polish Brigade nor French refugee pilots. Europe in the mid-1950s was something American schoolkids read about that happened *overseas*. Though two of my uncles served, and I never forgot the numbers tattooed on Aaron Wildavsky's arm,[11] World War II, Fascism, genocide seemed distant, unreal things to me as they did to most Americans when I left America for Cambridge. After two years there, and two months camping on the Continent before starting law school, they were real. Tried against European reality when I returned, American exceptionalism would seem a disingenuous myth, and my faith in it and its people less certain as well.

I had returned to Cambridge for my second and final year without my wife and possibly marriage. She had insisted she tag along my first year, though it meant she would have to work to support the household her presence would create. The College frowned on married undergraduates—I met only one other while I was up—and made no effort to accommodate spouses. I struggled to dissuade her, but she played the tearful high guilt card that ministering to me while I recovered from a broken neck had dealt her. It was a trump card then and for two more years.

Sharon took a secretarial job at Pye's, a Cambridge electronics manufacturer, shortly after we arrived in Cambridge. As anticipated, neither her nine-to-five job, college life, nor my inclination allowed her to participate in my student world. By the end of our Cambridge year together, we agreed she would return to America and live separately for the next year while we decided whether to remain married.

At the end of my first Cambridge year, now as presumptive MA Cantab, I applied for a second time to Harvard Law School. My scores in "prelims," two papers from part one of the Cambridge Tripos I took for practice, were creditable. I expected to be scuffing crimson and gold leaves from my path through Harvard Yard the following fall. So likely that apotheosis seemed, I applied to only one backup law school, the University of Virginia, selected on a whim for its reputed beauty. Harvard turned me down again.

Sharon had enrolled at Boston University when I returned alone to Cambridge in the fall of '65, betting I'd enter Harvard after Cambridge,

[11] See I, Childhood's Houses, 5141 Whitaker Ave.

and reunion more likely if we both studied in the Boston area. Ten days after I wrote her saying Harvard said *No* again, a letter from their admissions office arrived saying they hadn't taken account of my performance in the prelims and asking if I wanted my application reconsidered. Without asking or telling me, Sharon had bearded Harvard Admissions and persuaded them to look again. *Yes, please.* They did and rejected me a third time.

Thrice denied by Harvard, crushed, I again accepted succor from Sharon, though rejection made me no more suited to her. She lacked principles and ruthlessly stalked what she wanted. I felt more an object of her will than a beloved. From its beginning, our relationship had been transactional: first she traded her virginity for my companionship, later her care and devotion. Defeat, disappointment, abstinence, and loss of confidence engendering bewilderment again led me to accept the swap of her body and attentions for a life together. I agreed to reconcile when I went down, travel through Europe with her that summer, then cohabit in Charlottesville the coming fall while I attended my first year at UVA law school. The Harvard admissions committee had dealt her another ace. By the time I finally engineered an end to our commerce after my first year of law school, I had come to fear her as a succubus.

* * *

Just before going down, I bought an ancient Ford Anglia car to circumnavigate Western Europe—camping through Spain, Italy, and France with Tim Horsler and Sharon—and took it for repairs. The Royston Ford dealership completed them the day before we left, leaving no time to check that the fifteen-year-old car was roadworthy. We started for Pamplona on a late June Saturday in 1966, and next day, on a secondary road in Normandy, discovered it was not.

At speeds above thirty-five miles per hour, the Anglia began drifting uncontrollably from right to left across the tarmac. We crept to the first open garage and tried to explain the problem in French to the mechanic. He lay on his back on a crawler, scooted under the car, and after a minute or two, barked, *Merde! Les rotules, les rotules, sont mort.* I hadn't a clue what *les rotules* were but sure in hell knew what *merde* (shit) and *sont mort* meant; whatever *les rotules* were, they were shot.

After several minutes of mistranslation, and much gesticulation, I understood the bushings in the tracking rods, which steer the front wheels, were too worn to control them at speed. It would take a week or more to find new ones and get them to wherever in Normandy we were if you could locate them quickly for an old Anglia. So we drifted on, South East through France, destination Pamplona. After a few hours practice, I could antici-pate and correct for the Anglia's drift at speeds up to fifty miles per hour, but steering was more like helming a boat in a quartering sea than highway driving. And our speed on motorways, where sparkling new Citroens and Mercedes whizzed around and by us, was dangerously slow.

Pamplona at the first week of July, the week of *San Fermín*, was redolent of dusty towns in southern Georgia I'd driven through on my one trip to Florida, the *Guardia Civil*, sans reflective sunglasses, in the role of cracker[12] state troopers. Spain was a dictatorship that July of 1966, Franco its dicta-tor, the Guardia Civil its storm troopers—men in field gray uniforms set off by shiny black jackboots, holsters with flaps buttoned over pistols, Sam Browne belts diagonal across their torsos, tricornered hats, and rifles slung over their shoulders—who patrolled the streets, manned roadside check-points, and lounged out and inside bodegas (bars).

It was my first time in a police state. There were no gibbets bowed with rotting corpses, fewer than American quantities of flapping national flags, no tanks or armored personnel carriers on the streets, nothing to chill the heart in the bodega where we sat drinking beer and cheap sherry, fantasiz-ing about Jake Barnes, Ordóñez, and Papa H, until two Guardia walked in.

In the center of the room, ten feet from the bar, stood a tabletop foot-ball machine. A row of ten handles a fist's gap apart protruded from the table's two long sides, fastened to iron rods stretched across the table's sur-face, or pitch. Each rod skewered the shoulders of three-inch plastic men painted to look like football players, so they hung suspended feet down off the pitch. When activated, the machine ejected a miniature metal ball, fauxed to imitate a football, onto the pitch. Twirling the handles whirled the plastic figures, which "kicked" the ball. The rods had three inches of play between the inner table sides; pushing the handles in, or pulling them out, moved the figures left or right, allowing them to attack or defend.

The Guardias were young, perhaps early twenties. They approached the machine, took up facing positions on its long sides, and one put a coin in the slot. They each grabbed two of the rod handles, the ball shot from a hole at the end of the table, and it was game on! They frantically twirled

[12] A slur referring to poor, rural, southern U.S. whites.

the handles, slammed the rods from side to side, and the little plastic footballers revolved and darted back and forth, defending and attacking, while the armed sportsmen whooped and hollered like it was Barcelona vs Madrid. The game ended, the loser demanded a rematch, and another coin slid into the football machine's slot.

But no miniature football bounced onto the pitch. One of them shook the machine, then both. They punched it, hammered it with their fists, lifted and dropped it, but the little white ersatz football stayed in the belly of the machine. No one stared at them. No one said stop. A Guardia kicked the table's underbelly with the steel toe of his boot, first lightly, then harder. His comrade joined in, harder; they kicked till the wooden belly began to splinter. The frenzied policemen kicked the table's legs till one collapsed, then another, so the pitch sat tilted on two legs, its end resting on the floor. The vandals kicked and stomped the pitch until the dead football machine lay shattered on the barroom floor.

No one spoke; no one approached them. Spent, satisfied, the vandals sauntered from the bar. Patrons avoided eye contact with them as they left. The bartender and waiter began clearing the football machine's remains when you could no longer hear the departing Guardia Civil's footsteps. But brooms could not sweep away the lesson that in Pamplona, those armed striplings could do what they pleased, could on a pretext beat a passer-by to death as easily as a football machine. They were the State, and in Franco's Spain, the State went unchallenged. No Mr. Wolf[13] could dissolve the image of silent patrons averting their eyes as the thugs left the bodega. We were all afraid; we were all cowards. In the morning, we left Pamplona.

* * *

The mosquitoes attacked every day, a half hour before dawn, in Lloret de Mar. If the tip of your nose or an earlobe strayed outside your sleeping bag, they dive-bombed, pierced it, sucked your blood, and woke you with a sharp pain as they extracted their proboscises and zzzz'd-off, leaving you awake, skin red and swelling around their bites, and helpless to stop them.

We'd come to Lloret de Mar, a small town on the Med fifty miles northeast of Barcelona, for Tim to toast himself. He had an Englishman's insatiable lust for Mediterranean summer sun, to baste himself with oils and lie

---

[13] In the movie *Pulp Fiction*, Mr. Wolf is the almost superhuman fixer called to clean and dispose of a body and the car in which its brains were blown out.

in it till his pale, pasty, white English skin roasted to a tan he hoped would endure through November. He'd brought a gallon of tanning oil and an egg timer with him and, four hours every day, slowly spit himself in the sun, revolving fifteen minutes on left side, fifteen on belly, fifteen right, fifteen back, repeat, two hours in the morning, two in the afternoon. We spent three days there, then left Tim to the dawn dive-bombers and rotating immolation and drove northeast, toward the Riviera and Italy.

Two weeks later, shortly before twilight, we pulled into a packed camping site a few miles from Pisa and were directed to a site next to a twenty-foot-long camper (called an RV now), a behemoth in that pre-RV large-as-a-cross-country-bus era. Beneath a plastic awning cantilevered from the side of the camper's roof sat a large, fortyish White man on a camp chair, in his hand an open, cold, brown bottle of Budweiser beer grasped by its sweating neck; nearby, on another camp chair, his equally stocky White wife; between them, an arm's length from his chair, a white Styrofoam ice chest. Their three preteen children played catch nearby, while coals in a charcoal grill near the trailer's door rose to barbecue temperature. It might have been a beer ad.

Student camping is Spartan. We slept in a pup tent for two on air mattresses reinflated every night; washed, pissed, and shat at communal baths; pissed sometimes at the side of the road. A banana, orange, or apple with dry cereal was breakfast; dinner a packet of Knorr vegetable soup, heated in water on a single-burner Calor gas canister, bread, sardines, and, for a treat, cheap vin de pays. We skipped lunch. Somewhat thinner than we were a month earlier, we pitched our tent that evening and fished a soup packet from our stores for dinner.

Perhaps it was our accents, perhaps our ratty looks; it could have been simply neighborliness or kindness. But whatever the reason, one of the children came over and said their dad invited us to join them for dinner. Offer of a beer would have been a blessing; an American cookout, Christmas come early.

Our host was an American air force master sergeant from Ramstein Air Base, near Kaiserslautern in what was then West Germany. He fed us hamburgers—the only good ones I've had in Europe—as many as we wanted with relishes, ketchup, pickles, and onions. Massive bags of classic potato chips cooked in trans fats made the rounds, bags so large your arm sank to its elbow in them when you fished the last chips from their bottoms. There were three six-packs of Bud in the Styrofoam cooler; Breyer's vanilla, chocolate, and strawberry ice cream from the camper's freezer for dessert; fresh coffee to wash it all down; and Marlboros afterward to keep the mosquitos away. Levittown, Pennsylvania,[14] had materialized in Italy, five minutes' drive from the Leaning Tower of Pisa.

The sergeant had been servicing F-4 Phantoms[15] based at Ramstein for four years. Neither he nor his family spoke any German. The children went to the American school on the base. When my wife asked what living at Ramstein was like, he gestured toward the remains of our feast and said it was no different from life in America. There were Little League teams, bowling alleys, swimming pools, churches, hospitals, and dental clinics. His wife shopped at the PX (post exchange), which carried everything American from hot dogs to baseball caps, cigarettes, TVs and TV dinners to go with them, coffee, bicycles, medicines, and *personal things*, all at heavily subsidized prices; in short, everything a middle-class American family needed. Though military pay was low, the subsidized PX, free and excellent medical care, and base housing afforded service families a comfortable lifestyle.

Neither servicemen nor their families were encouraged to explore host societies; personnel and dependents looked inward, as Americans do. Foreign posting did not alchemize them into cosmopolitans. They believed in America and that it was exceptional, that they and their nation were superior to all others. They were no different from the butchers with whom I'd cut and sold meat and their families with whom I'd drunk and celebrated Fourth of Julys, America's Independence Day, in suburban backyards. Nineteen sixty-four was the apogee of the American imperium; our generous host and the base he hailed from manifested it, as British colonies in India, Egypt, and Singapore had the Raj before it. Our hosts mentioned neither Vietnam that evening nor Korea, secure in their faith.

* * *

Beginning in kindergarten, American children in the 1950s learned that the U.S. military was invincible, always had been, and their causes

---

[14] Levittowns were post–World War II subdivisions for returning GIs, inexpensive, mass-produced, cookie-cutter houses on small plots of land with white picket fences and small green lawns behind them. Federal Housing Administration lenders limited their loans to purchasers *of the Caucasian race*. They were called after the developer whose idea they were, William Levitt, and became a synonym for conformity, bigotry, and narrow mindedness.

[15] The F-4 was the U.S. state-of-the-art fighter jet of its day.

righteous. From the Minute Men—farmers and tradesmen in Lexington and Concord, Massachusetts, in 1775, who routed the British Regulars at the opening of the Revolutionary War—through the War of 1812, Mexican War, Spanish-American War, World War I, World War II to Korea, we knew U.S. wars were just, our troops victorious. We knew America won World War II. There was little mention then, or, I suspect, now, of Stalingrad, the siege of Leningrad, Russian tank and artillery factories beyond the Urals. The Battle of Britain was a romantic footnote to American military triumph. Modern history was red, white, and blue with white stars as I approached the Brenner Pass.

There, near noon, a German man—medium height, midforties, medium build—asked me how old was my dying Ford Anglia car. He and his son were waiting in the passport control queue immediately ahead of us, and after answering his question, we fell into conversation. My fellow traveler was the first German World War II veteran I'd met. He'd fought at Stalingrad, surrendered in January 1943 along with ninety-one thousand other German soldiers, and returned ten years later, one of only five or six thousand who saw the *Vaterland* again. He said Germany foundered on the eastern front and after Stalingrad knew it had lost the war, however long denouement might take. He did not blame the Russian winter but the Russian troops, who were tougher, indomitable, and more of them, with more tanks, artillery, and guns. He was pro-American, anti-Soviet, his parting words *Russki! Russki! Fook dem! Fook dem!* World War II wore a different cast a half hour later as I drove down into Inn Valley.

* * *

Three men looked down over the *Heiliggeistkirche* (Church of the Holy Spirit) and Heidelberg aglow across the river Neckar—Martin Kitchen, his father-in-law, me. It was the latter part of August, we'd had a fine dinner, and we men were sitting on the balcony of Martin's in-laws' house with after-dinner Eiswein,[16] coffee, and cigars. The low sun behind us fired the Holy Spirit's spire and Heidelberg University to the southeast; the scene looked like a tourist poster for a Rhine holiday, and *Gaudeamus igitur* rang in my mind's ear.

---

[16] Eiswein (ice wine) is an intensely sweet dessert wine made from grapes left on the vine as late as possible.

In my second year at college, I had roomed with two other students—both English, neither Johnians—in a small house. One, a historian, introduced me to his friend and fellow historian Martin Kitchen. Martin and his German wife, Brigitta, had me to dinner several times at their flat. When I mentioned I, and possibly my wife, would be wandering through south-western Europe after graduation, they said they'd be staying at Brigitta's parents' house in Heidelberg this coming August and invited us to stay a night should we pass through.

Brigitta's family home was large, set into a hill above the city on the Neckar's north bank. A new Mercedes sat curbside; a maid opened the door. I recall, dimly, that Brigitta's father owned a small, prospering *Mittelstand* (medium size) company, part of the *Wirtschaftswunder*, Germany's postwar economic miracle. But whatever he did, his establishment—and Germany—looked to have recovered from the war better than houses and families I'd visited in England.

Today, a few taps on a cell phone brings up the history of a place and people you visit; in the mid-1960s, that information was harder to come by. When we drove into Heidelberg, I didn't know it had been a Nazi Party stronghold, that its two synagogues were burned on Kristallnacht, what year it was declared *Judenrein* (Jew-free), or that lack of factories spared it allied bombs.

Dinner conversation touched on the war after I complimented my hosts on our surroundings and the impression of German affluence the drive from Munich fostered. They were proud of home and country, boastful about neither. Martin's father-in-law did not say how he had spent the war; I did not ask. But I was given to understand it had been a trial, a disaster, and their present comfort hard-won by the time the women left us and we men moved to the balcony.

Martin's father-in-law picked out sites across the river in the twilight and told us about them: the university's history, its current specialties, who lived where. I asked where the Jews had lived, and he pointed to a section of the *Altstadt* (old city) clearly visible across the river.

What happened to them?
We got up one morning, and they were gone.
Where did they go?
We didn't know. Nobody told us.
Did you ask?

No reply.

My wife and I left early next morning.

* * *

Cambridge had been an idyll. Immersion in a long-historied Britain, and the classical culture in which my Cambridge classmates were steeped, fed my Jewish hunger for perspective, to make sense of things, anticipate events, and, should the worst happen, survive. Leisure and ease of travel to the Continent slaked cravings for variety, novelty, excitement. In 1965, for the first time since I was twelve and a half, my summer was work free. I could sail the Atlantic on a small boat if I chose, and did.[17] Above all, the rage that attended me in America disappeared when I left it; my fists rarely clenched in Britain. There were powerful reasons to remain there.

Though Cambridge was an academic mountaintop, it was a British, not an American one. Cambridge had not given me the crampons to climb America's heights. With Harvard's rejection, any dreams I might have had to scale America's Brahmin peaks vanished. If I remained in Britain, a good, perhaps superior career and life were likely; my future as a Yankee was far less certain than as a Limey. Until the day before I enplaned for the States and law school, I worried at the idea of remaining in England. Time and again I decided to stay, and time and again resiled.

If asked, I said my reason for returning to America was *Because I'll never have a gut response to Guy Fawkes Day*; it was more than a flip rationale. Vulgar hunger to "make it" in America,[18] though strong, did not decide me, nor did the knowledge I'd be attending a top law school—albeit not Harvard—nor the prospect of an honorable profession, financial security, perhaps power. The black holes that dragged me back to America from Cambridge were childhood myths, the patriotic gore and exceptionalist doctrines pounded into all American schoolchildren, then and now: Indians feeding Pilgrims; Winthrop's *shining city on a hill*; George Washington confessing he cut down the cherry tree; Washington again, crossing the ice-choked Delaware at Valley Forge to surprise the British; Lincoln freeing the slaves; pioneer wagon trains *winning* the West; Sergeant York singlehandedly killing twenty-five and capturing one hundred thirty-two

---

[17] See II, Every Wrong Direction, Offshore, The Isbjørn Crøssing.

[18] See Norman Podhoretz, *Making It*, NYRB Classics, NY, 1987.

German soldiers in World War I's Meuse-Argonne offensive; the staged flag raising on Iwo Jima's Mount Suribachi; dogfaces (foot soldiers) lying under fire on Normandy beaches; the *Pledge of Allegiance to the Flag*, recited daily, to *one nation, under God, indivisible, with liberty and justice for all*, as we stood with right hands over our hearts[19]; the American triumphalist public holidays of July Fourth and Thanksgiving.

Negative tales reinforced positive. Once or twice a year in grade school, during assembly, we were shown the 1937 film *Man without a Country*. In it, a Lieutenant Phillip Nolan is tried for conspiring to commit treason with Aaron Burr in 1807. At trial, Nolan shouts he never wants to see or hear of America again. The judge grants his wish and sentences him to confinement for life aboard U.S. navy ships sailing beyond sight of the United States and to be denied news or mention of his homeland. Nolan is transferred from ship to ship on the high seas until he dies, an old man, decades later. He never sees or hears of America again.

The film ends with the interior of Nolan's cabin, revealed for the first time, the shot accompanied by music fit for a horror movie when the horror appears. *Old Glory*, patched from colored rags, covers one wall; cuttings about America scrounged from discarded newspapers bury a deal table, and the cabin sole inches deep. Lieutenant Nolan, we discover, made his ocean cell an *homage* to the land he scorned, then ached for, for the rest of his life.

That celluloid cabin scored my grade school mind. I see it as I type, its admonition as clear now as then: an American who abandons his country will rue it the rest of his life. The homily would have been less powerful had we been told it was a fiction, a filmic adaptation of a Civil War pro-Union propaganda piece, written by Nathan Everett Hale, published in the *Atlantic Monthly* in 1863. There was no Lieutenant Nolan, no patriotic cabin, no life sentence of patriotic regret, but I didn't know that when I was eight years old.

Cambridge had its faults. Though it educated me, as Hugh intended, it also left me deluded about what I would rediscover beyond its walls. It supplied an ivory template of civilized society to supplant the coarse dye I bore from Philadelphia but bred silly expectations of honorable behavior from

---

[19] The pledge I originally learned did not include the phrase *under God*, which was added in June 1954.

suited classes I knew nothing of and hoped to join. So armed, I foolishly discarded childhood's work-glove tutorials for a time.

Cambridge also did not deliver what I'd come for. *Pace* Gatsby, but MA Cantab after my name conferred no status or credibility in American legal, political, business, or social cultures nor stampeded the girl from Lower Merion into my arms. It has not trailed my name for half a century.

I bought three things when I left St. John's: contemporary art—an abstract painting and tiny clay head by John Blackburn; bone china—four settings of Wedgwood in a black-and-gold hippogriff pattern; and a bespoke dinner jacket. For fifty years, through four wives, eleven moves through ten cities on two continents, I carried the Blackburns and Wedgwood with me. I have them still. Only the DJ's gone, which somewhere along the road no longer fitted and was abandoned. Cambridge may have misled me for a time, may not have worked the alchemy on my American prospects I sought, but it dealt me an ace that I could keep: high culture as a choice rather than streets, bourses, and corridors of power.

3. Offshore

The *Isbjørn* Crossing

Meredith Jackson was sixty-two when I entered his set in St. John's Second Court in late May 1965. He rose haltingly to greet me: six feet, keg bellied, slightly jaundiced, very short crew-cut hair, and white, wispy goatee. He'd sailed small boats offshore from boyhood, enamored of crossing or attempting to cross oceans in them. His right hip's ball and socket joint was failing; he limped heavily but hungered still for blue water in little boats, like Yeats's Sligo uncle:

> But where is laid the sailor John
> That so many lands had known,
> Quiet lands or unquiet seas
> Where the Indians trade or Japanese?
> He never found his rest ashore,
> Moping for one voyage more.
> Where have they laid the sailor John?
> —"In Memory of Alfred Pollexfen," Yeats

In a few weeks, Meredith planned to sail *Isbjørn*—Norwegian for polar bear—his thirty-nine-foot converted Scottish fishing ketch, with three crew from Brightlingsea, Essex, to Annapolis, Maryland, via the North Atlantic low-power steamer route. I presented myself as his possible third crew member. He'd already chosen the other two, a Dane, Sven, and an Australian, Alan. Sven was twenty-four, a graduate engineering student at Cambridge. He'd raced Dragons—a twenty-six-foot keelboat—in the Baltic and North Sea, inshore off Copenhagen, and was the most experienced of the crew; Meredith dubbed him first mate. Sven's marriage had failed irretrievably a few months earlier, and his kit bag held texts by Kierkegaard and Sartre with which he planned to reexamine his life on the voyage, but didn't. Ocean crossings on little boats are too physically demanding for philosophizing.

Twenty-year-old Alan raced International 18s, also called Aussie 18s, in Sydney Harbor. They're the fastest mono-hull, nonfoiling skiffs in the world—the Ferrari of dinghies—sailed by three men suspended from trapezes attached to the mast, their feet on wings projecting from the port and starboard hulls. Aussie 18 sailors are the princelings of the sailing world. His father owned, or was a senior director of, a pharmaceutical company; Alan's kit bag bulged with medicines, especially antiseasick pills, which served him well.

Little recommended me. *Isbjørn* was just three feet longer than two Maybachs—Mercedes' most expensive limousines—parked bumper to bumper, a small craft for a three-thousand-mile sail over salt water deeper on average than the Matterhorn is high. My sailing experience totaled thirty-two hours, clocked that first year at Cambridge in two-hour weekly sessions in fourteen-foot dinghies on a nearby local gravel pit. Eighteen months earlier, I'd broken my neck, been paralyzed, and when mended, been warned off sports where I might fall or be knocked about. It would be a long way, over deep water in a tiny boat for a twenty-three-year-old with a dodgy neck, who had sailed little more than a day in total.

But Meredith needed one more pair of hands, however unreliable, after his twenty-year-old daughter, Mae Ling—an experienced sailor slated to be the third crewmember—canceled unexpectedly in late May. By then, most Cambridge students had fixed their summer's plans and were unavailable. I was candid about my tyro status but touted my offshore experience fishing, working, and skippering thirty-foot Jersey skiffs: how I could keep my feet, rig lines, and gut fish on the porpoising deck of a round-bottom charter boat; dead reckon a tuna trip ninety miles offshore and back; hold my breakfast when coastguards chucked theirs; run inlets through twelve-foot breaking seas in fog. I told him I learned *one hand for the boat*, every seaman's first lesson, at age eight and a half, and gave the sea its due. (Unstable vertebrae went unmentioned.) And so, by default, I joined the *Isbjørn's* complement, no sailor, but the one with sea legs schooled offshore.

Our skipper was Downing Professor of Law at Cambridge, his chef d'oeuvre, *The Machinery of Justice in England*, then in its fourth printing, now fifty years later in its eighth. Taciturn almost to rudeness, he told you something only once. He did not praise; had a gin-and-bitters when he woke at daybreak, scotch after the noon sun sight, three or four more after dinner; did not talk about himself; showed no interest in us. He was our Master, his word law, decisions unquestionable, competence unquestioned, and the only Englishman aboard.

* * *

Ebb tides left *Isbjørn* high and dry on the mud in Brightlingsea estuary twice a day—bilges, keel, and rudder bare to the world. She was a 1930s, double-ended, gaff-rigged work ketch, bow and stern ending in a point, a shape like a larger version of Grand Banks dories in the 1937 film *Captains Courageous* (based on Rudyard Kipling's novel and starring Spencer Tracy, Lionel Barrymore, and Mickey Rooney) or the boat depicted in Winslow Homer's *The Fog Warning*.

Isbjørn's headroom between deck and bilges was some six and a half feet. Her hull below the waterline looked like a plum cut in half. A thick oak keel shaped like a meat cleaver was bolted through to her oak hull, the cleaver's handle starting inches deep at the stem with the *blade* gradually lengthening till it hung five feet below the hull at the rudder post. The rudder was a door wide.

From her deck just forward of amidships, a wheelhouse rose like a camel's hump, seven feet high, eight feet long, and joined the cabin top that ran to the peak. Inside it, a forearm's length behind the helm, an oak trestle table seating two a side was bolted to the deck, and on it, we ate our meals. We sheltered in the wheelhouse from sun and foul weather and socialized there. Though we crew had little in common—and after the voyage never saw one another again—it was a long, slow trip, and we often lingered around the helm, talking of cabbages and kings, when the evening meal was done.

The main mast was two feet thick at the deck, the mizzen half that, both gaff rigged. Gaff-rigged sails are not the big white triangular sails

Interwar, gaff-rigged Scottish fishing ketch (PH from online)

people picture today but canvas trapezoids like those that hung from the yards of square-riggers a century and a half ago. The sail's head (top) is lashed to a gaff, a wooden pole almost as long as, a third the diameter of, and parallel to the boom. The gaff is raised in tandem with the luff of the sail, so it rises parallel to the boom till the luff, secured to the mast, is taut. Then the gaff is raised till the leach is fully extended, the jaws of the gaff tight against the main mast, and the gaff tip angled forty degrees higher than the boom, like a bullfighter's cape as the bull charges beneath it.

The *Isbjørn*'s canvas sails were thick as bath mats, stiff almost as boot leather when dry and crusted with salt. There were no winches aboard the *Isbjørn*, only blocks; we strained to raise sails and yards, as tars would have on that square-rigger, her blocks our only mechanical advantage.

Loaded, *Isbjørn* drew twelve and a half feet, displaced twelve tons, and slept four, two in the fo'c'sle and two in the main cabin. Except for an old four-cylinder Kelvin diesel that drove her at five knots max, she would not have been out of place with the rest of the fishing smacks off Galway in 1900.

Below deck, on the starboard side of the cabin beside the companionway, was a navigation table and seat just large enough for our 220-pound skipper to wedge himself in to use the ocean and coastal charts, sextants (two), chronometers, tide tables for the Azores, Bermuda, and the Chesapeake, protractors, compasses, and parallel rulers in fiddled shelves above. To help measure distance made each day, we trailed a log line. *Isbjørn* carried no radar or ship-to-shore radiotelephone; three decades passed before cruising craft carried GPS, cell phones, and weather-tracking computers. We would navigate as Drake had done.

The galley, on the port side of the cabin across the centerline from the navigation station, had a sink with a hand pump tap for fresh water, strictly rationed. A two-burner, Calor gas propane cooker, gimbaled and with high fiddles so pots and their contents didn't fly off the stove in rough weather, hung forward of the aft port cabin bulkhead. The cooker swung to and fro in rough weather, sometimes smacking the cook braced in the tiny galley. There were lockers for pots and pans, tableware, knives, stores, condiments, but no refrigerator. Meals would be simple.

Three weeks after I appeared in his set, Meredith drove me the two hours from Cambridge to Brightlingsea, showed me around the boat, and left me aboard alone to scrape, sand, paint, and caulk while he returned to Cambridge for the two other crew members. Between our mooring and Brightlingsea lay a narrow navigation channel; the current at peak tide flowed at four knots plus. Hundred-foot-long, broad-beamed coal barges swept up and down it with barely enough room for two to pass, doing seven to eight knots when a peak current was with them, nearly twice their normal speed. I did not look up from scraping paint as they steamed by.

We ferried skipper, crew, gear, and stores from Brightlingsea wharf in an inflatable ten-foot Avon dinghy, a sort of rubber bathtub with snub bow, broad stern, and wide sponsons (flotation tanks) on which passengers sat. A wooden board for the oarsman, slightly forward of amidships, sat athwart the sponsons, which had molded rubber oarlocks on them for stubby oars. *Isbjørn*'s Avon dinghy was no racing scull; with neither keel nor rudder, and a flexing hull, she meandered slowly toward her destination under oars, more driftwood than dory.

There were two hours of daylight left at the end of my first day aboard when I downed paint scraper and cast off in the Avon for a solitary pub dinner in Brightlingsea. I gave no thought to current as I rowed. Tides rose and fell less dramatically in my home waters than around Britain; channel currents ran more slowly. Powerboats are less affected by tide than sail; we heeded ebbs and floods primarily for their effect on the height of seas in the Barnegat Inlet or when fish were likely to bite. It was slack water, the tide just beginning to ebb, and the current dozing in the ship channel as I rowed across it did not affect my clumsy progress toward the pub.

It was dusk, drizzling, and I was three scotches to the good when I grasped the Avon's oars to struggle back. The tide was at peak ebb, current wide-awake and running more than four knots. It set me sideways faster than a comfortable stroke propelled me forward, and my distance across it to the *Isbjørn* began to widen rather than close. I picked up the stroke, began to inch ahead, and then heard a ship's horn. I looked to port and saw a coal barge three hundred yards away, closing fast. There was no room in the channel for it to avoid me without running aground; it could not stop. Even with engines reversed full, momentum and current would sweep the barge over me.

The horn again, like Gabriel trumpeting the Last Judgment. I swung the oars frantically back and forth, glancing left at the barge's black bow bearing down on me, a guillotine descending at nine knots, its speed plus the current's. The coaster swung ten degrees to starboard, as much as it could without leaving the channel; my oars frothed the water. I could number the barnacles below her waterline stripe, hear the thump of her pistons, see two crew leaning over her sides looking for debris as the coal barge pounded past. She was unladen, hence more maneuverable and drew less water, or I'd have been a statistic. Next evening, I checked the tide, looked up and down channel, and cupped an ear for the sound of engines before making for the pub.

The English Channel is a liquid motorway. More than five hundred ships—freighters, tankers, container ships, ferries, trawlers—daily pass up, down, and across it on their way to and from Belgian, Dutch, English, and French ports. A week later, we hoisted sail in the dying twilight and headed southwest into that scrum toward the channel and Plymouth.

Meredith called the crew to the wheelhouse to discuss standing night watches. We knew what green (starboard), red (port), and white (masthead or stern) running lights meant, as well as the basic rules of the road: power must yield to sail; pass port to port; if you can see a ship's port and starboard lights at the same time, you're about to be rammed. Then Meredith rewrote the rules.

A four-hundred-foot-long ship at night, in busy sea-lanes, can hardly see a thirty-nine-foot sailboat in time to alter course, he said, even with sea room to do so. If one rammed us, there'd be little left but blood and splinters, our bodies crushed in the collision, drowned in the wake, or hamburger if we were swept into the screws. Forget who has right of way; stay out of the way of ships. If we were confused, or a vessel seemed too close while on watch, he said to wake him.

He started down the companionway to the cabin, stopped, and recited,

Here lies the body of John O'Shay,
Who died defending his right of way.
He was right, dead right, as he sailed along,
And he's just as dead as if he'd been wrong.
—Old sailor's limerick

and then descended to his bunk. As I type this, I hear him reciting it.

* * *

We were fast to a wharf in Plymouth three days later, loading stores, fresh vegetables, fruit, bread, and gin, bitters, and scotch in bond. Meredith provisioned drink for five, on the theory he'd drink as much as two of us. It was more than ample; Sven and Alan found they had no taste for hooch at sea.

West of Plymouth lay our route down and across the North Atlantic: southwest to the Azores, from there due south to latitude thirty-two degrees north, then due west to Bermuda; from Bermuda, west-northwest to Annapolis, Maryland. We stowed stores and booze, paused for lunch, then set sail down the channel in a stiffening northeasterly breeze. Just before dark, we felt the first Atlantic swells, and Meredith called us to the wheelhouse for our safety briefing. *There's no lifesaving gear aboard: no life vests, radios, die markers, flares. If you go overboard in bad weather, you'll be hard, if not impossible to spot, and best dead soonest. Stay in the boat.*

* * *

Only we three crew helmed the boat, twice a day, four hours on, eight off. I had the helm from 8 p.m. to midnight our first twenty-four hours out of Plymouth. When I came off watch, a cold wind was blowing steadily at fifteen knots from the northeast. When I climbed from my bunk in the fo'c'sle to take the wheel at 8 a.m., the wind had picked up to twenty knots, still from the northeast. All day, we made our westing, and by the time I turned in that night, we had what proved to be our voyage's best day's sailing, nearly 190 miles.

The prevailing summer winds in U.K. latitudes blow from the direction we were headed, southwest; easterlies are an unusual, short-lived blessing, ours no exception. At dawn of our third day, as we left the western reaches of the Bay of Biscay, the easterly began to *back*, veer north to west against the circuit of the sun. It blew twenty-five knots from the northwest, strengthened, and continued backing to the west. Five hours later, it was *on the nose*, blowing thirty-five knots from the southwest, our course to Ponta Delgada, Azores, with gusts to forty-five, the glass falling. Unable to sail directly into the wind, or make headway on engine alone, Meredith told us to *heave to*[20]; we'd ride out the building storm, then head southwest again after it passed.

There are two ways for a small sailboat to weather a storm: run before it, masts bare, trailing warps (heavy lines) or drogues so you're sliding downhill before the seas; or heave to under storm sail, reefed main, and lashed rudder so the boat lies stationary in the troughs between and broadside to the oncoming, breaking seas while the wind pushes you away from them and they break under rather than over you. Running before a storm is a last resort, used only in the fiercest weather, because you can be carried hundreds of miles off course, pooped, or broached and rolled. I'd neither *run before* nor *hove to*, fishing offshore of New Jersey, because if it was blowing or forecast to blow too hard, you wouldn't leave the dock. Three hundred and fifty miles west of Lisbon at the western rim of Bay of Biscay, the dock was three days behind us.

First, we eased the mainsail so it didn't *draw* and drive us forward. We broke out the storm trysail—a small, heavy, triangular canvas sail flown from the forestay—and backed it so it caught the wind, like a sock or catcher's mitt, and tried to force us downwind. Simultaneously, we lashed the wheel to leeward, so the rudder kept trying to force the boat into the wind. The struggle between the wind in the storm sail blowing us away from the seas and the rudder forcing us into them left us in stasis, the *Isbjørn* parked broadside to the seas. Last, we had to reef (shorten) the mainsail so it did not *draw*, overpower us, or *flog* (flap uncontrollably in the wind) and

---

[20] See Wikipedia guide on *heaving to*, for detailed description, with image, of how to heave to.

tear itself to bits, but helped hold us steady in the troughs. Mainsail reefed, eased, and lashed amidships, storm jib backed, rudder lashed to leeward, we would be *hove to*, a cork bobbing in the ocean broadside to the oncoming seas, no more to do till the storm blew itself out than go below, drink if we could, read, or go to sleep.

We slacked the mainsail, raised the storm jib easily enough, lashed the wheel, but drew breath when Meredith told us to reef the main. Several reinforced holes, called cringles, were sewn into the back edge, or leach of our mainsail, spaced eighteen inches or so apart, starting from the clew (the point on the bottom of the sail farthest from the mast) and rising halfway up the leach. Reefing points, short thin lines, were sewn into both sides of the sail, also at intervals of eighteen inches, in a straight line from the cringles to the luff, the front edge of the sail hauled up the mast. To reef the *Isbjørn*, we'd have to climb onto the boom and walk to its tip, tie a strong line, the reefing line, through the highest cringle you could reach, carry it down to a block on the end of the boom, and pull it tight while another crewman eased the main halyard and lowered the luff, reducing sail area in slabs as if folding a rectangular blanket lengthways. Last, we'd tie the shortened sail's loose sailcloth around the boom with the reefing point lines.

The rub was rigging the reefing line. We had slacked the boom, as you must, to begin heaving to. Its tip hung over the sea just out of arm's reach from the boat and two to three feet above the two-story-high seas steaming under it, rising and falling like the end of a giant seesaw. One of us would have to climb onto the boom with the reefing line, walk to its end, tie the line to a cringle, run it down through the clew, then carry it back along the boom and draw it tight. The wind, now forty knots plus, keened in the rigging, a constant, buzz saw whine. The seas sounded like freight cars as they rumbled under us. You had to shout to be heard by the man standing a few feet windward of you. Who carried the reefing line would be out of earshot in the storm as soon as he was halfway to the boom tip. You would drown if you slipped.

Meredith emerged from the wheelhouse with the reefing line and offered it to Sven. The first mate shook his head. Meredith proffered it to Alan; he turned away. I was not spared a glance.

Wordlessly, the crippled, arthritic old man clamped an end of the reefing line in his teeth, clawed his way onto the wheelhouse, then mast end of the boom. His body unbent slowly, like a corpse stiffening into rigor mortis. He leaned into the sail and inched toward the boom tip seesawing over the seas. We watched, mute. Meredith reached the tip, tied the reefing line to the highest cringle, reeved it through the clew, bit down again, and the line end in his teeth, crept back along the boom to the wheelhouse. He slithered onto its roof, then the deck, threw the reefing line at our feet, and went below—no word, no glance left or right, where we stood shamed near the wheelhouse door.

For three days, we drifted in the Bay of Biscay till the storm passed. For two months more, we motored, wallowed, ran, and reached across the Atlantic, to the Azores, then Bermuda, and last, the Virginia Capes, Chesapeake Bay, and Annapolis. Near seventy days we worked, ate, and drank with Meredith Jackson, but he never mentioned the reefing—no scorn, reproof, even, perhaps, understanding. He left three young men who failed a test of seamanship and manhood to make their private peace with cowardice. No yellow *C* stigmatizes my chest, but the Reverend Dimmesdale often comes to mind.

*   *   *

A few hours later, I failed Meredith again. Doubts about how safe we were hove to drove me to the foredeck to watch the house-size seas bear down and wait for one to break over and sink us. My confidence in *Isbjørn* and heaving to grew as a quarter became half an hour, and the sets[21] continued to roll up to then under us until skepticism vanished and my customary comfort at sea returned. It was premature.

Dinners were simple: boiled potatoes, carrots or onions, stew from a can, one cup of fresh water—strictly rationed—coffee, and a shot or two of Scotch. That evening was my turn to prepare it, wedged in the galley with pots a third filled with boiling water, veg, stew and incarcerated in fiddles so the pots didn't slide off the two-burner Calor gas stove when the boat rolled, sometimes so far the cabin portholes were only inches above the ocean. The galley was fetid, the concentrated odor of heating stew almost nauseating, the wind screaming, the boat rail down every few minutes as seas rolled us over and rumbled under us. Fear, winds now near sixty miles per hour, and a small heaving boat suppress appetite:

---

[21] Storm seas come in sets of three or seven, with intervals or lulls between each set. See I, The Blue Guitars, Fool Me Once.

Sven and Alan passed on dinner; I ate a small portion, sans Scotch. Only Meredith chowed down.

Washing up was slow and cumbersome in the stamp-sized galley, the perimeter of its sink the size of a large dinner plate. You scraped uneaten food into the slops bucket; scrubbed dishes, pots, cups in detergent while seawater pumped from a small tap on the sink's edge; rinsed them in a blue plastic bucket of seawater; and piled them in the sink until you were ready to dry. The stew was sloshing in my gut, the slops smelled, and I dreaded washing up wedged in the galley as the boat heaved. I'd only been seasick once, when I was ten, on the *Jolly Roger* anchored beside the north jetty in the Barnegat Inlet, chumming stripers for the first time,[22] but thought my second bout might be at hand.

Perhaps there was a better way. Knee and waist high down the *Isbjørn*'s port and starboard sides, bow to stern, two quarter-inch diameter stainless steel wire safety lines ran through iron stanchions three feet apart. There was a second plastic bucket aboard, a yellow one, that could serve as a washing-up sink. I'd put the evening's dirty dishes in the blue rinsing bucket and carry it topside with the washing-up liquid to the lee rail (side away from the wind), lean against the safety lines, scrape the plates over the side, wash them in the yellow bucket, rinse them in the rinsing bucket, and *hey presto*, clean dishes, no scraps smell, no puking in the process.

The yellow bucket was yellow for a reason. Meredith rose several times in the night to pee. His gamey hip made climbing the companionway to exit the wheelhouse and piss over the side slow and painful; using the fo'c'sle head was even harder. So Meredith had a piss bucket. It lived during the day tied by a lanyard to one of the dorades (vents that allow air to circulate below decks while keeping seawater and rain out) on either side of the boat above the engine compartment, and rested beside Meredith's bunk when he lay down to sleep. He'd rise in the night, pee in the bucket, and lift the bucket to the wheelhouse deck beside the helmsman, who would quickly dump piss and bucket in the sea, pull it up, toss it in again to rinse, then pass it back to Meredith waiting below. We called it *Meredith's piss bucket*, and yellow proclaimed its sole function.

[22] See I, Shadow Maker.

Hove to, there was no need for a helmsman, and the wheelhouse was empty after dinner. I piled the dirty crockery in the rinse bucket, climbed with it into the wheelhouse, and left it inside the threshold as I slid the leeward wheelhouse door open to step outside to untie the piss bucket. I noticed the wind was a good deal stronger, the seas higher than when we'd heaved to five hours earlier.

Piss bucket lanyard in hand, I turned to reach for the bucket with the dishes in it when a sea rolled us over until the lee rail submerged. We righted, and I reached again for the dishes bucket when the second sea in the set, larger than its predecessor, rolled us until I stood calf deep in the sea and had to grab the top lifeline with my free hand. My quick-wash cycle was clearly a bad idea, but before I could secure the piss bucket and go below to wash up, the third and largest sea hit. The rail went under and kept going. The water rose over my calves and kept climbing. When it reached my waist, I let go of the piss bucket lanyard and grabbed the lifeline with both hands, afraid we'd be knocked on our beam-ends (completely on our side and near capsizing), I'd go under, and I'd be swept away or drowned. I took a deep breath, prepared for baptism, then the *Isbjørn* righted herself again, as she always did. But the piss bucket was gone.

In the lull between sets, I regained the wheelhouse, lowered the rinse bucket with its dirty dishes into the galley, and scrambled below to wash up. The other three were in their bunks and didn't notice me dripping from the chest down. A quick washup, wet clothes stripped off, and like the rest, I nestled in my bunk. A few hours later, Meredith prepared for bed. A roar came: *Where's my bucket?* Shtum I stayed. The rinse bucket did double duty till we bought a second yellow bucket in the Azores.

* * *

On the third day, the storm blew itself out, and we continued south-southwest to Ponta Delgada, winds largely unfavorable, heavily reliant on our Kelvin diesel during the eight more days it took to reach the Azores. There, we refueled, provisioned with fresh veg and potatoes, and a day later, cast off for Bermuda twenty-two hundred miles southwest.

We steamed due south for three days to latitude thirty-two degrees north, Bermuda's latitude, where we found the easterly trade winds[23]

---

[23] Winds are named for the direction from which they blow, so a wind blowing from the south is a southerly and blows toward the north.

blowing steadily westward at ten to fifteen knots, as modern weather charts and ancient mariners' logs predicted. We turned west, cut the engine, raised yardarms, unfurled the square sails,[24] and for eighteen idyllic days, ran our latitude down.[25]

It was South Seas weather, flying fish drying on deck at dawn, cloudless days, porpoises shadowing the boat for hours, red sun every evening,[26] and every day, 120–130 miles made good. We strung whipping twine between the two upright braces at the fore and aft ends of the wheelhouse table and, for hours, wove baggywrinkle (chafing gear) for the shrouds from strands of old hemp rope. Sven sunbathed while trying, and failing, to read Kierkegaard and succeeded only in frying his cock.

I enjoyed our evening Scotch, so much that, though only Meredith and I were drinking it, we had to restock it in Bermuda. On the helm at dusk, canned stew and Scotch in my belly, yards creaking in the trade wind as we rolled down to Bermuda, Tennyson's *In the afternoon they came unto a land / In which it seemed always afternoon*[27] often ran through my mind.

The Bermudas are a group of eight low-lying islands, linked by bridges, that peek from the sea around them, hard to see from the deck of a small boat until you're almost upon them. You can circumnavigate this archipelago on a push-bike in less than a day. Most of the houses lie close to the sea, generally no more than a bus length above the water; the highest point, Gibb's Hill Lighthouse, 117 feet. Cape Hatteras on the North Carolina coast is the nearest land, 650 miles west.

Navigating to this speck on the sea from Ponta Delgada, twenty-two hundred miles northeast—using log line, sextant, and chronometer—is a challenge for the best of navigators. Bermuda is in the North Atlantic hurricane belt, and late August, when we expected to arrive, begins its high season; it's a poor time to wander over the ocean for a day or two looking

---

[24] Yardarms are the poles fixed at right angles to the masts of a square rigger, from which the square sails hang. Square sails are most efficient when the wind blows consistently from the aft quarter or stern of a craft. They were the iconic rigs used on clipper ships. Meredith had fitted them on the *Isbjørn* to test their usefulness on a small boat almost a century after their desuetude.

[25] A boat *sails its latitude down* when it sails east or west along a parallel of latitude toward a destination on that same parallel.

[26] *Red sun at night / Sailor's delight* is a traditional, and accurate, weather-forecasting rhyme sailors repeat.

[27] Tennyson, *The Lotus-Eaters*.

for a pimple on the horizon. Our calculations showed we should make landfall sometime on our twenty-first day out of the Azores, and from dawn that morning, we craned our necks until it appeared, a small smudge on the sea, near noon.

* * *

Meredith was an honored member of the Royal Ocean Cruising Club and the Little Ship Club. The Royal Bermuda Yacht Club (RBYC) was delighted to offer him a courtesy mooring and the run of their club for our stay, and we picked up one of their moorings near teatime. I'd never been in a yacht club, country club, or similar establishment. The Independent Yacht Basin at Eighteenth Street and the bay in Barnegat Light, New Jersey, where the charter boats I worked on docked, was different from the "commercial" dock next to it only in not having scales to weigh catch.

Alan and Sven told me what to expect—freshwater showers, a bar, lounge, perhaps even girls—but did not mention a dress code. We had been three weeks without a freshwater shower. I threw fresh clothes and toiletries in a small kit bag; pulled on my dirty, tattered cutoff sailing shorts so crusted with salt they could stand by themselves; and rowed for the RBYC clubhouse in the Avon dinghy with Sven and Alan. That they had changed into clean, presentable T-shirts and trousers passed me by. We were one hundred yards from the *Isbjørn* when Meredith bellowed *You bloody fool. Get back here!* I was about to ignorantly breach decorum in an unfamiliar setting far from South Philadelphia's streets; occasionally, it happens still.

* * *

Far fewer sailors crossed oceans in small boats in pre-GPS days, and a thirty-nine-foot sailboat from England pitching up in Bermuda, captained by a distinguished professor of English law, was newsworthy in 1965. Local TV broadcast news of our arrival. The morning after the broadcast, a wooden motor launch as long as *Isbjørn* approached us and hailed. At its bow flapped the Governor-General's pennant, at its stern the Bermudan ensign. Three men in khaki shirts and shorts—Sam Brownes belted diagonally across their chests, naval insignia on their epaulets—stood erect at bow, helm, and stern. A young girl no more perhaps than twelve sat on the bench athwart the stern like Cleopatra on her barge, rose when they drew alongside, and requested to speak to Dr. Jackson. She was the vessel's commander.

She introduced herself to Meredith as the Governor-General's daughter and—with the grace, self-possession, and quiet social command of a Mitford sister—invited us to dinner at the residence that evening, dress casual in deference to our voyaging. I'd heard of Swiss girls' finishing schools but not met a product, had read *Le Grand Meaulnes* but formed no image of Yvonne de Galais until that herald princess rose from the stern cushions of the Governor-General's launch.

* * *

A one-hundred-foot schooner bound for the Caribbean winter charter trade from the summer charter trade in the Med lay moored nearby. She was spruce planked with oak timbers, three-masted, with long, low white sides and three cabin tops—fore, amidships, aft—rising two feet proud of her teak decks. She flew eight sails from sprit to mizzen in a fair quarterly breeze and wore faux, blue-painted gunports down her hull below them. She was the quintessence of romance, a titled gentleman's vessel from the late days of the British Empire.

Group Captain Archie Carr, a bona fide Spitfire veteran of the Battle of Britain, owned and skippered her. He sent his compliments with his boat-boy, and Meredith invited him to dinner aboard *Isbjørn*. After dinner, we lounged on the foredeck while Meredith and Group Captain Carr sat in the wheelhouse, reminisced, and drank and drank and drank. Meredith called us a few hours later to hand the hero back to his boat. We raised him from the table and supported him by the rail as he bellowed into the dark *Boy! Boy! Boy!* until his Black cabin boy came alongside in a dinghy. But the Group Captain was too drunk to disembark himself. We rigged a sling and lowered him gently into the boy's care. As they putt-putted into the dark toward the schooner's painted gunports, another heroic legend I no longer believed in disappeared with them.

We could not tarry in Bermuda. Peak hurricane season had just begun, and the Gulf Stream—a fast-moving river of warm water in the sea that works like a steroid for hurricanes—lay across the path to our destination, Annapolis, Maryland. Winds in the Stream are often light and variable. Midcentury weather forecasting—before satellites, ubiquitous super computers, exotic algorithms, and GPS—was not the science it is now, and *Isbjørn* was slow. You cannot happily heave to in a hurricane, and the prospect of drifting becalmed in the Gulf Stream as a hurricane bore down on us was terrifying. We knew we must cross now.

We fired the engine for the Virginia Capes before 8 a.m. on our fourth day in Hamilton Harbor. It died before we could slip our mooring. Meredith went below and checked fuel filters, lines, and injectors. They were clogged. We cleaned them, but still, the engine wouldn't start. Meredith and I went below, pulled the head, and discovered head, valves, and pistons badly gunked up; we'd been sold adulterated diesel in the Azores.

As well as injectors, fuel lines, and pumps, we would have to remove and clean the pistons—a delicate, arduous task due to the pistons' size, their rings' fragility, and the need to lie on your back in the cramped engine compartment in ninety-degree heat, sweat trickling into your eyes—to remove them. We did not dare cross the Gulf Stream without an engine. If we broke a ring, it would be ten days before new ones for our prewar Kelvin diesel could be located in England, shipped, and received, by which time it would be too dangerous to cross until October, hurricane season's end. Break a ring, and *Isbjørn* would winter in Bermuda.

Meredith chose to remove the four pistons himself and broke two of their rings. It was the only time we saw him crestfallen.

I asked if I could have a go at locating spare rings in Bermuda; we had nothing to lose. Near noon, I left in the dinghy, dirty engine-room shorts and all, to root around Hamilton. I was back with the rings by 4 p.m.

For hundreds of years, Bermuda had been a British colony. Bermudans bought British, and Kelvin was a famous Scottish marine engine maker. Diesel engine ferries *thrumped* across the harbor between Hamilton, Bermuda's main town, and the island's south shore; perhaps their maintenance people might know where I could find Kelvin rings. I walked the half mile from the Yacht Club to the ferry terminal, asked where—if anywhere—on the island I might find rings for an old Kelvin diesel, and learned the ferries used them. In their repair shop were two sets of unused, vintage rings for a four-cylinder Kelvin diesel like *Isbjørn's*.

It took several hours to install them. Meredith fired the engine, took the helm, slipped our mooring, and motored down channel into the Atlantic and nightfall, bound for Virginia's Capes, while I squared away the engine room. *Isbjørn's* companionway opened into the starboard side of the wheelhouse, next to the helm. I emerged from it greasy and sweaty for a seawater scrub on deck just as we began to roll in the Atlantic swell. Meredith turned to me, said, *Well done*, and returned his eyes to the channel. Three times in my life I've been proud: when I was eight years old and Captain Holmes Russell acknowledged me by name for the first time on the dock at the Independent Yacht Basin at Barnegat Light; twenty years later when Captain Louis Puskas told my father on that same dock, *Joe, if that was my kid, he could take my boat anywhere*; and when I stepped on deck for a seawater scrub as *Isbjørn* left Hamilton Harbor.

* * *

Isbjørn's complement stood on her foredeck in the late afternoon eight days later, swigging Scotch and swatting the mosquitoes. Anchored in a brackish cove at the mouth of the York River where it debouches into Chesapeake Bay, the Atlantic behind us, Alan and Sven rediscovered their taste for liquor. We took little time to down one bottle and begin a second.

We three young men were exaggerating about girls we'd known when Meredith, well oiled, uncharacteristically weighed in. He'd climbed mountains before his hip failed, and one expedition found him at the end of the day in a small Norwegian village at the base of a mountain he was to climb next day. The villagers were celebrating a holiday and invited him to join them. He drank and danced with a local girl till her capacity proved greater than his. He remembered being unable to stand, slung over her shoulder, carried upstairs to bed, further revels, and waking naked beside her in the morning, but couldn't remember her name. That she must have been a woman of parts—Meredith was six feet, and no bantam even then—made his moral the more sobering: *In time, you even forget the names of the women you've had.*

It was nearly 5 p.m. Virginia time, almost 10 p.m. in London, and Meredith went below to fetch the shortwave radio receiver from among his navigator's tools. Accurate time is essential for figuring longitude; every afternoon of the voyage, Meredith had been able to hear the six pips of the BBC Overseas Service at twenty-two hundred hours GMT, and on Sundays, Big Ben's chimes in their stead. Those pips grew fainter and fainter as we approached the U.S. mainland; Meredith doubted he could pick them up now we were in the Chesapeake. The bay's estuarine waters were well charted, we didn't need our time, and I puzzled why the skipper still wanted to hear those pips.

He came back on deck, twiddling the portable shortwave radio's tuning knob. It was Sunday, and at twenty-two hundred hours GMT, the first bong—rather than a pip—sounded, then five more in Big Ben's deep bass chimes. Meredith turned away as the sixth *bong* faded, but I'd glimpsed tears wetting his cheeks. It was my first inkling of how deeply British our eccentric skipper was and what that meant.

Sacrament's End

It was the third Thursday in November, Thanksgiving, 1963, and Joe and I were jigging weakfish on the Harvey Cedars Lump, a mile offshore of Long Beach Island. This was the last trip of the season before he laid up the *Dan-Rick* for the winter; every Thanksgiving, ritually, just the two of us fished it. The day was an unusually warm late fall day: high fifty degrees Fahrenheit, cloudless, a light chop from the fresh northerly pushing us southwest toward the beach. Side by side, we stood in the midmorning sun, braced against the starboard gunnel, rod tips rising and falling in unison, rocking over a slight rise in the ocean floor; two men alone on a boat, the boat alone on the sea.

The day before, I'd piled books, clothes, and records in a U-Haul, left my wife Sharon, and returned to my parents' house till I found a flat. We'd broken up often in the three years I'd known her, but this was the first time I'd left her since we married nearly a year earlier. My father asked, *Ya finally done?* I tugged my milled gold wedding band, the first and last I've ever worn, off my left third finger and flung it to sleep with the fishes. We said no more; there was no need. I had long reckoned the sea our common rite, the holy water that cleansed both our childhoods of beatings, failures, butcher shops—the bond between us. At sea, I confessed beliefs, hopes (though never fears) to him, sure he'd understand; the sea was our tabernacle, the only sacred thing we shared.

He had not always kept it undefiled. A few years earlier, when I was seventeen, he relegated me to the butcher shop as his deputy while he competed in the Atlantic City Tuna Tournament for the third time, a mate he'd picked up on the dock at his side rather than me. He said one of us had to watch the store.

The three-day Tournament attracted rich men with expensive boats and professional skippers. Their boats were far larger, faster, and better equipped than any *Dan-Rick* would ever be, with tuna towers, fighting chairs, state-of-the-art fish-finding electronics, and literally gold-plated reels; their professional skippers were more experienced hunting giant tuna than Joe could ever hope to be. He'd never have these rich men's wealth, and his harsh childhood, pride, and pugnacity made him desperate to show them up. I ached to bear his armor as he tried.

Joe had never boated a tuna much over eighty pounds, and he never would. He'd hooked, fought, and brought to boat four or five 150-plus pounders when I wasn't with him but lost them at the gaff, where most big fish are lost. The essence of gaffing a big tuna is self-control, remaining deliberate and steady as you lead a fish you've been fighting for over an hour—three or four times your weight and far more powerful—toward the gaff by the wire leader tied between the hook in its mouth and your fishing line while you drown in adrenalin. When the leader is within reach, you wrap it lightly half around your hand over the heel of your palm and clamp it with your thumb, so you can release it without its kinking or taking you with it if the fish spooks and runs again. You lower the gaff slowly until it's below the tuna as you draw it toward you, then—the fish above the gaff's hook—pull up smartly and impale it. Once impaled, skipper and mate slide the fish onto the deck through a gate in the stern, or slip a rope around its tail and drag it aboard over the gunnel.

If you clench, rather than wrap the leader, it likely will kink and break if the fish spooks, as they often do when they near the hull. Draw the creature to you too quickly, so the pressure comes off the leader for a few seconds, and the tuna throws the hook. Strike at the behemoth with the gaff from above or its side, and the tuna spooks, or you accidentally knock it off the hook. My father could not control his nerves when a giant neared the gaff and would make one or more of these mistakes. His frenzy—his screamed commands—unsettled his mates, who then botched the gaffing as well. I had endured twenty-one years of his panics and lost no tuna at the gaff.

On Friday, the Tournament's last day, an hour before the 3 p.m. closing gun, the *Dan-Rick* hooked a big tuna. None had been boated the first two days; there were no reports of one so far that day. The exhausted bluefin slowly swung its tail from side to side a few feet below the *Dan-Rick*'s starboard quarter an hour later, minutes before 3 p.m.; it was over five feet long, barrel bellied, perhaps 250 pounds, a sure winner. The mate lost it at the gaff.

Around 4:30 p.m. that afternoon, I was behind the counter at Pennsauken Meats, lifting a bag to a customer, when Tommy Anderson, the store's manager, said my father had checked in from the Tournament dock and mentioned he'd lost a big fish. I felt no schadenfreude, no vindication, only a deep filial wound. My father's disappointment, the certainty I'd have gaffed that fish or died trying, sharpened the shame and hurt of being kept ashore. But I excused his selfishness and thoughtlessness as I'd done often growing up by attributing them to deep-seated Jewish insecurity bred in him by shtetl parents and the Depression hardships he'd endured.

He did not talk about that lost fish and did not enter the Tournament again.

* * *

The Independent Yacht Basin's charter fleet rocked in its slips on a gray, chill, late May afternoon, jailed by a twenty-five mile an hour nor'easter that stacked ten-foot breaking seas in the Inlet and riled the ocean too much to fish. We were killing time in the stern of the *Dan-Rick* in sweatshirts and windbreakers, righting the world and repairing tackle, when an indigo-hulled thirty-five-foot skiff entered the marina and reversed into the slip beside us. She was a clinker-built, twin-engine, open-cockpit bass boat with a high-flared bow like an upturned plowshare and two wet men aboard, though the day was dry. The helmsman stood on a foot-high navigation platform, trousers wet to the calves; in the stern, the older man was soaked to the hips.

They and their boat were strangers at our dock. My father knew the elder man—casually, from the meat business—but not his son-in-law, Eddy Cuperman, a used-car dealer with a large lot on North Broad Street in Philadelphia. Eddy had chosen today to bring his boat closer to the superior fishing grounds off Barnegat—forty miles north of its homeport of Atlantic City—in the teeth of the nor'easter, despite small craft warnings and the perils of Barnegat Inlet. The older man, ashen, shaken, repeatedly used the Yiddish *meshugga* (crazy) and *meshugganah* (nutcase) to describe the passage and his son-in-law in answer to my father's *How'd ya get so wet?* The trip, normally three to three and a half hours, had taken six. They'd been pooped entering the Inlet, taken a large sea over the stern that filled the cockpit, and were lucky not to have sunk.

Cuperman was even less a fisherman than he was a boatman. He chartered the *Dan-Rick* several times to chum bluefish and once for a tuna trip. At the end of the tuna trip, he asked if I'd take him tuna and blue fishing on his boat when I wasn't mating for Joe, and I agreed. I was nearly twenty, pressing my father for permission to use the *Dan-Rick*, and hoped a stint as Eddy's captain might help my case. That it didn't was unsurprising as I learned more about Eddy.

My father and Cuperman became friends, but the friendship did not survive the season. A few weeks after he docked at the Independent, my father and Eddy stood talking by the *Dan-Rick*'s slip, when Dr. Fessman, another owner, approached them on the way to his boat a few slips on from ours. Dr. Fessman was six feet, rangy, slightly stooped as befitted his sixty-plus years, and every inch a Christian gentleman. It was a hot July day.

My father introduced them:

Dr. Fessman, this is my friend, Ed Cuperman, from Philadelphia.

How do you do, Mr. Cuperman? (They shook hands.)

Well, Mr. Cuperman, what do you think the weather looks like for tomorrow?

Looks like snow, spat Eddy. Dr. Fessman avoided my father after that; when they did meet, he merely nodded.

Cuperman sold my father a lightly used, metallic-blue, low-mileage 1961 Olds '98, Oldsmobile's top of the line. A few weeks after Joe bought it, the odometer began to skip one hundred miles at a time, irrefutable evidence it had been illegally tampered with. My father returned the car to Eddy and asked for his money back. The reason he fabricated for returning the car was that my mother caught him fornicating with another woman in its back seat and insisted either the fancy car went or she would, an excuse with which Eddy could empathize.

He had not been married to his present second wife long when he gave her a Cadillac as a gift. She disliked the color and said so. Eddy bragged that he drove the car inches from the house's parterre, so close to the front door you had to go through the car to enter or leave the front door of the house. He jacked it up, removed the wheels, lowered its axles onto four steel milk crates, and told his wife he'd replace the wheels when the color grew on her.

It was the beginning of fall when Eddy last saw his boat that first season at the Independent. His addiction was gambling, and he'd fallen badly into arrears on gaming debts. Gambling was illegal in Pennsylvania, hence the debts unenforceable, and Eddy refused to pay. It was high autumn, the maples gold and orange on our street, when my father mentioned Eddy had disappeared. A week later, an attendant at his used-car lot smelled a sweet sickly odor, like rotting meat, coming from the trunk of one of the Cadillacs on the lot. He found Eddy's decomposing body when he opened the trunk of the stinking car. The coroner said the cause of death was battery acid injected into the veins while the victim was alive.

* * *

By 1955, the end of the first half of my father's life, fishing was all of it. That year, he bought his first boat and laid older passions by—high-stakes crap shooting and poker, Scotch with pals, sharp clothes, cigarettes, and serious whoring. He became a charter captain in the early 1960s, taking parties game fishing offshore his only interest. He died, as we expected he would, at eighty, eighteen months after the coastguard declared him too old to keep his captain's license. We buried him in his fishing clothes. Chartering defined him; the *Dan-Rick* became him. I believed the sea was what we shared.

WHO HE WAS
    (i.m. Joe Burt 1915–1995)

The skeleton in a wheelchair props rented
tackle on the rail, stares down 20 feet
from a pier through salt subtropical air
at shoal water wavelets for blue slashes
flashing toward the bait below his float,
and misses one hit, two, a third, an inept
young butcher far from inner city streets
recovering from surgery, too proud
to bask with codgers, too weak to walk or swim,
a sutured rag doll whose one permitted
sport is dangling blood worms from a pole.
His father's plumb and adze, mother's thread and pins,
tradesmen, carters, peddlers, kaftaned bearded kin,
village landsmen from Ukraine, friends,
nothing in his life smelled of ocean; but cleaver
held again, he kept on fishing. Once a week
he drove 80 miles east to prowl the sea
with charter men, ever farther from the coast
till, white coat and meat hook junked, he trolled
ballyhoo for marlin eight hours run offshore.
Two score years and four skiffs on, by his command
we laid him down in fishing clothes, khaki
trousers, khaki shirt, Dan-Rick on the right
breast pocket, on the left Capt J Burt.[28]

I labored to make him proud: fished with him at every opportunity from the age of four and a half; mated for him the first decade he owned

[28] Dan Burt, *We Look Like This* (Manchester: Carcanet, 2012).

a boat (rigged lines, cut bait, gaffed fish, ran the boat offshore and back while he schmoozed the parties); traversed the Inlet with him half a thousand times. The imprimatur of his pride would be the day he shared the *Dan-Rick* with me, and I left the slip in her alone.

That day did not come, though not for want of asking, till I had crossed the Atlantic with three others on a thirty-nine-foot ketch and spiked any lingering argument I lacked offshore qualifications. He handed me the keys toward the end of law school, when I asked for them again.

The *Dan-Rick* cast off, me at the helm, shortly after sunrise on a late June Saturday, a year after my last class at Yale. We were headed forty miles offshore into the sun for tuna. Two former law school classmates, plus one's brother-in-law—all in their late twenties—were with me; none fishermen, none seamen. The previous afternoon at the dock, I'd rigged trolling rods and lures, listened to the captains talk about where they'd found fish that day, and before bed, checked the weather forecast—light southerly breeze in the morning rising to fifteen knots or so by midafternoon, when we'd have turned for home and have it on our port quarter. In ten minutes, we were at the Inlet.

The remnant of a hurricane a few hundred miles east was bowling long-interval swells west into Barnegat Inlet as we reached it. When the rollers neared the Jersey coast, and the sea floor rose, they steepened until they mashed against the Inlet's shoals and made up into twelve-foot-high breaking seas, higher than the wheel on the *Dan-Rick's* flying bridge behind which I stood gauging them. I idled in the Inlet's mouth a few car lengths inshore of the north bar with two or three charter boats and waited for the inevitable gap between sets, jammed the throttles forward when it came, cleared the bar, throttled back, and headed 120 degrees southeast by east into the Atlantic.

We ran *hooked up* (maximum cruising speed) for three hours, then slowed to trolling speed forty-five miles offshore. From 9 a.m. to 1 p.m., the *Dan-Rick* plowed larger and larger squares in the ocean, caught two small skipjack but no true tuna, then turned to three hundred degrees, our reciprocal,[29] and headed northwest by south for the Inlet, fifty miles away.

---

[29] A compass has 360°, and the reciprocal of any course is your course plus 180°. If your course out is 200°, its reciprocal is 20° (200° + 180° = 20° [380° − 360° (total compass degrees)] = 20°).

You had to choose which of two gauntlets to run—one on the north, one the south side—to go in or out of Barnegat Inlet: across the north bar or down the south side's buoyed channel. I'd run the north bar to the ocean at 6 a.m. that morning on our way offshore. Ten hours later, when we'd reach the Inlet again, it would be low water—the breakers a deal higher and closer together—and no room to recover if you miscalculated when to dare the north bar.

Some two miles away in a southerly arc from the north bar lay the Bell, a bell buoy that marked the offshore entrance to the channel. The channel stretched nearly a mile down the south side of the Inlet to a blinking green light atop a steel tower at the sea end of the south jetty. Inshore of it lay Barnegat Bay and home.

Charts prescribed the channel as the passage through the Inlet, and the Army Corps of Engineers dredged it every two years or so to keep it clear. It was a Sisyphean task; sandbars flowered there again within months. If you followed the channel through the Inlet, you'd have a long run across shoals in breaking following seas (seas at your stern), more dangerous than taking them bow on. But more water covered the channel's shoals at ebb tide than the north bar's. In rough weather, homeward-bound charter men—I never heard of a woman charter-boat captain on the Jersey coast while I fished it—paid their money, chose north side or south, and took their chance.

The storm-spawned swells were bigger than when we'd left, the seas breaking over the bars in the Inlet consequently larger and closer together. The Coast Guard had stationed its double-ender, a thirty-five-foot lifeboat that could roll through 360 degrees and right herself, a few yards offshore of the north bar. She had not been there that morning. Warm moist air blown west from the offshore depression spawned thick fog that lay a half to three miles off the beach; you would hear breaking seas before you saw them.

I switched on the ship-to-shore radio. The *Dan-Rick* was still thirty-five miles at sea when the first of the charter fleet reached the Inlet, and the radio filled with boat names I knew and their captains' voices:

Rascal, Rascal, this is the Mary M. II. *Come back, Beachy.*[30]

---

[30] *Beachy* was an older captain who acquired his sobriquet when he ran his boat ashore rather than run the Inlet one particularly rough day.

Rascal back.

What's it like in there, Beachy?

I'm at the Bell, Daryle, but the fog's not lifted much. Coupla hundred feet I'd guess. Big seas; close together.

Which side ya takin?

Dunno yet, Daryle. Seas on the north bar were real close together, breaking almost to the jetty. I'm checkin' the channel.

Thanks for that, Cap.

The radio continued to crackle and sputter warnings, comments, and advice on conditions in the Inlet as the *Dan-Rick* rolled west from offshore. Nine miles off, just past the lightship buoy, I decided to use the channel and set a course for the Bell. Ten minutes before I hoped to hear its clang, my father's guttural voice blasted from the radio. *Danny, it's dangerous in the Inlet. Wait. I'll come get you with the coastguard and take you through.*

* * *

He was transmitting from the coastguard station beside the Barnegat Light. Though it was Saturday, his butcher shop's busiest day, he left the manager in charge and drove seventy miles east from Pennsauken Mart to monitor my return. He was panicked—for his boat, or son, or both—and the whole fleet heard him, indeed anyone within sixty miles with a VHF receiver tuned to channel twenty-eight heard him.

Dad, I'm OK; I don't need help. I'm OK. Relax. I could not calm him.

Danny! Danny! Listen to me! Wait there, and we'll come get you. You hear me! Do what I say!

Charlie Eberle broke in on the radio: *Danny, this is Charlie on the* Doris Mae III. *I'm a mile behind you. Wait and follow me in.* The *Doris Mae III* was a seventy-foot, twin-screw diesel-engine head boat (a boat chartered for fishing trips and payment made "per head" for each person) with state-of-the-art electronics, including radar, and Charlie Eberle was her skipper. He had founded our dock, the Independent, in the early fifties with a few other charter men and pioneered bluefish chumming from head boats. The Independent's only better seaman, now Holmes had retired, was Louis Puskas on the *Gracee II*.

Before I could depress the send button to reply, the bell loomed from the fog, one hundred feet away, on the bow, where my dead reckoning said it would be. My father's voice again: *Danny! Danny!* The charter men's chatter was distracting, my father's fear contagious. I turned the radio off and started down the channel, listening for seas breaking on sandbars ahead.

You feel a wave make up beneath you before you see it, hear it, or it begins to carry the boat, a sensation like a toddler's sitting on her father's shoulders as he rises from his chair and strides off, of a power vastly greater than your own, beyond your control, lifting and propelling you forward. The bell was almost out of sight astern when the *Dan-Rick* lifted to a swell as it made up and powered down channel for the bars. My mind emptied of all but wave and boat: *Ease the throttles . . . ease . . . sit on the shoulder, just behind the crest. Ride it . . . ride it . . . as it heads for the jetty. More throttle, it's speeding up . . . careful . . . throttle back . . . don't overrun it, or you'll pitchpole.*[31] *Don't let it slide out from under you, or you'll slow in the wash and get pooped.*

The *Dan-Rick* rode the sea till it broke down in a welter of sand and foam 150-foot short of the south jetty. The wave's momentum, and a quick tap on the throttle, propelled us past the south jetty tower and into Barnegat Bay; color returned to my knuckles, shoulders slumped, jaw unclenched, adrenalin drained away.

Captain Joe Burt loomed from the dock as the *Dan-Rick* backed into her slip; his hail before the stern lines were secured: *Any damage? Is she all right? Anything broken?*

Dad, the boat's fine. He did not ask about me, my passengers, the trip; he said nothing about my boat handling in the Inlet or seamanship offshore. The chance to do so forced itself on him a minute or two later.

It was low water, our cockpit four feet below the dock's black top. He jumped down to inspect for damage himself, while I prepared to hose down the trolling rods with fresh water. Louis Puskas, one of the charter captains, walked over from where his *Gracee II* lay berthed four slips away. *Hey, Joe . . .*

There was no mate or skipper at the Independent who did not respect Captain Louis Puskas. He was the first to fish for tuna and marlin in the Hudson Canyon, eighty to one hundred miles offshore, and for tilefish there in the winter. He went to sea when no one else would; a local hero, a legend on the Jersey coast. He'd brought the *Gracee II* home that day across the north bar, the *Dan-Rick* clearly visible to the southeast coming

---

[31] A boat pitchpoles when it falls off a sea, its bow drops suddenly, and the following sea lifts the stern and tosses the boat stern over bow.

in the channel half a mile and a few minutes behind her, and tied up just before us.

Joe looked up. *Yeah, Louie?*

Joe, if that was my kid, he could take my boat anywhere.

No reply. Louie walked off toward his boat as my father resumed: *Yah sure she's all right? Yah checked the engines? The oil? Take any seas? Bust any gear?*

I crimped the hose, stopped its flow, and waited for him to offer what a stranger just had. He bustled about the deck, sputtering concern for his boat like Shylock his ducats but with no word for me.

I looked on a little longer, silent, then turned off the hose, laid it on the deck, gathered my gear, and like Ishmael, left without a word. Five years passed before we spoke or met again. After that, I saw him rarely, fished with him once, and did not ask to use his boat again.

The *Captains Courageous* father I'd created, the mystic cord of brine and scales that bound us, vanished when my seaboots left the *Dan-Rick*'s deck that afternoon. In their place, where he had always been, stood the violent, selfish, Abrahamic patriarch, my sire, an autocrat who could not praise a son for fear of fostering a challenger or luster brighter than his own, a shtetl family head whose children's duty was to serve him and for whom relationships were trades. I had conjured a phantom hero to bear abuse and exploitation, craving a father's affection he couldn't muster, and excused a man one could imagine a capo in the camps. My final fantasy—of paternal love forged at sea—vanished, and for the first time, I saw in full the fallible man who was my father.

Shame severed me from him when I left him standing on the *Dan-Rick*'s deck. I understood parents from the Pale, Crohn's disease, hard times, and hard life might have garroted his empathy and capacity to love but could no longer excuse what I saw. As a boy and teenager, I needed to believe in him to justify how I lived, and so connived in his excuses and gloried in his borderline sociopathy. But I was a man now. *Fool me once*, goes the apothegm, *shame on you. Fool me twice, shame on me.* Fooled since childhood, he could shame me no more.

* * *

Will and spirit in time bow to the body. Hard living—drink, cigarettes, butcher shop, obesity, and the sea—and sickness wore Joe Burt's heart muscle down. How much, I learned on a late spring day in New York City five years after cutting contact. My secretary broke into a midmorning meeting to say my mother was on the phone insisting on speaking with me. (I was surprised she knew where to find me.) I left the office to take the call.

Danny, your father's had a heart attack. They're gonna operate after lunch and give him a pacemaker. Will you come?

I don't know.

I cradled the receiver and called for a car to take me to the airport. On the short hop to Philadelphia, I drank several pony bottles of Jack Daniels, put three in my pocket for later, and was first off the plane. There was no open-armed reunion with waiting mother, brother, and sister when I emerged, reeking bourbon, from an elevator onto the ICU (intensive care unit) floor of the Philadelphia Methodist Hospital shortly after 2 p.m. My tipsy state offended my mother and sister and enraged my brother, who had donned Jacob's family role when I left five years earlier. The three of them watched me walk down the hall and enter my father's room alone. An oxygen tube was clipped to his nose; an intravenous tube fed a vein in his arm; other tubes taped to him monitored heart rate, blood pressure, pulse; above and behind him, screens flickered and danced as he breathed; a defibrillator stood by his bed: death's skirmishers had him pinned down. He was awake and watched me approach the bed out of the corner of his eye. No doubt he smelled the drink.

I pulled two pony bottles from my suit jacket and offered them to him. *Hello, mutha fucka, want a drink?* He smiled through his tubing, raised his right arm as if to arm wrestle, and grasped my hand, his grip strong. *I ain't ready yet, Danny*, he whispered, then grinned. The prodigal had returned, as Joe would have him, obeisant to the tough-guy myth by which Joe lived.

* * *

His pacemaker, then a second, gave him eighteen years more fishing, say two thousand more trips, but I was with him on only one. He'd bought a larger *Dan-Rick* after his first heart attack, a thirty-six footer, and begun fishing the Canyon, a two-day trip in the best of weather. Run east—hooked up six hours to its edge—fish what was left of the afternoon and through the night, head west for home shortly after sunup. The Canyon was a long way off for small-boat charter captains to fish, and few did; it was too far for an obese man in his late sixties with a pacemaker, little large intestine, and developing emphysema. Joe had suffered dizzy spells on prior Canyon trips and taken scopolamine pills to cope, but neither my acquaintances and I aboard the *Dan-Rick* nor anyone else knew he was downing them as we left the north jetty bound for the Hudson Canyon one August morning in the early 1980s.

Toward midnight, ninety miles at sea, we hooked something very powerful and fought it for hours without bringing it to boat or seeing what it was. During most of the fight, my father dozed below. Toward dawn, unable to move whatever it was we'd hooked, I cut the line and readied the boat for the trip home. I climbed to the bridge, my father after me, as the sun rose and headed her home with him beside me. Suddenly, he yelled,

Fish! Fish! They're break'n water. Look! Look!

And he gesticulated toward the rising sun at our stern.

Head for 'em, Danny! Chase 'em!

Dad, there's nothing there.

No! No, look, see 'em! Behind the boat! There they are! Turn the boat!

Dad, nothing's there.

He grabbed the wheel and tried to turn the *Dan-Rick* east into the sun, chasing the phantom tuna he saw farther offshore. He'd taken one scopolamine too many and begun to hallucinate. On the course he would have had me steer, there was nothing between us and Bilbao but saltwater.

He was too weak to wrench the wheel away and, after a few minutes struggle, calmed a bit. I persuaded him to go below and rest, promised I'd rouse him if I saw fish, and one of my companions helped him from the bridge. He slept most of the seven hours it took to reach the beach, waking when you could see the Barnegat Light. He rejoined me on the bridge, told me about the scopolamine, and laid his hallucinations at its door, an aging old man contending with inexorable decay. He went to the Canyon no more.

* * *

He dealt with life's degeneration the same way he had lived it. Strength deserted him, hearing failed, eyesight dimmed; he had to sail with an oxygen tank aboard to bring air to his starving lungs, but still, he fished. His failing frame endangered his parties as well as him; he should have stayed ashore but wouldn't. Mishaps—groundings, a wrapped propeller on the ridge, a broach in the Inlet—repeatedly brought the coastguard to his rescue. After one rescue too many, they yanked his captain's license.

Eighteen months later, he began to lose weight rapidly and underwent exploratory surgery, which revealed a massive, inoperable stomach cancer. At his funeral, his GP told me how he died. He came to in the ICU after the surgery and found a young intern marking his vital signs on a chart at the end of his bed.

Yah see the initials at the bottom of that chart?

Yes, Mr. Burt.

Whadda they say?

DNR.

Yah know what that means?

Yes, Mr. Burt. Do Not Resuscitate.

Lem'me tell ya, I got three kids, all lawyers, and if anything happens an' ya bring me back, they'll sue your fukk'n ass up one side and down the other.

He had a heart attack three hours later, and they did not try to bring him back.

Tales and memories of this hard, selfish, brutal man were my patrimony; it served me well in law, politics, and commerce. Pride in what he found of himself in me was his surrogate for love; it served me to eschew self-pity. Neither is much use now. He never understood the enduring gift he gave me was inadvertent, my first intimation of harmony that came when he took me to sea.

4. Trade Schools

> Let the sisters now attend her, who are
> red-eyed, who are wroth;
> They were younger, she was finer, for they
> wearied of the waiting
> And they married them to merchants,
> being unbelievers both.
>
> **JOHN CROWE RANSOM,** *Emily
> Hardcastle, Spinster*

Reject (UVA)

On an Indian summer's day in 1966, ignorance, arrogance, and aestheticism deposited me at Clark Hall, the white-columned, neoclassical building that housed the University of Virginia law school. A five-minute stroll northwest was the Lawn, the thirty-five-acre rectangle Thomas Jefferson designed in 1817 as the heart of his Academical Village, often called the most beautiful campus in America, and now a UNESCO World Heritage Site. At my back was all I loved: the sea two hundred miles east, Cambridge two thousand miles farther northeast across it. Before me stretched four decades of loveless labor—the brief study and long practice of law.

UVA, America's fourth oldest law school and one of its top ten, offered a place and a scholarship when Harvard turned me down a second then third time. Too late to reapply to Chicago and Penn, the Lawn an aesthetic enticement, me a presumptuous, impecunious, three-time Harvard-applicant loser, I accepted. It was a mistake, architecturally enchanting, but for me the wrong place, for the wrong reason, with the wrong people.

American law schools, with a few exceptions like Yale, are primarily trade schools. They prepare students to sell legal services to clients as business schools prepare fledgling company executives, or carpentry schools train cabinetmakers. UVA was not one of the exceptions, and Clark Hall's Georgian grace made the trade taught there no more appealing.

Among America's best law schools, UVA turned out a disproportionate number of partners in top corporate law firms but few famous jurisprudes, judges, or lawyers hankering to improve the world. UVA students talked little of jurisprudence or law as social policy's handmaid. The bruit was of which Wall Street firms were best, what they paid, how high in the class you had to stand for them to hire you.

The mid-1960s in the United States were the height of the Haight,[32] counterculture, civil rights strife, race riots, and the anti–Vietnam War movement. Johnson had signed the Voting Rights Act[33] into law in 1965; draft cards burned on campuses; pot was ubiquitous, LSD the drug of the daring. But UVA slumbered. That slaves were the first occupants of the ground floors of the lawn's pavilions, where UVA's honor students now lived, made that housing coveted no less. There were no Blacks in my UVA classes, no freedom marchers among my classmates, no smoldering draft

---

[32] The Haight Ashbury district in San Francisco was the heart of the West Coast hippie and drug scene.

[33] The Voting Rights Act of 1965 aimed to allow southern Blacks to vote, a privilege they held in theory but not in practice. Johnson told Bill Moyers, "I think we have delivered the South to the Republicans for a long time to come" after he signed it, and Richard Nixon, a Republican, duly won the presidency three years later. The act is contentious to this day, and Republican-controlled states continue to disenfranchise Black voters using myriad schemes.

cards or Stars and Stripes. Clark Hall smelled of Aqua Velva and Brut, not pot; Virginia law students did not *trip*.

* * *

I had had enough of trade—low or high, as a butcher boy in Philadelphia pushing pork-loin ends to the working poor for fifty-nine cents a pound—and had not come to UVA to learn one, however high, but to qualify in what I imagined to be a learned and honorable profession. I was to learn in time that profession was with Brandeis in the grave, buried under mega-firms with megaoverheads. My first day at UVA, I had no inkling of the high-value, amoral industry American corporate law had become. I had never heard of fabled Wall Street law firms—Cravath, White and Case, Dewy Ballantine, Davis, Polk and Wardwell, Breed, Abbott and Morgan—before entering Clark Hall; of eight-inch-thick, six-pound, incomprehensible bond indentures; of platoons of lawyers immured for months in unheated old brick warehouses, sifting millions of pages of documents; of seven-day workweeks; of two-thousand-hour annual billable hour requirements and injunctions to bill the time you spent in the john that alchemized a shit into a billable event. UVA fitted its students for this contemporary coalface, but my dream had not been to be a miner.

Worse, UVA stank of failure. Many of its three hundred entering class were ambitious Ivy Leaguers that more prestigious schools had spurned. For them as for me, Virginia was a fallback, a never-mentioned, omnipresent odor of rejection we trailed. One or two top students at the end of their first year customarily tried to transfer to sweeter-smelling schools; at the end of my first year, the third and fourth ranked made a break for it. Some didn't wait that long.

Near Christmas, while crossing the lawn, St. John's College scarf around my neck, a passerby with an English accent accosted me. *Sorry, but is that a John's scarf?* My British interlocutor, Kevin Tierney, had read law at John's and, three months earlier, enrolled at UVA as a graduate student in legal history. We hadn't met at John's and met only that once at UVA. After a month there, he applied to transfer to Yale, was accepted, and when the winter term began, had skedaddled to New Haven.

My background and politics differed too much from my classmates' for familiarity to blossom. They had *prepped*, or gone to toney suburban public high schools rather than a city public high. They *summered*, not vacationed. (At UVA, I first heard summer used as a verb.) No one I met, save the itinerant Johnian, had studied abroad; most were unmarried; there were fewer

Jews than you'd expect at a top U.S. law school; Christian believers were the rule; and my classmates' politics were mostly soft to hard right wing, where mine were left, almost *communist* by UVA standards.

* * *

Law professors use two tools to teach: the case and the Socratic methods. The case method uses casebooks containing leading cases, customarily organized chronologically in, say, Torts, Contracts, Property, Civil Procedure, and Administrative Law, the legal foundational branches taught in first-year law school from which a student may deduce the elements and evolution of that branch. Students are supposed to read and brief these cases—summarize facts, identify *holdings* (rules of law), distil ratio decidendi—and be able to present all three if called on in class. There are no lectures. In this wise, law schools hope, students derive the law themselves from its roots up in a process that attempts to replicate—more efficiently and better guided—how law clerks once gradually absorbed the law by toiling for years at firms like Tweedie and Prideaux.[34]

Notorious handmaid to the case method is the Socratic method, a teaching style akin to an intellectual rack, which can turn a law school classroom into a humiliation chamber. The beginning of class, a professor chooses a student at random to *stand and deliver*—summarize the facts of a case assigned in the casebook, give its *holding* and *ratio decidendi*. The professor does not say whether she answered right or wrong but instead asks questions to explore her understanding. These questions often suggest the interrogatee has misunderstood the case, even if she hasn't, and drag her down winding paths into blind alleys. This so-called Socratic method aims to teach students to *think like a lawyer* more than explore the history, meaning, and significance of case or legal principle. When a hapless respondent is unable to answer a question, the professor turns to the would-be piranha savants in the classroom waiting to feed on their stumped classmate's stupidity.

The more sadistic or insecure faculty use this technique to flush faces, and wring tears at times from embarrassed victims; grins on cocky classmates' faces tighten the thumbscrews. In the hands of some law professors, the Socratic method, satirized in the 1973 film *The Paper Chase*, is dehumanizing; at its best, it may help ready students for a courtroom very

---

[34] The firm of solicitors where Dickens worked as a clerk.

few will ever enter.[35] What it unfailingly does is turn law school classes into a blood sport, fouling the idea of law itself and education.

Law school flummoxed me. I read the cases, registered their dates, extracted their rule of law or legal principle, *ratio decidendi*. But professors' questions, classmates' aimless answers, convinced me I'd misunderstood the lot. No one told me the first year of law school attempts to teach critical thinking through misdirection until you question whatever you're told or asked. Both skepticism and analytical capability were assumed at Cambridge and developed in tutorials. No school I had attended set out to mislead; law school pedagogy was inconceivable to me. Even had the Socratic method been well explained before I matriculated, I doubt I'd have believed it, so unnecessary and wasteful it seemed.

The other students were either as confused as I or too smug and competitive to enlighten the rest of us. I burrowed into the rear of classrooms, third row from the back, two in from the windows, to avoid being called on, asked no questions, did not comment. For a month, I successfully lay doggo. The fifth week, I began exploring the possibility of abandoning law school for a graduate program in English Literature. In the middle of the sixth, in Torts class, I was asked to stand and deliver.

Our Torts professor was Calvin (Cal) Woodard, a thirty-nine-year-old, six-foot-four, ex–University of North Carolina football star, Yale law, Cambridge (Peterhouse), whose expertise and passion were the history of the English Common Law. He wore Harris Tweed sports coats with leather elbow patches, rimless gold *granny* glasses, and an ineffable air of sadness; his young wife had died the year before, leaving him with two girls under ten. He was kind and gentle, like many physically imposing men, avuncular, civilized, and spoke with a soft Piedmont drawl. His German and French, spoken and read, were good; Latin and Greek above the mark; he was an Anglophile. John Crowe Ransom would have welcomed him as an *Agrarian*,[36] though I didn't know any of that when he winkled me from the back of the room and called from the front,

[35] The vast majority of graduates of top ten law schools practice civil law, and less than 1% of civil cases go to trial.
[36] The Agrarians were an American literary school prominent in the '40s and '50s, who wrote nostalgically about the South. Among their leaders were Allen Tate and John Crowe Ransom, and their house organ was *The Sewanee Review*.

Mr. Burt? . . . Mr. Burt? My hand crept up. *Mr. Burt, would you please . . .*

I stood and delivered: facts, holding, rationale. The expected question followed, and I blanked. After a few silent seconds, the room filled with semaphoring piranha arms; the air pulsed as they swung back and forth, stirred almost enough to ruffle the pages in the casebook open on Cal Woodard's desk. I saw myself as a drowned goat, my classmates' arms slashing the air, so many incisors intent on stripping my flesh. *You may sit down, Mr. Burt*, said Mr. Woodard politely, then called on a waving arm to answer the question I hadn't.

At the end of class, the fiercest flesh-eater planted herself between me and the door as I slunk out. Product of a middle-class Long Island suburb and Pembroke, Brown's women's college, Nancy Buck was the class's loudest, caustic, cocksure student. The bane of the less assertive—and perhaps more thoughtful of us—contentious, a trial for professors, she was someone I would have shunned had not alphabetical organization at matriculation—*Buck, Burt*—assigned us the same classes and forced nodding acquaintance.

Boy, was that stupid! You got that case completely wrong, Miss[37] Buck rasped, arms akimbo before me. I stood speechless. My shoulders and head slumped farther, my face flushed as it had when Mr. Woodard dismissed me. After a few mute seconds, I circumvented her and trudged like Sad Sack (an American comic book character) from the room.

No one had called me stupid since second grade nor been so rude since high school. But to this day, I haven't learned how to counter humiliation or rudeness with anything but fists, an uncivilized, hence unthinkable riposte in the circumstances even had Miss Buck been a man. Worse, I was confused and demoralized and accepted her judgment, if not how she delivered it. I left Clark Hall for lunch, determined to leave law school.

Because I'd embarrassed myself in his classroom, I knocked on Professor Woodard's office door after lunch to apologize and say I was withdrawing from law school before anyone else found me out. I entered, introduced myself:

Mr. Woodard, I'd like to apologize . . .

For what?

---

[37] Ms. did not come into common use in the United States till the '70s.

Misstating that case. I'd prepared, but obviously didn't understand it.
Why do you think that?
Miss Buck said I'd . . .
Mr. Burt, you had it exactly right.
But Miss Buck . . .
Mr. Burt, this early in the first year, the ones who think they know what's going on are often the most confused.

He advised me to wait, ignore the know-it-alls, take the first term exams coming up in a month, see how I did before dropping out, and call on him again before decamping.

* * *

I took his advice to its logical conclusion. From that afternoon, I went to no classes, read the assigned cases, discovered and used hornbooks (one volume explanatory treatises on branches of law), and kept to myself. Whether my fellow students were as addled as I was or simply vicious like Miss Buck, there was no reason to look to them for help, and faculty did not offer tutorials.

At 10 a.m. on the first day of second semester, our exam results and class rank were posted on a prominent notice board by the main entrance to Clark Hall, and the law school cosmos was remade. Our first grades established each student's status on a concrete base, since status equaled class standing, hence likelihood of good jobs; defanged the piranhas, though not all of them had the self-respect to melt into the mangrove roots now they could no longer draw blood so easily; alerted the faculty to potential stars who would staff the *Law Review* (upon which the school's reputation partly depended), who might be useful research assistants, might have financial success and, it was hoped, generously remember their old law school.

The scrum around the notice board the first hour was almost impenetrable. I didn't bother trying. After the damned and saved thinned, I checked, found my class rank was eleventh, then visited Professor Woodard. Though my results assured success at UVA—automatic election to *Law Review*, faculty attention, job with a big firm—I was no happier there. Woodard heard me out, told me my results offered the possibility I could trade up, and suggested I apply to transfer to Yale. But Harvard remained the blinking green light at the end of the North Shore pier. Though Yale might suit me better and was ranked first in the nation, all I could see was that blinking green light, and the little cheerleader from Lower Merion who, I had somehow learned, was working on her PhD there.

Woodard asked if, given the chance, I'd visit Harvard to make my case for admission. *Yes.* He spoke with someone at Harvard and procured an audience.

My plane landed at Boston's Logan airport near noon a week later. I took a cab to Cambridge to meet Irwin Griswold, dean of Harvard Law School, in his office at the northwest corner of the Yard (the oldest part of the Harvard campus built in 1718). Large and dark, his office was more lair than workspace. I was called in, greeted curtly, and signed to a chair near where the great dean sat enthroned in a high-backed leather armchair, large and forbidding like Nabucco. He did not rise to greet me, did not say hello. As soon as I was seated, he began: *We do not accept transfers. However, if you were first or second or third in your class at the end of this year, we might consider you.* Then he showed me the door.

I had come 554 miles by car, plane, and cab, stayed overnight in a hotel—all at a cost that strapped me—to be told in a meeting that lasted no more than three minutes I was wasting my time. At year's end, ranked third, I applied to Yale, not Harvard, self-respect stronger than obsession, even than the lure of the girl from Lower Merion studying there.

* * *

The *Dan-Rick* had been tied up at her berth an hour earlier after a blue-fishing trip to the ridge, the party iced their fish and left, I'd scrubbed the fish box and was about to swab the decks when the bait-shop clerk walked over and passed on a message from my mother that a letter had arrived from Yale. I dropped bucket and brush, shouted I'd be straight back to finish, and sped home to open it. My father knew I'd applied to transfer and opposed it, since I'd excelled at a top-ten school already. As my car shot from the marina's parking lot in a cloud of dust and spray of gravel, I heard him holler: *Whaddya gonna do if they want ya?*

Others warned, *Stay where you are.* Roy Schotland—a thirty-two-year-old, short, roly-poly Jew from Newark—taught administrative law at UVA and was the *Law Review*'s faculty advisor. His BA was from Columbia; he'd been a *Harvard Law Review* editor, and a Supreme Court clerk. I would see a lot of him if I stayed at Virginia; my class rank made me automatically a member of the *Law Review*.

Schotland introduced himself shortly after first-year grades were posted. He'd heard of me, bet Yale would have me, and aimed to persuade me to remain if they did. We met for coffee or lunch five or six times before I left for Barnegat to mate on the *Dan-Rick* and await Yale's judgment. He rehearsed the same arguments my father made for remaining at UVA, plus one.

Good lawyers leave what they think is their strongest argument for closing, Schotland no exception. At our last meeting, he said, *Look, here you're known, a big fish in hardly a small pond. At Yale, you'll be unknown, a small fish in a big pond. Why risk it? Why leave a sure thing?*

The big fish argument had not occurred to me. It implied I overrated myself and should fear finding that out. It was an argument from cowardice that no one before Schotland advanced as a virtue. It said more about his self-doubts and the insecurity at the heart of UVA law than me. If I was second rate, now was the time to know.

Yale offered a two-year scholarship and loan. I telephoned their admissions office, accepted, and headed back toward the Inlet to finish cleaning the Dan-Rick.

To this day, an Oxbridge college scarf serves British undergraduates as a badge of rank. They are practical, warding off colds and worse in the dreaded, dark, glacially long English winter. But their most important role is signaling—I am a member of an Oxbridge college elite, the world mine.

The American counterpart, serving the same practical and symbolic purposes, is the Ivy League sweatshirt. Monochromatic—crimson for Harvard, blue for Yale, and so on—they pick their wearer out as elect on beaches, tennis courts, wherever people dressed casually gather. You can buy them in most of the tourist areas of east coast cities and towns, and many do, to memorialize a trip, or impress.

I hungered to wear one as of right, not merely from ego, stubbornness, or parvenu lust, but because the schools they signified gave a head start. More even than today, a law degree from Yale or Harvard opened doors and later partnerships on Wall Street, in DC, the courts and law teaching that were closed or not easily shoved opened by graduates of other schools. Coveted summer jobs on Wall Street and on Washington committees, which previewed those worlds, went disproportionately to Yalies and Harvards between their second and third law-school years.

Long Beach Island, the *Dan-Rick*'s home port, was a typical New Jersey barrier island, middle-class seaside resort. Its main road, the island's spine, from our dock near the Inlet at Barnegat Light to our two-bedroom bungalow near the bay in Surf City, was peppered with small shops selling postcards, curios, T-shirts, and sweatshirts with names of famous universities emblazoned across their breasts flapping on racks on the curbs outside. I stopped at one, bought a dark-blue sweatshirt with the word *Yale* in three-inch white letters on its front, pulled it on, and returned to complete my chores.

I pulled into a parking place fronting the *Dan-Rick*, where my father stood kibitzing with several other captains. As I hurried past to resume cleaning, he grunted, *Guess I don't have to ask what yur gonna do.*

D. M. Burt. Esq., "Enters into Heaven," cartoon by Bill Hannan, Dan Burt's UVA classmate

Half Called (Yale)

The Sterling Law Building—a Depression-era, collegiate Gothic mass of gray stone and brown brick—crowds the four sidewalks of a square block near downtown New Haven. No lawns lead to nor neoclassical symmetries frame it. Looming four forbidding stories above the asphalt streets of this small, dingy, dying Long Island north shore city, it prompts no thoughts of Inns of Court—from which it took its form—but of power, privilege, and exclusivity; not Washington, Jefferson, and Lincoln but Vanderbilt, Morgan, and Pew.

The street before it was empty when I pulled up to the main entrance on a Sunday afternoon in early September 1967. I had reached Yale Law School, 421 miles northeast and a culture away from UVA, come to what students and faculty called *The Law School*, the definite article and absence of identifying adjectival noun implying unrivaled superiority. Here they taught policy—what the law should be, not what it was—and that those who plaited policy into U.S. society's traces were lawyers.

YLS was for people who did not want to practice law. Robert Reich, Bill Clinton's Secretary of Labor and YLS alumnus, captured its ethos so: *Yale Law School was the kind of place you went to if you felt you needed to go to law school, maybe for your résumé. But you really didn't want to practice law. You wanted to do public policy or go into politics.*

At Yale, some dreamed of molding the law from tenured chairs at fabled law schools rather than advising clients of renowned New York law firms—Cravath Swain & Moore, Davis Polk and Wardwell, Sherman and Sterling. Others foresaw themselves rise for their first speech from the U.S. Senate's floor rather than addressing a company's board of directors. Not a few were headed to public interest law firms like the Sierra Club or American Civil Liberties Union, where they hoped to bring the case that saved the great spotted owl or legalized gay marriage. If you aimed to practice commercial law and make a modest pile, you kept mum about it at The Law School in 1967.

Faith in their coming consequentiality was not delusional. YLS graduates became presidents, Supreme Court justices, Cabinet officers, Senators and Representatives, state governors, mayors, and aides to these illuminati; they became TV talking heads. Many of the nation's best judicial clerkships from the Supreme Court down fell to them; they swelled the federal bench, held professorships and deanships at leading law schools and senior slots at policy shops and think tanks. The YLS class of 1969, my class now, reasonably believed it would fill these roles in turn; it was merely the natural order of things.

But Yale had a dark side. The Law School was intolerant and shunned those who doubted its liberal orthodoxies. I noticed few spoke to a decent, generous Baptist preacher's son who roomed in my dorm. He was bright, athletic (black belt in karate), a fair linguist, and had unusual experience. (I suspect he'd done a stint in the Agency [CIA].) He was pilloried because he supported the Vietnam War unashamedly.

Most of our 90 percent male class lugged privilege, prep school, and Ivy league backgrounds with them to their rooms as well as suitcases. Few had or would serve in Vietnam; the three U.S. presidents of an age to have fought there—Clinton, Bush, Trump, did not. My classmates had little experience or, at best, superficial knowledge of those they wanted to help. Policy at Yale was conceived and implemented *de haut en bas*.

These reformers championed undemocratic methods—litigation and regulation—to impose their policies. Judge and regulator-made law can be just that, a rule governing the many made by one, or a handful of jurists or regulators having tenuous justification in statute, common law, or constitution. When a case or regulation broadly affects society—say, on abortion, voting rights, environmental protection, immigration, or antidiscrimination—those opposed who had no right to vote on the decision, or its makers, can plausibly scream foul. From the late 1950s, cadres of bright, determined, idealistic lawyers, often Yalies, aggressively used the federal courts and agencies to shape and direct U.S. society in ways the legislature would not and, in the process, enraged a large part of the populace who were, perhaps, less *bien pensant* than Yale-trained public-interest lawyers. Fury at this use of the federal courts and agencies to force social change played no small role in the ascendancy of the U.S. conservative movement and election of Ronald Reagan; the Erinyes loosed can be seen chanting at Trump rallies today.

* * *

I entered YLS in the fall of 1967, the peak of the American counterculture storm. The highest waves broke over the Ivy League, even their law and business trade schools. The atmosphere reeked of utopian plans, heaved with conviction that superior research and advocacy could force change through agencies and courts unattainable through legislation. Dissenting voices were quashed or dismissed; the prevalence and corrosive effects of corruption on politics and commerce went undiscussed. I lost sight of the suitless racketeers of my mother's Kevitch clan left behind in Philadelphia, came to believe the bribery and dishonesty I'd witnessed was reserved to the lower orders, and foolishly laid aside my cynicism born watching them.

Cambridge had exposed me to political organizations and ideals of social justice alien to Philly's butcher shops and bars and my working-class Catholic college. At UVA, I glimpsed the role and potential of law to level inequality in America. By the time I left for Yale, long-standing anger at a game rigged for the elite, mated with possibilities seen at Cambridge for making that game fairer, fostered dreams of rewriting the game's rules. Bill Hannan, a UVA classmate and cartoonist manqué, drew the cartoon of me leaving for Yale that opens this chapter. It was his parting gift, the Trotsky pennant waving from its radio antenna graphic evidence of the future he foresaw for me.

But education, idealism, and revolutionary paroxysm could only muffle, not silence, my father's voice warning, *Hard times! Jew-haters!* The claxon he sounded continually overwhelmed my childhood with repeated tales of Depression-era poverty and his parents' exodus from a shtetl east of Kiev where the ones who stayed behind—paternal grandparents, uncles, aunts, nephews, and nieces—were murdered in a pogrom. Though I experienced no anti-Semitism at Yale, I still heard my father there, far from the Pale and South Philly's cobblestones. Infected with his fears, conditioned to dread want and a Jew's future in gentile society (the major U.S. white-shoe[38] law firms did not begin hiring more than the token Jew until 1969), unconditional surrender to idealism was impossible. I trimmed, and chose a cause that, should it fail, would leave me with expertise to sell. Encouraged by peers, exhorted by professors, swept up in the times but obeisant to the ghosts of want and the Diaspora, I only sipped the Kool-Aid and chose tax reform as calling and cause.

Yale's faults were not invisible, but my arrival in the land of the big rock candy mountain[39] dazzled me too much to see them. I abandoned Charlottesville for New Haven not solely to do policy law, but to burnish my résumé, bury failure, and escape the miasma of the also-ran that pervaded UVA. YLS satisfied all four.

Yale was not academic Elysium. No matter how utopian, in its marrow, The Law School remained a trade school, as law schools must since most of their graduates will at some point practice law, even if in time they become politicians or policy wonks.[40] Course work, casebooks, exams, and the labor required to cope with them were roughly the same at Yale as at Virginia. Even if your cause is to leaven inequalities by making taxes more progressive, you must understand in brutal, boring, dull detail on how the tax code works. Sweating to garner this knowledge is inescapable, legal studies implacably pedestrian. I liked neither the grind nor classmates' trade talk, notwithstanding its policy cast, any better at Yale than UVA

---

[38] Elite U.S. firm traditionally populated by WASPs. Derives from white buckskin shoes, historically popular at Ivy League colleges.

[39] Folk song about a hobo's idea of paradise.

[40] Fifty-eight percent of the current U.S. Congress have law degrees.

and was often away two hours west of New Haven by car at Vassar, one of the New England women's colleges known as the Seven Sisters, the female counterpart to the then all-male Ivy League.

For all Yale's opportunities, energy, and excitement, it proved anticlimactic. Your first year at law school rocks you because it surprises, bamboozles, befuddles, unpacks, and reassembles the mind. The last two years are progressively duller, disruption complete and what was novel familiar. Had I floundered or had to work harder, Yale might loom larger, but I didn't. Other top-five law schools would have showcased an LLB's varied uses, though perhaps none so dramatically. Another's degree would have opened doors, though none, perhaps, so wide as Yale's. Only one Yale friendship survived graduation, and it died twenty years ago, withered by time, distance, and the different roads we traveled. Confrontation with reality turned my idealism to dust in fifteen years.

Part III

Between the Kisses and the Wine[1]

● ● ● ● ● ● ● ● ● ● ● ●

> "Look Lou, let's stop this." "Can't I see you once?
> Just one more time? Tonight?" "No. I'll be late
> For work upstairs. Good-bye." Now that I know
> I won't see you again, an awful pain
> Of deprivation twists my abdomen.
>
> **L. E. SISSMAN,** *On the Island*

A Vassar girl was my main event at Yale; students, professors, classes, a sideshow. She dominated every day, her last act unforgettable. Law school has faded; she has not.

Friday night, end of the first week's classes at Yale: I'm riding shotgun to my first mixer in Saul Green's white, late-model Impala convertible, heading northwest from New Haven to Poughkeepsie and Vassar at eighty

---

[1] "Between the kisses . . ." Ernest Dowson, "Non Sum Qualis Bonae Eram, Sub Regno Cynarae," in *The Poems of Ernest Dowson* (London: Bodley Head, 1905).

miles per hour on Route 84. My quickie divorce filed a few months earlier will soon be final, unshackling me after eight years from the succubus
who at seventeen became my wife. Wind and tire-whine balk conversation.
It's a warm, Indian-summer's September night—the top down, setting sun
in my eyes—bound for a Seven Sisters college to meet young women only
read of. I'm Amory Blaine, two weeks short of twenty-five, the American
Dream in my grasp.

Cynthia Sonja Bauer is twenty minutes late. Saul and I have been talking to her friends Cassie Adams and Jet Mason while waiting in the sitting room at Strong House, a Vassar residence hall. The sitting room's high,
wide, arched entrance frames the dorm rooms' staircase just beyond. Cassie
spots Cynthia descending: *Sie kommt*. My head turns toward:

> the swish of nylon slip on dress,
> gray A-line, scarlet hem and cuff,
> collar fringed with white lace ruff,
> matching gray Alice band to snare
> her fall of shoulder-length red hair
> sashaying down a dorm hall stair
> at Vassar the autumn night we met,
> a half century ago....[2]

She sits on the sofa with her friends on the only free cushion, the one
nearest my chair. She does not apologize for being late. Introductions made,
conversation resumes. We engage, our talk strays from the group's, becomes
tête-à-tête. The others go to the dance; we choose to stroll the campus.

We walk, have a drink—cosmo for her, whiskey sour for me—talk.
She is a sophomore, German American, just returned from summer at
her grandmother's in Düsseldorf, to which she carried her recently dead
mother's ashes. Her maternal family are wealthy, long-established *Mittelstand* manufacturers the war impoverished, who have rebuilt their fortune.
Grandmother pays for her education, brings her to Germany in summers,
subsidizes her life.

Her father is a middle manager at a small plant near West Trenton,
New Jersey, where she lives when not at Vassar or in Germany. He was an

---

[2] Dan Burt, "Caballetta," in *We Look Like This* (Manchester: Carcanet, 2012).

American army captain of German descent stationed in Düsseldorf at war's end, where her mother met and married him. It was a marriage conceived in German postwar desperation, on the distaff side more than one social rung down. She says nothing more about her father, nothing at all about his family, and discourages questions about him.

I tell enough about myself for her to know my youth was charmless. We have sadness in common but time only to outline it. Soon after midnight, Saul and I drive back to Yale.

Waiting on my desk in New Haven is a half-inch-high, unedited first draft of a *Law Review* article. I collected it from the *Law Journal*'s offices the day of the mixer, obedient to the Admissions Dean's insistence that I try out for the *Law Review*. Candidates have seventy-two hours, the weekend, to edit the draft. Either I take my red pencil to it as soon as I return or rise early to attack it. Instead, I call Cynthia when I reach my room, and we talk till dawn. We talk all day Saturday after we wake and late into the night. We do the same Sunday. Monday, I return the unmarked manuscript to the *Law Journal*'s office. What flickering interest I had in joining the Journal winked out when I saw Cynthia coming down the Strong Hall stairs.

Love at first sight is a fact. Sensors and MRIs can measure the shock of its happening: adrenalin increases heart rate, dopamine lights up caudate, tegmental, amygdala, and hippocampus areas of the brain. Writers from Shakespeare to Richler testify to it. French, German, Spanish, Chinese, and Arabic tongues have a phrase for it; I suspect all do. I've experienced it twice: at sixteen and nine years later that first night at Vassar.

Cynthia was a natural redhead, fair skin nearly porcelain smooth, blue eyes in a regular face, high cheekbones, thin lips below a narrow, slightly pug nose. Twenty, just under five feet four, fine boned, flat bellied, near breastless with a slightly haughty mien, she was an almost ideal Nordic German beauty, or Yellow Book,[3] princess. For two years, almost to the day, we were a couple.

A month later, I'm among more than a million who swarm Washington, DC, to protest the Vietnam War. When Cynthia declines to accompany me, her roommate Barbara Cohen asks if she can come. Barbara arrives at

[3] A British literary periodical published quarterly in London between 1894 and 1897, associated with aestheticism and decadence.

Yale about 9 p.m. on Friday night before the march. We're to leave New Haven at dawn next day for the five-and-a-half-hour drive to DC.

Barbara has more than protesting in mind. About to separate for the night, she confesses attraction, embraces, and kisses me. I gently disengage, prepare to go to my room, when she grasps my arm, stays me, makes her pitch. She knows Cynthia well and is sure we're incompatible. Our backgrounds are too different; Cynthia's is upper-class German, mine working-class Jewish/Italian/American. Our politics and values differ. Cynthia is socially conservative, no feminist. She wants a traditional upper-class marriage, not career. She's prudish, still a virgin. In roots, experience, and outlook, I'm Cynthia's contrapositive. Barbara's the better match.

But Barbara has come to the game too late. I shoved my chips to the center of the table the Friday night Cynthia and I met and was all in when I put the phone down forty-eight hours later. Like every foolish gambler, I believed the next card would make my hand, and Cynthia mine, when the dealing was done. Had Barbara Cohen been Helen of Troy, I would not have left the table.

September to June for the next two years, mostly in New Haven, Cynthia and I spent almost every weekend together. The first year, there are quarrels and brief breakups, prudishness and absent intercourse the root cause. Though after dating for six weeks or so, we shared a bed, I never saw her undress. She slept in bra and panties. I never saw her naked. On retiring, the lights were always off. She came to my rooms a virgin and the first year remained one while I played Tristan to her Isolde, my satisfactions constrained to those a teenage boy achieves with his girlfriend on a basement couch, while his inamorata's parents watch TV upstairs. If Cynthia took pleasure from our fumbling, I couldn't tell.

* * *

On a crisp, New Haven Sunday morning in November, two months after we met, tree limbs nearly leafless, dawns frosty, I'm propped in the window seat of my sitting room, legs stretched halfway down it, back against a wall, facing west up Wall Street. To the right across the road, the tombstones' shadows in the cemetery pointed north. It was nearly 10 a.m. I'd eaten my McIntosh breakfast apple, had fresh coffee in the half-filled cup beside me and *The Well-Tempered Clavier* spinning on the turntable as I read Reston's latest antiwar jeremiad in the Sunday *New York Times*.

Everybody at Yale in 1967 read the *Sunday Times*, or so we assumed, and James Reston was the antiwar oracle all turned to first. We revered him and would quote him all week until his next pronouncement in the next *Sunday Times*. His argument that morning for ending the war seemed exquisitely dispositive.

Cynthia enters, showered, powdered, painted and fresh from the weekend women's bathroom across the hall (a sign hung from a nail on our dorm floor's bathroom warning *Lady Inside*). My world narrows to her. *Cynth! Cynth! Honey! Come read Reston's column. It's the best argument against the war I've read.*

Dan, you know I'm not an intellectual, and passes through to the bedroom. My cheek stings as if it's been slapped. I knew her politics. She could have begged off with *Later, darling* or *Not now, sweetheart*, rather than that barbed demurrer. Whether she was an intellectual or not had never crossed my mind. I was too besotted with her to have wondered and didn't care whether she was or wasn't. But my passion for her as is was not what mattered.

I had told her the night we met how I'd come to Cambridge and Yale from Philadelphia's inner-city streets; that my loves had become literature, art, classical music, opera; that I eschewed drugs in terror of addling my only asset, my mind; in short, that I was an intellectual. Now her mean reply—vocative form, accusatory preamble, *Dan, you know* . . . the *not* spat out just shy of a scream—reveals that what defines me galls her. That was the moment to let my deal go down, cash in my chips, and leave the table. Instead, I simply sat smarting, almost laboratory proof that love yokes the most mismatched human pairs till one cripples the other.

* * *

We're still a couple when the academic year ends in June. Cynthia promises that when schools resume after our summer's separation, we'll become proper lovers, then flies to her grandmother in Düsseldorf.

I cannot say good-bye to her at Kennedy because I'm thirty miles offshore of Sandy Hook when her plane takes off, delivering a sailboat from Greenwich, Connecticut, to Cape May. When I return to my rooms at Yale, an envelope of the finest Japanese rice paper, addressed to me, sits on the mantle; on the note inside, three words in large, perfect, cursive script—*I love you*—below them a capital *C*. I slip the note between the leaves of a notebook I travel with to jot down lines that come to mind.

In the last half of the 1970s, I'm an itinerant international lawyer, flying regularly to and between Middle Eastern, European, and American cities, Riyadh, Tehran, Zurich, London, New York, Houston,

Boston, more. A successor notebook, between its pages Cynthia's note, flies with me. Late spring, London, 1976, seven years after I last saw Cynthia, I check my suitcase—notebook cum love note—into a Berkeley Square hotel's cloakroom while I attend a business lunch. The case is gone when I return. For the next five years, I stop by that hotel whenever I'm in London and inquire if my case has been found.

The beginning of our second year together, on my dorm room bed at Yale, Cynthia redeems her promise. Squabbles diminish, there are no breakups; the first year's slights and tempests fade.

She gave me two more gifts that second year; they're with me still. On October 1, 1968, my twenty-sixth birthday, I unwrapped a one-foot-by-two pencil-and-charcoal portrait of Yeats. Cynthia, a fine draftswoman, had drawn it from a publicity photograph. Yeats was and is my lodestar poet, and her portrait of him has hung in libraries of flats and houses I've lived in this last half century. It looks out over the North Atlantic from my writing room at Schooner Head on the Maine coast as I type; when I'm there, I pass it every morning. Sometimes I pause, sometimes stare at the draughtsman's signature—*Cynthia Bauer, '68*, prominent in the lower right-hand corner—sometimes remember. Now my hair is white, guests often say it resembles me.

We attend midnight mass together on Christmas Eve at a church in West Trenton near her father's house. As I leave around 2 a.m. to drive the forty miles south to my parents' house in North Philadelphia, she hands me a facsimile edition of the *First Folio*, published a few months earlier. It sits behind my desk at Schooner Head, a few feet from Yeats's portrait. The flyleaf is blank. From time to time—often in early September, the time of year we met—I lug it from the shelf and turn its pages, searching for a dedication I know is not there.

FACSIMILE FIRST FOLIO

A blank flyleaf augurs pristine leaves
in the Folio you gave me three wives ago,
exhumed today, my birthday, where it lay unsleeved
beneath my present lady's books and clothes.
Once more my fingers trek first page to last
hunting an envoy from you there,
an endearment I fail to track
on luckless expeditions down the years,
the way a Qumran scholar's scalpel scrapes

encrusted Aramaic scripts for clues
that Jesus Christ to whom he prays,
was foretold by a splinter sect of Jews.
That searched for text I shall not find
a billet-doux writ only in my mind.[4]

I take the title of my first poetry collection, *Searched for Text*, from this poem's penultimate line.

Cynthia's drawing of Yeats

June 1969, my formal schooling ends. I've graduated and accepted a job as an associate at Morgan Lewis and Bockius, a large Philadelphia corporate

---

[4] Dan Burt, *Searched for Text* (Manchester: Lintott, 2008).

law firm, starting September 2. June and most of July will be spent cramming for the Pennsylvania bar exam.[5]

I've also signed on to sail the Atlantic again on a small boat, crewing with three others on the *Barbara*, a thirty-nine-foot centerboard Alden Challenger yawl. Immediately after sitting the bar exams, I'll join her in Bermuda for the long passage—two thousand miles—to Horta, a centuries-old staging post for transatlantic sailors on the island of Faial, in the Azores. Whether I leave the boat in Horta or stay with it for the short haul to Lisbon across the Bay of Biscay depends on Cynthia.

We spend the weekend in Barnegat before she leaves to summer in Germany. She is the first woman I've taken there. We visit the Independent Yacht Basin at Barnegat Light and the *Dan-Rick* tied up on the front row among the other charter boats. We walk around the Barnegat Lighthouse then out onto the south jetty from the beach at the Inlet. I point out the shoals and how we run them. After dinner, in the long mid-June day's dusk, we promenade along the tide line on the beach at Surf City, arms around each other's waist.

We agree I'll quit the *Barbara* in Horta and make my way to Düsseldorf to meet her grandmother and family. We talk of what she'll do next June when she graduates, of perhaps marrying. That night, for the first time, haltingly, she fellates me.

Fully bearded, heavily tanned, hair bleached blond from salt and sun, olive-drab stuffed army surplus kit bag over my shoulder, I knock at the door of her grandmother's house in Düsseldorf midmorning late in August. The graying butler shows me through to the garden, where Cynthia and her grandmother are taking tea. Expostulations, introductions, then to my room to shower and change. Later, *Mutti*, as Cynthia calls her grandmother, shows me around the grand town house: fine Persian carpets, prewar furniture, photographs of Cynthia's mother and grandfather; his cigar room, glass fronted, humidified, shelves packed with box on box of large, brown, best-quality hand-rolled Havanas. I'm invited to help myself. Though Mutti speaks little English, and I less German, I feel welcome.

---

[5] Each U.S. state requires lawyers who wish to practice in that state to take its professional qualifications exam called a bar exam. Lawyers justify this restraint on trade by arguing that each state's laws differ, hence lawyers must qualify in each jurisdiction in which they wish to ply their trade.

Twenty minutes away in the countryside lay the estate of Cynthia's cousin, Herr Langsam, where we arrive for a cookout in the early evening. He heads the family electrical products company: specialty wires, filaments, housings, connectors, and so on. No one mentions its wartime role, which was likely as a material cog in the Nazi war effort. When Herr Langsam learns I mated on and skippered sport fishing boats, and my father captains one, he produces photos from the mid-1950s showing him in Bimini with marlin and giant tuna he'd landed. I compliment him on his silver belt. *Nein, es ist Platin* (*No, it's platinum*).

Dinner is served on a veranda sunk beside the swimming pool. Behind us, a bar and stools run down one side of the pool into which, below the water line, are let two-inch-diameter portholes. The salacious thoughts those portholes spawn, the questions about what sort of laborers the family business used during the war, I keep to myself. It's still *Stunde Null*[6] at Herr Langsam's.

* * *

Cynthia, Mutti, and I, plus butler/driver and maid, leave next morning after breakfast for two days in Norderney, a traditional German North Sea beach resort some four hours northeast of Düsseldorf. Our first night, we visit a popular *Bierhalle* (beerhall). Mutti and the others leave around 10:30 p.m., in deference to our next morning's sailboat cruise casting off at 8:30 a.m. I'm enjoying myself and drinking heavily; Mutti insists I stay. By midnight, I am up on a trestle table's bench, arms linked with fellow drinkers either side, swaying left and right and bellowing German songs whose words I am not sure I want to understand. It's a scene from a prewar Nazi propaganda film, and all that's missing are the lederhosen and swastikas.

The *Bierhalle* closes at 3 a.m. and pours me, with the remaining inebriates, into a black street I am sure I haven't seen before but must have. For a few minutes, I stand there, a lost, bedraggled, English-speaking monoglot, stinking of beer, then sway off searching fruitlessly for our hotel. I stumble into a police station an hour later and beg directions, fall into bed close to

---

[6] *Stunde Null* (zero hour), the dominant German postwar cultural doctrine until the late 1960s, proclaimed a complete break with Nazi art, history, thought, and language as of one minute past twelve on the morning after Germany surrendered. It became an excuse, connived at by the Western Allies, for Germans to avert their eyes from their part in World War II's horrors.

5 a.m., but report as required for the sightseeing trip three and a half hours later. News of my predawn wanderings had got out, through the concierge perhaps, and my status rises when I show up on time.

Two days later, on the morning drive back to Düsseldorf, Mutti mischievously tries to augment my German. She teaches me that I am Cynthia's *Freund* and, if asked what my relationship to her is, should say, *Sie ist meine Freundin* (*She is my girlfriend*). Then turning to Cynthia, she asks, *Wann heiraten Sie beide?* Cynthia crimsons and screams, *Oma! Bitte!* The servants smile. When I ask what *heiraten* means, the chauffeur says, *to get married.* (Mutti—*Cynthia, when are you two going to get married?* Cynthia—*Grandmother! Please!*)

We reach Mutti's house in the early afternoon. I'm to leave for Frankfurt and a flight to Philadelphia next morning. Cynthia and I opt for a walk along the Rhine. On its bank, I ask her to marry me, and she says *Yes.* While walking back, we agree to keep our engagement secret until I leave, and she can tell Mutti and her father. On the cold, stone basement floor of her grandmother's house, we make love in the late afternoon, before the others rise from their naps.

Next morning, grandmother and granddaughter travel to Frankfurt to see me off. At the departure gate, I hold Cynthia until every other passenger boards, kiss her as the gate closes, then sprint down the jetway to the plane. I never see her again.

* * *

A week later, on September 2, 1969, I'm shown to my office off the walnut-paneled halls of Morgan Lewis and Bockius, introduced to the secretary I will share with Bill Macan—the associate in the adjoining office—and before close of business, I am assigned my first legal memo. I plan to take *meine Freundin* to lunch and show her around a few days after her boat docks in New York two weeks from now. (Mutti decided it was time Cynthia crossed the Atlantic by sea and booked her return, first-class, on a German liner from Hamburg.)

The day she's due back, I reckon how long it will take her to disembark and be driven home, call her house about 3 p.m. and am told she hasn't arrived. That evening around 8 p.m., I call again, and her stepmother tells me Cynthia reached home exhausted and went straight to bed. I ring a third time about 11 a.m. the following morning. Her fifteen-year-old brother, Alan, answers: *She's still asleep. She was out late last night dancing.*

Near 4 p.m. that afternoon, I shut my office door and dial her number. The stepmother answers: *Hold on.* She shouts, *Cynthia, he's on the phone.* Cynthia picks up: *Dan, I never want to see you again.* Click.

* * *

I run into Barbara Cohen in San Francisco five years later. We spend a day picnicking in the wine country northeast of the city. Naturally, Cynthia comes up. Barbara tells me that on the crossing to New York, Cynthia met a German economics postdoc on his way to Princeton and fell in love with him. They married a year later, when she graduated.

Barbara doesn't crow I told you so, but asks, *What was the attraction?* I ascribe it to class and cultural ambition. Cynthia was a symbol, I argue, an embodiment of the American dream. She was my *Daisy Buchanan,* my great shiksa (gentile woman) avatar of the WASP America I believed I'd join. I don't mention the most powerful driver—her looks. Red hair, blue eyes, alabaster skin, and sylph's body chained me to her with adamantine links of shape and hue; she had my number.

For months after Cynthia put the phone down, I'd leave work at 7 p.m., go home, and sit alone in my flat in the dark, no stereo, no radio, no TV. In time, self-pity runs its course; there are no more nights sitting alone in the dark. I have many liaisons in the following half century, some serious, and marry three times more, but at the time this memoir ends, I had never gone *all in* again; the end of none—liaison, affair, or marriage—leaves me more than briefly heartsick; none leaves me disconsolate.

For Cynthia, I shucked cuirass and buckler, forged from the age of five, as I had for no woman before and have for no woman since. I gave her what was unscarred in me after childhood and youth. When she hung up, there was nothing left unscarred. Ambitious Jewish-American boys often chase a *great shiksa.* The lucky ones don't catch her.

Part IV

Every Wrong Direction

● ● ● ● ● ● ● ● ● ● ● ●

> *Tout droit dans son armure, un grand homme de pierre*
> *Se tenait la barre et coupait le flot noir;*
> *Mais le calme heros, courbe sur se rapier*
> *Regardait le sillage et ne daignait rien voir.*
>
> **BAUDELAIRE,** "Don Juan Aux Enfers"[1]

Arrogance is a foul disease. Like cancer, it blows no trumpet to announce its presence. Success breeds confidence that rots to arrogance, the way colon cancer sprouts in an intestine and spreads through the peritoneal cavity till it kills you. By the time you realize you're cancerous, you've made the mistakes that will destroy you. Arrogance is the winner's cancer.

---

[1] *Erect in his armour, a giant stone helmsman / Grasps the tiller and cleaves the black water; / While the hero, collected, indifferent to all, / Leans on his sword and stares into the wake.*

Higher education, and what came with it, was a giddy ride. Few thought me college material in 1960, when the good offices of a high school teacher secured my place at a workingman's college in Philadelphia. Four years later, I'm at Cambridge; five more, and I graduate Yale Law School. Philadelphia's top law firm gives me a three months' signing bonus to choose them over competing firms.

In the summer of 1965, eighteen months after a broken neck will likely leave me a permanent quadriplegic, I sail the Atlantic east to west with three other men on a thirty-nine-foot ketch. Four years later, I sail it again, west to east, on a different thirty-nine footer.

Imperceptibly, I begin to assume I'll win every fight, get whatever I desire, except one woman's love. I dwell on that doomed affair with Cynthia for the rest of my life, a memento of what remains forever beyond the reach of will—shared romantic love. Superior, unhumbled, I show up September 2, 1969, for my first day as an associate at Morgan Lewis and Bockius, which we called ML&B.

1. Hucksters

When I left law school, the advent of the Nixon administration and my politics barred me from my job of choice, as lawyer in the Treasury's Office of Tax Legislative Counsel. Runner-up was lawyering in a prominent corporate law firm until I found a suitable government job. Lawyering in a major firm, you are a professional, I thought, like a doctor or a priest—a sea change from flogging pork-loin ends in a butcher shop—and a big firm's saving grace.

I found New York cramped, dark, and hostile working there as a summer associate. Too many people labor and live in too little space in Manhattan. Experiments with rats show penning them in small cages increases their hostility; NYC does the same to people. My hostility needed no enhancing on the Big Apple's packed pavements; I returned to Philadelphia, rather than Wall Street, after Yale.

Philadelphia's four or five top firms, with one exception, were peas in a pod: all had large corporate clients—manufacturers, banks, insurance, pharmaceutical, real estate developers, media, service businesses; had DC offices; had offered a signing bonus; had courted me. But only one featured in a film.

The Young Philadelphian portrays the rise of a working-class boy (Paul Newman) in post–World War II Philadelphia. He specializes in a new field, tax law, at the city's most prestigious law firm, makes partner, humbles the Main Line's *pezzonovante* (big shots), and wins the *great shiksa*. I read the book, saw the movie, and knew ML&B was the model for the tale's twenty-four-carat WASP law firm. Could I have gone anywhere else? I did not go to ML&B for their bonus, large DC office, or Republican political connections; I went because I dreamed it was my story.

ML&B, founded in 1873, looked the part of a leading white-shoe law firm, outside and in. It sprawled across high floors of a half-block-square, twenty-some-story gray granite building on the southeast corner of Broad and Sansom Streets, a few blocks south of William Penn's hat. The building's twelve-foot-high bronze-bound doors were so heavy that when the wind blew hard from the west in winter, a man had to use both hands to pry them open. The elevators debouched onto the firm's nineteenth-floor reception lobby, walnut-paneled, thickly carpeted. A walnut desk the size of a block from the base of Cheops' pyramid confronted arrivals. From behind this fortification, a prim, thin, fiftyish receptionist, skirt three inches below her knees, cleared visitors into the paneled waiting room to her right or chirped *Good morning* to the senior partners as they strode to their offices down the paneled corridor to her left, where somber portraits of the firm's founders stared sternly down at them. She smelled of attar of roses, the walnut paneling of lemon-oil furniture polish with which cleaners stroked it daily at dawn. Morgan Lewis' offices smelled of old money and looked like a lumberyard.

* * *

On the northwest corner opposite preened the Union League, a *Dèuxiéme Empire* style, rusticated brownstone-and-brick Civil War mansion. Founded in 1862, the Union League was the city's most exclusive private social club, the in-town watering hole for male *Black Book*[2] listees; no women, Jews, Blacks, nouveaux riches, or arrivistes were welcome as members or diners. My maternal grandfather, then a corrupt member of the Pennsylvania state legislature, was refused entry for lunch as a member's

[2] The *Black Book* is the U.S. social register in the '60s with some thirty-five thousand names of the bluest of blood.

guest in the 1940s. When I joined ML&B, the League had been their lawyers' club of choice for ninety-six years.

Partners, and most associates, lived on the Main Line—in townships like Merion, Bryn Mawr, Radnor, Villanova, Devon—where Philadelphia's upper crust had lived and been rich together for more than a century. They summered in Northeast Harbor Maine, yachted, foxhunted, played tennis, golfed, and held debutante balls in their restricted country clubs. Female issue prepped at Holton Arms and The Baldwin School, male at Choate and Andover; the young ladies went on to Vassar and Smith, the young men to Princeton and Yale.

Associates joined ML&B straight from law school, became partners, and never left. The firm had counseled many of their clients for decades, some almost from its founding. Until the mid-1960s, clients rarely had large in-house legal departments and, even rarer, substantial in-house tax groups. ML&B did all some big corporates' legal work, and major clients paid them an annual retainer to be on call, whether they used them or not. Partners served on clients' boards as directors and sometimes left to become their senior executives. These hoary, intertwined relationships—the retainers, relatively low overheads, the firm's ethos, stable partnership, and reputation—freed it to advise honestly, unconcerned whether its advice would lead to more business, or protect a relationship.

There was no expressed policy that associates bill a minimum number of hours a year when I joined the firm. Eighty-hour working weeks were neither routine nor encouraged. ML&B had not tried to grow by hiring laterals, partners from other firms with portable books of business. The Bar Association forbade lawyers to advertise; the firm deemed it unseemly to shill for clients or hustle work. Male lawyers were gentlemen, the few female lawyers ladies; all were counselors, not service providers. Practicing law at ML&B had long been an honorable profession, rather than a hustle, when I rounded the receptionist's desk to my first day at work, but the tectonic plates beneath corporate law practice had shifted, commercialization had begun, and in their wake, abasement to a service business followed.

* * *

ML&B's tax department was nine strong in 1969, five partners, four associates; in law firm argot, it was top heavy. The three senior partners were gentile gentlemen with long-established, secure practices: Tom Lefevre, the department's head and a specialist in reorganizations; Al McDowell, an expert in controversies—civil and criminal tax audits, investigations, and litigation; H. Peter Somers, an estate and gift tax guru who handled the tax and other affairs of the Campbell Soup heirs. They were counselors and prized as such by clients. But Tom and Al would soon retire; H. Peter was midfifties and absorbed in his practice. They were the past. Top-heavy firms of gentile gentlemen would not survive in the emerging world of corporate law practice; the status quo was not an option.

The remaining two partners were the Odell brothers, Stuart and Herb. Both were Jews, under forty, and not to the manner born. (ML&B penned its Jews in the tax department fifty years ago.) Neither had attended prestigious colleges or law schools, but had done well at the nation's best graduate tax programs. Stuart had been top of his LLM tax class at NYU; specialized in partnerships, equipment leasing, and tax shelters; and was a nationally acknowledged expert in all three. Herb was a litigator, and smoked cigars.

Their practices were transactional, either in newly developed areas of tax law (Stuart's) or tax controversies (Herb's), both less secure than the senior partners' practices. Retainers in Stuart's area were rare and vanishing; in Herb's, illogical. Both had to scurry for new business and were better equipped for it than their seniors. Stuart succeeded Tom Lefevre as head of the tax department before he was lured to a New York firm. Herb remained behind.

No one at ML&B had mentioned billable hours when I interviewed. There was no minimum billable requirement until some time after I left; but there might as well have been. Within days of starting work, I gleaned from associates that partners hoped we would bill a minimum of eighteen hundred hours a year. "Less is more" was not a rubric applied to billing. Partners as well as associates were on deck well before 9 a.m., Mondays through Fridays. Most associates worked a half day Saturday, as often did the Odells, and not infrequently senior partners. Associates vied to bill the most hours and to be seen too.

To bill an honest 35 to 40 hours a week (1800 ÷ 49 weeks) meant spending 55 to 60 hours in the office in those precomputer days. The pressure to bill more was palpable and increasing. We understood copious billings greased the rails to partnership and weighed heavily in deliberations on your annual bonus. No junior kept banker's hours at ML&B.

Minimum billable requirements, formal or not, are unprofessional. It assumes, wrongly, there is always adequate work to be done. Suppose not;

do you spin out what you do have—cheat? If you're faster than others and spot an answer quickly by chance or ability, should you be penalized or the client denied the benefit? If a partner responsible for feeding you work doesn't, should you be faulted? Is every minute spent thinking about a client billable; is taking a shit a billable event? I understood overheads and that associates were well paid; partners had to pay school fees and club dues, hence billing was important. But I expected emphasis to be on advising well first and billing second, not the other way around. Billable requirements are unsurprising in service businesses like accounting and management consulting. I hadn't expected or been led to expect them at ML&B.

I must have heard the phrase "rainmaker" before I lowered myself into the standard-issue swivel chair behind my desk at ML&B, perhaps during my previous summer's stint on Wall Street, but it did not come readily to mind. A few hours later, David O'Brien—a civilized, decent, corporate law partner aged just over fifty—assigned to be my mentor and familiarize me with the firm, introduced me to Bill Goldstein. As we left Goldstein's office, David told me he had come from a policy-making position at Treasury, was well regarded in the firm, and especially prized as a *rainmaker*.

What's a rainmaker?

A lawyer good at getting new clients or work.

Lawyers and accountants use the term routinely. I've not heard it applied to other professionals, like GPs, surgeons, architects, or academics.

Not only partners were supposed to make rain. Associates were urged to write trade articles, entertain likely clients, socialize with them in the right clubs. We saw the firm's heroes were rainmaking partners and heard they got the largest shares of the partnership pie. We watched associates quickly become partners if they brought in business. So we chased possible new business ourselves. Client snaffling was another topic unmentioned when I interviewed.

Shortly after I joined the firm, another associate rushed up to me as I was leaving one evening and thrust a tabloid in my hand. *You've GOT to see this*. It was a trade journal whose front page bannered *Top 20 Law Firms' Profits*. Inside were listed the leading twenty firms by billings, profits, and per partner income; ML&B was there. His almost breathless prurient interest was unsurprising; the firms' two legal castes, partners and associates, were fixated on how much their peers made, a fixation ubiquitous at the big law firms. An image from boyhood trips to schvitz popped into my mind: my father and two other ghetto butchers wrapped in sheets and towels, only their eyes, noses, and mouths bare, reclining on deck chairs *schvitzing* (sweating) after a *platza* and exaggerating to each other how much they made.

* * *

With client getting and money the measure of men, envy was rife at ML&B. Status fixed by salary and bonus, or share of partnership profits, discouraged friendship, camaraderie, and mutual assistance. Jealousy and envy burbled just below the firm's surface; occasionally, it boiled over.

William A. Macan IV—WAM IV, as he initialed memos—labored in the office next to mine. He was thirty, a Penn law grad, married with one child, and lived on the Main Line. Like the younger tax partners and associates, excepting me, he came accredited to ML&B, with an LLM in taxation and clerkship on the U.S. Tax Court. He understudied Stuart Odell on leveraged leasing deals, which were often tax shelters and a hot area of tax practice. To become a partner was his all, a common quest among associates.

WAM IV was a florid, barrel-bellied man who appeared always to be hurrying, his breastbone thrust forward like a snowplow's blade, or fast strutting like a turkey avoiding danger or Mussolini leading his Fascisti. He looked half again older than he was, a look he cultivated. He had a temper and deployed it against juniors and staff. We shared a young Italian American secretary whose skills needed burnishing. More than once, he reduced her to tears after she mangled a draft. Angered, which he often was, he flushed British pillar-box red. Superiors he flattered, juniors ignored, disdained my paltry tax expertise and me, and refused to help me the one time I asked. ML&B made him a partner in due course, after which he jumped ship for the New York office of a London firm.

We started at ML&B the same day. Even with our office doors shut, which mine rarely was, we could hear the other's phone ring through our common wall. Cambridge supervisions had taught me if I couldn't explain a problem and solution so a layman could understand it, I didn't understand it myself. So I strove to simplify tax issues as much as possible; clients welcomed the effort. Years in the butcher shop may also have helped me discuss tax with clients because it had given me a good grounding in business, and corporate taxation is all about business. It can be understood as, essentially, the answers to three questions: *Have you made a profit? If so, how much do you owe Uncle Sam? Can you avoid that debt without doing time?*

Perhaps, as some said, clients found me intelligible because I oversimplified, being a tax neophyte lacking, say, WAM IV's specialized knowledge, and ignorant of the subtleties of a problem. Or perhaps they just appreciated my predilection to say bluntly what I thought they should do and opine on their chances of success if they did it. (I'm often wrong, but never in doubt.) For any or all these reasons, or because I was a colorful cuckoo in a nest of subfusc suits, clients often called for advice.

One afternoon, after a morning when my phone had rung incessantly, WAM IV stormed into my office, slammed the door behind him, and screamed, *Why does your phone ring all the time!* He knew the answer. *Well, clients call me. Don't they call you?* He slammed the door again on the way out. That my ringing phone drove WAM IV mad on the other side of the wall caused me no undue regret.

*   *   *

Shortly after 10 a.m. one morning, we were all summoned to an emergency meeting in Tom Lefevre's corner office. The chief executive of the firm's largest client had just called to say he had won a new car in a charity raffle the night before, and the value of the car, which was taxable income to him, would push him into a higher tax bracket and cost him more than the car was worth. What should he do?

Our nine-man tax department scrambled *en masse* for the answer. The search was fraught; would we find an acceptable solution PDQ. Within an hour, we had it: refuse to accept the car. At today's billing rates, that blitz cost either the CEO or his employer $7,000 (£4,500), assuming it was billed, or the firm if it was written off as PD (practice development), the euphemism for wining, dining, and generally pandering to clients. The taxpayer was the CEO, not the company, and the amount at issue could not have been great. The panic to satisfy him demonstrated his power to take the public company's business elsewhere, and the partners' slavish fears that if in the least dissatisfied, he might. Peers and partners dwelled in anxiety about whether clients might move to another law firm. In the case of the largest clients, anxiety rose to hysteria.

Most mornings around 11 a.m., a bent old man shuffled through the tax department toward the corner offices where the senior partners sat. Perhaps twenty-five minutes later, he passed by again on his way to the elevator bank. His hands were stained a chestnut color, as was the apron he wore over work shirt and pants. In his left hand, he lugged a worn shoeshine box.

I never learned his name, or anything about him, though I think he was Italian. He crept from office to office, offering to shine the lawyers' shoes. Some regularly accepted. Herb Odell and I were discussing a problem he'd assigned me when the shoeshine man appeared in the doorway. Herb crooked his finger to motion him in, swiveled his chair, swung his legs from under to the side of his desk, and received brush and polish from the old man at his feet without pausing our conversation or dousing his cigar.

Shoeshine men on their knees at a partner's feet were a common tableau in big firm law offices. One made the rounds at the Wall Street firm where I'd worked the summer before. Associates often aped their betters and had the shoeshine man spiff up their shoes as well; I was not among them.

ML&B was not unique; what it was becoming, the other big firms were too. America's 1960s economy powered changes that ineluctably sapped the professional foundations of big-firm law practice. By the mid to late 1970s, corporate law practice was fully commercialized, a service business, not a profession. Six engines, economic and social, torpedoed traditional firms—the growth of in-house law departments, fee pressure, death of the retainer, plethora of new laws and regulations, rise of the accountants, and distrust of outside counsel. The first three led to lower billings at old-line firms, the second trio to competition from the new. The net effect was to sink firms that couldn't adapt. Today, forty-nine years after I worked there, ML&B is the world's ninth largest law firm with two thousand lawyers in thirty offices around the world generating $2 billion per annum in revenue—a complex international service business, not a professional law practice—its practitioners service providers with revenue generation (partners) or billable hour (associates) targets to meet.

* * *

I realized only gradually, over weeks and months, that I'd become a piece-worker like my grandmother, my garments memoranda and opinions instead of frilly ladies' blouses and, once again, the huckster I'd had to be at Pennsauken Meats. I felt I'd been had, lured with attar of roses and walnut-paneled walls, with ninety-six years' honorable history and distinguished reputation and with gentile gentlemen like Tom Lefevre, Al McDowell, and H. Peter Somers. ML&B had not deliberately deceived me; like all the big firms, market pressures were forcing it to commercialize, perhaps insensibly to its seniors. Nevertheless, I felt baited and switched, like the wife who believes she's wed a paragon and in days discovers he's a cheat. Disillusioned and angry, my anger and arrogance showed.

I flaunted my contempt in ways small and large. Back in Philly, I rented a flat in a very slowly gentrifying south-center city area a few blocks from where I'd been born. My birth block was unreconstructed slum, a street too far south for gentrification. No ML&B lawyer lived near me, and I wore my inner-city digs as a badge of egalitarian superiority,[3] neglecting to mention that my flat was broken into and stripped of all worth taking within a month of moving in.

My inner Trotsky had not died when I joined ML&B while I schemed to win the policy job at Treasury I wanted. Pending that, with several non-firm lawyers, I opened a free legal clinic to represent poor tenants in fights with slumlords. I held its organizational meeting in ML&B's main conference room so my somewhat scuzzy pro bono cocounsels might shock my uptown peers. The clinic generated squeals of outrage from sued landlords and favorable stories in the city's press. ML&B's seniors were not amused by the publicity or the clinic's anticapitalist slant.

Shortly after I'd been shown the article on big-firm partners' profits, my mentor, David O'Brien, called me to his office to ask how I was getting on. He knew that private practice had been my second choice, had seen the pro bono lawyers file into the conference room, that I lived far from the Main Line and did not attend the first several firm functions, so he could not have been surprised when I blurted out, *Dave, we're not practicing law. All we're doing is selling pork chops.*

Italian immigrant tailors in South Philadelphia advertised in the local papers, an ad of theirs caught my eye, and I decided to have a three-piece suit made for the office. The wool suiting was a light denim blue with wide, bold, purple-red stripes, like material for a baseball team's uniform. Firm gossip soon dubbed it the baseball suit. The receptionist's eyes widened, the corners of her mouth drooped into a frown the first morning I passed her kitted out in it. Its broad colored stripes, too light for business blue field, and tight waistcoat gave it a 1930s gangsterish air. It did not give off wealth or pomp, and was like nothing else at ML&B. The baseball suit spat *Fuck you!* to everyone at the firm, lawyers and secretaries alike. I retired it from service when I left ML&B.

---

[3] See Billy Joel, *Uptown Girl*. Available on YouTube.

WAM IV, and I in the baseball suit, were waiting for the elevator one lunchtime. As the elevator doors parted on a car packed with partners—including Mr. MacIntosh, the firm's Managing Partner—Bill whispered, *Please, don't say anything to me while we're in the elevator.* I turned to him as the car began its nineteen-floor drop and said in a raised, clear voice, *Bill, what do you think about squirrels?* Heads swiveled; alarm appeared on a few faces. Mr. MacIntosh ostentatiously looked away. WAM IV turned boiled-lobster red and, except in tax meetings, never spoke to me again.

Tax season, the four months before corporate then individual U.S. tax returns are due, runs from January to April 15. Partners were often in the office on Saturdays from February on, helping answer the flood of questions that arise while returns are prepared. My office was first on the left as you entered the tax department, so I could see whomever came in. Snow was threatening on a late February Saturday morning around 10 a.m. when Tom Lefevre passed by my office with a copy of *I and Thou* tucked under his arm; Buber's book of moral philosophy was on the bestseller list at the time. Tom said, *Good morning*, as he passed. Instead of a greeting, I blurted, *What are you doing with that book?* Tom paused, turned, stared at me for several seconds, then said, *I read, too, Dan*, and walked on.

A few minutes later, I knocked on his office door, entered at his *Come in*, and apologized. He raised his eyes, fixed me with a doleful stare, lowered them again to the Tax Court Reporter open on his desk, and motioned me from the room. The dried sweat smell of my shame still wreathes me, forty-eight years later.

2. Knaves

I believe in America are Amerigo Bonasera's first words to Don Corleone as he pleads *for justice* in *The Godfather* movie's first frame. Growing up, I heard something like it from my father; it's something I might have said my first day as a lawyer at Treasury's Office of International Tax Counsel (ITC). The Don gives the undertaker *justice* in exchange for the fealty he swears. I gave justice to no one during my eighteen months at Treasury and did not believe in America when I left.

A year earlier, ML&B had rewarded me well at bonus time, despite my contemptuous behavior and protenant advocacy. Clients continued to call for advice; my billables were healthy. But everyone at ML&B knew I was incorrigibly unclubbable and, no matter how much rain I made or hours billed, would never make, nor wanted to make, partner. They also knew ML&B had been my second choice; first was a policy job at Treasury. A few months later, they corralled it for me.

At a weekly ML&B tax department meeting soon after I started, Tom Lefevre asked for a volunteer to specialize in the Internal Revenue Code's (Code) foreign sections. When no one else volunteered, I raised my hand. Two years at Cambridge had made me less provincial and convinced me business's future was global. If business was going global, international tax lawyers had a future.

The foreign sections overlaid on the Code's economic and accounting foundations three nontax concepts—jurisdiction,[4] antiavoidance,[5] bilateral tax treaties.[6] These sections do not redefine income and expense for foreign contexts; rather, they allocate them between jurisdictions and attempt to prevent offshore tax avoidance. Most U.S. tax lawyers shied from learning the foreign sections. The few who didn't formed a small, close-knit Acela Express coterie.

Stan Weiss was one of their brotherhood. A partner in ML&B's DC office, he had worked in international tax at Treasury and with me my first year at the firm. Stan heard of an opening on the ITC staff, asked if I was interested, and when I said *Yes*, recommended me for it. ML&B seconded his recommendation. I interviewed with Bob Cole, ITC's head, in mid-February 1971. A few weeks later, he offered me an attorney-advisor slot on his staff, to begin in June after a routine FBI background check.

* * *

Cole's offer did more than offer me worthwhile work. A year earlier, I had married Leslie J. Scallet, a plump, bright, kind, twenty-four-year-old entering her third year at the University of Pennsylvania law school. Like me, Leslie was Jewish and interested in a policy-law career, but there, the similarities ended. Her mother, an heiress to a St. Louis department store fortune, was happily married to the head of research at Budweiser. They were socially prominent and lived in a gated community in an imposing, faux-antebellum-style house, like Tara in *Gone with the Wind*. Four

[4] I.R.C. §§ 861–864, source of income and expense rules.
[5] I.R.C. §§ 951–954.
[6] Treaties with other countries to avoid double taxation of the same item of income.

two-story white columns flanking the front door raised expectations Mammy would open it when you knocked.

We met shortly after I joined ML&B. That first date, I told her I was damaged goods, and if I had an affair, it would be on the rebound. Undeterred, a week later, she took me as her first lover, and for the three years we were together, she salvaged what she could of my capacity to trust.

The FBI's background check proved not to be routine. The information they uncovered led Cole to withdraw his offer; I'd been hired and fired in six weeks without working a day. Leslie and I were deep into moving to Washington. We had pledged some of her inherited stock to secure a loan, with which we bought a three-story, four-bedroom, brown-brick town house at Thirty-Fourth and P Streets in Georgetown, the smartest part of town, and had set the date for the movers. I'd promised Leslie that I would bear any loss when we sold the house, but any gain would be for her, since it was her stock she pledged. Not only would I be unemployed but would lose money reselling the house we'd just bought.

I appealed to ML&B for help, reasoning that if I didn't get the Treasury post, it would reflect worse on them than me; when word got out, clients might want to know what kind of associates they were hiring who couldn't pass a routine FBI character check. The firm made inquiries and discovered it was my pro bono work for poor tenants that scuppered me, not traces of my misspent youth; policy staffers who'd represented poor people were unwelcome in Mr. Nixon's government. Mr. MacIntosh, ML&B's managing partner, called his friend Hugh Scott, U.S. senator from Pennsylvania and Republican Senate Minority leader, and a few days later, Cole renewed his offer.

Nixon by then had been in office two years, and my experience at the sharp point of his right-wing government did not augur well. I should have thought carefully before accepting Cole's offer a second time. But we owned a fancy Georgetown house, I was twenty-nine, and winner's cancer was already devouring my judgment.

* * *

At 7:30 a.m. on a warm morning in late June 1971, I head my bike down M Street in Georgetown toward Main Treasury, a grand whited sepulcher at Fifteenth and Pennsylvania Ave. This Greek revival building fronting Pennsylvania Ave—with a 350-foot north facade, Ionic-columned portico, and White House next door—is familiar to anyone who's looked at the back of a U.S. $10 bill. Pedaling past the White House fence toward

Treasury's underground garage, I grow a tad taller, my voice deepens, and I'm Rick Blaine, pistol in hand, about to tell Captain Renault, *Not so fast, Louis.*[7]

I report to Cole's third-floor office suite, and a secretary shows me five doors north up a hushed, high-ceilinged corridor to mine. To the south from my office window, I can just see the Washington Monument on the National Mall. Cole comes in an hour later, welcomes me, and hands me my first project: analyze a draft private member's bill to bail out some mining companies, and tell the Assistant Secretary whether Treasury should support it.

The U.S. Constitution's origination clause says, *All bills for raising Revenue shall originate in the House of Representatives.* Even presidents must use a friendly member of Congress to introduce tax legislation they want. Not infrequently, large corporates avail themselves of this rule and have their congressman or woman introduce a private member's bill to fix one of their tax problems or give them a tax benefit to which they would otherwise not be entitled.

In that summer of 1971, Anaconda Copper, Kennecott Copper, and Cerro (AKC) had a tax problem they needed fixed. A few weeks earlier, Salvador Allende, democratically elected Marxist president of Chile, completed the nationalization (expropriation if you like) of AKC's copper mines. They received nothing in return. General Augusto Pinochet led a U.S.-sponsored military coup a few years later that toppled Allende, who committed suicide, or so we're told. But in 1971, Allende sat tall in the saddle and inflicted a collective $80 million capital loss on AKC ($500 million in 2018 dollars). The copper companies realized no tax benefit from the loss of their mines; the Code only allowed them to take their losses against capital gains, and not unusually, they had none. Now they wanted Congress to allow them to deduct these losses from their ordinary income, which would have given them a roughly $40 million tax benefit (a quarter billion in 2018 dollars) and halved their losses.

The Code's treatment of AKC's capital gains and losses was symmetrical and fair. Had AKC had a $500 million capital gain, it would have been taxed at the much lower 15 percent capital gain rate rather than the 48 percent ordinary income rate. AKC wanted it both ways—plusses taxed at the

---

[7] *Casablanca*, 1942.

lowest rate, minuses allowed at the highest. The private member's bill I was to analyze was their begging bowl.

I detailed in a memo why the law change AKC wanted was a Treasury raid, and recommended we oppose their bill, which would kill it. A private member's bill that goes to the Hill without Treasury's imprimatur is DOA, dead on arrival. Wednesday at day's end, I sent the memo to the Assistant Secretary's office, and next day, Jack Nolan, Deputy Assistant Secretary for Tax Policy, asked me to meet him at 10 a.m. on Saturday morning to discuss it.

The offices of high-ranking Treasury officials are large and imposing, Nolan's no exception. He sat behind a seven-foot-long, three-foot-wide mahogany desk awash in papers. The tax world regarded Nolan as the real Assistant Tax Secretary and his putative boss—Edwin S. Cohen, Assistant Secretary for Tax—no more than the Administration's front man. Nolan was in his late fifties, slightly above middle height, balding, colorless, formal, and efficient. He had been a senior, highly regarded tax partner at Miller and Chevalier, DC's preeminent white-shoe tax firm.

He began by thanking me for meeting on a Saturday morning, then larded praise on my memo. He picked it from the paper heap before him, read conclusions and recommendation aloud, then said, *I agree. We'll oppose the bill.* I'd stopped a theft, balked the forces of evil, was Wyatt Earp at the OK corral, a smoking gun in each hand. Adrenalin whipped through me, and I thought, *So this is what power feels like.* I'd been given morphine injections for months, aged twenty-one, to quell pain from a broken neck; this felt better.

I rose, was half turned to the door, when Nolan said, *Is there anything we can do for them?—We?* Should Treasury warp the Code to subsidize behemoth mining companies? The glow Nolan's compliments and concurrence kindled faded along with my presumption of power. Reality flooded back; once again, I was standing on the Tabriz before his desk. This was Nixon's first-term Republican administration, enraged that a Marxist had won a fair election in America's backyard, confronted with a plea for help from American miners who'd had *their* copper stolen by a *commie*; what did I expect?

A way to appease Nolan and still thwart the copper companies came to mind; I answered: *Maybe they could get a ruling.* IRS will rule on matters of law at a taxpayer's request if the question involves a tax principle of general interest. It will not rule on facts, or mixed fact and law questions, like whether AKC's stock in their nationalized foreign subsidiaries was wholly worthless; normally does not initiate a ruling but waits for a taxpayer to request it; and will not alter standing interpretations of law to accommodate a taxpayer. The IRS has complete discretion to rule or not, for or against the taxpayer.

To rule that Chile's nationalizations entitled AKC to an ordinary loss would require the Service to investigate facts surrounding the takings and expand existing law in AKC's favor. I thought it would be an arctic day in hell before they did either, which was why AKC had come knocking on Treasury's door begging for a statutory change.

* * *

But Nolan seemed pleased, which should have worried me. I assumed the ruling idea appealed because it was sufficiently plausible to fob off the miners. A more experienced, humbler Treasury lawyer would have reflected that Nolan was an old Washington hand who'd forgotten more about applicable law, rulings, and how the IRS worked than this twenty-nine-year-old Washington ingenue before him would ever learn. But I was young and snotty, no use to talk to me.

Nolan and three AKC representatives were in the Secretary's grand third-floor conference room when I entered two days later on Monday morning at 11 a.m. The three older men were chatting familiarly. A man my age, clearly the miners' bag carrier, stood two steps outside the clot of elders and their conversation. Five people meeting in so large a room—nearly a tractor trailer long and one and a half times the width of one—was incongruous and injected a lugubrious note. A meeting in Nolan's office conference room would have been more comfortable, but Nolan presumably wanted to impress the AKC reps that Treasury took their problem seriously.

The older men were Ray Sherfy, Fred Peel, and Nolan. Sherfy was chief lobbyist for the American Mining Congress and brother to Larry Sherfy, one of Jack Nolan's ex–law partners at Miller and Chevalier. Peel had written the four-volume bible on consolidated corporate tax returns and was also an ex-partner of Nolan's at M&C. The gathering was more a cousin's club than a business meeting.

Nolan introduced me to Sherfy and Peel. Sherfy introduced me to the bag carrier, and we all sat down at the twenty-five-foot-long conference table: Nolan at its head, Sherfy at his left hand, Peel next to Sherfy, and the bag carrier next to Peel. I sat, ignored, on Nolan's right some way down the table, within earshot to hear and take notes, but not participate in the conversation.

Nolan spoke first. *Ray, Treasury will not support your bill.* The suppliants' faces fell simultaneously, like the gartered legs of a chorus line. Sherfy began to argue; Nolan cut him off.

I'm sorry, Ray, but the Administration cannot support legislation to help you out.

Jack, is thar anythin yuh kin do fur us?

Well, we think you might be able to get a ruling.

Jack, rulin's take a long time, and we need help quick.

Nolan swiveled right, looked down the table at me, and said, *Dan, how long do you think it will take us to get a ruling for them?* The others' heads snapped left from Jack to me, but they were too far away to notice my flush. *Us get a ruling for them?* Surely, Treasury didn't procure rulings; taxpayers did that. It hadn't occurred to me Treasury would run interference for the mining companies with the Service (the trade term for IRS), heavy it, put Treasury's ponderous finger on the scale, do covertly what it refused to do openly. It seemed the Nixon administration did not object to bailing out the miners, so long as it was done without the public noticing.

We rose, and Ray Sherfy hurried down and around the long conference table to shake my hand. He gripped it less perfunctorily than at our introduction fifteen minutes earlier, held it for a moment or two, clutched my elbow with his left hand, pulled me a little closer, and said, *What was yawh name again, young man?*

Dan Burt.

Waal, wuh'll have lots tuh talk about tuh get this rollin'. Y'all free for lunch tuhmorrah? I had a new best friend.

* * *

On the corner of Eighteenth and K Streets, the heart of the lobbyist gold coast, stood the marquee of the Maison Blanche, the capital's premier French restaurant. I arrived there on time at 12:15 p.m. next day, sweaty from the heat of the sun after a seven-minute pedal from Treasury; chained my bike to one of two thin, steel curbside poles supporting the marquee; and entered. Mine was the only bike in sight.

Ray, Fred, and the bag carrier were waiting. The restaurant was almost wine cellar cool, paneled in dark wood, with a burgundy-red, thick nap wool carpet. The ceiling was high, the tables sufficiently far apart, the carpets absorptive so that it was easy to hear your dining partners, but not another table's conversation. There were no food smells. This was ground zero of the three-martini lunch.

Jean-Pierre, the owner, greeted me like a relative, though we'd never met. Clearly, he'd been told to look out for me, and certainly knew *Monsieur Sherfy*. He showed me to an ample, round table in the right rear corner of the dining room farthest from the entrance, the most private spot in the restaurant. I shook hands with my hosts and settled down to my first, long, boozy lobbyist's lunch.

Surely, Treasury rules forbade staff accepting expensive lunches of the sort I was about to have, but no one at Treasury had told me about them, and I would have ignored them in any case, confident I couldn't be bought and already fond of fine French food and wines. A lifetime's dinners at *La Tour d'Argent* in Paris could not have suborned me to help my hosts obtain their ruling nor curb my plans to scuttle it. But the Maison Blanche's Camparis, *canard a l'orange*, 1959 clarets, maroon plush chairs and sparkling linens, the irony of being feted by people I was trying to screw, added a spy's piquancy to this and frequent future lunches.

That first lunch lasted until the staff began discreetly trying to prepare the tables around us for the dinner sitting. I remember my two double Camparis, my aperitif of choice at the time; our two bottles of claret; *coupe aux marrons*, my first experience of the dessert and a favorite ever since; port; and superb, blacklisted Havana cigar, but no appetizer or entrée. I remember Sherfy leaning toward me as soon as I was seated and saying, *Yuh shur look young. We thought yuh were a summer intern when we first saw yuh*. A little later, he told me how bright my future was, how keen the big DC law firms would be to hire me, especially if the Mining Congress recommended me. The contrapositive, how bleak my way would be if I disappointed the miners, went unsaid. I left in a haze of bonhomie, wobbled my way back to Treasury, and slept at my desk till almost quitting time two hours later.

But business had been done, between the bouquets and the port. AKC were to draft and submit a ruling request to IRS's Branch Five, the foreign sections specialists, within two weeks. A blind copy would be sent to me, and after a few days, I'd call the branch's head so that he was aware of Treasury's interest and desire to expedite the request. I'd bird-dog the ruling thereafter until the Service issued it.

* * *

Following that lunch, until just before Christmas, I delayed, dissembled, leaked, and undercut the ruling's progress every way I could. Treasury sent a letter to the IRS commissioner supporting AKC's request a day after IRS received it. I met with Branch Five's boss, Ed Goldwag, a looming, gentle, six-foot-plus-tall career civil servant, gave him an unvarnished history of the ruling request's provenance, and promised to help derail it. Branch Five opposed issuing the ruling after they studied it and dragged their feet.

A Treasury economist, Marcia Field, introduced me to her husband, Tom, who published *Tax Analysts and Advocates*, a fledgling, muckraking journal for tax specialists dedicated to giving an unvarnished, generally left-leaning, reformist account of tax news. I told Tom in detail about the AKC ruling request, and he printed a piece critical of what was happening. But the mainstream press didn't pick the issue up.

Branch Five dug its heels in deeper. I defended them when Nolan complained about how long the ruling was taking and continued enjoying long, sybaritic lunches at the Maison Blanche on the Mining Congress's tab, sometimes with Sherfy and the bag carrier, or, more frequently as the process dawdled on, the bag carrier alone. Invitations to Maison Blanche lunches dwindled as Indian summer turned to proper autumn and the ruling remained bogged down; they stopped completely when the trees were nearly bare and there was still no ruling.

Nolan's frustration mounted. He was scheduled to end his two-year stint at Treasury early in the new year and return through the revolving door to Miller & Chevalier, where he and his partners would profit from his knowledge gained, enhanced reputation, and contacts made or improved during his Treasury sojourn. In November, Secretary of the Treasury John Connally—former Texas governor and passenger in the front seat of the limousine with Kennedy in Dallas eight years earlier, who had taken a bullet as well—wrote to the Commissioner about the ruling, to the effect of *Get this done!* In late December 1971, the IRS published Revenue Ruling 1972-1,[8] the first ruling of the coming year, giving the miners what they asked for. The reward for my quixotic labors was a jaundiced view of the American way of making law, my first experience of fine clarets and Burgundies, and a penchant for *coupe aux marrons*.

* * *

[8] IRS Rev. Rul. 72-1, 1972-1 C.B.; p. 52.

Sunday, August 15, 1971, my crew, Anne, and I had been racing my 5-0-5, a two-person trapeze dinghy, off Galesville, Maryland, and were stowing the boat when news from a car radio announced Nixon had upended the global economy. Anticipated delights of the coming evening with my crew vanished. (Though I was married, Anne was not my wife. None of my four wives have been sailors). I quickly put the boat to bed and headed home.

America had a large trade deficit in 1971, as it does as I type almost fifty years later. The deficit's root cause is the dollar's role as the world's reserve currency. International trade, in oil, for example, is conducted in dollars, which creates demand for dollars independent of U.S. economic performance, and inflates its value. The powerhouse countries could not agree on how to solve the problem then, any more than they can today. That Sunday, alone and unassisted, Nixon tried to cut this Gordian knot by eliminating dollar convertibility to gold, enacting an export subsidy called DISC, the acronym for Domestic International Sales Corporation, and introducing wage and price controls, a triad that history recalls as the Nixon Shock. I was the ITC staffer responsible for DISC at Treasury.

For several years, Treasury and Congress had mooted enacting DISC to help reduce the chronic U.S. trade deficit. The leading economists said DISC wouldn't work. America's trading partners complained it was an illegal export subsidy under the General Agreement on Trade and Tariffs, to which the U.S. was a signatory, as well as the World Trade Organization's rules, of which the U.S. was a member, and vowed to challenge it in international trade tribunals if enacted. No one in DC thought it had a hope of passage, so no attention was paid to it. I was handed the DISC watching brief when I joined ITC, but had barely familiarized myself with it when Nixon hurled DISC into the Congressional hopper.

Literally overnight, passing DISC was the administration's top legislative tax priority, damn its legality under GATT or WTO rules, damn squeals from America's trading partners. The country's manufacturers were dithyrambic at the thought of a tax regime that might cut their taxes by half or more, depending on how much they exported. But few knew much more about DISC than its acronym; my phone rang off the hook.

* * *

DISC aimed to boost manufacturing exports—Caterpillar backhoes, IBM computers, Clarke drill presses, Boeing airplanes—but it was unclear what was *manufacturing* for DISC purposes. However, common sense, policy, and the DISC's drafting history decreed that mining minerals in America was one thing *manufacturing* was not for DISC purposes, nor intended to be. Freeport Gulf Sulfur's lead lobbyist thought otherwise.

With a roughneck's grip and a brawler's gait, burly Bill Byrne was an atypical corporate legislative affairs director. Slightly over middle height, in dark blue and gray expensive wool off-the-rack suits, he eschewed a DC office and emollient manner for bluntness and determination. Freeport mined soils and seas across the globe, in some of earth's most inhospitable places, including vast sulfur deposits in the Louisiana bayous, and Byrne fit the image of the hard, implacable global miner he championed.

When Treasury sent DISC to the House, it didn't cover Freeport. Byrne saw to it that when the House passed DISC and sent it to the Senate, it did. The United States has a bicameral Congress; tax bills must originate in the House then go to the Senate, the upper chamber, for consideration. If the Senate disagrees with the House, it passes its version of the legislation, and the two chambers work out their differences in a joint conference. Senate Finance would have to cut the Freeport provision from the DISC legislation the House sent it if it wished to conform to Treasury's original legislation. Bill was only halfway home when the Senate Finance Committee took DISC up.

Bob Cole walked Byrne up the hall to my office almost immediately after Senate Finance started considering DISC, introduced us, and left him to make Freeport's case. Byrne trotted out his arguments calmly, without threats, or job offers bald or subtle. Nothing he said countered the facts that neither Freeport nor the mining industry was suffering from foreign competition. DISC's aim, to help U.S. manufacturers suffering from that competition—not sulfur mining companies that were not—was why miners had been excluded from DISC in the first place. Freeport just wanted a handout.

Though noncommittal, I was clearly unpersuaded. We had another meeting, and a lunch in which Byrne and his DC law firm pressed their case, then parted on polite terms as Senate Finance prepared to vote.

Hugh Scott, Senate Minority leader, was managing the bill for the Administration in the Senate. I was Treasury's DISC expert. Late the afternoon before Senate Finance's evening vote, I persuaded Cole to strip Freeport's amendment from the bill. Cole checked with Nolan, who said it was Cole's call. Cole sent me to Capitol Hill, alone, to tell Scott the Administration wanted the Freeport amendment cut from the Senate's version of the House bill.

It had been dark for two hours when I arrived to beard Scott. Old Glory was flying from the flagstaff above the Capitol's north wing, the Senate side of the building, proclaiming the Senate in session, much as the Union Jack flag flies above Buckingham Palace only when the Queen is in residence. Senate Finance would vote DISC out of committee in a few hours, and I was shown in to Scott immediately.

His Capitol office suite was the size of a small ballroom; 150 people could have comfortably enjoyed cocktails in it, as they no doubt occasionally did. Ranking minority member of Senate Finance, slack skinned, jowly, run to fat, and looking older than his seventy-one years, Scott was waiting for me. He skipped the pleasantries and asked what Treasury wanted him to do. I said we wanted Freeport out and explained why. He accepted what I said without question, said he'd take care of it, and turned to an aide who had appeared about the next item of business. The meeting lasted less than five minutes.

It was after visiting hours, and the tourists were gone as I marched across the empty Capitol Rotunda floor to the double-height bronze east doors. I listened to my heel plants echo from the frescoed canopy 180 feet above me, the height of three mature oak trees laid end to end, glanced one hundred feet across the Rotunda to the House side, and felt neither awed nor diminished but rather comfortable, as if I belonged here. Outside, I paused beneath the east portico, took a deep breath, and exulted in the crystalline late-October night. Washington's humid evenings were gone with summer; the glow from a full, yellow-orange harvest moon to the south fired the Capitol Dome, while thirty feet below me at the bottom of the east Capitol steps waited my wife. It was not the first time I could have used a slave at my ear whispering, *Memento mori*, nor the last when his absence brought me grief, but it was the first time megalomania had gripped so tightly.

In my mind's ear, the Marine Corps band played the "Halls of Montezuma" as I paraded down the Capitol's steps to my wife's brown Chevrolet sedan. Almost breathless, I jumped in beside her, shouted, *I fucked them! I fucked them!* hugged and kissed her fiercely, and exulted as we sped down the drive from the Capitol to celebratory Bloody Marys and curry dinner at our favorite Indian. That night, I made love to her with a passion often lacking.

* * *

Russell Long—son of Huey Long, the late populist governor of Louisiana assassinated in 1935—was the long-serving senior U.S. Senator for

Louisiana, a Democrat, and at the time, chairman of Senate Finance. All tax legislation must pass through Senate Finance, and Long was commonly conceded to be the second most powerful tax legislator in Congress, after Wilbur Mills, chairman of the House Ways and Means Committee, where all tax legislation originates. Freeport was one of Louisiana's largest as well as most powerful businesses.

ITC's secretaries didn't start work till 9 a.m., an hour after I was at my Treasury desk, so when my phone rang a few minutes after eight the following morning, I picked up the receiver myself. No hello, no how are you; before I could say a word, the caller growled, *You did that, you little son-of-a-bitch! Well, son, lemme tell yuh, in a half hour, you're gonna change your mind.* Click. I recognized the angry voice but did not expect Byrne to be happy nor care that he wasn't.

Bob Cole appeared in my doorway some forty minutes later. *Dan, I'm sorry, but Senator Long's chief of staff called and said if we don't put Freeport back in, Long will vote against the bill*; Cole didn't have to add, *And we won't have one.* If Chairman Long voted against the bill, it would be dead, but there was too much else in the DISC legislation that Long, America's manufacturers, and the Nixon administration wanted for Long to scuttle it. It was a bluff.

But as Byrne foretold, "I" had already changed my mind. Cole had called Scott's office and told them to include Freeport before he crept down the hall to lean against my office doorjamb and tell me. A few weeks later, IRS prepublished the Chilean ruling. My quixotic charges had failed; unhorsed, routed, the arms of the windmill continued to turn as the long decay of my American faith began.

3. The Revolving Door

I cast about for an exit from the lists, and spied three: private practice, the *commentariat*, teaching, the first best signposted and most used.

Bob Cole, my first boss at Treasury, was a thin, bandy-legged, mincing man. Slightly under middle height, say five feet seven, thirty-nine years old, he wore a five-o'clock shadow at 9 a.m. and spoke in a reedy, nasal, Queens whine. He squirreled credentials: accounting from Wharton, law from Harvard, two years U.S. Air Force, a Master's from the LSE. In the late 1960s, he quit a New York law firm to pick up another, International

Tax Counsel to the U.S. Treasury, burnish his reputation, and cultivate future clients.

The U.S. government has no senior civil service. From the Secretary of the Treasury through Under, Deputy, Assistant, Deputy Assistant Secretaries, staff heads like ITC, to me seven levels down, Treasury employees are political appointees. The federal government is run as a spoils system; among the spoils are senior agency jobs.

Accountants, businessmen, bankers, economists, agronomists, scientists, lawyers, PR specialists, all manner of professionals migrate each year from private sector to public, shoals of them, like herring, in the year after a presidential election. There they fin for two or three years in upper-level federal jobs at the big regulatory agencies—Treasury, IRS, Commerce, EPA, et al.—fatten their résumés, then return from the federal pond to tributary law firms, banks, consulting firms, to earn far more than when they left them. These transitory bureaucrats issue rulings, regulations, standards, and advice governing U.S. and foreign businesses; negotiate government contracts; allow or deny mergers and acquisitions, drug sales, advertising, safety requirements, pollution controls; tax or spare tax; absolve, penalize, and prosecute. They bet that when they root around for a private-sector job at the end of their agency stints, the corporations and major law, accounting, and lobbying firms who appeared before them will remember and reward the expertise, contacts, and *understanding* they showed. It's a bet they rarely lose. This hallmark of the federal spoils system is called *the revolving door*, and companies dealing with senior agency employees often remind them subtly—or baldly, as Sherfy did me—how it spins.

ITC was updating the Code's source rules when I arrived, and Cole assigned me to work on them. These rules classify items like sales proceeds, royalties, interest, and capital gains as foreign or U.S. by applying U.S. tax principles regardless of how a foreign country treats them. They affect all international businesses, some banks among them, more than others. A bank can use a favorable source rule change to avoid most, sometimes all U.S. tax on its worldwide income; an unfavorable one can increase its taxes dramatically. The New York money center banks were intensely interested in Treasury's source rule revisions.

The first thing John Stollard, tax director of Globalbank, one of the world's largest, said to me when I joined him and Cole for coffee at the Washington Hotel across from Treasury, was how lucky I was to be working on the source rules. He had asked to meet the new boy in charge of redrafting them when he shuttled down from NYC, and Cole arranged our coffee klatch. Stollard oozed charm and friendliness, offered help should I have any questions, then detailed Global's worries about how our treatment of guaranty fees and original-issue discount would affect certain Global financings. He hoped the new regulations would assuage the bank's fears. Cole assured him they would.

I was less sure. Cole dismissed me; he and Stollard went to lunch, and I recrossed the street to work. For the next few weeks, I studied the source rules—Global's *ask*, relevant policy, and the rules' history—but found no basis for accommodating the bank. Cole had ordered me to give him my conclusions orally before depositing them in print. I did; he told me not to bother writing them up and, a few days later, reassigned the source rules project to another ITC lawyer. Stollard I never heard from again.

Cole had given me a plum, by his lights, assigning those rules to me. Constantly in touch with the New York banks, he knew they paid handsomely for ex-Treasury staff, and that their outside law and accounting firms paid even better; he expected gratitude. He didn't get it, nor did the companies he prodded me to help. I hadn't come to Treasury to beef up credentials and land a Wall or K Street corner office. While ITC opened the doors to those offices, and the people in them seeking my help dangled jobs before me like zookeepers feeding seals, I didn't jump for them; life as a performing seal seemed charmless.

After the Freeport DISC amendment, and the copper companies ruling, my contempt for Cole and tax politics was unmissable. I challenged him in meetings and tête-à-têtes, refused to adopt a position I thought wrong, groused to all who would listen about what I'd seen and experienced, and manifested my contempt in color. Treasury allowed their lawyers to choose their office walls' color; all were satisfied with the white on them when they joined. I painted mine a decadent lilac redolent of Oscar Wilde and *À Rebours*, then left the door open so passers-by from the Secretary of the Treasury to visiting bank chairmen to cleaners could not help but see them. Cole and his deputy, Bob Patrick, averted their eyes when they passed, and my five peers on the ITC staff avoided me.

*   *   *

Cole hadn't the courage to fire me for general bolshiness, or bad taste. Instead, he had me kicked upstairs in early 1972 to be attorney advisor to Eddy Cohen, then Under Secretary for International Tax. America's major trading partners had sued America under the General Agreement on Trade and Tariffs, claiming DISC was an impermissible tax subsidy, as they vowed they would when Nixon proposed it. My job was to defend the indefensible, which I did, poorly.

My brief on behalf of America was sent to the GATT tribunal in late spring, and a few weeks later, I followed it to Geneva with Cohen et al. for three days of hearings on our trading partners' complaint. Cohen argued DISC was GATT-legal, though he, I, and everyone else knew that was false. Several years later, the GATT judges ruled for the complainants. The U.S. replaced DISC with FISC, Foreign International Sales Corporation, which, a few more years later, the GATT tribunal also declared an illegal tax subsidy. What little faith I might have had in American government when I began advising Eddy Cohen had vanished by the time I departed Geneva.

Cole left Treasury several years later and hung his shingle out. His first client was Globalbank. But insider lore, like payback debt, is short dated. His law firm was no roaring success, and a few years later, it closed. He ended his career as the embodiment of Uriah Heep, a lobbyist in the DC office of a large international law firm.

* * *

When I started at Treasury, I gave no thought to a job when I left. If I had, muckraking journalism would not have occurred to me. After being steam-rollered by taxpayers, their Senators, and Representatives, after dissembling for America in the DISC/GATT hearings, it did.

Phil Stern, an heir to the Sears fortune, left-wing member of the commentariat, Washington gadfly, needed help locating the business weevils in the Code's foreign tax sections for his forthcoming book *The Rape of the Treasury*. His first—*The Great Treasury Raid*, detailing for the uninitiated how the rich used tax shelters to avoid tax—had been a best seller. He hoped to repeat the feat by exposing tax perks available to multinationals. Marcia Field referred me to him, and I agreed to help as soon as he contacted me.

Stern was less than a tyro about how the U.S. taxed foreign profits, an area arcane even to most tax professionals. I spent several months explaining the rules to him, as well as the wheezes with which American companies exploited them to lower or eliminate U.S. tax on not only their foreign but on U.S. profits as well.

* * *

Stern proved more interesting than his nascent book. He drove to my house for education and drafting sessions in an old, rackety Mercedes, wearing a disguise, wig, false mustache, dark glasses to protect me from Treasury censure and retaliation, he said. He insisted our clandestine meetings at his Massachusetts Ave mansion on DC's embassy row begin after dark. In his foyer hung an eight-by-ten-foot Lichtenstein Ben Day dot painting of a U.S. jet fighter with red tracers and a trademark comic book yellow *Whaam!* where the enemy exploded. It was the first time I'd seen famous contemporary art hanging in a private house.

The Rape of the Treasury came out in 1974. Stern acknowledged me in its credits, since I was long gone from Treasury. But the book was no best seller, and the Code taxed multinationals' foreign earnings ever more favorably. I'd changed nothing.

* * *

Tom Fields, Marcia's husband, was a former Treasury lawyer turned crusader who, in 1970, started *Tax Analysts and Advocates*, an investigative tax newsletter. He launched *TA&A* on a shoestring and now, two years later, it needed money. I'd leaked to him when I tried to stop the Chilean ruling, and he knew I'd helped Stern. He offered me the editorship of *TA&A* if I could raise the capital to keep it going.

His offer's timing was perfect. I was searching for a new job. Practice was out, bureaucrat frustrating, teaching or think tank—tweed jacket, leather elbow patches, law journal articles critiquing the Code—toothless. But muckraking tax journalism perfectly suited my idealistic fantasy of delousing a filthy system, and my thirst for action.

Helping with Stern's corporate tax exposé had earned me, if not a call on him, at least a right of audience. I touted Tom's tax journal and Tom to him, introduced them, and Stern quickly agreed to fund *TA&A*. Capital found, Tom reneged; in a brief, last meeting at twilight, he said he'd continue editing his newsletter himself. I met few spotless white hats in DC.

That night with a lover, I was impotent, too dejected to be roused despite her tenderest, protracted attentions. Nothing had unmanned me before: not South Philly and the Pennsauken Mart; not quadriplegia, while I lay healing my broken neck for three months in Crutchfield traction and Nora Kinsler, a sympathetic young nurse, or my wife ministered to me; not Harvard's rejections; not the *great shiksa*'s scorn. A welsher accomplished what mean streets, wreck, rejection, and heartbreak had not.

4. Garret and Chalkboard

Three years out of Yale, I'd played three roles: big-firm tax lawyer, and felt soiled; swaggering DC bureaucrat, and been soundly trounced; muckraker, and had the job jerked from under me. I learned the difference between my mother's racketeering family and DC's power elite was that the latter wore suits and ties; watched the romantic reformer's faith that justified mastering a wearisome, servile trade dissolve in the acid of reality; and discovered my deepest fear was to fail at writing.

As Evelyn Waugh's Lord Marchmain fled the God he was desperate to embrace, so I fled writing down the days. From the mid-September Monday morning at La Salle in 1960, when I realized words of mine might hold a reader, my philosopher's stone was *writing well*. When Claude Koch, the La Salle English faculty's resident writer, asked me what I wanted to do when I graduated, my unhesitating reply was *write*.[9] I worshipped language and forgave *all of those by whom it lives*,[10] even Eliot the anti-Semite; drafted poems in flyleaves and margins of books, kept notes, notebooks, and wrote wherever I found myself. But at each crossroad, ogres on the path that led to desk, paper, and pen appeared, howling, *You'll starve!* or *You'll be no good!* and ran me off. After Treasury, I could cope with fear of want but shrank from confirmation I was a talentless poseur, that I would be judged unworthy of the only God I've ever had. At each fork, I chose the road more traveled that led away from the typewriter and the morning's blank A4 sheet.

MANQUÉ
Through fog blown inland off the sea
by tumbled walls amidst old trees
summoning verse from memory
that others wrote, I walk my land,
a stiff kneed quondam businessman
fixed on Ulysses, lesser men,
faded notes, a dry pen
and fear, push come to shove,
I am no good at what I love.[11]

[9] See II, Credentials, John's; W. H. Auden, "In Memory of W. B. Yeats."
[10] Auden, original version of "In Memory of W. B. Yeats."
[11] Dan Burt, *We Look Like This* (Manchester: Carcanet, 2012).

With all the certainty of ignorance, I thought teaching law would allow time to write. Teaching was not a career choice, but a straw grasped the evening Tom Field yanked the editorship of *TA&A* from under me, and with it my deliriums of reform, and left me to confront my fundamental hunger to become a writer. I had no debt, had a year's income in the bank, and was qualified to teach law. The law professor market was hot, the pay good; teaching law would assuage the reformer in me by encouraging legal tyros to achieve what I had not, and I was free to move without regard for my second wife, our marriage only a kind fraud, easily ended, perpetrated to quiet her parents who objected to her living in sin. Not to take a job that offered all this and a year's hard scribbling would be to admit I turned aside from my dream out of cowardice and pride.

In the fall of 1972, I attended the annual law school meat market, the National Law Faculty Recruitment Conference in Washington, DC, and interviewed with several schools. A few weeks later, my first choice, Boston University Law School, offered me an assistant professorship for the academic year beginning September 1973. BU ranked in the top 10 percent of U.S. law schools, serving as a class A farm team for law teachers with sights fixed on top-five schools. Young male professionals ranked Boston above all other U.S. cities as a place to live: women outnumbered men, it was home to some of the best sailing in America, and was thirty minutes by air from NYC. The BU law tower rose seventeen stories over the south bank of the Charles River, opposite MIT and the Charles' practice course for MIT and BU's sailing teams. Professors in northeast-facing offices had unobstructed views up and down the river—west to Harvard, east to the Longfellow Bridge to Cambridge, northeast across the Charles River basin—where from March through October, the college sailing teams in two-person dinghies practiced arabesques in the afternoon. BU promised me a third floor, northeast-facing office, a skybox for the sailing, and I was theirs.

My wife and I agreed to divorce amicably, and in September 1973, I moved my possessions—campaign desk, stereo, sixteen-foot 5-o-5 trapeze racing dinghy—from DC to a furnished one-story, four-bedroom winter rental (September to June) on Bass Rock Lane in Marblehead, Massachusetts, seventeen miles north of Boston. Marblehead is one of America's preeminent sailing venues, Bass Rock Lane a half block long, fifty-foot-wide granite point jutting east into the Atlantic just across the town line from Swampscott.

My rental stood at the sea end on the point's southeast side. Bluefish trapped menhaden against the rocks, their feeding frenzy churning the water white with thrashing, the sky gray with gulls diving on slashed menhaden corpses. Sailboats, cruise ships, tankers slid north, east, and south beyond the cottage's south-facing wall of windows. The sea murmured or chortled or boomed, depending on the strength and direction of the wind; a strong nor'easter sent sea spray over house and Lane. To the south, Boston's downtown commercial towers loomed out of the smoky afternoon haze and autumn tang of rotting leaves. The stage set, props perfect for a writing idyll, what was supposed to be a romantic drama quickly descended to farce.

* * *

The BU faculty drifted in and out of the faculty lounge on the floor above my office midmorning to midafternoon Mondays through Fridays. There, the tenured professoriate sipped coffee, met, kibitzed with, and measured their colleagues and new hires. Halfway into my first term's tenure, I hadn't entered the lounge. One day, the professor in the adjoining office delicately mentioned that participating in the coffee ritual was important to an aspiring first-year professor's career. I left BU still a faculty-lounge virgin.

Disgusted with the gulf between my subject's noble pretensions and venal practice, disappointed with the students, I was a disgruntled teacher as well as a poor colleague. Though I'd taken the job to buy time to write, I had expected to reprise at least some of the late 1960s' student idealism I'd found at Yale. But times had changed, and BU law students were less idealistic than their slightly older Yale counterparts; few BU students in 1973 were ravening to improve the world. What excited them was commercial success, that each week I donned a three-piece suit and flew to NYC for two days to consult for Touche Ross (TR&Co), a Big Eight international accounting firm. Three years into the 1970s, 1960s' utopian reveries were becoming risible.

I wrote nothing at BU. I shied at the first fence and sold the writing time teaching was to buy by agreeing to continue consulting for TR&Co, begun six months earlier in San Francisco. Come the end of my first year's teaching, I did not ask, and BU did not offer, to renew my contract.

5. Bean Counters

The DC10 banked southwest over Sacramento in the afternoon sun and slid down toward San Francisco airport (SFO). The city materializing beyond my cabin window stunned me. It stretched west beside the bay from downtown toward the Golden Gate, the bay white-capped and flecked with white triangles, though a workday. The Transamerica Pyramid sparkled in the sunshine, and City Lights, cradle of the Beats and America's version of *La Joie de Lire*, stood open where North Beach met Chinatown. Two decades before the dot-com boom, three before Facebook's founding, 'Frisco's residents were, or pretended to be, laid-back. The wind blew steady, often hard, off the Pacific almost every afternoon. It was February 1972, my first time west of Ravenna, Ohio, and I had come to the land where the "Sunflower Sutra"[12] and the Free Speech Movement were born.

DISC sent me there. The U.S. Treasury was begging exporters to take its money, and they were panting to oblige. But DISC was unprecedented, and companies were unsure how to exploit it. So Treasury lawyers fanned out to major industrial centers across the land to explain and promote it, and learn what problems manufacturers foresaw to address them in the regulations they were drafting. I was the government's first DISC envoy to the West Coast, for the nonce the law's viceroy, high priest, and oracle.

Next morning at 10 a.m., I stood in a St. Francis Hotel ballroom before an overflow crowd of tax executives, accountants, lawyers, and business-people. The ballroom held 750, and my talk was piped live into an adjoining ballroom where another seven hundred or so listened. I'd have lured a smaller crowd had I stood on Union Square and passed out $100 bills. High on lack of sleep, the Bay Area's scenery, and the crowd's size, I was on form.

I spoke for twenty minutes, then, what the crowd had come for, took questions for sixty minutes more. My listeners were familiar with the law or wouldn't have been there. They came for advice, how to apply this law to their company. The Q and A part is where they found out. DISC Q and A sessions resembled business school seminars; attendees described real-world transactions, and I explained how the law applied to them.

---

[12] Alan Ginsberg wrote his poem "Sunflower Sutra" in Berkeley in 1955.

Promoting DISC throughout America, and writing its regulations, became my MBA.

* * *

Dozens swarmed the lectern and showered me with their business cards when I finished. One stands proud in memory among the flock that fluttered onto my lectern, André Aversa's. André was a Sicilian immigrant eight years my senior, who began adulthood as a seminarian with a BDiv (bachelor's degree in divinity) from the Seminaire Adventiste de Haute Savoie, and had found a different God after emigrating from Sicily to America in 1956. He became a lawyer, accountant, international tax partner in Peat Marwick Mitchell's[13] Houston office and, just weeks before, had joined TR&Co's San Francisco office as their first international tax partner. Though he had lived seventeen years in the U.S. when we met, his Italian accent was still strong, perhaps because it bolstered his international tax credentials, and helped seduce American women. André was a competent Lothario and gifted salesman, the most charming conman I've known. In the following months, he focused his charm on me.

He called with DISC questions shortly after my return to Treasury. Within the month, he visited DC, invited me to lunch, and there asked what my plans were for after Treasury. I said perhaps teach, gave him no encouragement to make the job offer he then did, and heard little more from him until late fall. In November, I told him I'd be teaching at BU nine months later. He pressed me to reconsider, finally offering to fly me to the U.S. Virgin Islands for the weekend to discuss his offer under sail.

André was no sailor, but the thirty-six-foot bareboat he chartered was easily single-handed. Sailing with him changed nothing until, reaching back over the Caribbean to St. Thomas on Sunday morning, he made me an offer I couldn't refuse—try TR&Co in 'Frisco for six months, January through June, before returning east to prepare for my first semester at BU. For kicker, he promised the fast thirty-foot sloop he intended to buy would be floating in her berth in Sausalito—minutes across the Golden Gate Bridge from my new office—when I arrived, mine to sail when he was, as often, away on business. I'd be twenty-nine years old, a single male living in a romantic hill city by the Pacific, paid twice my Treasury salary with a boat

---

[13] Peat Marwick Mitchell, now part of KPMG, was one of the Big Eight international accounting firms in 1972.

to sail and an excuse to funk writing for six months more. Christ would have been tempted. *Deal.*

* * *

The Big Eight accounting firms dominated international tax practice in the U.S. Their networks of foreign offices enabled them to advise on how foreign as well as U.S. jurisdictions would tax cross-border income. U.S. law firms in those days didn't have commensurate foreign networks, so they could only advise on the U.S. taxation of this income. Seven of the Big Eight had large international tax groups, mostly composed of lawyers, in their New York offices. Without them, a firm couldn't consider itself truly *international.* TR&Co, the exception, had only the newly arrived André in San Francisco.

He had boosted himself to TR&Co as an international tax star, boasting he devised the international tax strategy for Schlumberger, then as now the world's largest oil services company and among the globe's most sophisticated tax avoiders. He moved to TR&Co for San Francisco's scenic glories and lifestyle, he claimed. He did not mention that at TR&Co, he would be the only fish in the pond, *the* international tax partner in a firm without one, with remit to build their international tax practice.

But André was no star. Though he saw the forest where most saw only trees, technicalities were not his forte. He had a marrow-deep understanding of international commerce, a vestige perhaps of growing up on the Straits of Messina, but was not known for expertise in any area of foreign tax law. He could almost feel how U.S. tax rules and double tax treaties interacted with the rhythms of international trade but did not write, speak, or belong to panels of industry experts on them. Had he the essential detailed knowledge of the relevant Code and treaty rules, he would have been formidable, but his name rang no bells in New York or DC international tax circles. So far as the tax world was concerned, André was *all hat and no cattle* (full of big talk and no action: in English idiom, "all mouth and no trousers").

I had the deep knowledge of U.S. laws and treaties, what the tax trade calls technical expertise, that he lacked. I was to supply it as his first hire for the international tax group he'd been tasked to build. But as a green technician, the underlying patterns and policies of the international tax system were still opaque to me. André saw them and taught me to see them too. Within a month, I learned what he had to teach and was building a following among the TR&Co offices and their clients.

* * *

I gave Treasury my notice on December 1, 1972. Neither superior nor peer shed a tear. A month later, I swaggered like Rupert of the Rhine into TR&Co's offices in a tower on the Embarcadero to start work. Kelly, office manager and executive assistant to the Managing Partner, greeted me, showed me to my office, introduced my secretary, arranged for a TR&Co credit card and building pass. She was thirty, saucy, working-class Scots Irish with a high school education. She joined TR&Co as a junior secretary at nineteen and rose through its ranks on the back of intelligence and charm. Young for the two important office roles she played, and good at both, the office and boss's affairs ran smoothly.

She was also a freckled, five-foot-one hourglass with shoulder-length flaming-red hair cut like a helmet and aventail. Two weeks later, we were living together.

From a photo, none would call her beautiful. In the morning, before ablutions and makeup, she was plain. Her shoulders and breasts were large, nipples tiny, legs a tad short for her body—stumpy some would say—arms and legs hirsute. She wore bronze-tinted glasses that darkened in daylight. But all who met her thought her a beauty. Sparky, always flawlessly dressed, game for new experiences, she was a quick study. She learned the rudiments of sailing from me and was a help on a boat. She enjoyed sex in all its heterosexual guises, was attentive and unpromiscuous. I recall no headaches.

Yet style, charm, intelligence, and sexual allure could not quite silence the blues singing inside her. Soon after we met, I learned she was infertile, for a reason alluded to but never clearly explained. My guess is a teenage-botched abortion left her barren. Though she neither whined nor pitied herself, there hung about her a just perceptible air that chance had treated her harshly.

* * *

Our six-month ménage was idyllic. Kelly would pick me up at the airport on Friday evenings when I returned from frequent trips to the firm's offices around the country, and we'd drive to a bar on Russian Hill where a balladeer sang rock 'n' roll hits from the 1950s. I'd down three or four whiskey sours with my hamburger and double fries, then, slightly drunk and completely nostalgic, drive us home to make love. Up at dawn, fifteen floors above the bay, I'd watch the sun behind me fire the Golden Gate Bridge, stretch, leave Kelly sleeping, and go for a run. She would be waiting, showered and shining when I returned.

We quarreled seriously only once, after I flirted too obviously with a friend she'd invited to dinner. Despite apologies, even a tear or two from me, Kelly still took a week to forgive me. It wasn't jealousy that racked her, but wounded self-respect, and doubt about the depth of my affection. She sighed for a settled, late-1950s-style marriage, a union inconceivable to me, and nurtured the hope until I left that happy months with her by the bay would work a sea change in me.

Kelly and local business friends threw me a party the day before I left for BU. Her parting gift was a 1924 French translation of Swinburne's *Laus Veneris*,[14] its rice paper pages still uncut, its original wax paper dust jacket yellowed but untorn. On the flyleaf, this inscription in French:

Dan—

je t'aime et respect vous [sic]

"le tortoise"

Dan—I love you and respect you. "Turtle," my nickname for her. This sad, apt token lies beside my right hand as I type, pages still uncut. We did not meet again.

* * *

André kept his word. His new Jensen Cal 2-30 was bobbing at her berth in Sausalito when I arrived. At least two weekends every month, I'd sail her with Kelly, and sometimes acquaintances, aboard. A building sea breeze off the Pacific rolled in from the Golden Gate most afternoons as the fog lifted and blew twenty knots or more for hours, ideal conditions for the boat. She was all glass (fiberglass), a new boat-building material at the time, her hull thicker than comparable boats today because no one knew when she came from the mold how well an all-glass boat would weather. Had her hull been a quarter inch thinner, I'd have sunk her one Sunday afternoon on the bay.

A friend's ex-wife, her new boyfriend, Kelly, and I were beating past Alcatraz one Sunday midafternoon in an eighteen-knot westerly beneath a cloudless sky. We were flying main and 180 degrees genoa or *genny*, a large foresail set from the forestay whose foot extended aft some twenty feet to a point even with the end of the tiller. The only visibility to leeward, the side opposite the wind, was through a three-by-two-foot clear plastic patch

---

[14] *Laus Veneris* is Swinburne's take on the Tannhauser legend, a tragic hero who must leave his mortal love to be imprisoned in the love mountain with the goddess Venus.

sewn just behind and above the tack, the forward bottom angle of the sail; with genny set, you were sailing blind to leeward.

With the genny strapped in tight, I bore off south on a tight reach toward the St. Francis Yacht Club across the bay. The St. Francis housed the town's richest establishment sailors. That afternoon, members on the club's docks, public behind them on the esplanade, clumped in knots watching the racing fleet, rails down, slash across the bay.

We were making seven knots, fast for a thirty-foot sailboat. The declining midafternoon sun, low in the afternoon sky, bounced off the genny's plastic view port and turned it opaque. Had we been racing at seven knots, a crew member would have stood in the thin stainless steel bow pulpit, gripping the forestay and looking around the genny to leeward for obstructions. But neither were we racing nor was there anyone aboard other than me who could safely stand lookout in the bow, or helm the boat if I did. Moreover, we were on starboard tack, with right of way over other boats. I was high on speed, wind, sun, and Kelly's blowing hair whipping against the right side of my neck as she sat beside me.

An eight-foot-high red bell buoy marked the entrance to the St. Francis Yacht Club channel a quarter mile inshore. It weighed more than four thousand pounds and was moored to a ten-thousand-pound mushroom sea anchor. Buoys are not supposed to move; the seven-plus tons St. Francis' channel buoy and anchor was no exception.

Our port bow smashed into it going full tilt. The crowd watching the race snapped their heads right toward the splintering fiberglass and clanging metal cymbal crash a quarter mile offshore, adding shame to danger. I put the helm over and spun the boat onto port tack to keep the impact side as high out of the water as possible. From my place at the tiller, I could see the mangled bow pulpit, knew there'd be no repairing it, then sent two of the passengers below to report damage. The collision ripped a three-foot-long, six-inch-wide hole in the port hull running aft from the bow where it joined the deck. Because the boat had been hull down when we hit the buoy, the junction of the hull and deck almost in the water, the hole was a good foot above the waterline; there was little danger of sinking, provided the boat stayed on port tack or upright. We wedged two bunk cushions in the hole and tenderly sailed her home to Sausalito.

* * *

San Francisco was an unintended experiment in pleasure's worth. The fog retreating daily toward the Golden Gate before the rising sun dramatized

San Francisco mornings. Berkeley and Stanford were, respectively, twenty to thirty minutes away by car. The city was abuzz with art—good opera, museums, classical music in the streets. One Tuesday afternoon, returning from lunch to my Embarcadero office, I heard singing and saw a crowd gathered on the approaching street corner. Four men and two women stood on a truck's flatbed singing the sestet from *Lucia di Lammermoor*, a favorite ever after. The sea breeze fluttered the Coors beer bunting decking the flatbed, the voices were good, the noon crowd enraptured. My passion for bel canto opera took root then; I've had no street experience like it anywhere else in the world.

Kelly, André, the firm, clients, and acquaintances pressed me to stay. André was easy to work with and away much of the time; Kelly and I cohabited happily. My time on the bay—in the city's bars, restaurants, and beds—had been joyful. The firm offered double my handsome pay and a principalship (partnership status for nonaccountants) in two years to sign on permanently; within five, at thirty-four, I'd be rich. With every reason to stay, I departed for BU as planned.

San Francisco was too perfect. A tragic sense of life, social complexity, a historical sense were wanting; tethers to Europe were too slight; cosmopolitans should gaze east not west, I thought; London, Paris, and Berlin were too long a jet ride away; the locals were callow and parochial. Life was too easy; it seemed lotusland, where it was *always afternoon*.

Moreover, San Francisco didn't and could never quite seem home. The sun was in the wrong place, at my back in the morning close-hauled heading offshore, at my back under spinnaker coming home. On the Jersey coast I came from, the sun was in your eyes going and coming; you were always headed into the light. I remember the San Francisco sojourn fondly, like the first weekend with a new love in the spring, but did not tear up when my Boston-bound jet tucked its wheels into its belly.

* * *

Manhattan, August 1973. A nondescript, slip-gray steel-and-glass tower creeps skyward five car lengths back from the west curb at 1633 Broadway a few blocks north of the Theater District. Surrounding buildings throttle the sunlight before it reaches the tower's lower floors. Hot dog and pretzel vendors choke the adjacent curbs, cramming the air with the reek of fried onions, steaming chili, boiled hot dogs, spilled mustard. Police horses piss and shit, and the rising stinks swirl with the fast-food smells into a nauseating miasma. Sewer steam, taxi, and truck exhaust drift from the tarmac roadway over the hot concrete sidewalk. Passers-by in conversation shout to be heard above the horns, screeching brakes, cursing drivers and deliverymen. Everyone sweats.

On weekdays, white-collar workers swarm 1633's sidewalks between 8:30 to 9:30 a.m. and again nine hours later. Few smile or greet you as they scurry through the glass doors into the forty-eight-story building, shift from foot to foot in churlish clumps before the elevator banks, pack the cars, and ascend to their labors. No seagulls, seafront or harbor, no ship horns or ferry bells, no fog peeling from Golden Gate towers as the sun rises, no rotting seaweed or sea smells distract the daily scrum washing in and out of Touche Ross's New York offices.

Ira Hefter, a stocky, forty-year-old Brooklynite tax accountant lured me here. He headed TR's New York tax department, which should have been the firm's flagship but lacked essential international tax expertise. Ira asked me to supply it when he heard I was to teach in Boston. He dangled a sumptuous hourly consulting fee, expense account, partner's office, secretary, weekly traveling costs to and from Boston, and freedom to run my own show if I would spend a day and a half each week for the next nine months in New York, initiating willing tyros into the mysteries of international tax.

I'd loathed the city since my summer stint clerking in a Wall Street law firm five years earlier, but could bear a day and a half a week of it on the terms Ira offered. Aged thirty, three-and-a-half years out of law school, chuffed and mercenary, I bit without first visiting the New York office, meeting its partners (except Ira and the junior staff who were to work for me), or understanding how an international accounting firm ran.

At TR San Francisco, André had given me plum assignments and shielded me from the daily vexations and pressures of Big Eight life in the hope I'd renege on my teaching commitment. Almost my only work during six months by the Golden Gate was helping companies use DISC to avoid tax. The August day I stepped into the elevator and pressed seven for the New York tax department for the first time, I had not prepared a tax return, participated in a financial audit, vetted a company's financial statement, advised on foreign tax and business rules, defended an IRS challenge to foreign income reporting, or struggled to recast tax evasion as benign avoidance.

The car's doors opened on a half-block square, windowless bullpen—no walnut paneling, no wool-carpeted floors, no paterfamilias lowering from the walls, no flowers, no wooden desks, nothing natural at all, and no art on the walls. Work pens—euphemistically dubbed workstations, with low, opaque partitions separating them—packed the open-plan staff area. In them, secretaries and junior tax accountants sat like so many battery hens on stainless steel adjustable chairs with spring-loaded backs and thick plastic wheels at Formica desks by thin steel filing cabinets, typing or filling out forms. Sound deadening, off-white acoustic tiles stippled with holes covered the ceiling. Ranks of flat, flush-mounted fluorescent ceiling lights long and wide as small bath mats shed garish light on drudge and partner alike. Rubberized dun-gray tiles covered the bullpen floor and the corridor between it and the partners' offices.

The firm's senior professionals—Supervisors, Managers, Partners—were CPAs (certified public accountants). Supervisors, the lowest management grade, worked in eight-by-ten boxes, more finished closets than offices, interspersed between the pens like battlements in a castle wall. In them was space for a metal desk, filing cabinet, and visitor's chair, plus a hook for outer clothing on the backside of the door. The walls were too thin to hold picture hooks or conversations, which seeped out even with the door closed.

Managers', and Partners' offices the size of a dining room for ten, lined the seventh floor's perimeter, their exterior walls opposite the offices' doors perforated with windows; only Managers and Partners knew if it was day or night. At one end of each office, a wood veneer Partner's desk, two armchairs for visitors drawn up before them; at the other end of the office, two low, contemporary Italian-style love seats, each with a glossy Formica end table and lamp, furnished these premium spaces. Beige faux-wool, wall-to-wall carpet covered the floors. Opposite each Partner's door in a pen sat his secretary, where buzz or bellow could summon her.

Professional staff were male, predominantly Jewish New Yorkers from Brooklyn, Queens, Bronx, Staten, and Long Islands. They held degrees in business or accounting from local branches of the tuition-free City University of New York. None had attended private secondary schools, Ivy League or Little Ivy universities or colleges; none had graduate degrees; few were lawyers as well as CPAs.

Their second language, if any, was a smattering of Yiddish, picked up at home when parents spoke it to conceal the meaning of a conversation from their children. Softball, handball, touch football, and golf were their sports, or watching baseball, football, basketball, hockey. They holidayed in the Poconos, Long Island, or the Jersey shore; neither they nor their children *summered* anywhere. They played poker or gin rummy, frequented comedies or musicals, and married *in*, young, to Jewish girls from similar backgrounds.

Partners differed from staff only in being older and better paid. They lived in nearby New Jersey and Long Island suburban Jewish neighborhoods. Little traveled, if at all, outside the U.S.; none had studied abroad or staffed a TR office in another country. They worked sixty-to-eighty-hour weeks, drove Cadillacs and Chrysler Imperials, swaddled their wives in mink, counted on a good pension at sixty, and aspired to a beachfront retirement condo in a Miami, Boca Raton, or Palm Beach high-rise. How the firm functioned reflected who they were.

In current dollars, TR was a $1.5 billion a year, bureaucratic business in 1973, with HR, practice development, advertising, quality control, legal, insurance, and executive cost centers. Overheads swallowed 80 percent of the firm's yearly revenue. To crack a nut that large, management constantly squeezed Partners and, through them, everyone else, to increase billings and cut costs. The firm scrimped not only on space, furnishings, decoration, and travel, but also on tax libraries, lunch hours, and vacation. Professionals other than management and some Partners had to bill a minimum of two thousand hours a year. Ira's secretary prowled the department on Friday mornings like a baton-wielding warder, hectoring professionals to complete their time sheets by COB (close of business).

Partners had PD (practice development) quotas to bring in new business or extract more work from existing clients, as well as annual billing quotas. Garnering business from new or old clients counted more than billings toward promotion and pay. The higher Partners rose, the longer they worked, the faster spun the gerbil wheel, till they fell off, or retired at sixty, limp and puffy like rotten fish. I was exempted from both quotas as a part-timer.

* * *

TR and its Big Eight siblings battened on their corporate audit bases. Public companies worldwide must file annual financial statements certified by independent auditors; as a practical matter, so must any business that borrows from a bank. The cost of these obligatory audits is akin to a tax corporation's pay for the privilege of selling their stock to the public, or borrowing from a bank; their public accountants akin to ancien régime tax farmers. Audit fees pay the overheads and more; they accounted for over seven of every ten dollars of TR's revenues in my day. Fees from tax ($1.5

of every $10), management consulting, IT, mergers and acquisitions, and other money-spinners were merely icing on the audit cake.

TR pandered to and jealously guarded its audit clients; few left. Nominally independent, the firm would torture facts, law, and logic to certify clients' financials cleanly[15] or produce tax results they wanted, for fear of losing not only the audit cake but the consulting fee icing as well. Audit partners leaned on tax partners to bless questionable tax provisions in clients' public financial statements or devise aggressive tax-avoidance schemes. This desperation to please could cross the line into criminal conduct, with potential to destroy a firm, as it did Arthur Andersen in the 2001 Enron scandal.[16]

Partner and junior alike felt this pressure and either knuckled under or quit, went unpromoted, or were fired. The constant kneading of facts and law to support clean opinions and favorable tax results sapped analytical accuracy, devalued the firm's opinions, and spread a mist of disingenuousness. The pretense that the firm was not practicing tax law without a license because it did not represent clients in court, though it opined and advised on tax law no differently than law firms, thickened that mist.

* * *

Ira offered me a one-year, full-time, consulting contract as my BU teaching year wound down, a rich offer with a downside: the plus—compensated and perked like a new Partner; the minus—living and laboring for a year, Monday through Friday, in Manhattan. I told myself New York might be tolerable, even enjoyable, in a superior apartment a short walk from the office; that after a week or two, the tax department bullpen, with its human battery hens pecking at typewriters and forms, probably wouldn't register as I crossed it to my office; that my commitment was only for a year, after which I'd abandon the coalface for a seaside cottage north of Boston to try to write, enough in the kitty to live comfortably for five years. If I proved a dud writer, I could descend into the financial pits again.

* * *

Consulting a day and a half a week for ten months had been too little time, the demands of building an international tax group from scratch too great, to fully fathom the distasteful fundamentals of TR's New York practice.

---

[15] A clean audit certification means the auditor found no material problems to bring to the public's notice.
[16] Arthur Andersen, one of the Big Eight, illegally helped its client, Enron, hide financial problems from the SEC and public. The ensuing prosecution caused its demise.

Being a short-term part-timer insulated me from some pressures to varnish the truth and scant analytical integrity. I had worked somewhat closely with only one Partner and not at all with the Managers and Supervisors. It would take several months working daily with the TR tax men until sniffiness rotted to smug scorn for their slipshod research; ungrammatical, inarticulate memoranda; and superficial opinions.

The last, heaviest standard weights nestled at the bottom of the balance pan, were the changes two incomes, from teaching and consulting, together with an expense account wrought. I swapped yellow taxis for black limousines; each week, a car and driver waited at LaGuardia as my plane flew in from Boston; thirty-six hours later, it idled by the curb at 1633 to return me to the Boston air shuttle and home. At least monthly, my expense account treated a law school friend and me to the best chicken Kiev I've eaten, at Jimmy's La Grange, a luxury restaurant on Sixty-Third Street between Park and Lexington Avenues, where Jimmy, the restaurateur, was celebrated for drawing his signature dish on the edge of the spotless white tablecloths as he promoted it to newcomer and regular. I flew first class, stayed at five-star hotels and tipped concierges well, skied at St. Moritz, Zermatt, Vail, and Jackson Hole. I no longer knew the price of a gallon of gas or of limousine rides to meetings, always picked up the check if I dined out with others, and did not ask the price of bespoke suits, cashmere sweaters, or haircuts in fine salons. I became a stereophile, my music system evolving toward *reference* quality. A secretary paid my bills; balanced my checkbook; arranged dinners and trysts; booked opera and concert tickets, appointments with doctors, dentists, and tailors. A travel agent arranged my trips, accountants prepared my tax returns, a maid cleaned house and laundered, a yard maintained my boat. I did nothing I could pay someone to do for me.

* * *

Suborned, I accepted Ira's offer and took a year's lease on a corner penthouse on the twenty-fifth floor of a building on Central Park South, east of the junction of Sixth Avenue and Fifty-Ninth Street. It had three bedrooms with en suite baths, living room and library with working fireplaces, patio, a clear view north for three miles over Central Park to its northern border at 110th Street and west to Columbus Circle and stretches of the Hudson. Grander than I needed, cheaper than I could afford, fitting for a young, big swinging dick, I moved in at the end of June.

In the relative cool of deserted 7:30 a.m. Gotham summer sidewalks, I'd leave the flat, turn left, cross Sixth Avenue, walk a block west on Fifty-Ninth, left again, then wade nine blocks south on Broadway through trash, beggars, deliverymen, garish storefronts, screaming signage and enter my office twenty-five minutes later, depressed. At the violet hour, if I wasn't dining out, a car and driver bore me home. There, I sat reading in the library in air-conditioned isolation rather than on the patio, where soot and particulates breaded you as you sauna-ed in the 100 percent humidity and 90-degree heat. Nights, the interminable, echoing sirens warned sleep away.

Within two weeks, the city was intolerable. Four more, and I surrendered the lease, abandoned my three-month security deposit, and returned to a Marblehead winter rental. Midday on Mondays for the next ten months, I boarded the Shuttle to New York and, Thursday afternoons, returned on it home to the sea.

* * *

International bean counting offers a postdoc in avarice, a global green eyeshade, a grand tier view of high commerce. January 3, 1974: a lover and I stood on a Bahamian beach, sand squidging through our toes, staring at a queue of VLCCs (very large crude carriers), waiting a mile out to offload their Libyan light crude for the shivering masses of New England. Three months earlier, King Faisal ibn Abdulaziz al Saud had joined the OPEC oil embargo against states supporting Israel in the 1973 Arab-Israeli war and cut Saudi oil production by 10 percent. He pledged to keep cutting so long as the West helped Israel. His father, Abdulaziz ibn Saud, had come out of Arabia's Eastern Province in 1902 like a wolf on the fold, conquered Riyadh—in the next thirty years, the Nejd and Hejaz—founded modern Saudi Arabia, and, on one hundred children by twenty-two wives, raised the House of Saud. Now his son Faisal would beard the West and bestride the planet's oil markets.

Oil quadrupled in a few months from three dollars a barrel to twelve. Gasoline at the pump followed crude up. America panicked; runs on gas stations quickly drained them, stranding quarter-mile lines of fuelless cars at stations waiting for resupply; the media forecast heating-oil shortages and freezing masses in winter; government buildings lowered their thermostats to sixty-eight degrees Fahrenheit; gas-guzzling car sales plummeted; wood-burning stove sales spiked.

But the motionless VLCCs in the Caribbean off the BORCO (Bahamas Oil Refining Company) refinery, their Plimsoll lines under water, testified that OPEC's embargo had not corked the flow of crude. The doomsayers were wrong. There was no oil shortage; America could buy all the oil it wanted but *for a price, Ugarte. For a price.*[17] The industrial world would neither freeze nor seize up, just pay four times more than it had a few months earlier to stay warm and be able to commute.

Oil producers would reap a windfall; the quadrupled oil price shifted more wealth from rich states to poor, and faster, than ever before in history. The bulk of this windfall went to Saudi Arabia, by far the largest, lowest-cost producer. America fell into recession.

* * *

Detonating the *oil weapon* didn't balk the Israelis from again defeating the Arab armies. But its blast wave rocked BORCO, and hence New England Petroleum Company (NEPCO), its majority (65 percent) shareholder. BORCO was NEPCO's engine. It refined Libyan *sweet* (low sulfur) crude and sold it to New England electric utilities under the cosh to reduce emissions. Libya had nationalized its oil fields in September 1973, crimping the flow of crude to BORCO. Faisal's production cut a few weeks later choked it further. BORCO's profits sputtered, and financial markets wagered NEPCO would fail and take with it NEPCO's owner, Ed Cary—older brother of Hugh, New York's Governor. It didn't; NEPCO staggered on for another five years. It wouldn't have, had the business suffered another financial holing in 1974, like a multimillion-dollar additional U.S. tax liability.

NEPCO claimed BORCO's profits were not subject to U.S. tax, though solid arguments said they were. NEPCO played *audit roulette* and reported no tax due on these profits in the tax returns it filed. Audit roulette is the metaphor tax accountants use for filing tax returns containing questionable positions; wagering IRS examiners are too few to find them or too dumb to understand their flaws if they do. It's a common practice companies facing financial shortfalls use to help themselves to what is, even if discovered, effectively a low-interest government loan. Provided the facts of the position are sufficiently disclosed, it's not fraud. The worst the taxpayer must fear is that it will have to pay the tax plus interest and, in egregious cases, a negligence penalty if the IRS discovers and successfully challenges its filing position.

Touche Ross NY audited NEPCO, valued not only for fees, but also for the prestige that auditing a significant oil company conferred on a

---

[17] *Casablanca*—Rick's reply to Ugarte in the gambling room when Ugarte tells him he's going to sell the letters of transit he stole from the two German couriers he murdered.

TR office that had few industrial audit clients. Theretofore, TR had not challenged NEPCO's tax reporting; had NEPCO not been in financial trouble, TR still might have had no reservations about it chancing the audit wheel. But NEPCO was in trouble, its lenders hovering. If it went under and a large hidden tax liability that TR should have flagged was discovered, lenders were sure to sue TR for their losses.

This risk put the wind up TR. It could refuse to certify NEPCO's accounts, or qualify its opinion of them to avoid being sued if NEPCO failed, but if it did, lenders would spook and call their loans or at least curtail NEPCO's credit; even a qualified opinion might be NEPCO's coup de grâce. TR sent me to BORCO to decide whether the blade should fall.

Were BORCO's profits taxable in the United States? If likely, could BORCO make minor or cosmetic changes now to reduce that risk? A few hours wandering the refinery, a few more in BORCO's Freeport offices, allayed my worst fears and sparked ideas for simple, pro forma changes to BORCO's business to armor its faulty but legal attempt to avoid tax. I reported by phone to the TR tax partner responsible for signing off NEPCO's tax reporting and, work done, sped to our hotel for three days of palm tree passion with my lover Carla.

* * *

Carlotta (Carla) Altschloss: twenty-five years old; alumna Miss Chapin's[18] and Radcliffe; first-year law student BU; listee, New York Social Register; home, parents' east seventies Big Apple brownstone; sailor (Captain, Radcliffe sailing team), ice-skater (divers silver cups); ballroom dancer; cook; traveler; fluent in French and Italian. This résumé was not pinned above her small breasts when we met; it unspooled slowly after we became lovers. A practiced, upper-class, Knickerbocker social eye would have taken her measure in a trice when she first entered my BU office with a question about coursework; not-too-tight skinny jeans on long WASP legs (thirty-inch inseam), well-pressed denim work shirt opened to the third button down from the top, bright silk Hermes scarf tied insouciantly around her pale white neck. But the type in the flesh was new to me; all I saw was a five-foot-seven, flat-chested, cat-walk woman with green eyes, blond hair in a bun, in flats, not trainers, with an almost imperceptibly imperfect face,

[18] Miss Chapin's School for Girls in NYC consistently ranked in the top-five American private elementary and secondary schools. Many of its alumnae went on to Radcliffe, then Harvard's coordinate school for women.

slight dorsum bump like Jill's between bridge and nose tip the more visible because she was otherwise flawless. My sister, who met her once, continues to rhapsodize about her beauty four decades on.

Carla and I met a few weeks into my first term teaching, went for dinner, then to bed at Bass Rock Lane, my rented Marblehead house by the sea. What faults she had were not obvious to me. I was working flat out, preparing law lectures for the first time, and flying weekly to NYC to consult for TR; she was diligently trying to master first-year law school's first term, the hardest. We lived apart Monday mornings to Thursday nights, at Bass Rock Lane the rest of the time, without, when there, leisure or energy to delve deeply into each other's character.

We sailed my 5-0-5 the last two Indian summer weekends before first frost. She hung comfortably from its trapeze wires riveted just below the spreaders, feet wide apart on the gunnel, moving as much of her 105 pounds outboard as possible. She unhooked from the wire before sliding inboard to tack, kept us flat till the last possible moment, crossed the boat with me, hooked in, and sprang outboard again on the wire as I sheeted in. She flew the chute from the wire and could unhook, come inboard, gybe the pole, and be ready to hang from the wire again as I pulled the main across to gybe. A list of the perfect paramour crew's particulars described Carla.

Person trapezing on 5-0-5

Ballroom dancing learned as a girl, practiced as a deb, a favorite pastime since, was something she longed to do with me. I had never learned to dance, had attended no cotillions, did not aspire to learn. The images I carried of the practice came from the polonaise in Tchaikovsky's *Eugene Onegin* and ball scenes in period films like *Il Gattopardo* (*The Leopard*) with Burt Lancaster as the aging Leopard whirling around a palace ballroom with Claudia Cardinale as Angelica, the mayor's glorious daughter a third Lancaster's filmic age, in his thinning arms.

I had no call for suede-soled dancing shoes the first two months we were an item. Then Christmas returned Carla to New York and her set's dances.

* * *

The night before New Year's Eve, I am to pick her up from one of these. I leave work at 7:30 p.m., walk to the dance's midtown hotel venue, hear an orchestra playing Strauss as I push through the revolving door. At parade rest on the ballroom landing, wearing a Eugene Onegin-ish expression, I peer down at New York's jeunesse dorée in DJs and ball gowns waltzing across the floor. The women shimmering in the arms of black-suited male partners are neon-bright, saltwater tropical fish, red, yellow, blue, green, orange, peach, and more. Outside the aquarium, I stare through the glass at this foreign species interweaving in an alien element.

An arcing *threadfin anthias*[19] in scarlet and pearls separates herself from a drab fin and rushes up the steps to grasp my hand, flushed, drops of sweat just below her hairline, breathless. She entreats and tugs to drag me down onto the dance floor. But it's Carla, perfectly finished Carla, not Onegin's Tatyana, or my Jill or Cynthia. However much she may care for me, I'm not besotted. I know my place; I'm no romantic fish, merely a puffed-up urchin gasping on the strand. I beg off, press her to stay till the ball is over, and watch her dive down the ballroom staircase to rejoin her kind as I turn toward the revolving door and freezing night. This is not my world.

---

[19] Threadfin anthias is a dark-scarlet salt-water tropical reef fish found in the western Pacific.

A threadfin anthias

Extrapolation failed me, or perhaps I needed more information or didn't want to know; the ball was a tell that I should have read. But come morning, my freshest memory was of our night together, when she joined me after the ball in the flat she'd borrowed for our three-day stay. We saw in the New Year, then on New Year's Day served brunch in our pro tem flat to a small group of her East-Side friends, a few years my junior and new to me. The day before, I'd gone to Zabar's,[20] bought ample corned (salt) beef, pastrami, lox (brined salmon), cream cheese, bagels, rye bread, and the rest of the accouterments of an Ashkenazi Sunday brunch, as well as champagne, red and white wines. To the East-Siders, it was unfamiliar fare in unfamiliar abundance, but they wolfed it down. I had no common experiences to share with them so said little, merely smiling and nodding, as a host should while guests gobble, drink, and drivel on.

Alone on a sofa near a window sat a young man I'd not met. I walked over, introduced myself. He replied, *Richard Merrill*, and offered his hand. As I searched for small talk, he cheeped, *That's Richard* Merrill, emphasizing the patronymic. When my face remained blank, he went on, *Merrill, as in Merrill Lynch Pierce Fenner and Smith*. My lineament continued to say,

[20] Zabar's is a fabled West-Side New York deli beloved of New York Jewish intellectuals.

So? I did not bow. After a few minutes dull talk, I excused myself to wait on other guests. Merrill looked surprised.

* * *

He came to mind three days later, after twenty-four hours in Freeport alone with Carla, unbowed by TR duties or preparing classes. Familiarity hadn't dimmed her accomplishments, pride swelled no less when men eyed her covetously, her sexual hunger matched mine at least, yet I skimmed my eyes for the emergency exit. Carla was neither intellectual, artist, scholar, nor imaginative conversationalist. A figure in a Gobelin tapestry—an intricate, beautiful, expensive hanging—but static and slight, an elegant decoration to celebrate a dynasty or class, to dress a wall, diminish drafts, deaden sounds, but lifeless. Carla was the work of glorious craftsmen, not Bernini. Divorced from that tapestry, the world that made her and she was made for, Carla did not fascinate. She embodied for me the distinction between illustration and art; I found no raw truth in her or her world.

Carla and her friends opened their clubs' doors to me, as have others down the years, but I kept to the pavement. Even had her evanescent social glitter promised riches, it would not have made her and her society more interesting. Our affair petered out a few weeks after we landed back in Boston on the plane from Freeport.

* * *

For a century, the U.S. Navy has lured recruits with the slogan, *Join the Navy, see the world*. Substitute TR for Navy, and you have my two years with their New York office. Understood but unstated in the Navy's exhortation is *and you'll serve your country*. No such understanding ennobled my travels for TR.

In the service of clients trying to avoid tax, or sometimes jail, TR flew me to London, Amsterdam, Toronto, Dublin, Brussels, Luxembourg, Tehran, Hamilton (Bermuda), Zurich, and Vaduz (Liechtenstein). I learned to use U.K. companies to avoid U.S. tax and U.S. companies to avoid U.K. tax; exploited differences in how nations treat the same commercial facts, that what is a dividend, say, in the Netherlands, may be interest in the United States; cut *sweetheart* tax deals with Irish, Swiss, Belgian, Luxembourg, Dutch, and U.K. tax authorities who promised not to tax the income of locally registered companies so long as they were only headquartered, or nominally operating, in their countries. I accrued a smattering of knowledge about European and Middle Eastern tax, corporate law, and double tax treaties; met Americans, Brits, Germans, Iranians, and a host of other nationals striving to avoid or evade tax, as well as lawyers and accountants around the world who helped them; discovered that if your business was international, paying tax was optional.

What tax avoiders, complicit governments, and I were doing in those days was neither illegal, unusual, nor, in general, condemned. The prevailing attitude toward international tax avoidance—even evasion, among national revenue services, boardrooms, and practitioners—is best summed up in a colloquy between Friar Bernardine and Barabas in Marlowe's *Jew of Malta*:

> BERNARDINE Thou hast committed—
> BARABAS Fornication; but that was in another country;
>   And besides, the wench is dead.
> *Jew of Malta*, IV. 1.

Dead wench schemes, where profits earned in substance in one country are reported, and untaxed, in another, and favorable private tax deals with cooperative fiscs, are to international tax advisors what a hammer and saw are to carpenters. With TR, I mastered the fundamentals of the sophisticated, complex, international tax version of three-card monte, a skill with which to build a fortune and sap faith in finance, law, and the comity of nations. On a buck-slip among notes dated around the end of my TR days lay this doggerel published some forty years later:

> SUMMA
> Ethics distills to three *wills*:
> If I do it, will I go to jail?
> If I do it, will I get paid?
> If I do it, will I get laid?
> The rest is a charade.[21]

Dublin was misty, drizzling, just above freezing as I walked across St. Stephen's Green from law offices in a row of gray eighteenth-century Georgian houses with Alfred E. Gregory, a prominent Irish solicitor, to lunch at the Shelbourne Hotel. The morning before, I'd arrived from

[21] Dan Burt, *We Look Like This* (Manchester: Carcanet, 2012).

Boston, Christmas a week away, to play Mr. Wolf[22] for an American tax evader. My assignment: disappear the problem.

Several years earlier, Gregory had formed a Gibraltar company for a U.S. client of TR. He and a law partner held all the company's stock, were its only directors, and had a handshake understanding with the client that the company would do what he wanted. A foreign businessman who owed the client $5 million wired it to the company, which invested the money in tax-free, offshore accounts.

It was garden-variety tax evasion. The client had a duty to report the company's formation, and his interest in it, to the IRS, but didn't. If they discovered the scheme, he would have to pay the taxes he tried to evade, plus interest and penalties, and perhaps be jailed.[23] TR came across the subterfuge while preparing the client's tax return and refused to continue unless he came clean.

The solicitors and I met at 10 a.m. that morning to launder this linen, if possible. *How had they formed the company*, I asked. *Did you dot all the i's, cross all the t's?* They hadn't or, when they understood where I was headed, told me they hadn't. Not having been legally born, the company never existed, which, for U.S. purposes, meant there was no company to which the $5 million payment could have been paid. U.S. law would treat the solicitors as agents holding the funds for the client, who could file amended tax returns, declare the $5 million as income rather than dividends from a foreign company, for which various IRS reports and forms should have been filed, and ignore the attempted tax evasion. Relieved, Gregory, his firm's managing partner, proposed lunch—on the client's tick, of course—to celebrate a good result.

The 162-year-old Shelbourne hotel was Dublin's finest and Gregory's favorite lunch venue. The maître d' recognized him when he entered and bowed and scraped us to a table. The work had gone well, and we were going to do no work after lunch that Friday five days before Christmas. I chose foie gras for starter, accompanied by toasted brioche and sauterne. My first course was wild Irish salmon—not to be missed, I was told—with

[22] Mister Wolf was the legendary fixer in the film *Pulp Fiction* sent to dispose of a body and bloody car.

[23] Paul Manafort, Donald Trump's 2016 campaign chairman, was convicted in August 2018 of eight counts of U.S. tax fraud for a similar scheme, using Cyprian rather than Gibraltarian banks, and awaits sentencing.

a bottle of Hock for the table. The entrée was venison, the wine with it '64 Grands Echezeaux. Cheese, coffee, port, and cigars closed the merry feast.

Lunch over, we processed through the hotel's doors like King George I boarding the Royal Barge for Chelsea—lords of the earth laden with all the holiday joy the Nativity, Friday, a successful meeting and fish, game, and Burgundy can bring—turned right, and headed back to Gregory's offices to collect my bags. A girl, perhaps fifteen or sixteen years old, sat huddled on the slick curb two car lengths to the right of the hotel's entrance. She was a classic colleen, not Roma, blue eyes, straight red hair, fine boned, porcelain skin, a Celtic beauty in the rough; think *Molly Malone*. She wore a thin, dingy cloth coat and skirt, cloth kerchief over her hair; in her arms, a swaddled infant, perhaps a few months old. There was no mat or tarp beneath her.

The drizzle had turned almost to fine sleet, and the girl shivered slightly. Gregory, on my left, was closest to her as we walked by; their eyes met, she extended her right hand toward him, palm up, while her left clasped the infant tighter. He cursed her, readied a kick, checked himself, then as we drew away, launched a diatribe about filthy beggar whores and work-houses. Perhaps she made him feel guilty—the cost of his camel hair top-coat, bespoke, twelve-ounce merino worsted, pin-striped suit, plus our lunch would have housed and fed beggar and babe for a year—or disturbed his solicitor's due order of things. I'd not seen anyone spurn a mendicant as he had, though I have since; my father would have decked him. To my shame, I didn't stop, dig in my pocket, and give her the pittance my host had not.

I retrieved my bag, ignored his hand, left, and never saw or spoke with him again.

* * *

Thirteen thousand feet below Mount Tochal, the gated, guarded villas, tennis courts, and pools of Elahiyeh sprawled in the spring sun. They lay so close, the mountain would have shadowed them if the sun rose in the north. It was late March 1975, the streams clear, cold, and swollen with snowmelt, the air clean, cool, dry.

I sat on the Royal Tehran Hilton's patio, gazing north at the Alborz range, sun on my back, drinking Camparis and soda, eating caviar har-vested in the Caspian beyond the mountains. The only bearded men in kameezes and chador-draped women in this northern quarter of Tehran were dailies tending lawns and kitchens, who trekked south to their poorer neighborhoods at night. Elahiyeh's resident wives, daughters, girlfriends wore neither chadors over fashionably short skirts nor hijabs atop their Jackie O sunglasses. The bespoke-suited men in the back seats of passing Rolls, Mercs, BMWs, were clean-shaven. Rich Tehranis did not have to go to Paris to shop, London to gamble, or Courchevel to ski.

In this part of town, there were few fellaheen to ask whether life for them was good as well. That question was answered four years later when most of the ruling class scarpered to Paris, London, LA in the wake of the fleeing Shah. Among them would be the lawyer we had come to see, Fouad Mahjoub, who decamped, classic cars and wealth in tow, to live in a large country house near Cheltenham.

American Hospital Supply (AHS) was the United States' largest distributor of medical supplies. The wealth Sunni Saudi Arabia showered on Shia Iran and the rest of the world's oil producers when it had deployed the oil weapon six months earlier lured AHS to set out their stall in the peacock empire's bazaar. Don Hausman, a TR Chicago tax partner—AHS's tax director, their CFO—and I came to Tehran to write the agency contracts AHS needed to tap this market and plan to minimize its taxes if it did. The four of us were newcomers to Western Asia; we'd rely on Fouad Mahjoub to guide us.

I left Boston at night for London and a connecting flight to Tehran. It was night again when I landed at Mehrabad International Airport, six-thousand-plus miles east, seven-and-a-half time zones ahead of Boston. The other three flew from AHS Chicago's HQ, a farther one thousand miles west and one time zone behind. Jet lag inescapable, we took a lay day.

Next morning at 10 a.m., we gathered in the Hilton's lobby to meet our driver and play tourist. He described the section of the city we were in, identified the mountains behind us, asked what we'd like to see while we walked toward his black Mercedes sedan parked at the curb. As we stood by the car debating, a figure materialized out of the midmorning sun, like Sherif Ali in the opening desert scenes of *Lawrence of Arabia* or Clint Eastwood cantering toward Lago in the first frames of *High Plains Drifter*. The man staggered toward us, stooped under a rolled carpet balanced on his left shoulder, its ends drooping four feet or so before and behind him. His face was crevassed, sun-leathered; perhaps a third of his teeth were missing, the rest almost as brown as his skin. He wore a traditional *shalwar kameez* over his short, skeletal frame, was sockless in crude leather sandals

The hajji's Bukhara

with small loops for the big toe at the tip of each insole, and was dust coated; an anachronism bucking the passing cavalcade of modernity—cars, motorbikes, glass-and-steel Hilton.

The rug bearer halted a few feet from us, said something in Farsi to our driver, stood there. *Hajji*, the driver said, a tribal villager come many one hundred miles by foot and bus to flog his carpet on Tehran's streets. For perhaps three years, his wife, daughters if he had them, would have woven, knotted, tied, and cut the carpet's threads, spun from wool gathered and stained with vegetable dyes, in the village where they'd lived all their lives. He'd use the money from selling it to make his hajj, the pilgrimage to Mecca the Koran enjoins every Muslim to make at least once in their life.

The romance of buying a Persian carpet in Persia off the shoulder of a Persian hajji whose family had woven it, of walking daily across the warp and woof of faith I'd never have, was irresistible. The hajji unrolled on the pavement a classic five-by-eight-foot Bukhara carpet teeming with red-, blue-, and sand-colored octagons. It was cheap, there being no middlemen.

I paid his asking price, dumped the rug in the Mercedes's trunk, and went sightseeing. It lies today by the sea in a room in Maine, vegetable dyes long faded by a western sun.

BUKHARA
Backlit by the sun
on a boulevard in Tehran,
a tribesman tottered towards us,
rolled rug over his shoulder.
Three years his daughters
wove, knotted, and cut the threads
he lugged from Turkmenistan
to raise money for the Hajj.
Spread at our feet, five wool rows
of octagons, berry-dyed molten lava,
flecked with terracotta,
fixed the eye within the selvage.
I bought it for those colors;
witless, laid them in a skylit parlor,
where sunshine bled to beige
the palette that entranced me.
Only a thin black band stood fast
around each pale polygon
marching in field and borders
like pilgrims circling the Ka'aba.
In that swarm I glimpsed the faith
that whipped the weavers' fingers,
sallow flags in a faded token
praising a power past my ken.[24]

* * *

When our work for AHS finished three days later, Fouad shanghaied me to help one of his clients. The Chicagoans boarded a British Airways flight to Heathrow for a connecting flight to O'Hare; I headed to

[24] Dan Burt, *Salvage at Twilight* (Manchester: Carcanet, 2019).

gnome-land[25] for the first time to set up a virtual vault called an *Anstalt*[26] for Mozafar Panahpour.

Mozafar was rangy, short haired, beardless, no more than thirty-five years old, and owned a local construction company. Mohamad Reza Pahlavi, Shah of Shahs, used the oil dividend to accelerate Iran's modernization. But Iranian contractors often lacked the necessary expertise, size, and experience to realize his projects, so for cosmetic and legal purposes, they bid for them as prime contractors, then subcontracted the brick and mortar work to foreign companies if they won.

The prime/sub arrangement helped hide kickbacks and payoffs, useful in lands where bribery was endemic, like Iran. Say NIOC, the National Iranian Oil Company, solicits tenders to build an oil storage terminal. An Iranian contractor promises to pay NIOC's contract officer 5 percent of the contract's price under the table if its bid wins. A foreign subcontractor offers to build the terminal for the Iranian prime for $100 million. The Iranian bids $115 million for the contract, is awarded the contract, slips $5.75 million to the NIOC official, pays $100 million to the foreign sub, and keeps $9.25 million for itself ($115 million − $100 million − $5.75 million = $9.25 million). All three—Iranian prime, foreign sub, NIOC executive—keep shtum; bribery may have been rampant, but no one wanted to advertise it.

Mozafar and Iranians like him had a more pressing reason than cloaking bribes to own a secure, confidential, offshore virtual strongbox. In 1975, Persia's ruling class—nouveau riche, westernized, secular—feared their sun might be setting. If darkness fell, as it did three-and-a-half years later, their moveable wealth, black and white,[27] had to be housed beyond the grasp of revolutionary mullahs and international criminal courts if they wanted to keep it. Shortly after the mullahs seized power in January 1979, the international press published lists of Iranians each of whom recently

---

[25] UK Prime Minister Harold Wilson coined the term *gnomes of Zurich* to refer to bankers and financiers shorting the pound during the 1964 UK currency crisis.

[26] An *Anstalt* is a Swiss law hybrid entity with limited liability, unlimited life, no shareholders, and no distribution requirements, whose founders, owners, and beneficiaries are confidential. Control inheres in a Founder's Rights deed, which effectively converts the *Anstalt* into a bearer bond.

[27] *Black money* refers to proceeds from bribes, kickbacks, tax evasion, and the like whose existence must be hidden; *white money* the reverse. The terms in Yiddish are *shwarz* and kosher.

had transferred more than $100 million (in 2018 dollars) from Iran. Some of the names I knew.

The day after we arrived, Mozafar landed a large contract and subcontracted its performance to an FTSE 250 company. The British company insisted it be segregated from Mozafar's other business and kept confidential. Mozafar had no offshore legal structure to take contracts—prime or sub—and no offshore hidey-hole for wealth. Fouad asked me what I could do, and quickly.

*　*　*

Neither law school, Morgan Lewis, Treasury, or Touche Ross offer courses in bribery, black money, or burying assets, but I needed no instruction in their principles. *All I really need to know I learned in kindergarten*[28]: as a boy on Philadelphia's streets, from my maternal grandfather and uncles Meyer and Al, from the butcher shop. It took me fifteen years to suss out the rules of my post–law school political and social worlds; I recognized the aims and rules of sophisticated corporate machinations and third-world business practices on sight.

Washington, DC, is a greasepaint city of marble, limestone, granite, columns, pediments, domes, boulevards, monuments, and grand white buildings built to present the nation's capital as a pure, noble, enlightened successor to an idealized Roman republic. In the age of Ike, the 1950s, schoolchildren were taught their legislators, presidents, and cabinet secretaries were honorable men who conducted the nation's business honestly. Seventy-two percent of Americans trusted the federal government in 1964, when I graduated from college. Fifty-two percent still trusted it when I joined the Treasury in 1971, the height of the Vietnam War.[29]

Sure, I knew local politics were corrupt—knew a bribed judge spared me a criminal record when I was seventeen, that when I was ten, Uncle Meyer had killed a criminal tax investigation into my father's business—but I had been taught national government was different, better, and wanted to believe it. I knew DC politics were seamy but not fundamentally corrupt. That I learned shortly after I joined Treasury. Business I never saw through rose-tinted spectacles.

---

[28] *All I Really Need to Know I Learned in Kindergarten*, title of a popular book in the 1980s, passed into U.S. lexicon.
[29] Pew Research Center, *Trust in Government*, survey, November 23, 2015.

But boyhood taught nothing about the details of trusts, *Anstalts*, or offshore asset protection. In Philadelphia, you kept black money in your pocket in a roll with a rubber band around it, under a mattress, or in a safe-deposit box; no acquaintance of mine had a trust fund or knew what a trust was. Liechtenstein, the Turks, and Caicos Islands, Mauritius, just names on a map.

The specifics of offshore finagling I picked up through reading and hear-say during eighteen months at Treasury and almost twenty-four consulting for TR. In these two classrooms, I learned the ideal characteristics of a tax haven: impenetrable bank secrecy (no one, individual or government, may be told what you have), political stability, no taxes, major banks, strong legal tradition, central location, financial expertise, flexible trust laws, reliable trust companies, English fluency. I met U.K. and Dutch tax specialists with long experience in using havens, though had never worked with one. Only Liechtenstein and Dr. Marxer, then just names to me, ticked all tax haven boxes. I was about to find out if they lived up to their reputations.

* * *

You can fly into Zurich at 9 a.m. with a suitcase of cash, deposit it with Centrum Bank in Vaduz, and by 1 p.m. be rising with your skis on the St. Moritz funicular to the top of Piz Nair. It's a trip many make. From Fouad's office, I called a TR London tax partner for the name, phone number, and referral to Dr. Marxer and, next morning, boarded an Iran Air flight to meet him.

Vaduz, Liechtenstein's capital, is a town of 5,400, an hour by car south-east of Zurich off the A3. At the appointed hour, my driver turned left off Heiligkreuz Strasse onto the covered, ground-level parking area under Marxer & Partners' four-story office block. I took the lift to the reception area, announced myself, and was shown to a large office where Herr Dok-tor Marxer, seventyish and Vaduz's leading lawyer, sat behind a Jugendstil desk in front of a window. The sun at his back silhouetted him, and I could not see his features clearly. He did not rise to greet me or shake my hand, motioned to an armchair in front of his desk, asked why I'd come.

Dr. Marxer, I represent Mozafar Panahpour, an Iranian contractor, who would like to organize an Anstalt. He's a prominent builder based in Tehran and . . .

Marxer cut me off with a wave, and in accented English, said, *Yung man, I dun't care who yur client iss or vhut he duss. I haff only to ask two qvestions, und I don't care vhut yur answers are. Duss your client deal drugs, or sell arms?*

No.

Here, complete dese forms—name, phone and telex numbers, bank, founder's rights—giff them to my secretary, und ve vill contact you in a few days vhen the Anstalt iss formed. Gut afternoon.

I took the stairs down to the ground floor, turned my collar up against the late March mountain cold, walked to the open car door to be driven across the Rhine and north to Zurich. I burrowed into the Mercedes's rear seat, asked the driver to increase the heat; neither car heater nor my scarf dispelled my chill. Dr. Marxer's *und I don't care vhut the answer iss* echoed over and over. I had met Arendt's *banality of evil.*

It is not a crime in Liechtenstein or Switzerland to bribe foreign officials, evade foreign tax, or sequester foreign wealth. Marxer had behaved punctiliously, asked the questions Liechtenstein law required, treated me no differently than he would a drug kingpin or merchant of death. He bribed no one, evaded no tax. He had followed the rules and obeyed the laws of his principality and was at peace facilitating bribery and tax evasion somewhere else; his conscience was clear. Was I complicit too? I could argue the question either way, as tax lawyers do. But in the half century since I passed the bar, I've never answered, *I'm an international tax lawyer,* to the question, *What do you do?*

* * *

Liechtenstein was my last foreign trip for Touche Ross & Co. Ira Hefter called me into his office a few months later, in late July, to review my performance and tell me my bonus. My one-year contract with TR had required me to develop the seedlings of an international tax department for their New York office. If successful, I was to receive a bonus of 20 percent of my annual consulting fee.

When I started, the New York office had no international tax specialists. The day Ira called me in, it had five, three of whom subsequently worked at the Treasury in the post I'd had there. My foreign tax group was more than 100 percent chargeable, meaning its billings exceeded TR's hourly billing requirements; the practice was booming. I'd done well, too, in the five years since leaving law school. I had my stake, enough saved to live comfortably the next five years without earning, enough to set tax regulations and virtual vaults aside. At our meeting, I planned to thank Ira for my time at TR, and resign to write. When I knocked on his door, it hadn't occurred to me I'd not receive my full bonus.

Ira saw things differently. He said though I'd satisfied the contract's requirements and more, I *had not been a team player*, so he was giving me a 10 percent bonus, half what had been agreed. Our contract said nothing about playing for the team. My irises changed from blue-green to gray; the skin over my cheekbones tightened. I stared at him a moment, said, *That's unacceptable*, and left. Next morning, my office was locked, my key did not open it, and a box with personal belongings from my office waited for me behind the receptionist's desk. With them was a message to see Mr. Padwe on the tenth floor.

Jerry Padwe, the firm's National Director of Taxes and Hefter's boss, asked me to join the National Office as its head of international tax, for more money, almost before I was through his door. But when I began bemoaning how shabbily Ira had treated me, Padwe interrupted. *C'mon, Dan. You tortured that guy.* I grinned, thanked him for his offer, declined it, and left for the Boston shuttle, never again to enter a U.S. office of Touche Ross. Deloitte Haskins and Sells merged with TR in August 1989. The new firm, Deloitte and Touche, fired Ira soon thereafter for the same overbearing behavior I would not abide.

It was not hard to guess some of what I'd done that might have infuriated Ira; the *peanuts meeting*, the *binned business cards*, the *librarian affair* came quickly to mind. The tax partners were addicted to meetings. Whenever a sensitive client matter arose, they met, not from love of consensus but from fear of being individually blamed for a mistake; corporate decisions insured cock-up culpability would be spread among them all. Generally, these meetings wasted time; all were too long. Working two jobs—one a new trade, commuting 220 miles weekly to the other—insufferably arrogant, I'd no time to spare.

One afternoon, gobbling a late lunch at my desk, my secretary brought in a note from a partner insisting I attend a meeting about to convene. Dessert in hand, a bag of Planters salted peanuts, I took my seat in the conference room. After ten or so minutes of chatter, I began tossing peanuts at the attendees. The partner chairing the meeting asked what the hell I was doing? *Feeding the monkeys.* I was excused and invited to no more meetings. I walked proudly from the meeting, but that pride is laced with shame as I tell the story now.

* * *

The firm printed embossed Touche Ross business cards for me, as for all professionals, shortly after I joined. I threw them away. A few weeks later, a client new to me asked for my card. I apologized for not having one, wrote my contact details on a buck slip, and handed it to him. When the client left, the partner whose client it was asked if the firm hadn't supplied me with business cards. I said they had, but I tossed them.

Why?

They implied I'm an employee. I'm not, just a consultant; I don't want anyone to think I work here.

* * *

Kathy Santagata, the tax department's librarian, was a stringy, black-haired, sloe-eyed Italian girl from Staten Island, an innocent, but with a sultry air. Her father was a Calabrian immigrant shoemaker. She had attended Catholic schools from kindergarten through college and had hardly been outside the five boroughs. Her prominent *nu yawk* accent, which I loathed in others, charmed me in her, as did her feistiness and bookishness.

She accepted my invitation to an evening concert performance of *I Masnadieri* at Carnegie Hall, mounted by the Opera Orchestra of New York under Eve Queller's baton. Afterward, we walked uptown to her apartment through lightly falling snow, which obscured the city's dirt and softened its phalanx of buildings and shop fronts. Arms around each other's waist, slipping along almost deserted blocks, the brash, vulgar city alchemized to an urban version of the forest of Arden, a stage set for passion. She invited me in when we reached her third-floor brownstone walk-up in the high east Eighties. We became lovers. Passion spent, I noticed *The Joy of Sex*[30] open on a chair beside the bed, half covered by the bra and panties she'd cast off. When I asked about it, she said she was an ingenue and did not want to disappoint.

We remained lovers till I left TR, the tax department's open secret we were unashamed of. I was fond of her then and am today.

---

[30] Alex Comfort, *The Joy of Sex* (1972). An illustrated sex manual for tyro and expert, fourteen weeks on the NYT bestseller list in 1972, it remains an international favorite.

6. Arrogance and Rage

D M Burt & Associates in Saudi Arabia

In the middle of the road of life, I lost my way. Nine years I labored at law—
two schools, three practices, government, teaching—to buy a few years'
silence and slow time, only at closing to refuse the freedom I'd earned.

A six-string acoustic guitar leaned, body down, in a corner at Bass Rock
Lane by a sliding glass door onto granite and sea. Morning coffee in hand,
looking southeast over the chop to the horizon, I fancied myself picking
it before a November fire, once I'd learned how. No law firm or corporate
desk stood bare for me; my résumé lay in no hiring partner's briefcase;
TR's last check had cleared; my taxes were paid; there was neither debt,
wife, lover, nor child to mind. The $50,000 ($350,000 today) in my savings
account would buy four scrimp-free years. Bridges burned, exits blocked,
excuses exhausted, a pristine, portable, red Olivetti Lettera manual typewriter on my campaign desk, I had foreclosed all but writing.

I began riffling through scraps of paper accumulated with casual notes
for, or the beginnings of poems on them, a line or two, maybe six or eight,
to choose one to work seriously. At least five of these scraps—on a College dinner, deracination, the Holocaust's long shadow, chance, and an
affair—became published poems in my first chapbook, *Searched for Text*,
thirty-three years later. But before I typed a word in revision, two former
clients called for advice, though I'd been gone from TR for weeks: Denny
Crispin, Boeing's tax director, and Marc Leduc, Northern Telecom's. I fig-
ured they'd swallow no more than a few hours a month, pay me for my
time what TR had charged them, and stretch savings but not filch writing
hours. No noncompete barred me. *No brainer*, I thought and shied at the
first hedge. A few weeks later, I fell at the second and did not address
the hedge again for thirty years.

* * *

By the mid-1970s, the Gulf oil producers were issuing frequent international tenders for projects to modernize their countries. There were no
corresponding programs to alter their cultures. The second Saudi Five Year
Economic Development Plan teed up the Kingdom to feverishly build
roads and microwave towers, ports, schools, hospitals, housing, and office
buildings to catapult its oases and mud-walled cities—Jeddah, Riyadh,

Dharan—from nineteenth to late twentieth century in a half decade. Foreign contractors were to build the catapult.

TR clients began asking about Gulf business and tax laws, especially Arabia's, as the international tenders appeared. These queries often found their way to me, TR New York's international tax guru, and someone who at least could find Tehran and Riyadh on a globe. From pamphlets, articles, business guides, calls to TR affiliates in Arabia, Iran, the Emirates, Kuwait, and my four days in Tehran, I tried to answer them. The advice was often sketchy, *but in the kingdom of the blind, the one-eyed man is king.*

By fall 1975, America was nearly two years into a recession hallmarked by stagflation, caused in large part by the Saudi jolt to oil prices. New England's contractors—road builders, construction companies—were especially hard hit; they slavered to win Saudi work. While I was still a consultant to TR, the New York office promised the Boston office that, come fall, I'd give a seminar for their clients on doing business in the Middle East. When the nights grew crisp, and though I'd left TR two months earlier, Boston asked me to honor that promise, and I complied, thinking, *keep options open.*

The moon was yellow, and the leaves were falling, and the conference room was packed. My thirty-minute talk stretched to ninety as I took questions from some fifty contractors and exporters. Almost all were about Saudi Arabian agents, business laws, taxes, communications, visas, payment. Men—many with the red necks and rough, browned fists of outdoor workers—rushed the dais when I finished, shoving business cards in my hand and asking for my phone number.

The surrounding crowd gave human form to the recession. This was not my first rodeo: I'd promoted DISC, Treasury's then new export subsidy, to thousands of financial executives, accountants, and lawyers across America in 1972. Those audiences had been keen to hear me, the men encircling me now almost in a swivet to hear what I had to say. These Yankee contractors, none of whom had worked outside their home state or region, were desperate enough for work to shoot crap in a primitive desert peninsula three-and-a-third times the size of Texas, sixty-five hundred miles and eight time zones away, that they knew nothing about and lacked the physical infrastructure they relied on to build in the U.S.; desperate enough to chance their companies in an Arabic-speaking, nomadic Muslim land with rudimentary roads, ports, and communications and subject to Sharia law; desperate enough to rely for advice on a monoglot Jewish tax lawyer who'd made one four-day trip to Iran and never been within twelve hundred miles of Saudi Arabia. For some, it was build a Saudi road or school or go bust.

At 8:30 a.m. next morning, Tuesday, in my winter rental at Bass Rock Lane . . . *ring, ring, ring. Ring, ring* . . . 6:50 p.m. there that night. *Ring, ring, ring, ring* . . . through Friday afternoon. Some callers, when we spoke, complained the line was always busy. A week later, New England companies hunting information on Mideast business rules still clogged my phone. As word spread of a Marblehead lawyer who knew about Levantine commercial and tax laws, calls came from further afield. My path diverged beside the sea.

* * *

I'd come to Marblehead to live a dream of the pen. All my short adult life, from first week at La Salle College fifteen years before, my heroes had always been writers, my hunger to join them. I believed then, and believe now, that writing one lyric poem that *pass[ed] into the memory of the race*[31] justifies a life, that making millions, billions, building commercial empires, ruling nations, doesn't; that one day, with money and time enough, I'd try to tread my heroes' path. So I'd told wives and lovers, so I'd told myself.

I rigged conditions to force me to write. A winter rental on a spit of Massachusetts's rock braving the North Atlantic might be a fine place to draft lyrics, hunt, and peck well enough to type a sonnet, but would be useless for law practice. Bass Rock had one phone line, no answering machine, no telex, no stationery, no secretary, and only me to research, draft documents, answer questions. Marblehead was a sailing town seventeen miles north of Boston, not Wall Street. It lacked straw for the bricks of practice: pools of lawyers and legal secretaries from which to hire, case law reports, nearby law and commercial libraries. The internet for online research was a quarter century in the future.

The chalice shone before me. Ex-wives and lovers murmured, *Do what you love.* Circumstances—youth, money, health—cleared the way. No one held a Police Special[32] to my temple and threatened, *Keep practicing law or*

---

[31] My recollection is that Yeats said this of his own work in the preface of the *Oxford Book of Modern Verse*, 1936 edition, but I have been unable to locate the quote.

[32] Colt Police Special is a .38 caliber, six-round cylinder revolver. Uncle Al carried a .38.

else. But I'd already turned aside and taken the road more traveled; I told no caller, *Sorry, I don't practice law anymore* or *I'm on sabbatical.*

I covered every mirror I could in which I might see myself creeping down the road to law practice. Rather than search for a secretary, I asked my part-time housekeeper, Bev Hower, if she could type. At her *Yes*, I hired her full-time to answer the phone, type, and collect mail from my PO box, as well as clean house. I installed no second phone line, no telex, hired no lawyer to help me, though already, there was work for two. My mantra was *I'll handle this crush, pick up a quick few thousand, and in a few weeks, reopen the Olivetti's case*. Deceit, all self-deceit.

Every practicing lawyer needs two things: stationery, for invoices if nothing else, and a system for recording billable time, the indisputable hard evidence of private law practice. At my request, Bev ordered both. The stationer asked what the letterhead should say, to prepare a proof. I scribbled *D M Burt & Associates* on a yellow pad, added the Bass Rock phone number and my PO box, and handed it to Bev.

There were no *Associates*, the trade term for lawyers below partner level in a firm; there was no *D M Burt*. I never used my middle initial. The letterhead puffed a flyspeck, accidental practice, and its practitioner. My first thought in the morning, last at night, remained, *soon I'll pound that Olivetti*, but the mint letterheads and time sheets in my desk drawer gave that the lie. Within the month, my dream lay buried at the back of a storage closet with the Olivetti and guitar.

On a Saturday morning, a generation earlier, aged twelve and a half and a butcher's apprentice at Pennsauken Meats, Marty Goldfield, my father's partner in the butcher shop, came into the back room where I was slicing boiled hams. He watched me whip slices from the stacker while the slicer ran and platter them. After perhaps thirty seconds, he said,

Danny, there's a nickel on the floor. I looked, saw nothing.

There, just in front of your shoe.

Marty, I can't see it.

Look, you're almost stepping on it.

Marty, there's no nickel.

He bent down and picked up a slice of ham from the sawdust covering the floor. *Danny, this is worth a nickel.* Shamed, face flushed, I stifled tears, washed the slice, added it to the platter, and for the next half century, picked up whatever fell but could still be sold.

The companies calling for advice were ham slices, money lying on the back-room floor. My father's tales of selling apples with his father on Depression-era street corners, of being beaten at thirteen for buying a pair of new shoes with part of his first paycheck; my nine years a butcher boy at Pennsauken; tales of Jewish grief and hardship handed down from grandfather, to father, to me, were etched on my bones. My conditioned response was to let no ham slice lie.

If asked why I exploited the practice I'd stumbled on rather than try to write as intended, I blamed childhood's indoctrinations. But the excuse was not the reason, just words to cover shame. Fear of being poor, the insecurity every post-Holocaust diaspora Jew feels, was not my dispositive terror. Experience and history had scored me, sure, but in 1970s New England, neither poverty nor pogrom was a real worry for a Cambridge-educated, Yale-trained, experienced lawyer with a modicum of capability, repute, and an iron will to win.

The bogeyman I fled lay ahead, not behind. He was the risk I would fail at the only thing I rated; he was fear of defeat on my only field of dreams. I'd chickened out, knew it, was mortified. From the day Bev ordered D M Burt & Associates letterhead until I gave up law three decades later, if a stranger asked, *What do you do?* I'd hesitate, mumble, *A bit of business*, and change the subject.

* * *

The Cessna 340 rolled to a stop a football pitch away from Logan's private air terminal. Two men deplaned almost before the chocks were set and walked toward the terminal: one, fair-skinned, heavyset, six feet plus with thin, stringy hair and the dry, red-scabbed skin of an eczema sufferer; the other swarthy, chunky with thick, curly hair and a head shorter; both mid-fifties. It was late morning, last Sunday in November 1975, as I waited for them inside the terminal's door.

The big WASP was Tom Dunbar, CEO of R. P. DeSantis, Inc., a New York road builder; the short Italian, Tony Salvei, CFO. In the 1950s, DeSantis had paved a fair portion of the roads and airport runways in eastern New York state and southern Connecticut but fell on hard times. Tom and Tony were running the company when the founder died in the mid-1960s and bought it cheap from his heirs. Tony had called Bass Rock Lane twenty-four hours earlier to introduce himself and ask to meet next day.

DeSantis was paving little in New England as we shook hands. In one of the terminal's private meeting rooms, Tom said they'd been to

Saudi Arabia a few months earlier, appointed a Saudi agent—al-Mohsin Establishment—tendered on a Saudi Ministry of Transport road contract, and a few days ago, received a telex saying they'd won. They were returning to Jeddah three days after New Year to sign it and mobilize for construction. They asked me to go with them to deal with problems they were having with their Saudi agent, as well as create a legal framework to avoid U.S. taxes on their hoped-for Saudi profits.

You needed a visa to visit Saudi, and the application required two things I hadn't: a Saudi sponsor and a religion. Al-Mohsin supplied the first, the second was my problem. My grandfather and father were atheists, though strong ethnic Jews, as was I. If called yid, kike, or sheeny, I'd fight, but did not observe Jewish holidays, eschew gentile lovers and wives, or know a rabbi who would supply a good-standing certificate. I also doubted the Saudi embassy would look kindly on an application with Jewish in its religion space. After a brief call with Tony's visa expediter, and a $100 donation, I became a Unitarian, whatever that was, shielded by my atheism from apostasy and ethnic guilt.

Arrivals Hall, Jeddah, January 3, 1976. It had been scarf and gloves weather—thirty degrees Fahrenheit, little humidity—twenty hours and six thousand miles ago at Boston's Logan. It was T-shirt and shorts weather—eighty degrees, clammy (seventy-five percent humidity)—and nearly midnight, as men in expensive business suits or spotless white *thawbs*, swinging Connolly leather briefcases, emerged from the forward door of our L1011 from London. From the rear doors poured stained, coarse thawbs and burqas, many lugging plunder from London shopping sprees in large cloth sacks or cardboard boxes. The sticky tarmac between plane and terminal was dark; passengers left the pool of harsh halogen light from construction lamps at the base of the stairs and shuffled cautiously, single file, toward what looked like a warehouse. I peeled off my sweater as my feet hit the ground and straggled with them, jet lagged, into the Arrivals Hall.

Between Arrivals Hall doors and Passport Control five hundred feet opposite was nothing; no baggage carousels, no signs identifying areas for luggage from arriving flights, no baggage trolleys, no uniformed porters, only gray stained cement floor and foot-wide steel columns supporting the roof. Fluorescent ceiling lights spread a green, ghastly glow over dyspeptic knots of the deplaned. The thawbs and burqas waited fatalistically for luggage to appear, some of the men telling prayer beads. The suits sweated, paced, peered into the black on the tarmac.

From time to time, scrawny fellaheen in dingy thawbs and sandals dragged baggage carts into the hall, piled with luggage high as they could throw a bag. They picked an empty spot on the terminal's floor, dumped the luggage so it formed a small hill, and straggled back to open cargo holds for more.

The passengers gathered around the baggage handlers like maggots on roadkill and peered at the luggage hills as they rose, looking for a familiar strap, tag, or material. If you spotted your bag, you shoved through the milling crowd to rip it free; if you didn't, you clambered up the hill in search of it.

ARRIVALS HALL, JEDDAH, 1976
Wool suit and cotton kameez
jostle on luggage mountains
for their Samsonites, Louis Vuittons,
string-bound cardboard cartons,
like rag-pickers on a dump.
At their feet, russet fellahin
from the Horn, or huts in Yemen,
bare-toed in sandals and soiled thawbs,
add to the piles from LIOIIS.
In the scrum, six centuries elide;
Huntsman and hajji,
Bell Labs and prayer rug collide.[33]

We reached our hotel at 1 a.m. It was the height of the Saudi building boom, a gold rush for recycling petrodollars, Jeddah what San Francisco had been in 1849.[34] Our packed plane was one of four crammed international flights that landed there that night. The hotel, the best in town, was the equal of a Times Square whore hostel renting rooms by the hour. Several western businessmen were asleep on couches in the moss-green tiled reception area. There was no bellhop. Our reservations were lost until

[33] Dan Burt, *Salvage at Twilight* (Manchester: Carcanet, 2019).
[34] James Marshall discovered gold at Sutter's Mill in 1848. The California gold rush followed as the news slowly spread, and by 1849, San Francisco was morphing from a sleepy pacific coastal village to a city.

Tom helped the night clerk search the reservations ledger for them, using a $100 bill as a pointer. My clients went to their rooms to sleep; I to mine to work.

After lunch on our flight from London, Tony had handed me a copy of DeSantis' agency agreement with al-Mohsin. Twenty minutes later, I knelt beside his seat and told him the agreement had three clauses that put DeSantis at al-Mohsin's mercy. First, al-Mohsin had the right to receive road-building payments due to DeSantis from the Transport Ministry, deduct its commission, then pass on the balance to DeSantis. If DeSantis and al-Mohsin disagreed on something, al-Mohsin was able to withhold payments from DeSantis. Second, Sharia law applied by a Saudi court governed the contract rather than ICC arbitration.[35] Third, al-Mohsin would hold the passports of DeSantis' in-country employees. Saudi agents had used foreign employees as bargaining chips in disputes with their employers by preventing them from leaving the Kingdom. *Tony, this contract's commercial suicide. You've got to renegotiate it.*

That's your job, Dan.

Across the table was Raymond Nakachian, a.k.a. Raymond Nash, al-Mohsin general manager, forty-three years old, Lebanese, polyglot (Arabic, English, French, German, Russian), charismatic, and notorious. It was customary for non-Saudis—Lebanese, Syrians, most often Palestinians—to manage international and daily admin of a Saudi agency's business. These managers spoke English as well as Arabic, often French and German; were cosmopolitan, experienced international businessmen; and loyal only to money.

Their employers, the agency owners, often spoke only Arabic, had little if any education, were untraveled, and in at least one case, were illiterate. They managed the Saudi side of things—including bribes to secure contracts, permits, visas, and on-time payments from the government. Saudi law required every foreign company working in the Kingdom to hire one.

---

[35] Substantial international contracts customarily provide that disputes shall be resolved in a neutral country under the Rules of the International Chamber of Commerce.

The local agent ostensibly guided foreign principals in local ways, supplied admin and logistical help, and kept them in-line in-country. But Saudi agents had neither staff nor expertise to help foreign contractors execute contracts. Builders supplied their own expertise, equipment, and personnel. King Fahd's government didn't need the agents to control foreign contractors. Ministry contracts gave the government ample rights and power, and once a contractor put its personnel and equipment in the Kingdom, the government had all the leverage it needed. So what did agents do for their commissions?

They arranged and paid the bribes necessary to procure and execute contracts. A standard Saudi agent's commission was 5 percent of contract value, for example, $2.5 million on a $50 million contract. There was no maximum; commissions were often 10 percent or higher, depending on contract size; I've seen them breast 25 percent. The worldwide rule of thumb for the percentage of a contract an in-country representative agent is due is the higher a contract's value, the lower the agent's percentage, since the agent does roughly the same amount of work for a $50M as for a $500M contract. The reverse was true in Saudi; the higher the contract's value, the larger the agent's percentage. This anomaly spotlit the agent's true role; commissions in Saudi and other Near Eastern countries were higher the greater the contract value because the more a contract was worth, the more senior the Ministry employees, and more of them, who had to be paid off.

Agents implied, sometimes bragged, that much of their commission went for bribes. Foreign principals rarely witnessed a bribe being paid, but circumstantial evidence argued they were. Agents supplied no admin services, office space, housing, or employees to contractors to justify their commissions. Gulf country government employees and kin stayed at Paris's Ritz and London's Dorchester hotels and shopped at Chanel and Versace, Givenchy and Hermes, Graff and Boodles, Huntsman and Tommy Nutter, whose suites, scents, silks, sparklers, and suits no government employee's salary in the world could have paid for. Experience, logic, and local lore testified the agent's function was to bribe.

* * *

Dawn broke as I added the last words to a revised agency agreement for DeSantis. A chant floated across the rooftops of the two- and three-story buildings below and through my open window. I couldn't make out the words or, for a few seconds, guess what it was. Then the sound raised an echo from boyhood of synagogue chazans leading diaspora faithful in high-holiday prayers, and I realized it was a muezzin calling flock of another faith to sunrise hosannas. Ever after, Jeddah felt less foreign than the clay tennis courts and parquet dance floors of New England's WASP yacht clubs.

I went for a run through ancient Jeddah's shattered streets to clear my head. Within a few strides, I was weaving through hordes of honking, careening white Toyota flatbed pickups, like a forward striker through defenders; forty years later, television viewers around the world became familiar from ISIS videos with these same Middle Eastern workhorses, fifty calibers rather than rebars behind their cabs. Wood-framing planks, cement sacks, steel cabling, gas cylinders for welding torches, chains, compressors, jackhammers, Yemeni, Somali, and Pakistani laborers in kaffiyehs bounced on their heaving cargo beds. Piles of concrete, steel, and plastic pipes were heaped on every street. Yellow Komatsu and Caterpillar backhoes, mobile cranes, and tractors jostled for space in a competition it looked like Komatsu was winning. Rolls of steel cable, plastic water and waste piping, electrical conduit cable were strewn among portable generators, lumber piles, and concrete mixers.

Passing heavy equipment had uncobbled streets, if they hadn't been excavated already to lay pipe, pour foundations, or replace open sewers with buried conduits. Craters gaped where once houses stood, flanked by half-demolished mud walls. Newsreel footage of London's East End during the Blitz spooled through my mind. The stuttering *pow! pow! pow!* of jackhammers followed by the *whoosh! whoosh! whoosh!* of exhaling compressors driving them, soprano of screams of power saws and drills, grunt of tractor diesels, crash of falling walls, builders' shouts and curses combined in a cacophony that forced would-be speakers to shout. Diesel fumes mingling with dust from demolished buildings and excavations and stink from open sewers fouled the air. It was 7 a.m., work was in full swing.

SITE WORK

Yellow Komatsu backhoes
rip chunks from mud-brick walls;
pneumatic drills chew stones
pre-Islamic masons spalled;
swarms of Toyota pickups
swallow rebars spewed from ships.

Hydro-carbon hunger
unleashed these beasts
remorselessly devouring
Jeddah's ancient streets.[36]

Jeddah's harbor was clogged with ships waiting to offload heavy equipment and building supplies, the wharves piled to impassibility with freight waiting to be cleared. The demand from foreign contractors for Ro-Ros—roll-on roll-off ships, which could land cargo on the beaches of Obhur Creek, twenty-two miles north of the city beyond the choked harbor—drove international Ro-Ro charter prices stratospheric.

Jeddah was not unique; construction convulsed all Arabia. The Saudi masses looked on silently as foreign contractors demolished and rebuilt their cities, flouted their customs, ridiculed and disdained them. Four years later, in November 1979, those silent witnesses applauded Wahabi fundamentalists who seized the Masjid al-Haram—the Grand Mosque in Mecca, the Muslim world's holiest site—and lit the blue paper for the Muslim fundamentalist explosion whose shock waves still rattle the world.

Tom, Tony, and I arrived at 9 a.m., on schedule, at al-Mohsin Establishment to meet Raymond. He arrived at 11 a.m. and then kept us waiting another half hour. When I complained, Tony told me Saudi businessmen turning up hours late for meetings, always unapologetic, was usual in the Kingdom. Business here, he explained, was done the IBM way: *Inshallah* (*God willing*), *Bokra* (*tomorrow*), *Malesh* (*no problem*). One of these three words was the invariable, interchangeable reply to questions such as when a meeting would begin, a payment made, a shipment cleared. *When will Raymond get here? An hour, Inshallah. When will the ministry pay our last invoice? Bokra. Can you clear our bulldozer through customs today? Malesh.* But God was often unwilling, tomorrow never came, and every clearance proved a problem.

Raymond was medium height with a refrigerator's build, shaved head, snarling voice, penchant for bragging about his karate black belt; he swaggered, was abrupt, and given to shouting at and cursing subordinates. Calumny became him. He was railing about *that sand-n-----*, his dark-skinned

---

[36] Dan Burt, *Salvage at Twilight* (Manchester: Carcanet, 2019).

boss and al-Mohsin's owner, Sheik Mohammad, when we entered his office near noon. It was the first time I'd heard the slur, ironic as Raymond was dun-olive colored himself; dark skin is an affliction even in a khaki-hued land. Twelve years earlier in London, as Raymond Nash, he had owned the El Condor Club with Peter Rachman, the eponymous slumlord.[37] There, royals, toffs, and politicians mingled with show girls and models like Christine Keeler[38] and Mandy Rice-Davies, criminals like the Kray brothers, and Russian spies in the stew that became the Profumo scandal;[39] Raymond was reputed to be a money and gambling man, something of a heavy, in the mix.

* * *

Tom introduces me as DeSantis' lawyer, says I have concerns about the agency agreement, and hands me the con. I begin, *There are problems with the agreement. . . .* Raymond cuts me off. *Come back tonight*, he barks and then hollers for someone to show us out.

Most serious business with agents in Arabia is done after dinner, between 10 p.m. and 1 a.m. Their offices are too chaotic, interruptions too constant for serious negotiation during office hours. An hour before midnight, Tom and Tony sit on either corner of a large, deep, knackered sofa in Raymond's office, me between them. Raymond presides from a leather chair opposite. A coffee table almost as long as our sofa, heaped with papers, separates the parties.

There are no pleasantries. I tell Raymond the agreement has three unacceptable terms: al-Mohsin's right to receive DeSantis' payments from the Ministry, retention of DeSantis' staff's passports, governing Saudi law, as well as a number of minor faults. I reach into my briefcase for the revised contract to hand to Raymond when he shouts, *No! You signed it; the deal's done. Who the fuck do you think you are? That's all. Leave!*

---

[37] Peter Rachman, a Holocaust survivor and resistance fighter, came to the UK from Poland in 1948. Infamous for renting slum flats at outrageous rents, his surname became an English noun for heartless slumlord. Both Christine Keeler and Mandy Rice-Davies were at one time or another his mistress.

[38] See Christine Keeler and Douglas Thompson, *Secrets and Lies* (London: John Blake, 2012), chap. 5; and the Profumo scandal.

[39] In 1963 UK Tory Minister of Defence John Profumo admitted to sharing the favors of Christine Keeler with a Russian spy. Profumo resigned; and the Tories lost the next general election.

Tom and Tony blanch, press their spines and sides against their respective sofa corners as if to pass through them to anywhere else, say nothing.

Raymond, I've told my clients they can't work under this contract; they'll leave Saudi first.

He sits wordlessly for perhaps thirty seconds, leans slightly toward me, says softly, *You know, Saudi's a dangerous place. Something might happen to you, maybe walking back to your hotel tonight.* As he speaks, he pushes some of the papers off the coffee table to expose what looks like a Beretta.

C'mon, Raymond. If I go missing, you'll be the first person questioned. I'm an American, and the Saudis will care a hell of a lot more about what happens to me than they will about you. Here's the revised contract. We can discuss it tomorrow.

We rise, leave; Tom and Tony are silent on the short walk to our hotel. I'd seen killers since I could recognize faces; my Uncle Al was one, a hit man. A .38 hung by its trigger guard on a nail below the till at my father's Fourth Street butcher shop; a .22 lay in the top drawer of his bedroom dresser. I played with the .22 when no one was home. Raymond is no killer, at least not in Saudi Arabia. He signs the contract, unchanged, the next day.

* * *

The cookie jar rule is the first a criminal lawyer learns. *If your hand is in the cookie jar, don't say it ain't.* You may be counting the cookies, discarding broken ones, gathering crumbs, cleaning the jar, fixing a crack, estimating how many it will hold, but your hand is in the cookie jar, proudly and rightly. Pithily put, the rule is, *admit the act* or *confess and avoid*. If caught, don't deny what you're doing or have done; explain it away. Deny what you've done, and you lose credibility; the jury won't believe you when and if you tell the truth. Worse, they'll believe the prosecutor, and you'll do time. I introduced Tom and Tony to this rule four years after I'd put Saudi behind me.

The FBI pounced on the two drug dealers as the buyer closed his car trunk. He opened fire; the seller fled in his car, pursued by the feds. They forced him off the road a few minutes later several miles south of Wilmington, North Carolina, and he died in the ensuing gun battle. In the trunk of his car, the agents found a suitcase stuffed with several hundred thousand dollars in $1,000 bundles of $20s. The name of the bank on the paper band around each bundle was South Bridgeport Savings Bank (SBSB), a small southern Connecticut state bank 658 miles due north of where the drug dealer's corpse bled onto I-95.[40] Tom and Tony owned SBSB.

Federal bank examiners showed up at SBSB's teller windows a few weeks after the drug bust. They wanted to know how the drug cash came to have SBSB bands around it. Was the bank financing or laundering money for Bridgeport's thriving drug trade? The manufacturing city's glory days ended thirty-eight years earlier with World War II's last shots; SBSB would not have been the only Bridgeport bank involved in drugs. The examiner's search was fruitless; SBSB was in full compliance with all federal regulations and uninvolved with trafficking. But they disinterred a consolation prize.

I hadn't spoken to either Tom or Tony since November 1979, when I'd surrendered my interest in Burt & Taylor, the law firm hatched as D M Burt & Associates almost four years earlier. I'd seen Tony last in 1978, on the steps of DeSantis' Jeddah villa, where we swapped avuncular warnings as we said good-bye.

His—*Dan, you know this ain't going to last. I hope you're putting some of it away.* Tony was talking about my law firm battening on fees from the Saudi construction boom, the *it* being my share of the firm's profits. *Yeah, I know, Tony, I ain't pissin' it away.*

Mine: *Remember, Tony, don't bring it back in brown paper bags. Call me when you're ready, and we'll find a way to bring the money home tax-free.*

I heeded Tony's caution; he ignored mine.

DeSantis' Saudi road building and equipment rental businesses operated as branches of DeSantis, Ltd., a nondomiciliary U.K. company incorporated in the United Kingdom, but managed and controlled in the United States. This arrangement, state-of-the-art international tax avoidance at the time, exempted DeSantis' Saudi profits from U.K. tax and deferred any U.S. tax on them until DeSantis returned the profits to the U.S. There were ways to use the deferred profits in the U.S. without triggering U.S. tax, but that took careful planning, hence my warning not to try to spirit the Saudi profits home.

Washington, DC, midmorning, March 1983, several months after the federal bank examiners left SBSB. The receptionist at Capital Legal

---

[40] Interstate 95 (I-95) runs 2,000 miles north-south from Maine's border with Nova Scotia to the tip of the Florida Keys. It's the main north-south highway on the U.S. East Coast.

Foundation, the public-interest law firm I then headed, put a call through from Tony. I hadn't spoken to him or Tom since I'd sold my law firm interest four years before. He skipped the pleasantries.

* * *

Dan, we'd like to talk to you.
  Sure, Tony, about what?
  We'll tell you when we see you. Can we meet?
  Of course, when?
  How about tonight?
  OK. Where?
  We'll be at The Fairfax, on Massachusetts Ave by 8 p.m.

It was the second time Tom and Tony had flown in their plane to meet me. But rather than talk in their suite when we met that night, they insisted we stroll down Massachusetts Avenue and told me what had happened as we walked. Shortly after receiving the road contract, they opened an equipment rental business in Jeddah, Brett Crane Rental, to capitalize on the shortage of heavy equipment the Saudi infrastructure program created. It was a galloping success; the first few years—say, 1976 to 1979, the height of the building boom—they had no effective competition and made millions, most of it in cash. The business tailed down from 1980, and they planned to close it. Three years before, they'd instructed Brett Crane's Saudi-resident American manager to bring back cash in tranches of $100K or more each time he returned to the U.S. He'd hauled back more than $2 million in his luggage, literally in brown paper bags, by the time the Feds had the boards up at SBSB.

Tom and Tony divided the cash, kept it briefly in their personal lockboxes, then dribbled it into their bank accounts at SBSB in roughly $9,000 tranches per deposit. Federal banking rules require a bank to file a cash transaction report when someone deposits more than $10K in cash. SBSB did not report Tom and Tony's deposits because no single deposit exceeded $10K. But the Feds discovered the suspicious three-year pattern of $9,000 deposits, by then totaling over $2 million, when they scrutinized SBSB's books. The bank examiners referred the matter to the IRS's criminal tax division, which smelled attempted tax evasion. They opened an investigation, judged the facts showed Tom and Tony had committed tax fraud, and referred the case to the U.S. Justice Department for prosecution. Tom and Tony received summonses from the U.S. Attorney for the Southern

District of Connecticut, ordering them to appear before a grand jury in ten days, the morning before Tony called me.

Federal grand juries weigh evidence of a crime. If they reasonably believe sufficient evidence exists, they return an indictment, after which the U.S. attorney arrests the accused and asks a judge to set a trial date. Grand jury proceedings are secret. Witnesses must appear alone, without their lawyer. The grand jury needs little evidence to indict; reasonable belief the accused has committed a crime is enough. It's often said a federal prosecutor can get a grand jury to indict based on a ham sandwich. Lawyers do all they can to keep their clients from testifying before one.

* * *

I asked Tom and Tony if relations with their Saudi agent, Sheik Mohammad, had remained fraught from the time I'd last talked with them. They said that they had, and worsened as the good times waned. Had he threatened to confiscate Brett Crane's assets? Yes, and have their American manager jailed. Had he put his threats in writing? Tony thought he had.

A lawyer may not tell a client what to say but can offer his understanding of what happened and ask if it's accurate. I said it seemed to me that Sheik Mohammad, on whom their right to work in the Kingdom depended, had been greedy and hostile from the first. His constant threats had grown more serious and frequent as the construction boom, and profits, waned. By 1980, there was a real risk he would seize Brett Crane's cash and equipment, possibly have its U.S. manager imprisoned, and force DeSantis from the Kingdom. Saudi authorities and courts offered no protection. DeSantis might lose most of what it had earned there. To protect themselves, Tom and Tony spirited money from Saudi operations to the U.S. They didn't spend it. Instead, they deposited those profits in SBSB with the intention of holding them in escrow (transferring money from A to B via a neutral third party), pending the final accounting for their Saudi business, and Sheik Mohammad would be paid anything he was due from this escrow. *Is that what happened? Yes*, they said, *that's what happened.*

I asked Tony to find and send me Sheik Mohammad's threatening telexes. Meanwhile, I organized an escrow account in the Channel Islands to hold the amount sneaked back to the States, pending an agreement with Sheik Mohammad on what, if anything more, he was owed. *Determine how much you brought back, and wire that amount to the Channel Islands escrow,* I told them.

The following day, Tony faxed me a number of telexes from Sheik Mohammad demanding more money. Several threatened to shutter Brett Crane, seize its equipment, bank accounts, and jail its in-Kingdom manager. I set up the escrow, and Tom and Tony wired $2M into it.

* * *

The U.S. attorney had graduated from Yale law a few years after me and knew who I was. I called, told him what had happened, and volunteered to produce my clients and evidence confirming their story, if he would quash the subpoenas. He agreed.

Three weeks later, we met in his offices in Bridgeport's federal building. Tom and Tony described how they had tried to protect themselves from Sheik Mohammad. I outlined the escrow, now holding the peripatetic Saudi dough, gave him copies of the escrow agreement, and tabled the threatening telexes. He questioned Tom and Tony, read the telexes, then asked my clients to wait outside. Alone, he said he'd drop the tax fraud case, reopen it if the government discovered evidence inconsistent with our explanation, and sent us on our way.

Tax evasion is a U.S. federal crime whose penalties include substantial jail time. Offenders are vigorously pursued. To convict, the government must prove intent to evade beyond a reasonable doubt. The U.S. attorney let Tom and Tony walk because he doubted he could meet that standard. No jury was likely to believe it was beyond a reasonable doubt they were trying to evade U.S. taxes rather than protect their business in the face of Sheik Mohammad's grim telexes. Their tale may have been bullshit, but it was compelling bullshit.

* * *

In the mid-1970s, buccaneers—swarms of them, Europeans, Americans—prowled Jeddah for deals to broker. They packed the hotels, company villas, restaurants, and *Doing Business in Saudi* seminars at the U.S. consulate. Some were U.S. lawyers but not touting legal advice; like the rest, they were business-suited freebooters, aspiring middlemen lunging for brokerage commissions, brass rings worth millions if you snagged one. None I knew did. Brokering Saudi government contracts—negotiating kickbacks, bribes, payoffs necessary to win them—was reserved for Saudis and their Arabic-speaking cousins, Palestinians, Lebanese, Syrians, and Egyptians, not Yanks and Europeans. Nevertheless, tales of deal-broking jackpots, like reports of the philosopher's stone, lured counselors to down quills and join the hunt for golden fleeces.

An ant among grasshoppers, I stuck with what I knew, lawyering. There was little competition. Several companies met in Jeddah during my first visit. I was hired on the spot, and I returned to Marblehead with more business than when I left. A week after landing back at Logan, D M Burt & Associates hired its first associate. New clients called. Perhaps there was a brass ring for lawyers but fashioned out of subfusc contract drafts, legal opinions, tax plans rather than glittering deal fees.

Six weeks after my first visit, I returned to Saudi, for two weeks this time rather than one, representing three or four clients in addition to DeSantis. There were even more foreign companies wanting legal help than on my first stay. But to satisfy this demand required a Saudi office, which meant finding a Saudi partner, because foreign lawyers could only practice in the Kingdom under a Saudi lawyer's sponsorship. I knew none.

At the time, there were perhaps fifteen Saudis in the Kingdom trained in secular as opposed to Sharia law, hence able to sponsor foreign lawyers. The U.S. Consulate kept a list of them available for the asking. I began cold-calling the names on it, starting from *A*. Some wouldn't speak to a foreign practitioner from an unheard-of firm; one, Saleh Hejalain, already in a loose relationship with Sherman and Sterling,[41] cursed my presumption in ringing and hung up. But the name after Hejalain's on the list was willing to listen, and I flew to Riyadh next day to pitch him.

Mohamed Hoshan was a son of the Nejd, the central section of Arabia—provincial, fundamentalist, and tribal home of the ruling al-Sauds. Born into a nomadic Bedouin family, first of it to be schooled, he studied law in Cairo in the late 1950s and fell in love with Nasserism. He was a good lawyer and read people quickly.

Slightly below middle height, fat, pale mahogany skin, wiry steel-gray hair, Mohamed's choleric demeanor hid a rather kind, avuncular, middle-aged man. He was acutely sensitive to and infuriated by condescension, like many Saudis of his generation, and uncomfortable among the uptown crowd. His weaknesses were women, alcohol, cigarettes, and a penchant for spoiling his children. We were a match; analogous backgrounds, leftish leanings, at least one weakness in common. A handshake, and D M Burt & Associates had a Saudi sponsor and Riyadh address; a handshake, and I tapped a pool

---

[41] S&S was and is among the largest blue-chip, white-shoe Wall Street law firms.

of clients, wealth, and experiences that poisoned me for a decade, drip by imperceptible drip. *Look on my Works, ye Mighty, and despair!*

When Dr. Hoshan agreed to sponsor me, only Burlingham, Underwood & Lord, a stodgy Wall Street maritime law firm, had a Saudi office. They looked to be a milk toast competitor in a seller's market. I hired a second associate immediately on returning to Marblehead.

D M Burt & Associates didn't need capital, nor was it hurting for business. It did need more lawyers to handle the business it had, especially a senior who could supervise the juniors. Word had got around Boston that there was a burgeoning international law practice based, improbably, in Marblehead. A few weeks after I hired the second associate, Jack Gray—who was a diplomat's son, lawyer, stranger, and fifteen years my senior—paid court.

He invited me to lunch at his Beacon Hill Club, which barred Jews, Blacks, and scions of the working class, and there petitioned to join D M Burt & Associates as a partner. Jack was eking out a living as an Of Counsel to a small Boston firm, had some expertise as an international trade lawyer, and knew a meal ticket when he saw it. The firm's name changed to Burt & Gray when he joined, but he was partner in name only. I retained 90 percent of the profits and voting power, but Jack's 10 percent profit interest made him three times what he'd been making when he joined.

Eighteen months after Gray joined, Fritz Taylor, a just-retired senior Aramco executive, signed the partnership agreement, and the firm's name changed to Burt, Gray & Taylor, then a year later to Burt & Taylor. I took Fritz in because he held the promise of more business. However, the majority of profits and control remained mine, and would for several more years.

Clients multiplied from five to fifty plus in four years, a fair number of public companies—Comsat, Boeing, Fluor, GE, International Harvester, Northern Telecom, Pan Am, Racal Electronics, Westinghouse. Lawyers grew from one to fifteen by October 1, 1979, my thirty-seventh birthday. The *New York Times* published a flattering half-page profile of the firm, above the fold on the front page of the business section. It featured a quarter-page picture of me at my campaign desk, staring out over harbor and sea.[42] My share of Burt & Taylor's 1979 profits was just shy of

---

[42] Tom Goldstein, "Mideast Tapped by Small Firm," Business and the Law, *New York Times*, May 11, 1978.

$2 million in 2018 dollars, ten times what TR had paid me to consult for them four years before.

Each new client, lawyer, dollar minutely dulls my senses that have registered risk and danger from childhood. I walk flat-footed where I once trod on the balls of my feet, the least bit less crouched, less ready to strike or run. Gradually, expectations that tomorrow may bring disaster, that the clients will all take their business elsewhere, that greed will impel men I know only slightly to betray me, diminish. Fight or flight reflexes relied on since the age of five atrophy. Without being aware of it, the wariness I learned in childhood fades.

* * *

Too much success too soon transforms confidence into arrogance. I expect the practice to grow, and when it does, the confirmation of my judgment makes me more certain I'll be right next time, no matter the subject. As the firm and my reputation grow, clients second-guess me less and less until I'm advising ex-cathedra (with full authority of office) and assume clients unquestioningly will do what I tell them. Associates and partners flatter continually and almost never challenge me. As Dale Johnson, one of my first hires and only Partner promoted from in-house, said to me one day, *Dan, I don't believe you can walk on water, but I'd go down to the beach and watch if you tried.* With shame, I recall my delight when he said it, and how it chuffs still. Little by little, a grain at a time, I feel infallible and correlatively invulnerable.

D M Burt & Associates bought a house at the top of Cliff Street on Marblehead Harbor with a lawn that ran down to its own dinghy float. A contractor client remodeled the house into offices and residence, and I lived above the store for six months until new business and hires squeezed me out. During long summer lunch breaks, after work and on weekends, I sailed the Laser[43] stored on the float.

Global clients, large deals, a Saudi office, and control of the firm demanded constant travel. My life passed on planes between the U.S., Saudi, London, and Europe. When not headed overseas, I circumnavigated America, from Boston to NYC, DC, Atlanta, Miami, Houston, San Diego, LA, Chicago, and cities large and small in flyover states between. Six weeks did not pass without boarding a 747, DC10, or L1011 in Boston

---

[43] A Laser is a fourteen-foot, single-handed mono hull racing dinghy with lateen-rigged sail.

headed for London, then another two hours later to Jeddah or Dhahran. A steward greeted me at their cabin doors and escorted me left to my seat, except where the door was forward of first class or on Concorde, where we all turned right. Hall porters at Europe's grand hotels remembered my name: London, *The Berkeley*; Paris, *Le Bristol*; Rome, *Hassler*; Geneva, *Hotel President Wilson*; and Zurich, *The Dolder Grand*. My 1977 business travel expenses were more than six times that year's median U.S. income. The constant motion, and the cocoon in which I traveled and lived, muffled and disguised the fast-approaching end of the Mideast business boom, and my partner's building jealousy.

* * *

When the practice absorbed the whole of the Cliff Street house where I also lived, I moved out and bought a seaside mansion at the top of Rolleston Road, a private road ten minutes' pedal south from the Cliff Street offices: eight thousand square feet, six bedrooms, in four acres on a bluff above the Atlantic. A local architect helped me gut and redesign the spread: strip floors; raze walls; add new bathrooms, a library with a fireplace on the sea, new kitchen, sauna, gym, wine cellar, safe, and study for whomever might be cohabiting. I'd gone from winter renter to man of property in 360 days, though my paramour at the time did not bed the architect, so far as I know.[44]

Most of the accouterments of this new life came from Europe. England supplied contemporary British paintings, early nineteenth-century Spode, contemporary Wedgwood, bespoke suits, Sea Isle cotton shirts with French cuffs, silk ties, and Winston Churchill Havana cigars, the latter carried to America in my luggage. Wines came from France—vintage clarets, Burgundies—and old ports came from Portugal. America supplied contemporary studio ceramics and a hand-hammered silver dinner service. Saudi gold guineas fashioned into cuff links rested in a jewelry box on a table by my bed. My British partner craved a piano, and a Steinway baby grand materialized beside one of the Persian carpets covering the drawing room's blond oak floor. I never heard her play it.

Property, possessions, and demands of work spawned servants and staff. An executive assistant arranged my business and personal life,

---

[44] See Irene and Bosinney in John Galsworthy's *The Man of Property* (London: Literary Press, 1906).

appointments, travel, trysts. A driver chauffeured me to meetings, the airport, home. A housekeeper cleaned, laundered, and shopped for food and household supplies. A handyman mowed, clipped, and fixed. I was Mr. Burt to all.

Romances and vacations suffered a sea change. Relentless travel to major European and American cities meant more women met, in more places, so there were more liaisons. If business left no time to romance a lady where she lived, I transported her to Marblehead. One I met in London with time only for introductory drinks came to Bass Rock Lane a few weeks later on the air ticket I sent her. Others in cities I strode through briefly on business flew to Marblehead for weekends or with me on business trips when I could tack on a few days at the end for pleasure.

Kissinger said, *Power is the ultimate aphrodisiac.* Wealth is a close second. I had at least the appearance of the former, reality of the latter. Feminists were fewer on the ground in the late 1970s, and an unmarried lawyer in his midthirties, head of his own firm with a national reputation and no debt was a catch whatever his personal qualities; beauties would have flocked to Quasimodo had he been fixed as I was then.

The Englishwoman who'd flown to see me was a keen skier. The first winter after we met, I said, *Book wherever you've dreamed of skiing*, and found myself at Badrutt's The Palace in St. Moritz in January 1977, enduring the most expensive, worst ski holiday of my life. Skiers took a three-minute, thirty Swiss Franc taxi ride in the mornings from the hotel up to the tram, then stumbled slowly back down the main street from the tram in ski boots on wobbly après-ski legs, bowed beneath the skis on their shoulders, to the hotel in the afternoon. The palace's lounge divided into two sides for après-ski drinks: one reserved for the glitterati, one for the merely able to pay, a segregation new to me. Jacket and tie were de rigueur at dinner, the food unexceptional, everything overpriced. I remember fondly only the glaringly bright, starched, and ironed sheets and duvet covers changed every day, or more if needed. St. Moritz, Badrutt's Grand Palace Hotel, were places where royalty went to be with royalty and plutocrats so they could say Prince X or Princess Y, whose hand they'd shaken once, were their best friends.

The same woman later led me to Zermatt, Aspen, Vail, and Alta for ski breaks; to Barbados, the Bahamas, and British Virgin Islands for sun and sand. Her roots were the scullery rather than high table; once I was paying, she would stay only at the poshest high-class resorts she'd read of—

the Canyon Ranch, for instance. With her, I visited all the best places. I've never been again.

My Ozymandian decade was exciting, replete with beauty and elegance, but ultimately destructive. Few men in their midthirties would not have enjoyed my tour of the western world's plutocratic precincts, the money, possessions, fawners, and sex. But even though business and its trappings were corrosive, because they eroded fear and self-doubt, without something more, they would not have led me to the public combat that came within a whisker of undoing me. That *more* was the mix of power, novelty, intrigue, and, at times, danger my mid-East practice supplied, the heady notoriety acquired on my early-1980s strut through DC, and the rage simmering in me since high school.

* * *

It was after 7 p.m., and the Queen's Building, the smartest business address in Jeddah, was almost empty. A Saudi lawyer of Syrian descent, Hassan Mahassni, and I were negotiating the final legal points of a subcontract between his client, a prominent Saudi establishment businessman, and Collins Construction, an Ohio contractor, to build a large hospital in Jeddah. Collins had given me full power of attorney, notarized and plastered with Saudi Embassy stamps, to conclude the deal as I saw fit, its construction elements having been already agreed.

Shouts, wails, chains clanking in the alley five floors below Hassan's office interrupted negotiation. I turned my head toward the windows and asked, *What's that noise?*

Prisoners being taken to the punishment square, and the crowd going to watch.

I'd heard of Sharia law penalties—say, flogging for an adulterer or severing a thief's fingers or hand; the passing tumult made them real.

When I turned back to Hassan behind his desk, he asked, *You're a Jew, aren't you?*

Yes.

And you're flying to Riyadh tomorrow? (Hassan knew my partner, Mohamed Hoshan, and where he practiced.)

That's right.

Aren't you afraid?

No. Why? Should I be?

He waved his hand toward the alley. *Jeddah's enlightened compared to Riyadh.* Negotiation resumed, my demands undiminished.

We struck a deal and then went to Hassan's house for dinner while our agreement was typed in final. Hassan was a leading Saudi lawyer representing some of the Kingdom's wealthiest businessmen,[45] and his villa, cars, clothes reflected his stature. He was also effortlessly charming, a not unusual asset of sophisticated Levantines. We'd met on my second trip to Jeddah, and he'd visited me in Marblehead when in the U.S. on business shortly after. This was my first time in his home.

* * *

Hassan showed me into a small room with a bar adjacent to the dining room and asked, *What would you like to drink?* Before I could answer, he said, *Perhaps a Campari?* Though Saudi is *dry*—as Sharia decrees—rich, westernized citizens like Hassan discreetly maintained fully stocked bars. From his Marblehead visit, he knew I drank Campari before dinner. But Campari is an uncommon tipple, and I was surprised as well as delighted he had it. I asked how the trick was done.

He said smugglers regularly visited their Saudi customers and took alcohol orders. They filled them in Europe and shipped the wine and spirits in bond in sealed containers to Jeddah on Arabia's west coast for transshipment to Dhahran on the east, where they would proceed by sea to, say, Mumbai. The booze lorries stopped for the night at a secure depot in Jeddah. Customers alerted to the stopover several days in advance came to the depot in the dark for their orders. The smugglers cut the container's seals, distributed the drink, then resealed the containers for hauling east to Riyadh, where the process was repeated, then on to Dhahran. There, the now-empty containers were loaded on a ship bound for Mumbai. Hassan had known for a month I was coming to negotiate and added Campari to his standing order.

A driver entered with the final typescript of the hospital contract. Hassan skimmed it, said it looked in order, laid it on the bar, and asked,

Shall we sign?

Of course.

I picked up the contract to double-check the final points agreed that night had been correctly inserted, then recoiled.

Hassan, I can't sign this. It's in Arabic.

---

[45] His best-known client was Ghaith Pharaon, a high-flying, controversial businessman extremely close to the royal family, immensely rich, and, after BCCI collapsed, an international fugitive from U.S. justice.

Dan, don't you trust me?

My signature would bind Collins to whatever the contract said, and I had no idea what that might be because I couldn't read Arabic. It would be worse than foolhardy to sign a document I couldn't read; it would be malpractice. But Hassan had given me his word, which, in Saudi, meant much. If I signed it, and all was in order, I'd have secured a friend for whatever further dealings with him I'd have. My *gut*, and perhaps a bit of the Campari, said, *Chance it; show faith.* I signed.

By midmorning next day, I'd had the contract translated, found it accurate, and whipped the English version around to the Queen's Building for Hassan to sign. He laughed when he saw me; I'd had the document translated in a hell of a hurry for a trusting colleague. We worked together over the next three years on other deals, the way smoothed by trust established over Campari and Arabic text.

If there'd been a ringer in the Arabic version, I could have confessed malpractice to Collins, who could have disavowed the contract for lack of mutuality, meaning they couldn't possibly have agreed to the contract because their agent, me, had acted beyond his authority by signing a contract he didn't understand. They would certainly have sued me. Though the contract's Arabic text proved fine, and the willingness to take Hassan's word bore fruit in future, as I'd bet, it remained a foolish risk, since it is even more difficult to disavow a signed contract in Arabia than in England. It wasn't a chance I would have contemplated, let alone countenanced, before my practice bloomed in the Saudi desert. It was the first consciously arrogant chance I remember taking in my invincible decade but not the last.

* * *

Newly shaved, showered, dressed, and cologned, I emerged from my Riyadh hotel near 10 p.m. on a Friday night and, my driver unavailable, hailed a cab. I got in, said, *As-salaam-alaikum (Peace be unto you)*, handed the cabby a paper with my destination's address in Arabic, and settled into the back seat.

We'd been hurtling over a newly built, wide, unlit boulevard for less than a mile when the driver asked, *Bint? Bint?* I stared at the back of his head. *Bint? Bint?* more emphatically this time. I shook my head to signify incomprehension. He almost shouted, *Bint? Bint?*

Please, I said, *English. No Arabic.* Without slowing, he half turned to me, raised his right arm parallel to the car's floor—fingers and thumb aligned to form a spade—and thrust it rhythmically down and up, down and up while almost screaming, *Bint! Bint! Want Bint?* The pantomime worked; the penny dropped.

Bint is Arabic for girl, or woman, though in the present context, meant something coarser. I'd never knowingly had sex with a prostitute. I was in the capital of Wahabism, most fundamentalist of Muslim sects. Fornication with a prostitute is haram (forbidden) in Islam, the penalty one hundred lashes. Though not a religious crime that men were often punished for, imagining what the *Mutawe'en* (Islamic religious police) might do to an American, Jewish atheist caught in Riyadh fucking a Muslim hooker was sufficient for a lifetime's nightmares. Perhaps the cabby was an agent provocateur. I shook my head vigorously, repeated, *No! No!* and longed for the ride's end.

* * *

Weekends in Arabia when I worked there began at sundown Thursday. If Riyadh boasted public entertainments other than restaurant dining and watching public punishments, no one mentioned them to me. Social life and entertainment took place in private, like the party to which the cab was taking me, thrown by fashionable Palestinian expatriates in their large villa in an expensive Riyadh neighborhood.

My host was Aboud Abdulrahman, a Palestinian Lebanese and deputy general manager of Adham Establishment. Aboudi, as all called him, was more playboy than businessman. His gift to me when he visited me in Marblehead was a long-sleeved, dark-blue, collarless, three-button silk Yves Saint Laurent shirt, printed with playboy bunny logos—I suspect how he saw us both. His wife was the tall, fashionably thin daughter of Lebanon's ambassador to Syria, who was also chairman of a major Arab bank, substantial PLO funder, and father-in-law to reckon with in the Arab world.

Aboudi was Adham's front man; his partner, Mahdi Saifi, its general manager who ran the place. Mahdi, too, was Palestinian Lebanese, but there, the similarities ended. An engineer, experienced road builder, good with numbers, serious, he was the brains of the pair. Mahdi made the daily business decisions, vetted contractors, and saw to Adham's finances. Both were in their early forties, near six feet tall, black haired, fair, and flat bellied; they made a good pair.

Aboudi opened the villa's door at my knock and ushered me through the vestibule into a thirty-by-thirty-foot drawing room whose furniture had been pushed to the walls to create an ersatz dance floor. On it, some twenty Levantine men and women, arms linked, rotated in two segregated circles—men in one, women in the other—to traditional Arab music. The dance superficially resembled an Ashkenazi hora, to which I'd danced at bar mitzvahs as a boy. But this was no hora, where men and women link arms and circle to plaintive klezmer clarinets and violins to celebrate harvest, wedding, or coming-of-age. This was a *dabke*, a Levantine dance pulsing with suppressed sexuality in which two single-sex circles, side by side, rounded to twanging ouds, lilting shawms (primitive oboe), and pounding *davuls* (double-headed drums). Klezmer music is drumless, the mixed-sex hora chaste; the *davul*'s drumbeat at the heart of a *dabke* infuses a primitive, palpable sexual tension foreign to klezmer.

Aboudi brought me a drink, introduced me to a few people on the chairs lining the dance floor, and then left me to link arms with the circling men. After several circuits, he filched one of his wife's scarves from her as she passed in the women's circle, slipped his arms from the men either side of him, and advanced to their circle's center. He stretched the scarf between his hands to simulate a handkerchief or veil, held it a few inches before his groin, and moved it from left to right in time to the music as would a belly dancer. The men clapped and shouted in time to the music. The women joined in as they circled to the *dabke*'s beat. The tempo quickened; Aboudi swayed faster. His wife broke from the women's line, entered the center of their circle, and with another scarf, mimicked Aboudi. The dancing went on for perhaps another ten minutes, the music louder and louder until it climaxed in a burst of orgiastic drumming, clapping, stomping. Husband and wife stopped in their circles bull's-eyes; fervent applause; sweat beaded on Aboudi's brow. The dancing continued for hours, but the evening's climax almost certainly came later, when couples went home to bed.

* * *

Crist Road Contractors (CRC), out of Phoenix Arizona, had introduced me to their Saudi agent, Adham Establishment, and its general managers, Mahdi and Aboud. Bill Crist owned CRC and gave his life to it. From one man with a bulldozer, he built it into a major southwest road builder, specialist in blasting, moving dirt, and paving blast furnace deserts. He was illiterate, missing three fingers on his right hand, one on his left, a constant stubble before the look was fashionable, gaunt, middle height with watery-blue Celtic eyes and sandy hair. Almost always smiling, no terrain too tough, no deadline too short, he was the type of American *can-do* frontiersman lionized in World War II U.S. propaganda films about the Navy's Seabee construction battalions. A verse from "Ridin' Old Paint" came to mind whenever we met:

> Now old Bill Jones had two daughters and a son,
> one went to Denver, the other went wrong,
> the son got killed in a pool room fight,
> still Bill keeps singin' from morning till night.
> —"Ridin' Old Paint"

Bill sent Clay, his twenty-three-year-old son, and Bob Norman, general manager in Crist's Tucson headquarters, to supervise their Saudi road contract. Neither had been out of the U.S. before. They could push sand all day with a D9 in 130-degree Saudi desert, but Saudi customs and character flummoxed them. For everything to do with their Arabian operation—except blasting, grading, and paving—Crist relied on Mahdi and Aboudi. I handled their contracting and tax work and advised generally where necessary.

It's 10 a.m. in Al-Khobar, where I am, and midnight in Tucson, eighty-two hundred miles west, when Bill Crist reaches me:

Dan, Mahdi and Aboud are in jail, and I'm worried about Clay and Bob. Can you meet with them ASAP and figger out what's goin' on?

What happened?

I'm not sure, but Clay'll explain.

I'll be on the next flight.

No one talked about sensitive subjects on Saudi phone calls, assuming the *Istikhbarat* (Saudi General Intelligence Directorate), as well as America's NSA, could monitor them. It was unusual to hear from Bill rather than Clay or Bob on a purely Saudi matter, especially at midnight Tucson time. Whatever the problem, none of them wanted to talk about it on the phone. Moreover, there was a tremolo in Bill's sixty-year-old voice I'd not heard before; Clay was his only son.

Bob and Clay were pressed against the arrivals gate, scanning the disembarking passengers for me when I deplaned in Riyadh from Dhahran late that afternoon. On the drive to Crist's villa, they said Sheik Adham, Adham Establishment's owner, had Mahdi and Aboud jailed the day before for skimming and taking kickbacks from the Establishment's contractors. The Sheik demanded Clay and Bob meet him in his office the next morning, passports in hand, to delve into their role, if any, in the fraud. He promised to find and jail them if they were no-shows.

I asked had Crist paid the jailed managers any kickbacks or bribes in the Kingdom, or given them traceable funds. *No.* I did not ask whether Crist kicked back to the pair in some other way or place and didn't want to know. I left Clay and Bob at their villa, told them to secure their passports, not bring them to the morrow's meeting, and went to brief my Saudi law partner, Mohamed Hoshan.

Next morning, we sat in the Establishment's outer room for an hour before the sheik arrived. All stood when he entered. He hurried past us into his office, barking orders in Arabic to staff scurrying after him. His long gray prophet's beard preceded him like a pike. A soiled gray *thawb* billowed over his chest, stretched taut over his big belly; he was sockless, sandaled, hair unkempt. Arabic his only tongue, unable to read or write, you would have taken him for an old, nomadic goatherd had you bumped into him on the street.

But Sheik Adham was no bumpkin; he could do numbers like a rocket scientist and had been at his ease in a London boardroom with Goldman Sachs' investment bankers across the table. He'd weighed the value of his principals' contracts, guessed how many millions he should have reaped, estimated the Establishment's costs, came up within $50,000 of what Adham Establishment should have earned. It was some 20 percent less than what was on the Establishment's financial books, the books Mahdi and Aboud kept.

Dr. Hoshan and Sheik Adham knew each other; Mohamed assured me they were friends. Crist agreed Dr. Hoshan could offer to open its books to Sheik Adham and reimburse him for amounts, if any, he should have received from Crist but didn't. We were shown into the Sheik's office but not offered the customary tea or coffee. The two Saudis spoke briefly in Arabic, Sheik Adham motioned to an assistant, and we were shown out without more. Outside, Mohamed told us the Sheik was mollified but not happy, knew almost to the penny what had been stolen, and would look first to recover from Mahdi and Aboud. For the time being, Clay and Bob should carry on building the road, and keep their passports close.

Aboudi's father-in-law secured his release from jail a week later, and he quickly left the Kingdom with much less than he'd expected. Mahdi had no powerful intercessor to arrange his release and wasted behind bars another

three months before he squared Sheik Adham. Mahdi, too, left the Kingdom hurriedly after walking out of his cell and, like Aboudi, with far less
money than hoped. Mohamed and I agreed Clay should return to Tucson
as soon as possible and stay there; he left two days after the meeting with
Sheik Adham. Crist finished building their road and built no second in
Saudi. The Sheik sailed on: whole, satisfied, unchallenged.

* * *

Traveling the Middle East held more threats than thuggish agents, taxi
pimps, and cheated sheiks; angry locals, for example, or nervous soldiers and faulty planes. I ignored them all, and all the risks I took proved
worthwhile. But the fact that a risk is successful isn't evidence it should
have been taken, any more than *post hoc ergo propter hoc* ("after this, there-
fore because of this," often referred to as the post hoc fallacy) is true. Worse,
the arrogance these victories bred spread through me like tea spilled on
cotton, dimmed my sight, tainted my judgment.

* * *

Tehran. The Iranian New Year begins not in January, but when the land
first breeds new life. It's early evening March 21, 1978, the spring equinox,
Nowruz eve. For weeks, Tehran's streets have heaved with protests against
the Shah and his westernizers. Ten months later, he abdicates and flees
in the face of the Islamic revolution. Yet the Tehran Hilton's grand ballroom glitters with hundreds of *Nowruz* celebrants, insouciant men, and
bejeweled women accoutered in the best from Paris and London bou-
tiques. Neither before nor since have more women in one place, at one
time, beguiled me. I'm sitting at a table with some of them, all polite, cosmopolitan, and indifferent to me. I go to bed early, alone. Their flawless
English, Western fashions, and cosmetics disguised their ethnic clannish-
ness, a gulf between us that made romance impossible.

At 8 a.m. next morning, *Nowruz* day: I hustle through the empty
lobby, turn right out the door headed southeast in brilliant sunlight
beside a broad boulevard, and within a block, hit my stride. The streets
are empty of people, only the occasional car, and dry—perhaps sixty-
eight degrees Fahrenheit, cloudless, smogless air—a perfect high plains
spring runner's morning. Right across a grass strip, perhaps 250 feet
away, four youths walk toward me. As they approach, one yells, aims a
stick, chucks it at me, and they close. I break into a full run; the distance
between us doesn't lessen. After a few hundred yards, they quit, resume
their route, walk off. I don't slow till they're dots in the distance. I haven't

witnessed the demonstrations against the Shah and America but just met some of the demonstrators.

* * *

Damascus. I like souks; they remind me of Fourth Street in Philadelphia, where I was born, a cobbled shopping street packed with pushcarts. Al-Hamidiyah souk in Damascus was one of the best, packed with stalls selling jewelry, gold, food, clothes, rugs, and mother-of-pearl marquetry tables, trays, chessboards for which Damascene craftsmen are famed. I spend several hours there in the late afternoon after a meeting, hoping to find the perfect chess set and board. Tired from the hunt, I'm early to bed and rise before dawn for a run before my flight to Paris.

Hafez al-Assad had seized control of Syria six years earlier, in 1971, and ruled ruthlessly. Soldiers in pairs patrol his quiet Damascus streets, Kalashnikovs slung from their shoulders. Togged in a red tracksuit, dawn a half hour off, I set off at a fast clip from the hotel down an ancient street well lit by modern, incandescent lamps, and keep the pace up. To my left, on the pavement across the street, a pair of soldiers approach. As we draw abreast, one shouts, *Waqfa!* (*Halt!*). I keep running. Another shout. I hold my pace. The *click* of a round being chambered sounds; I continue to pull away from the patrol. They don't fire.

There was light enough for the soldiers to see I was weaponless, and terrorists don't often wear red running suits. Twenty years earlier, fourteen years old, hanging with a gang of older boys, I'd stood on one of their shoulders an hour before dawn to steal some bunting from above an Atlantic City boardwalk shop. My booster slipped, and my feet kicked in the plate-glass shop window as I fell. In the predawn stillness inside the lobby of the Chelsea Hotel 150 feet north, you could easily hear the crash and tinkle of heavy glass. I hit the ground running, darted left twenty feet from the store at the ramp to the street, and pounded down it past the Chelsea, headed for the boonies (boondocks, meaning rough or isolated country). A figure burst from the hotel as I passed and shouted, *Halt!* I didn't break stride. *Crack! Crack!* Two pistol shots in the air. I stopped and waited to be collared. I've bet the Syrian soldiers are at least as disciplined as the Chelsea Hotel security guard a generation earlier, and there'd be warning shots this time too.

* * *

Thirty-five thousand feet over southeastern Turkey. Saudia is a dry airline, no alcohol served or allowed on board. I fly it on internal flights, but

BA takes me home. I spent two weeks out of every six, except in July and August, in our Saudi offices; two weeks enough. As I turn left after boarding the London-bound BA TriStar in Dhahran, I'm impatient for wheels up and a drink.

There are only five or six of us in First Class this morning, few enough for everyone to have a two-seat row to themselves. But BA has plonked me on the plane's port side beside a large, gray-haired American, a Texan perhaps from his accent. Immediately after takeoff, I take advantage of the two-thirds empty cabin, move to the vacant row behind him, and wait for a drink.

I sip my second double Campari before lunch, daydreaming while gazing at the approaching Taurus Mountains. *Brraaat!* A sound like a truck backfire from the starboard wing. The plane lurches forward; the seat's lumbar support hits my kidneys as if someone kicked my seat back. The starboard wing dips, I spill my drink, we drop perhaps five thousand feet before leveling out. Ashen, wiping Campari from my crotch, I'm startled when the gray beard I'd sat beside in the row ahead twists so he can see me and drawls,

Son, y'all evah bin tuh Turkey?

No.

W'aal, yur goin thar tuhday. We just lost our starboard engine.

I've read that three-engine Lockheed TriStars can fly on only one if necessary but am not reassured. The captain comes on, confirms the Texan's diagnosis, and tells us we're making for Istanbul an hour north. I ask Tex how he knew what happened and am told he'd been a U.S. Army bomber pilot in World War II who'd spent a lot of time ferrying B-17s from the U.S. to Britain. His calm is infectious. I ask if I may retake my seat next to him and, with his assent, spend the hour as we limp toward the Bosphorus lost in his war stories.

This is the captain speaking. We've begun our descent and will shortly be landing. My heart races. The runway appears, white with fire-retardant foam like a broken sea. A gauntlet of lime-green crash trucks and ambulances line its sides. I cinch my seat belt till it bites, grip the seat arms, wait. Touch down, a slew left, and the plane rolls to a stop in an empty area far from the Ataturk International terminal. The passengers applaud.

* * *

All booms end. There was less construction work in Saudi by the beginning of 1979, as initial major infrastructure projects completed. By then, too, the U.S. economy had been recovering from recession for three years, and U.S. contractors and manufacturers turned their sights inward again. Lastly, the

1977 U.S. anti-Arab boycott law (ABL) and the Foreign Corrupt Practices Act (FCPA) had come fully into effect, erecting additional hurdles for U.S. companies trying to do business in the Arab world.

American business had lobbied hard against the ABL and whittled it to a mere annoyance. But no company lobbied against the Foreign Corrupt Practices Act when Congress debated it; even oil companies shrank from publicly championing foreign bribery. So the FCPA had teeth, and SEC and justice would sink them deep into violators.

The FCPA forbids a U.S.-controlled company, wherever based, to give anything of value to a foreign official. Something of value is undefined, but paying an agent more than a 5 percent commission on, say, an Omani, Mexican, or Nigerian government contract or giving an Indonesian general more than $5,000 is problematic. To pay an agent 25 percent commission on a Saudi airport maintenance contract would buy a ticket to jail. This imperial attempt to export American commercial morality to endemically corrupt lands failed, but injected me into the heart of American deals and intrigues in the Persian Gulf.

Kansas Oil Field Equipment Corp (Kofeco) built and supplied 95 percent of the compressors, valves, sensors, and gauges NIOC (National Iranian Oil Company) used in Iran's oil and gas fields. A British company had supplied these to NIOC until the mid-1970s, when Kofeco hired Mahsood Almadani as their Iranian sales agent. Within months, the British company was out, Kofeco in, and Mahsood receiving a commission of 25 percent on every nut and bolt it sold NIOC. Kofeco paid him $55 million (in current dollars) on these sales the first year, which rose steadily thereafter.

North Tehran is green, leafy, and warm in early June 1978, a few months after the passage of the FCPA. Mahsood's villa, tennis court, swimming pool, lawns, and garages sprawl behind an eight-foot-high stone wall and delicately interlaced iron fence. A security guard mans the gate. Kofeco has sent me here to tell Mahsood he must renegotiate his commission and reduce it by 60 percent; under this dispensation, he would have received $22 million rather than $55 million his first year as their agent.

With me is Fred Kroger, Kofeco's fledgling general counsel. He's come to Kofeco from farm, cow college,[46] law school, and the assistant U.S.

---

[46] A provincial college, sans culture, sophistication, and tradition, often specializing in agriculture.

attorney's office; he has no business experience. His ten government years were spent in Topeka, Kansas, prosecuting drug dealers, armed robbers, and insurance fraudsters. Less than one hundred thousand souls then dwelled in Topeka, the capital of a Bible Belt state whose main industries are cattle, corn, and Evangelical Christianity. The film *Elmer Gantry* (1960; starring Burt Lancaster and Jean Simmons) was set there. Fred receives his first passport a week before he sits with me at dusk on the patio of the Tehran Hilton, drinking his first ever Campari, before we meet Mahsood next day. You don't have to sniff to smell the cow shit on his shoes.

A servant shows us into a drawing room—marble floor, replica Empire furniture seating thirty, crystal chandeliers, silk Isfahani carpets, Sèvres tea and coffee services. A tennis-thin man—perhaps five feet eight, clean-shaven, in open gossamer silk shirt, silk-wool summer trousers, dark-blue linen blazer—rises to greet us from a group of five male retainers. He's all Eurasian charm and hospitality. We sit, are served coffee, tea, and cakes, talk generalities for ten minutes. Then Mahsood stands, excuses himself, and asks me to accompany him. We leave the others talking about cars and climb the stairs to his second-floor library. Its door shuts behind us; we're alone. Business begins.

Mahsood, the U.S. has just passed an antibribery . . .

I know about that. What does Kofeco want to do?

Well no one is going to go to jail for you, that's for sure. They can't keep paying you a 25 percent commission.

How much will they pay?

Ten percent at best, and that will have to be justified.

Can you do better?

If I can find any way, I will.

It's a short meeting. We rejoin the group, tell them negotiations will resume in Geneva a week from now, and prepare to leave. I'm headed for the airport for a flight to Crete and a seaside villa I've rented for a five-day holiday. We are standing at the door shaking hands when Mahsood says, *Wait*, signals; a servant appears and hands me a thick plastic carrier bag. *A gift for you.*

Beyond the villa's gates, I open the bag: two round stainless steel tins, unmarked, taped shut, nestle in enough dry ice to keep the two kilos of best black market beluga caviar inside them cold till I reach Crete. The caviar's market value is $2,500 ($10,000 today), the then price of a pound of gold. There was no gift for Fred.

At the villa, I refrigerate the caviar, buy biscuits to eat it with, a liter bottle of Campari, two dozen bottles of Schweppes soda water, and several lemons. Shortly after dawn next morning, I swim, then sit drying in the sun above the Aegean eating caviar and drinking Campari for breakfast. Three days later, I'm two-thirds through the first tin, nearly finished the Campari, and bilious. The remaining kilo and a third of caviar become brunch for the fishes.

Mahsood and I meet in Geneva, negotiate, but I won't offer more than a 10 percent commission. He warns NIOC will replace Kofeco as a supplier, but it does not. Seven months later, Mahsood follows the Shah into exile. A month after, he flees when a news report appears listing the names of scarpering Iranians who have transferred money, and how much, to Western banks. Mahsood's name and the amount he transferred, $100 million ($400 million today), appear near the top. Five years later, he sues Kofeco in U.S. federal court for unpaid commissions, reasoning the company would rather buy him off than have their possible bribery exposed in a trial. My judgment, and advice, is he's bluffing. Kofeco doesn't pay. Mahsood drops the suit and slinks away.

A smidgeon of power, the rush with it—prestige, wealth, luxury— refashion me, though not so the morning mirror shows; Caesar syndrome does not reflect. I take greater risks, play bit parts in affairs of state, discount great and good, and am pissed if a client doesn't take my advice. I grow my law firm cavalierly. Years later, a law student I had been seeing at the time said her friends had dubbed me *Lord Marblehead*.

* * *

Boardroom, top floor, COMSAT building, Washington, DC. The conference table stretches to the horizon; an aircraft carrier's flight deck comes to mind. Halfway down its right side sits Lucius D. Battle, COMSAT's senior vice president for corporate affairs, who will chair the meeting. Arrayed on his left are seven or eight COMSAT top brass. At his right hand is Lloyd Cutler, senior partner of Wilmer Cutler and Pickering (WCP), one of DC's preeminent law firms and COMSAT's outside general counsel. Battle is a former U.S. ambassador to Egypt, Middle East expert, State Department doyen. Cutler (BA, LLB Yale), one of WCP's founders, is an international law specialist. In a few months, he will be Carter's White House counsel; fifteen years later, Clinton's. These powers have convened to act on a recommendation for COMSAT's Saudi agent.

COMSAT was born out of the U.S. Congress in 1963, like Athena from the head of Zeus, to develop satellite communications systems. Part publicly funded, wholly privately owned, its board is replete with political, scientific, and business grandees; in provenance and profile, it is the bluest of blue-chip companies. COMSAT's government roots, funding, and ongoing connections make reputational risk a major concern; a scandal or illegal activity at COMSAT is a quasi-governmental one. It must not only behave lawfully but be seen to do so; it must be Calpurnian.

Communications satellites figure in the plan for the Saudi national communications net. COMSAT wants to supply, install, and/or service them. The business team recommends Adnan Khashoggi for their required Saudi agent. COMSAT hires Burt & Taylor to advise it, and this morning, I'm to say whether they should enter Saudi on Adnan's arm.

I had met Khashoggi and worked with directors from his Mayfair offices on Upper Brook Street, a half-block east of Park Lane in London. Magazines advertising shoulder-fired, heat-seeking antitank missiles and 50-caliber machine guns littered the reception room's coffee table. Adnan Khashoggi is the best-known, most flamboyant Arab agent in the world. His Turkish father had been personal physician to King Abdul Aziz al Saud, the Kingdom's founder. Adnan grew up with Abdul Aziz's favored sons, the Saudi princes, one of whom is king, his younger brother waiting in the wings. He flies the world in a DC8, sails it aboard *Nabila*, a superyacht the size of a small cruise ship. His homes span the globe; his offices dot London, New York, Paris, and LA. Adnan is the world's largest and most powerful arms dealer and one of its richest men, Saudi royal family contacts the source of his power and wealth.

I had eaten with two of his directors at his local, Le Gavroche, London's best French restaurant, fifty yards east from his offices; been a weekend guest at the country estate of another director on the River Test. Adnan is the Saudi agent for some of our clients, his commissions at least double or triple 5 percent. This morning, I'm to tell COMSAT how he does business.

*   *   *

I arrive with an associate, am introduced, seated opposite the company contingent. There are no preliminaries; we all know why we're here. Battle asks, *Is Khashoggi effective and responsive?*

He's both, I say, emphatically, and explain. Battle again: *Is Khashoggi reputable?* My lawyerly answer begins: *Large, sophisticated international agency . . . major clients across the globe . . . financially secure . . . never indicted or charged . . . if you're careful. . . .* Cutler interrupts.

We didn't ask that! Is he corrupt?

Aah, c'mon, Lloyd, you know the answer to that as well as I do! Of course he is. You don't get a government contract in Saudi or sell arms internationally without a bribe, and Adnan is agent for some of the biggest Saudi contracts and international arms deals.

There are no more questions, and I leave a few minutes later. COMSAT does not retain Khashoggi.

A few weeks later, Cutler invites me to lunch at his club, The Metropolitan, at Seventeenth and H on the northeast corner of Farragut Square, the White House prominent to the south across the park a five-minute stroll away. The club is one of Washington, DC's oldest, august, exclusive, all male; it's my first visit. The invitation flatters me, and I'm curious to see the club's interior and experience its atmosphere.

Cutler doesn't talk about COMSAT. He explores, gingerly, sotto voce as befits the Metropolitan's dining room—double height, cavernous, crystal chandeliers and wall sconces, walnut walls interspersed with crimson, watered-silk-covered panels—my joining WCP. But the prestige membership in his firm confers hold no interest. I don't share Cutler's vain, pompous assessment of himself, his firm, DC lawyering, and business law itself. We don't meet again, nor do I reenter The Metropolitan Club.

* * *

Hong Kong, winter, 1979. From an elevator on a high floor of a hotel in Central, the business district, I exit right and walk down a dim hall toward a corner suite to meet a stranger. I'm to brief Mr. Smith, if that's his name, on Pan Am's chances of winning a contract to manage the King Abdul Aziz International Airport (KAIA), five square miles of new runways and terminals nearing completion nineteen kilometers from Jeddah.

Five years earlier, Saudi Arabia broke ground for KAIA, touted as a state-of-the-art airport and high-tech tent city intended to ease the journey of millions of Muslim Hajj pilgrims, some 2.4 million in 2018, who pass through Jeddah to and from their pilgrimage to Mecca an hour and a quarter's drive away. But Mr. Smith is interested in KAIA's second, less ballyhooed role, as base for the Royal Saudi Air Force's Eight Wing.

The Saudis had neither the people nor experience in 1979 to operate and manage the infrastructure, including KAIA, built or abuilding for them. Once completed, they outsourced the operation of these facilities, and hence day-to-day control, to experienced international companies. The CIA is keen the outsourcer that runs KAIA be American.

Pan Am crowned itself *the world's most experienced airline.* However, America's unofficial flag carrier, its blue globe logo instantly recognizable everywhere, is no longer atop the world in 1979.

Pan Am logo

Hobbled by overcapacity, a lack of intra-U.S. routes, and the '73 Arab oil shock, Pan Am has been losing money since the early 1970s; it will fold in 1991. William Seawell becomes its chairman and president in 1975 and, by decade's end, has turned the company briefly profitable. He dreams of glories ahead funded by revenues from managing KAIA, a steady revenue stream untethered to bums on seats.

But first, Pan Am must bid for and win the contract, which will depend on the answer to two questions: how large a commission must they pay a Saudi agent, and will the FCPA allow them to pay it? I'm hired to answer both, and then report not only to them, but to the CIA as well. The intrigue infuses excitement, a drug I need in ever-larger doses.

From the start, building D M Burt & Associates in a distant desert kingdom with alien laws and culture drew me more than the money, which alone wouldn't have held me. But after four years, the practice was routinizing, negotiations less fraught and unpredictable, Saudi commercial culture westernizing, investment bankers and asset managers from London and New York thick on the ground. Hunger for something new, novel, especially with a soupçon or more of risk inherent in it, had driven me since childhood. My taste for the new and at least a semblance of adventure in part underlay my decision to go to St. John's, and Yale after that. It drives me still.

On my first trip to Riyadh in 1979, I suss out that the successful bidder for the KAIA management contract will have to pay a commission much higher than 5 percent of the contract's value. This surprises neither me nor the Saudis and others with whom I discuss it. KAIA is a visible, high-value, national and international prestige and strategic project, involves the Saudi Ulema, Muslims everywhere, and the Saudi and U.S. military. It will attract swarms of bidders. By the time I prepare to leave our offices in the Eastern Province for meetings in Korea, it's clear a successful bidder will have to pay a minimum 25 percent commission to their agent.

An Aramco executive, an American, asks me to coffee while I'm finishing my stint in our firm's Al-Khobar office before flying to Seoul. I'd met him through Fritz Taylor, who'd joined my firm from Aramco a year earlier. Over sweet Arabic coffee, he says he knows Pan Am wants the KAIA contract, of my inquiries about it, and asks me to stop in Hong Kong on my way to Seoul to meet a gentleman who is also curious about it; this Aramcon serves two masters.

At my knock, Mr. Smith, a middle-aged Caucasian American with mid-Atlantic accent, answers the hotel suite door. He's alone. His first question, How much commission will Pan Am have to pay its Saudi agent? His second, Will U.S. law allow them to? I answer, leave, never to see him again, learn if his real name is Smith, whether he's CIA, or to return to Hong Kong.

Next day, I fly to Seoul, attend meetings, then twenty-four hours later, board a Pan Am 747 Clipper to New York. At Kennedy, a stewardess in

Pan Am blue preempts the other departing passengers and escorts me from the plane, down jetway stairs, and into a waiting limo. I've checked no luggage, am excused passport control, and in less than an hour, another Pan Am flunky opens my limo door in Manhattan at Forty-Fifth and Park, the Pan Am building, and shows me into an elevator to Bill Sewall's office.

Sewall and a younger man are waiting for me. I report Pan Am will have to pay a minimum 25 percent commission, which still might not win the contract. Moreover, the threat of prosecution for bribery under the FCPA makes it too risky for the airline to contemplate paying more than 10 percent. The meeting lasts less than ten minutes, after which I, as well as Pan Am's plans for KAIA, depart.

On the curb moments later, I pause a moment before entering the limousine to eye Park Avenue up and down. I stand like Caspar David Friedrich's wanderer on his precipice; only, I'm surveying cars, limos, taxis, skyscrapers, passing salarymen rather than mist and mountains. On certain subjects, the world's great companies heed me, my firm is ascendant, *New York Times* reports my success. Eighteen months later, practice, partners, firm, and all with them are gone.

The Partners

Dan M. Burt in his law office overlooking the harbor in Marblehead, Mass.   The New York Times/Ira Wyman

Dan M. Burt in his law office overlooking the harbor in Marblehead, Mass.: "Mideast Tapped by Small Firm," *New York Times*, Friday, May 11, 1979.

You make your mistakes going in, Dale Johnson told me soon after he joined D M Burt & Associates. In his case, and that of the other two lawyers I hired to be partners—Fritz Taylor and Hynrich Wieschoff (collectively, the Partners)—the mistake I made going in was hiring them. Three years later, they proved the saying's truth when they ganged up to turf me from the law firm I'd started and built.

It was nearly seventy degrees Fahrenheit as I ran in Riyadh at dawn that morning, bone-dry, cloudless, little traffic, an unforeboding start to a late October day in the Gulf. The firm continued to grow, though more slowly than its first two years; the critical relationship with Dr. Mohamed Hoshan, my Saudi sponsor and partner, was solid; the morning cloudless and still comfortable when I entered my office shortly after nine and found this telex on my bare desk: *Dan—Come home immediately, the Partners. Signed Fritz Taylor.*

The peremptory, unprecedented command shocked me. Adrenalin-induced nausea roiled my gut. I guessed instantly, knew viscerally, what was happening—a coup. I'd had no inkling of their attack, launched when I was ten thousand kilometers away. A few days earlier, automatically, without discussion and as long agreed, my partnership interest had reduced from 50.1 percent to 49 percent, only a tad below 50 but 100 percent below control if the partners decided to act in concert, as their telex showed they had.

D M Burt & Associates had grown like kudzu its first two years, adding a new client on average every three weeks. The lawyers to service them swelled from one to seventeen. Abroad almost half the time servicing clients, I had to scramble when home to hire them, and scanted their vetting. Rather than conduct reference checks and multiple interviews that might have kept vipers from the nest, I installed rat guards to balk them. Legal control of the firm remained mine; if an associate or partner proved a problem, I fired them. Financial decisions and bank accounts stayed under my thumb; every check over $5,000 required my signature. But these protections were due to vanish in a few years, when my partnership interest dropped below 50.1 percent, because I was doling out pieces of the firm to new recruits to attract them and to existing lawyers to reflect their contributions.

But my best defense against revolt, I thought, would be the financial consequences to my partners if they ejected me. The partnership agreement required them to pay me so much that if they tried to depose me, it would be near impossible for the firm to continue if they did, unless they had substantial capital to invest, which they didn't. My calculations suggested it would be economic lunacy to remove me once I no longer had legal control of the firm, until my partnership interest shrank below, say, 35 percent. That the partners might miscalculate the financial risks of deposing me, or not understand them, did not occur to me. Secure behind this bulkhead, my head lay still on the pillow at night.

I had never indulged the fantasy of building an enduring law firm. From the start, I was sure that the glory days of the practice were numbered. My sense that I had a short-dated lease on a cornucopia[47] heightened my indifference to hires' backgrounds and ambitions; character would matter less in the short term. Once the first wave of Gulf infrastructure construction completed, the Oil Shock absorbed, the Levant would allure international businesses less. Major law and accounting firms inevitably would twig to the amount of business available and develop the expertise for which clients now used us. With their staffs, capital, international office networks, and the preference of publicly held companies for large firm advisors, multinational advisories in time would sweep aside D M Burt & Associates and its later iterations. My mantra was *Nem da gelt!* (literally, *Take the money!*), a Yiddish tradesman's phrase learned as a butcher's boy; skim the cream in the fat years and move on.

The pain I felt at the partners' power grab came not from lost money or prestige, but from the unforeseen betrayal and humiliation of being heaved from the firm I'd founded. Betrayal requires dissembling and premeditation, deeper grievance or jealousy than differences over policy or profit shares. Realizing how strong was the Partners' animus against me, and that I'd not detected it, was painful and worrying. Moreover, their betrayal dredged up memories of betrayals past by parents, lovers, businessmen, that intensified my hurt. Worst, they humiliated me before the rest of the firm's lawyers, staff, and clients, and before my wife, father, and acquaintances, who would know, or guess, defenestration had not been my idea. The Partners demonstrated my business acumen was flawed, my vision limited, my judgment poor; they had dressed me in motley.

My solitary passions—poetry, art, solo sailing, running—bared my throat, as did my background and aloofness, because they frustrated the chance for casual interactions with the partners that might have hinted

[47] "Dan Burt and Fritz Taylor had the whole world to themselves over there." *New York Times*, May 26, 1981.

at their hidden thoughts. I shared no social meals with the firm's lawyers; played no ball sports with them like baseball, touch football, hoops, bowling; joined in no holiday cookouts or office parties where an unguarded glance or comment might have tipped me off to a budding plot.

But my greatest vulnerability was my belief that reason dominated business decisions. It seemed nuts, hence quite unlikely, that the partners would risk upsetting what was a highly profitable, smooth-running practice. Why would they resent my take when I'd founded the firm, secured its client base, and was willingly reducing my share each year to reflect their contributions? I ignored how jealousy and greed well up, swell where shared in a group, join with ignorance, and, like a rogue wave, swamp judgment. That the men I employed might be unusually ambitious and mercenary lawyers should have been obvious, or they would not have left secure positions in good firms to throw in their lot with a start-up dependent on an unstable part of the world, no matter how successful at present.

I did not notice the partners frown at the sight of me, a short, slight, young Jew striding from Terminal Five at Boston's Logan Airport to meet his driver and be driven to his mansion on the sea. If a lawyer hailed from a well-regarded firm or, in one case, might bring business with them, and they impressed favorably at first, I'd hire them. On the morning the Partners' nine-word telex waited ticking on my desk in Riyadh, I had been eyeless in Gaza, blind among enemies for years.

The phone in the Taylor house on Marblehead Neck rang shortly after 3 a.m. Fritz answered:

Dan? He sounded unsurprised.

Fritz, what's this about?

Dan, we want you out. Come back now.

Since you've made up your minds, there's no sense cutting my trip short. I'll be back in ten days as scheduled. Click.

Six hours later, when it opened at 9 a.m., I called Randy Goodwin, President of the National Grand Bank in Marblehead, told him what had happened, and asked him not to process any Burt & Taylor transfers in excess of $10,000 until my return. The firm was by then the bank's largest client, I'd been a customer since coming to Marblehead, and I owned stock in the bank. As a favor, Randy honored my request.

Next, I called a lawyer at Mintz Levin—a superior, large Boston litigation law firm—and retained him. That evening, I told Dr. Hoshan what had happened and asked him to do nothing for the moment. I finished my work in Arabia and was at my campaign desk overlooking Marblehead Harbor eleven days later when, at 8:30 a.m., Taylor, Wieschoff, and Johnson entered my office.

They'd heard nothing from me since I'd hung up on Taylor in the predawn. Perhaps I'd contacted my clients, told them I was starting a new firm, rented temporary space in Boston, and persuaded loyal associates to follow me; or in order to pull down the pillars on the whole shebang, called all the clients and told them that Burt & Taylor was in chaos and headed to litigation. When a law or accounting firm's clients sniff turmoil, they flee.[48]

There was a whoosh of expelled breath when I told the conspirators I'd forgo litigation and resign immediately if they honored the firm's termination rules. These entitled me on the day I resigned to 49 percent of outstanding client receivables, unbilled work in process with no expenses to be set against completing it, cash in the firm's bank accounts, and the purchase price of our Cliff Street offices—in all, $1,450,000 in today's dollars. The partners would have to hand me a check for $950,000 of it as the ink dried on my resignation letter and the $500,000 balance within some eight weeks as clients paid their bills.

But the partners wanted more than just to see the back of me. They asked to retain my name on the letterhead, bar me from competing for two and a half years, and not bad-mouth them. In addition, they wanted me to litigate the tax case I'd filed for S&L Entertainment, ostensible employer of an entertainment stable including actors Lawrence Olivier and Jack Higgins and rock bands Led Zeppelin and Bad Company. If I won the case, the success fee of $1,250,000 due from S&L would belong to the Partners, not me. Disputes were to be settled by arbitration, with appeal to a court. In exchange, I would receive a note for $1,500,000, payable in $50,000 tranches on the first of each month for the next two and a half years for the balance of which each partner was personally liable.

I agreed. If all went perfectly, I'd leave with $2,950,000, half within eight weeks, the balance over the next thirty months; if all went perfectly, I'd leave with what I might have earned as a partner over the next three years, assuming those years were as good as the one ending, the firm's best.

---

[48] Arthur Andersen's clients dropped them, and the firm collapsed within a year of being charged with obstructing justice. The Supreme Court later held they hadn't, but by then, the firm was dead.

But all was unlikely to go anything like perfectly. When I left, half the firm's current cash reserves, receivables, and work in process would leave with me. The Partners would have to pay $300,000 for my share of the purchase price of the Cliff Street offices, as well as $50,000 per month for not competing. Their overheads would rise some 20 percent at the same time as billings fell by the amount I'd been billing. Money would be drumhead tight for at least six months and possibly much longer. Yes, the Partners now would share 100 percent of the firm's profits, but it would be some time before there was much profit to share.

Perhaps they hoped quickly to merge with O'Melveny & Meyers, a large international law firm where Taylor had been an associate before working at Aramco; perhaps their projections were rosier than mine. Whatever their plan, it would need luck, which absented itself. The *New York Times* reported the fall of Burt & Taylor as they had its rise. As the *Times* put it in a follow-up article on Burt & Taylor, "*After Mr. Burt left the firm in 1979 Mr. Taylor and its other key figures, Dale Johnson and Hynrich Wieschoff, ran into problems.*"[49]

A month almost to the day after I slunk from Burt & Taylor, Islamic fundamentalists attacked the Grand Mosque in Mecca, captured and held it for two weeks before French special forces, presumably all Muslims, recaptured it on behalf of the House of Saud. King Khalid tightened Islamic religious observance, delegated more authority to the Ulema (religious leadership) and *Mutawa* (religious police), which made Arabia less hospitable to western workers. The rise of Islamic fundamentalism, explosively displayed in the seizure of the Grand Mosque, as well as the Iranian Islamic Revolution eleven months earlier, cast a pall over Western business interest in the area. Just when the Partners needed Saudi business to expand, it began to contract.

* * *

Some clients deserted the firm because I was gone. I did nothing to encourage them to stay. While I was bound not to disparage Burt & Taylor, I was not bound to praise it. If clients asked why I'd gone, I'd say, *I can't talk about it* or *There were differences*, nonanswers hinting at malevolent machinations sufficient to send them scurrying to others for their Saudi advice.

[49] "U.S. Lawyers Frustrated in Saudi Arabia," *New York Times*, May 26, 1981.

The Partners bet I'd encourage clients to stick with them to protect my $50,000 monthly note payments. But every morning, I woke smarting, the humiliation and shame of expulsion harder to bear than pain from a boot to the groin. It wasn't more money I wanted; I had enough to need never work again. I wanted revenge. I briefed Dr. Hoshan on what the Partners had done, how they'd done it, said that all my ties to them were severed and I could no longer guarantee him a fair accounting. His relations with them deteriorated. After a few months, one of them went to Riyadh to negotiate a new sponsorship agreement with him. Talks went poorly, Dr. Hoshan threatened to jail the emissary, and he fled the Kingdom.

After Dr. Hoshan chased the Partners from the Kingdom, they failed to make the next note payment. Twenty-four hours later, I sued for its balance, some $850,000, and filed liens on the partnership's and the Partners' assets—bank accounts, homes, cars, insurance policies, investments, partnership shares. A week later, we were in arbitration. The Partners chose to represent themselves, perhaps to save money. After two hearings, my counsel urged me to settle. In exchange for canceling the note, I kept the $400,000 paid on it so far; the Partners waived all restrictions on my practicing law, removed my name from the letterhead, freed me to say what I pleased about them, and surrendered the right to the fees from the S&L case if I won it. Because information about the case was privileged, the Partners didn't know that a few weeks earlier, the U.S. had conceded the case; all that remained was to file the necessary joint stipulations with the court. Two months later, S&L paid me $1,250,000. In seven months, the Partners transmuted three years of speculative earnings into cash for me.

The Partners held a yard sale shortly after the settlement. They erected picnic tables on the Cliff Street office sidewalk, and on or beside them spread the tools of Burt & Taylor's trade: desks, office chairs, lamps, file cabinets, typewriters, staplers, staples, typing paper, yellow pads, pens, pencils, erasers, paper clips. All day, neighbors, secondhand dealers, scavengers, and passers-by picked over the offerings like starlings in a harvested cornfield. When night fell, almost a year to the day after the Partners had commanded my return, Burt & Taylor was no more.

Last Flight from Dhahran

My last trip to Saudi begins in Jerusalem. Mount Zion and the Old City's tawny walls loom ahead as we drive up from Tel Aviv's coastal plain to lunch. Early spring, 1980, my first time in Israel, I'm not here as a tourist.

The man beside me at the wheel is short, three fingers taller than a dwarf, stocky, broad, high forehead below bald, domed skull too big for his body, nose large and bulbous, skin pale, a sabra born unaltered from shtetl ancestors. He could have sat for the Nazi poster of *Der ewige Jude* (The Eternal Jew), were it reflective and smiling. You can imagine a *Meister aus Deutschland*[50] mocking him as he trudges to the death camp showers, or a corner thug from my childhood spitting some anti-Semitic slur as he knocks him out of his way, which would have been a mistake.

Avi Dvorkin is an Israeli paratrooper; there are no Zyklon B showers in his future. In the Six-Day War in 1967, he fought in Sinai; in the Yom Kippur War in 1973, the Golan and Jordan. A few years later, he did a tour in Lebanon. Quick, cool, confident, with the upper-body strength of a butcher or stevedore, he's friend and recruiter.

We met six years before, when he was Scientific Counselor at the Israeli Embassy and I head of international tax in Touche Ross's New York office. The firm had volunteered to help the Israelis negotiate a new double tax treaty with America and deputed me to advise them. Avi was one of the Israeli negotiators.

The United States and Israel sign their double tax treaty November 20, 1975. Avi returns to Israel but stays in touch, perhaps because I've told him during our treaty labors that if ever I could help Israel, I would. In fall '79, he visits me for an afternoon in Marblehead, but not to talk taxes.

On my deck's edge above the sea, legs dangling in the Indian summer midafternoon, we sit watching sailboats materialize from the haze a few miles offshore, westbound for Marblehead Harbor into the sun. Avi asks about Saudi. What's the practice like? The clients? Am I comfortable there as a Jew? Are the Saudis friendly; how do they feel about Israel, Jews, neighboring countries, especially Iran? Usually well informed, Avi's

---

[50] "Tod ist ein Meister aus Deutschland" (Death is a Master from Germany) from Paul Celan, "Todesfuge," in *Poems of Paul Celan*, trans. Michael Hamburger (Manchester: Carcanet, 2002).

knowledge of Arabia seems skimpy. When after maybe a half hour's Q and A, he broaches his visit's purpose, I realize why.

Don (Dan with an Israeli accent), there's something we'd like you to do.

What?

Open a back channel for us to the Saudis.

In the fall of 1979, the world knew Israel and the Arab world were enemies, knew Israel has no diplomatic relations with any Arab country except Egypt, knew the Iranian Islamic Revolution turned Iran vociferously anti-Israel. The world did not know what Avi tells me next. Israel has *back channels*, secret channels for diplomacy with all its regional enemies, even the most implacable, with Iran and all the Arab states, except Saudi Arabia. The Wahabi kingdom—the richest, most important Arab state—is dark to Israel; a back channel to it is essential. The Jewish homeland has sought and failed for thirty years to open one.

Israel will guarantee all communications with Saudi are secret, Avi says. Israeli representatives will meet anywhere, with anyone, at any time the Saudis designate. Cutouts will assure deniability. There will be no phone or telex traffic to be intercepted, no writings to leak. Israel will deny even to the Americans that they have a back channel to the Kingdom. Do I know a sufficiently well-placed Saudi to whom to make such an offer? If so, will I? *Yes.*

* * *

Spring, 1980. Avi and I lunch in DC. He asks me to fly to Israel to meet about the back channel. *OK.* He recommends I fly El Al airlines. In Israel, I'll stay with his family at their house outside Tel Aviv. *OK.* As I rise to leave, he presses a slip of paper in my palm, handwritten on it a phone number with a DC area code. *Don, if you have any problems with El Al at the airport, ask them to call this number.*

In my customary travel gear—jeans, fine gauge, black cashmere roll-neck, black leather zipper jacket, track shoes, luggageless but for a beat-up, soft leather, prune-brown briefcase and brown suede, two-suit carry-on—I stand at El Al's first-class check-in counter for the nonstop night flight to Tel Aviv, no one ahead or behind me. The agent: *Passport please.* The young man riffles through it, asks to check my bags. He opens, paws through them, then asks if he may take them into a back room for closer inspection. *Yes.*

My passport is a thumb thick with visas, entry, and exit stamps from Arab lands Israelis can't enter: Iran, Kuwait, Syria, Jordan, Saudi Arabia.

Passport control stamps from the world's crossroads—Amsterdam, Brussels, Berlin, Dublin, Geneva, Hong Kong, London, Paris, Rome, Zurich—swamp its dog-eared pages. The clerk's expression didn't alter as he checked my passport, but his request to inspect my luggage granularly doesn't surprise.

Ten minutes later, time enough to unpack and search my bags and all in them, the agent returns, accompanied by another man, also in his early twenties and fit. The agent lifts my bags onto the counter: *We're sorry, Sir, we're not going to allow you to board the plane*. Dumbstruck, I start to object and then remember Avi's scrap of paper. *Here*. I thrust it at him. *I was told to give you this if there was a problem*. The second man, a supervisor perhaps, takes the paper, looks at the number, walks to the end of the counter but within earshot, turns his back, dials. He speaks in Hebrew with someone, says, *Don Boort*, a few more words. In under two minutes, he's back. *We're terribly sorry, Sir. Please, let me take you to the V.I.P. departure lounge*. Around the counter, he rushes, my two bags in hand, escorts me to the lounge, introduces me to the attendant, makes sure I'm settled, apologizes again, and bowing and scraping, leaves.

* * *

I am the only passenger in the first class, upper deck of the El Al 747. The captain leaves the cockpit, introduces himself, offers to have a bed made up on the floor after takeoff. A steward appears as we level off over Nantucket, removes seat cushions, spreads sheets and blankets over them, produces pillows, and I bed down and sleep for seven hours before waking somewhere over the Med as we descend to Ben Gurion. Boarding stairs are wheeled first to the forward door on landing. A steward with my cases follows me down to a waiting car, and I'm in its back seat, where waits Avi, before the plane's other doors open. He's listing sights to see tomorrow, a lay day to recover from jet lag, as we exit Ben Gurion's gates.

* * *

Late morning, two days later, I follow Avi into a paper-napkin Jerusalem restaurant—bare ceramic tabletops, dim fluorescent ceiling lights, perhaps twelve tables, the one in the rear beside the kitchen especially dark. At the dark table, huddled over coffees, I can just make out two men. There are no other patrons; outside, little traffic on the drab commercial street. No sign announces the spot, just a line of Arabic lettering on its glass door.

The coffee drinkers don't rise as we approach. Avi introduces me, I catch the big man's name, now long forgotten, but not the small one's; I'm not sure it's offered. Fresh coffees arrive; the little man begins. Have I been briefed? *Yes.* Do I understand what they want me to do? *Yes.* Tell me what you understand we want. Our coffees are still hot when, preliminaries finished, he says, *You're on your own, do you understand? If there's trouble, we don't know you. We'll deny we ever heard your name or anything about you. We will not help you in any way, for any reason. Is that clear?*

Yes.

Are you sure you want to do this?

Yes.

He asks whom I plan to approach and why. I say Prince Fahd's private secretary. Crown Prince Fahd is next in line to the throne behind King Khalid, his older brother. Khalid is sick and dies two years later; Fahd holds the real power. Private secretaries to royal figures are as close as you get to Saudi royals. They rely heavily on them and their loyalty. I've heard rumors of disloyal ones thrown from planes at ten thousand feet over the Empty Quarter, sans parachute.

Maren Malhas, as she then was, an American graduate of the University of San Diego School of Law, is Dr. Hoshan's legal assistant. Her husband, Sam, is brother to the Crown Prince's private secretary. Several times, Sam has offered to introduce me to him if there's something with which I think he might help. Sam, of course, hopes to see a fee from any business an introduction produces. I've called Sam to say I'll be in the Kingdom in a few weeks. He says there'll be no difficulty arranging a meeting.

The small man studies me, then, *You understand except for the four of us at this table, no one in Israel knows about this, that there's no record of our discussions or anything else about you other than your help on the treaty?*

Yes.

And you're absolutely sure you want to do this?

Yes.

Good luck.

The two men rise and leave. Avi and I order lunch. We agree I'll fly to Amsterdam next morning, stay there twenty-four hours, then board a flight to Saudi. I'll stay two days in Riyadh, meet Sam's brother, and a day or two later, leave from Dhahran for London. Avi drops me at the airport next morning, his parting words, *Don, remember, if you change your mind, it's OK.*

* * *

I am no unthinking Zionist. By Halakha, rabbinic law, I am not Jewish; my maternal grandmother Catholic, my mother never a convert. By logic, observation, and family custom, I am an atheist. Israel holds no special interest as culture or country. I never contemplated aliyah (emigration to Israel) and dwell among atheists and gentiles. My Jewish friends are few, even fewer my Jewish lovers. But experience—and reading in Nazi-period German history, the Nuremberg Laws, and the sorry tale of anti-Semitism down the ages—insists that others define you no matter how hard you resist, that blood, not belief, makes a Jew. Whatever rabbinic law says, I am a Jew. My handlers had good reason to be concerned; any approach I make will mark me, if not spy, certainly an unwelcome Israeli sympathizer in the Kingdom. I don't hesitate for a heartbeat. Why?

Yes, I tell myself, a back channel will benefit both countries, perhaps even help cool a volatile region. Geopolitical logic argues Saudi and Israeli interests dovetail. Unlike Iran, Israel does not covet and, as it turns out, has no need of Saudi oil. Jewish Israelis and Muslim Saudis, both people of the Book, are not sectarian enemies, as Shiite and Sunni have been since CE 632. I know no Kingdom secrets to betray and will ask for none to pass on. But these are lawyerly reasons, makeweights. Even if I more than half believe myself clothed in invisible adamantine armor, the Israelis' concerns are real enough to have made me reconsider. They didn't; a ghost drives me, not reason.

At five years old, my mother hauled me down our back steps to fight a gentile bully who was tormenting me. At eight, my dying grandfather sat me in our kitchen and, in Yiddish-accented English, told me how Cossacks in the Pale murdered my paternal forbears.[51] As crew on my father's charter boat in my teens, I heard the Jersey charter captains taunt him with anti-Semitic slurs over the ship-to-shore—*Christ-killer*; *Ikey*; *Hey, Joe! We're starting the ovens!*—and his promises to wreak mayhem on them in reply. All my life, I heard tales of him decking and bludgeoning anti-Semites. The lesson was a Jew must fight. Joe, my father, had; now in my own way must I.

My father would not know what I planned; if successful, what I had done. Had he known, he would have tried to stop me. But what he knew didn't matter. An imperative to prove to myself, I am his equal as defender against anti-Semites compels me. Chickening out would cut a wound in my psyche; the stink of cowardice would never leave my

---

[51] See above, I, Ancestral Houses, Fourth and Daly.

nostrils. I could not have met my father's gaze again and would have had to cover all the mirrors, as I had at Bass Rock Lane when I funked writing five years earlier.

In a newly built part of Riyadh, at 11 a.m., Mr. Malhas, Crown Prince Fahd's private secretary, awaits me; punctual, somewhat stiff, a sniff haughty. A servant asks if I'd like coffee, how I take it, but before it comes, I'm on the street again. When Sam's brother understands I'm proposing a back channel to the Israelis, he throws me out; no discussion, no question how it might work, no who sent you or why, just, *Get out!*

On the curb, my head swivels up and down the street for dark-skinned men in smoked glasses and western clothing headed purposefully toward me. I'm not crestfallen; it's enough that I tried. I keep to schedule, and around 8 p.m., a few evenings later, I check in at Dhahran International Airport (DIA) for my flight to London. There, I'll report my overture's reception and, my bit done, return to America.

* * *

A tracery of thin columns supporting wavy roofs rises from the desert. The columns suggest palm trees, the roofs tent peaks or elegant mosque tops. Loosen your imagination, and you're approaching an oasis rather than the air traffic hub of Saudi's Eastern Province. DIA is a jewel among Saudi public buildings, a source of architectural inspiration across the Arab world. Completed in 1961, it amply accommodates Arabia's Eastern Province air traffic in 1980. At three in the morning, it will be near deserted.

DIA's international passengers enter the terminal, check baggage if any, receive a boarding pass, then proceed to passport control. There, uniformed Saudi passport officers—all men, dour, as passport officers worldwide are, with little or no English—glance at your travel documents, rarely ask a question. Satisfied, they cancel your visa and motion you through passport control into the departure lounge.

I always entered Saudi on a sponsored, two-week visa. Once canceled, and I pass into the departure lounge, I'm in no-man's-land, trapped till the plane leaves. I recall no public phones in the lounge, and these were pre–cell phone days. You're marooned till your plane goes wheels up off the runway.

The BA night flight to London didn't originate in Dhahran. DIA was a connecting stop en route from cities south and east, Bombay, Karachi, Singapore, Nairobi. It often arrived late from them by an hour or more. Scheduled to depart at 10:30 or 11:00 p.m.—after arriving late, unloading passengers and baggage, refueling and servicing—the flight for London-bound travelers might not take off until two or three in the morning. In the midwatch of the night, lounge almost empty, the terminal feels desolate, eerie.

The passport officer takes my thick, scuffed, eagle-fronted blue passport, riffles through it, finds the current visa, studies it. *Boort?* I nod. A few more seconds. *Dawn Boort.*

Yes.

Yoor passepoort?

Yes. A few more seconds, he cancels the visa, returns the passport. I've left the Kingdom more than twenty times in the preceding five years, and it's the first time a passport officer asks me anything.

There are perhaps three hundred people in the lounge waiting to board flights. By midnight, only passengers for London are left, perhaps seventy-five or so. Our BA L1011 doesn't land from wherever it comes from till almost 1:30 a.m.; we're unlikely to leave before 3 a.m. At 3 a.m., an announcement sounds: boarding begins in twenty minutes. I head to the toilets for a last pee.

The water closet is the size of two college classrooms. Some twenty urinals—say, in two lines of ten, small modesty panels between them—hang on the left and right walls. Perhaps ten stalls line the back wall between them. It's a clean, well-lit loo, smelling slightly antiseptic. There's no door; a U-shaped entrance—enter, turn right, four steps, left-hand U-turn—preserves privacy and eases wheelchair entry. Birds dart about near the ceiling, in and out through what I think are clerestory windows. Except for their beating wings, the room is silent. I'm alone.

I walk to the left bank of urinals, address the one nearest the entrance wall, unzip, start to piss. A man comes in behind me and takes up a stance facing the second urinal to my right. I don't realize he's there until he says,

Don't come back.

Whaddya mean, "Don't come back?"

You know what we mean. Don't come back.

Before I can store my tackle, zip, and turn to look at him, he's gone, as noiselessly as he came. I do not come back.

* * *

South Kensington, London, twenty years later. In the library of a large house a few blocks from the Natural History Museum, I stare at a famous image in a book on the Holocaust of a boy in short pants, hands raised, rousted from the Warsaw Ghetto. Behind him, a Waffen-SS man points his EMP submachine gun at the boy's back as he herds him and a crowd of mostly women and children to the transports to Treblinka, sixty-seven miles northeast of Warsaw. There will be no selection for work details at Treblinka; it's a *Vernichtungslager*, an extermination camp only. The little boy will be gassed within three hours.

Eight or nine years old when I first saw the picture, the boy's image has haunted me since, perhaps because when I first saw it, I looked like him. Had I been conceived in the Pale, like my grandfather and father before me, that boy might have been me. The image has become famous as the embodiment of the Holocaust in the half century since I first saw it. I want to understand why; what elements stamp it in memory?

In a few minutes, Paul Hodgson, a young digital artist, will join me to begin to answer that question. He's accepted a commission to attempt to expose the sinews of its emotional power. Paul paints with pixels, and our hope is that as he rearranges them in the image, its genius will play out.

Paul requires a version of the image digitized from the actual photo, a print from the negative, not a newspaper or magazine reproduction; only a digitization of the original photo will supply detail sufficient to work

SS driving Jews from Warsaw Ghetto after the uprising, 1943. *Source:* Yad Vashem.

with. A Nazi war photographer photographed the ghetto's eradication for a report to Himmler from General Jurgen Stroop, SS commander in charge of the *Aktion*. Stroop made five copies of his report, each containing the picture printed from the negative. One survives. *Where's the picture? At Yad Vashem.* Paul doesn't know if the Museum will digitize and send him the image, what their views may be on copyright and alteration, and, even if they will, from whom and how to request it. At the least, he expects it will take a long time to obtain.

When Paul leaves, I call Avi, to whom I haven't spoken in years. Next morning, when Paul opens his computer, the digitized image is on it. If my approach to the Saudis bore fruit, in even the most minor way, I never asked; had I done so, I would not have been told. But someone in Israel remembered.

Westmoreland v. CBS, et al.

Rosslyn, Virginia, conference room, Alcalde, Henderson and O'Bannon, June 1982.

Burt—*General, if you're lying, CBS will slit you open from cock to clavicle on prime-time television, hang you by your heels like Mussolini so your entrails dangle, and there won't be a fuck'n thing I can do to stop them. Do you understand me?*

Westmoreland—*I do.*

Burt—*Is the broadcast true?*

Westmoreland—*No.*

Sans due diligence, sans reflection, his *No* clanging in my ears, I commit Capital Legal Foundation (CLF) to sue CBS (Columbia Broadcasting System) on behalf of General William C. Westmoreland, U.S. commander in Vietnam 1964–1968, for libeling him in *The Uncounted Enemy: A Vietnam Deception*. It is a mad decision. My enduring indignation at America's elite has crystalized in the lot of a courtly, old, southern soldier humiliated on prime-time TV by the nation's largest network. Defending Westmoreland is not business for me; it's personal.[52]

---

[52] See David Margolick, "Legal Drama of Westmoreland Suit," *New York Times*, May 31, 1984, ¶¶ 26–29.

CBS sent *The Uncounted Enemy* into America's living rooms on Saturday night, January 23, 1982, five months before I meet the general, fourteen years after he's removed as COMUSMACV (Commander U.S. Military Assistance Command, Vietnam), and kicked upstairs. It claims in his last months as COMUSMACV, he led a military conspiracy to underreport the enemy's size to support his recent rosy take on the war: *This program* (The Uncounted Enemy) *will present evidence of what we have come to believe was a conscious effort—indeed a conspiracy at the highest levels of military intelligence—to suppress and alter critical intelligence on the enemy in the year leading up to the Tet Offensive.*[53]

When General Westmoreland returns to Saigon from reporting to a joint session of Congress in April 1967, his G3 (head of intelligence) hands him a draft cable to send to the Pentagon with MACV's new best estimate of the enemy order of battle (EOB), the number of fighters MACV (Military Assistance Command, Vietnam) reckons it faces. It's twice the number MACV estimated when the general reported to Congress days earlier. He takes issue with the new estimate, does not send it forward. *The Uncounted Enemy* claims the general suppressed the new estimate to avoid undermining support for the war, cut the size of the EOB's cadres, dropped a category of guerrilla fighters, and shrunk the new estimate to roughly MACV's old estimate.

Westmoreland sends this revised, lower EOB to his superiors in DC. It's deceptive, says the broadcast, and leaves the American public psychologically unprepared for the ferocity and initial success of the Viet Cong's attack in January '68, known as the Tet Offensive. Tet, though a massive Viet Cong military defeat, breaks America's will to fight.

When Westmoreland led his five hundred thousand U.S. troops in Vietnam, CBS was America's premier national TV news network. When CBS broadcasts *The Uncounted Enemy* a decade and a half later, it is still America's premier network, Westmoreland just an old soldier, fading away. Ever since Walter Cronkite declared the Vietnam War a stalemate and turned America against it after Tet, the general blames the TV media, CBS especially, for transforming his victory in the field into a home front defeat by undermining his countrymen's support for the war.

[53] Opening of *The Uncounted Enemy: A Vietnam Deception.*

At a press conference three days after the broadcast organized by Dave Henderson, a PR man and Westmoreland hunting companion, the general returns fire. He, senior MACV, and CIA intelligence specialists who'd supervised the EOB say the broadcast is false. CBS stands by it; the general continues to smart.

A disgruntled member of *The Uncounted Enemy*'s production team leaks the outtakes, the complete transcripts and tapes of the interviews, not just the on-air portions CBS used to make it, to *TV Guide. TV Guide* uses the outtakes to publish "ANATOMY OF A SMEAR: How CBS broke the rules and 'got' General Westmoreland" ("Smear"), an exposé detailing how the network used false attributions and unfair and misleading edits to indict the general. CBS conducts an in-house investigation, excoriates *The Uncounted Enemy*'s production values, but stands by the truth of the broadcast, then buries the in-house report.

* * *

At first, General Westmoreland didn't think to sue; the almost zero chance of a public figure successfully suing for libel in the U.S. well known. *Smear* changes his calculus. The article is clear third-party evidence from the heart of TV media that CBS unfairly attacked Westmoreland, and sparks hope in him and his supporters that a libel suit stands a chance. They argue that, biased and ratings-driven, the network cast a legitimate intelligence debate about the Viet Cong order of battle as a plot by Westmoreland to deceive the President, Congress, and the American people.

The general's friends and colleagues from the 1960s and 1970s, America's most senior movers and shakers, counsel against suing; none offer to bring the case or find someone to bring it on his behalf. Westmoreland turns to Dave Henderson to find a lawyer to represent him pro bono.

I'm running Capital Legal Foundation (CLF), a not-for-profit, public-interest law firm. Two years earlier—my ego too bruised after being chucked out of the law firm I founded to contemplate abandoning law, remarried to a British woman—I needed a base on which to rebuild a career as well as supply the excitement to which I've become addicted. I've covenanted not to compete with my ex-Partners at Burt & Taylor, so my options at law are few. The head of a former client's DC lobbying office is also Chairman of CLF. He approaches me to run Capital before the ink dries on my noncompete, which does not bar me from running a public-interest law firm.

Clientless U.S. public-interest law firms, whether right or left, are essentially culture warriors. CLF is one of them, a dozy, underfunded, one-lawyer entity. It offers a return to the policy practice that drew me to Treasury a decade earlier, as well as a crane to raise my career. I sign on as CLF's president, provided its remit is limited to pursuing libertarian-oriented economic policy. Two years later, CLF is financially sound and respected as a credible, open-markets, oriented, economic watchdog when Les Lenkowski calls me.

Lenkowski runs Smith-Richardson Foundation, a substantial CLF contributor. He asks if CLF will represent Westmoreland in a potential libel case against CBS. I say I've not seen the broadcast, read the *TV Guide* article, heard, or know anything about the controversy, think the Vietnam War history and libel suits about a general's behavior in prosecuting it not the kind of case CLF brings, but I'll watch the tape of the broadcast and read the *TV Guide* article he sends as a courtesy.

After watching *The Uncounted Enemy*, I believe Westmoreland rigged the EOB for political reasons. In close-ups called tight shots, he sweats, licks his lips, stammers, stumbles through answers, and looks away, as if nabbed with red pen poised to slash more enemy troop estimates. Interviews with his former intelligence officers admitting they'd rigged the EOB on orders from superiors explain the general's guilty bearing.

After reading *Smear*, I'm skeptical about his guilt. The people on camera admitting to skullduggery are not who the broadcast claims they were. CBS didn't interview Westmoreland's intelligence chief (G3) who revised the EOB sent to DC. Mike Wallace, who interrogates the general on air, feeds him cables that seem to confirm rigging but omits later cables that explain and defang them. The broadcast omits the general's exculpatory explanations and mischaracterizes the military significance of Tet. When I lay down the *TV Guide* autopsy, I believe a pensioner has been hatcheted, and the abuse of power that hatchet job represents troubles me.

I tell Lenkowski I'm willing to learn more. A few hours later, Henderson, whom I've never heard of, calls to arrange a meeting. In his offices next morning at 11 a.m.—on a swampy mid-June day, the Capitol dome shimmering in heat haze two miles north across the river—a gracious, erect, trim six-footer the capital's humidity has not withered, nor time weathered, offers his hand. When I shake it, all I know about Westmoreland is his name, about the intelligence dispute at the heart of the broadcast what I gleaned from watching it the night before, and about the making of the show itself what I read in *Smear*.

* * *

Westmoreland would have been my commander when I was called up to serve in Vietnam in 1966 had not army doctors rejected me as unfit after they viewed X-rays of my misshaped spine, the permanent damage from my car wreck years earlier. He's central casting's version of a four-star American army general. Full head of inch-high, white, brush-cut hair; well-trimmed bushy eyebrows; prominent cheekbones framing a clean-shaven jut jaw and slab-sided cheeks; topping six feet with no flab anywhere, he exudes command. If Mattel made a seventy-year-old Ken doll, he'd look like Westmoreland. The general moves without the stiffness you expect in a senior. Older than my father by two years, they have the same coiled energy. He greets me politely—slightly wary, perhaps a tad diffident—southern patrician charm unmistakable in grasp and smile. If this is a guilty man, he hides it well.

Born into an upper-middle-class Charleston, South Carolina, textile family, he was an Eagle Scout, devout Protestant, and First Cadet in his West Point class. He marries a colonel's daughter, has three children, does not philander. In World War II, he fights courageously in Sicily, France, and Germany and does the same in Korea five years later. He does not swear or talk smut. A graph of his career would show an unbroken arrow upward to the right, until Tet.

He sits opposite me at the boardroom table's end nearest the door, Henderson on his right. I have two questions before I can consider whether to represent him: why did he look so guilty on camera, and what happened when his then G3, General Joseph McChristian, gave him the new, doubled EOB?

He explains his on-camera demeanor as a function of how he came to be interviewed. Mike Wallace, the famed *60 Minutes*[54] "gotcha" interviewer, called him at his home in South Carolina, said CBS was preparing a program on intelligence during Vietnam, including the EOB debate, and wanted his input. Since leaving Vietnam, the general has made himself available to anyone who wants to hear him on the war. He knew Wallace, liked him, and flew to New York anticipating a fair discussion of military intelligence, despite Wallace's reputation as a hostile investigative reporter. (Kitsy, the general's wife, is prone to say *Wes still believes in Santa Claus*.)

---

[54] *60 Minutes* is an hour-long, prime-time Sunday news program featuring four fifteen-minutes, often investigative pieces. Mike Wallace was its star interviewer, renowned for his hectoring interview style.

At Black Rock,[55] the general discovers he's the accused in a star-chamber process. He says CBS took a scholastic argument among intelligence analysts about shadowy Viet Cong cadres—who, if they even existed, were not fighting his troops in the field—and hyped it into an intelligence deception that lost the war. Wallace had not hinted he wanted the general on camera as the deception's chief deceiver. Unprepared, sandbagged, and angry, what the cameras caught were Westmoreland's anger and frustration, not guilt.

What happened at MACV when you returned to Saigon from briefing Congress at the end of April 1967? I ask. The general says he was focused on the fight in the field and paid no attention to the EOB revisions percolating in G3. On his return, McChristian hands him a draft cable with new, doubled EOB estimates. The general says he scanned it and then said, *Joe, I can't send this back. We're not fighting these people.* He was in the field often and believed the irregular cadre strengths and new categories McChristian proposed to add to the EOB, if they existed, played no fighting role and could not be accurately or even roughly estimated.

What happened to the cable?
I said, "Leave it with me, Joe."
Did you send it back to Washington?
No.
What did you do with the cable, General?
I don't remember. Probably filed it.
You have no recollection, one way or the other?
No.
Are you sure?
Yes.

Shortly after handing him the draft cable, McChristian transferred as scheduled to Fort Hood, Texas. McChristian's successor at G3 reviewed and revised the new EOB downward based on Westmoreland's perception of what MACV was fighting. Westmoreland sent this revised, lower estimate back to the Pentagon.

The Uncounted Enemy suggests Westmoreland conspired to deceive President Johnson, Congress, and the public. The accusation pierced Westmoreland's heart. He's adamant and correct that the President, Joint

---

[55] CBS's black steel headquarters on West Fifty-Seventh in Manhattan was known as Black Rock.

Chiefs, and CIA knew all that happened, as it happened, in Vietnam; the general's superiors were not deceived by the argument over the EOB. Voice cracking slightly, and with a dying fall, Westmoreland says, *They accused me of treason. No one had ever called me a traitor.*

The boardroom goes quiet. Perhaps a half a minute passes in which no one speaks. Then, *General, we'll take your case.*

*   *   *

I hadn't planned to take the case on the spot. Yet without doing due diligence—talking to participants in the EOB debate, the general's superiors, peers, and friends, or researching the relevant history; without securing funding, identifying local counsel, approaching libel specialists; without telling my wife about what is likely to preoccupy and take me from home for the next several years; without watching the broadcast a second time; and despite the controversy surrounding Vietnam, Westmoreland, and the broadcast, I instantly commit CLF. His word, the slight tremolo in his voice, and lineaments of this white-haired soldier strafed by a broadcasting behemoth trigger an emotion that compels me to volunteer CLF and myself to serve him, pro bono, without concern for CLF's board, its lawyers, or my personal life.

My wife's reply when I tell her that night is *Why you?* I reel off a half dozen reasons the general should have come to me and I should take the case, including that it will be good for my career, hence her as well. But the only convincing answer is the one I won't countenance: *Because no one else would.* If the case had merit, why hadn't one of the general's famous friends in a giant law firm stood up for him? If suing CBS made sense, why hadn't some nationally known trial lawyer taken it on? Her question infuriates me because it highlights the cloud over the case and my dangerously obsessive reason for signing on.

I brought the Westmoreland case because I hated bullies and the smug intolerance of the liberal intelligentsia like my former Yale classmates and their glib assertion of moral superiority. In the general, I saw my father and myself. To America's eastern elites in 1982, Westmoreland is part of a dim, disreputable, violent caste, as to Boston Brahmins and New York *Yekkes* are working-class South Philly Jews. In CBS's scorn for Westmoreland, I see the disdain Jill Rubinson's father, Yale classmates, and Wall Street law firm partners had for me. As Westmoreland is to CBS, so I am to members of the Union League and Northeast Harbor Club, foul, with blood-smeared hands and dress. The *New Yorker*'s logo dandy peers haughtily through his monocle at both Westmoreland and me beyond the picture plane.

While there were subsidiary reasons to take the case—gild credentials, propitiate contributors, bask in notoriety the case is sure to generate—these would not have made me do it. But the general's humiliation by CBS seems to me to be the sum of all my slights. Rage roiling since high school erupts, and I spring to revenge myself on an entire culture in the guise of the Columbia Broadcasting System.

* * *

CLF's directors and staff object to bringing the case. They argue that *The Uncounted Enemy* is unlikely to be false. Even if it is, U.S. law contains a special *public figure* protection rule that makes it almost impossible for the general to sue successfully for libel. Bringing libel cases is not CLF's business. The parties' capacities to fight are grotesquely mismatched: CLF's 1982 contributions may reach $1 million; CBS's 1982 revenue is $9.3 billion, nine thousand times that of CLF's. But I had breathed life into CLF and raised all its money. CLF's board and lawyers must back me or resign. Blind and clenched-jawed, I march on. Capital Legal Foundation sues CBS for libel on behalf of General Westmoreland in Federal District Court in Greenville, South Carolina, on September 13, 1982. The general asks for $120 million in damages ($260 million in 2019), roughly $2.50 for every person who watched the broadcast, and promises any amount he's awarded to charity. The size of the damages asked for are calculated to rivet press attention. They swoop on the case like kites on carrion.

General Westmoreland's courtroom chances are too slim to rely on a trial to redeem him. Redemption will depend on trying CBS in the press for unfair reporting. If I succeed, the public will assume the network had to junk fair journalism to hang the general because he did nothing wrong. In that case, I expect CBS to sue for peace rather than suffer ongoing reputational damage. It's classic public-interest lawyer's low-cost, asymmetric warfare, possible because in America, losing litigants don't pay winners' costs. From inception, I arraign CBS before its brethren.

I'll feed the media information passed to me by sources, as well as what I winkle from the network, to try to convict CBS in the public square. *Westmoreland* is a large civil lawsuit and, like all such suits, has three stages: filing, discovery, and trial. Discovery is the long, superficially quiescent phase between lodging suit and trial, when each side demands relevant documents from the other, and deposes—questions persons under oath outside the presence of a judge—the other side's witnesses and relevant others. To the outside world, little appears to be happening, but below the public's

Cartoon of Westmoreland suing CBS

purview, the lawyers paddle furiously like swans gliding upstream, accumulating evidence and formulating proofs.

Before discovery begins, I use facts gleaned from sources inside CBS to whet the media's appetite. Several times in the first few weeks after filing, I spend the night in New York. Minutes after checking into my hotel room, someone leaves a package containing outtakes and other material outside my door. An hour later, I meet my sources for dinner and graphic dissections of *The Uncounted Enemy*'s fabrication and how CBS executives have criticized it. The next day, and every opportunity after, I pass what I learn to interested reporters while advocating how this information supports Westmoreland's case.

When discovery at last begins, it's raucous. Because CBS is a leading, sanctimonious media group, it dares not ask the court for a confidentiality order to prevent me from revealing documents they are forced to give me. Discovery occurs in full, clamorous view of the press and generates damaging story after damaging story, because I ply reporters with documents helpful to the general as we receive them, along with explanations of why they matter.

In the long pre-trial period, lasting nearly two years, CBS News became the Beirut of journalism, each day bearing the possibility of a bombshell. Burt deftly worked the press, leaking damaging titbits here and there . . . When [the judge] . . . ruled that CBS would have to turn over the Benjamin report[56] *to Westmoreland, Burt had a field day. The flaws of the broadcast got a new round of treatment in the press.*[57]

National dallies and wire services flock to the spectacle. Upscale magazines do features on the fight. The country's other TV networks air segments about the case.[58] I adopt a persona calculated to heighten press interest, dramatize an unequal fight, and humanize and elicit sympathy for the general: me, the crude, profane, street-fighter-tough David confronting a buttoned-down, blue-blooded, sniffy Goliath.

Photo of author in Washington, DC, for *TWA* in-flight magazine, 1984

[56] *The Benjamin Report*—CBS's critical, internal report on the broadcast that it refused to release on completion.
[57] Peter Boyer, *Who Killed CBS? The Undoing of America's Number One News Network*, 1988.
[58] See September 1982–June 1985: *New York Times, Washington Post, LA Times, Wall Street Journal, New York Post*, et al.; *The New Yorker, Columbia Journalism Review*; and NBC, ABC, PBS.

Eventually, it becomes hard for the media to find a benign explanation for why CBS exhumed an abstruse, fourteen-year-old intelligence analysts' debate, ten years after the end of the war it was part of; claimed it was a conspiracy to suppress information; and jettisoned good journalistic practice to finger an old general as its culprit, except as a false, calculated smear. *The Uncounted Enemy's* production, timing, and hype reek of malice and, to that extent, argue the general's innocence.

"*These disclosures, lawyers following the case say, have done more than secure the general a measure of rehabilitation unusual in a libel case. They have helped him shift the focus of the debate from the original charges against him to CBS, and its methods and motivation in putting the broadcast together.*"[59]

* * *

The press focuses on the lawyers as well as the case. My incantation that the fight is one of *might against right, a huge network with its formidable Wall Street Lawyers against a tiny law firm and its long-forgotten client*[60] is widely reported. Commentators say I seem personally involved, as if CBS had attacked me as well as Westmoreland, that it *represented . . . a personal cause, a symbolic struggle of the little guy versus privilege and power.*[61]

The *New York Times* reprises an anecdote I'd recounted from law school days.[62] A few weeks after matriculating at Yale, a fellow student who'd clerked for the summer at Cravath, Swain & Moore invited me to lunch at Mory's with John Barnum, a young star partner at Cravath. Barnum was at Yale to interview potential summer associates. I'd never been to Mory's or met Barnum or anyone else from Cravath or any other Wall Street law firm, and was thoroughly uncomfortable. The four of us—Barnum, my friend, another potential summer associate, and I—sat in a booth along the wall. The booth was large, designed for a six-foot-four-inch crew who'd *prepped* at Choate and Andover, not a five-foot-six-inch, slight, former Jewish butcher's boy from a state high school. To break the ice and calm myself, I joked, *Boy, these booths are sure big. I can hardly reach the table.* Barnum shot back, *Yes, Dan, that's the story of your life, always three inches away from the table.* The insult was gratuitous.[63] I can hear Barnum uttering it as I type.

[59] Margolick, "Legal Drama of Westmoreland."
[60] Jenkins, "The Right's Tough," *TWA Ambassador Magazine*, 1985.
[61] Boyer, *Who Killed CBS?*, 188.
[62] Margolick, "Legal Drama of Westmoreland."
[63] Margolick.

The press was right; *Westmoreland v. CBS* could not have been more personal. A few months after we filed suit, a *USA Today* reporter asked what I thought of a just-aired PBS report on the case highly critical of CBS. My tongue loosened by the champagne that CLF's staff and I had been drinking as we watched it, I snarled, *You may be watching the dismantling of a major media network.* The media repeated that quote ad nauseam to prove I brought *Westmoreland* to damage broadcasters, not restore the general's reputation. But I'd not taken aim at CBS because I harbored some grudge against the media. CBS for me was every American who ever sneered, insulted, or disdained me, every *restricted* club, every real estate broker showing me a seaside home in an exclusive community who asked, *What kind of a name is Burt?* It was against them I wanted revenge. Tom Wyman, chairman of CBS when the case ended, said I'd gotten it: *We came out of that case with a somewhat damaged image—and all the research we did proved it.*[64]

* * *

Capital Legal Foundation, Washington, DC, early September 1984. In an unupholstered, straight-backed armchair before the fireplace—shoulders squared, hands in his lap, stiff—sits General Westmoreland. To his left by the door and halfway between us, a court reporter waits in front of her shorthand machine for us to begin. It's a warm, drowsy, September Saturday midafternoon, the street quiet, we three alone in the building. I'm about to drag the general through a mock cross-examination to prepare him for trial.

If the trajectory of the Westmoreland case describes a parabola, this is its max point. The judge has refused CBS's requests to dismiss the case; trial is to begin October 9. The media believe CBS acted reprehensibly; there's a sense that the general's reputation has recovered. Ten minutes later, the trajectory heads south.

The case turns on what the general did with McChristian's draft cable and why. When we first met, the general said he didn't send the draft cable forward because he wasn't fighting the shadowy categories included in the new EOB, but didn't remember what he'd done with the draft itself. I described what had happened to Oscar Wilde when he falsely claimed the Marquess of Queensberry had libeled him and warned the general in

---

[64] Boyer, *Who Killed CBS?*, 198.

harsh, profane language the same would happen to him if he were lying. He was unshaken, and I took his word. I didn't consider what effect my warning might have on a man who'd spent his life at war.

Now, two plus years later, I'll press Westmoreland about that cable to prepare him for cross-examination. My questioning will be harsher than he'll face in court, where the judge will enforce civility, and opposing counsel fear to turn the general into a sympathetic figure by badgering, hectoring, and insulting him.

I begin gently. What had he told the President in spring 1967 about how the war was going; what had he told the Joint Chiefs?

Increase pressure. Did he know McChristian was producing a new EOB? When? Did he realize the EOB would be McChristian's swan song before transferring to Fort Hood? Had McChristian asked to meet alone? Was that customary? Was anyone else in the room when McChristian brought him the draft cable? Did McChristian think the new EOB was sensitive?

My office was courtroom still; the only sound a muffled thud of keys on the court reporter's shorthand transcription machine and the faint thrum of air conditioning condenser on the roof. Westmoreland fidgets slightly in the mock witness chair.

Lay on. *General, what did you do when you read the draft cable?*
I told Joe we weren't fighting those people.
What did he say?
I don't remember.
Really?
Yes.
Did you tell him to revise the numbers down?
No.
What did you say?
Leave the cable with me.
Then what happened?
He left.
What did you do with the cable?
I don't recall.
It was an important cable, wasn't it, General?
It contained a new estimate of the enemy's size.
That was important, wasn't it?
Well, not if it wasn't accurate.

You didn't send it back to the Pentagon, did you?

No.

Then what did you do with it?

I, I . . .

Ah, c'mon, General. What happened to the cable? Why didn't you send it back with a note saying you didn't agree with it?

Well, I . . .

You hadn't faulted McChristian's intelligence before, had you? But you overrode him about the EOB this time, didn't you? That was a pretty big deal, overriding your G3, wasn't it?

Uh. . . .

Do you expect me to believe you don't remember what you did with his cable? General, don't lie to me! What did you do with McChristian's draft cable after he left?

General William Childs Westmoreland exploded.

I'll tell you what I did with it! I threw the damn thing in file 13![65] I wasn't going to send that back to Washington! It would have been a bombshell. Those doves in the Pentagon would have got it and . . .

He stopped midsentence, aware he had just admitted *The Uncounted Enemy* was true.

I walked to the court reporter, asked for her shorthand tape and backup cassette that runs with it, then told her we were done for the day. After she left, the general rose, said good-bye, and left. I never again mentioned the cable nor prepared him further.

I lit a fire in the fireplace and burned the shorthand tape and cassette. Their status as privileged *work product* would not prevent them being stolen and/or disclosed sooner or later. I stood watching the tape burn and cassette melt, nauseous from my adrenalin rush that followed his outburst.

The case was lost. Cravath would prove the broadcast broadly true. If the general lost on the issue of truth, the blame would be mine. His supporters would fall on me like wolves on the fold. CLF's contributors, foundations, and individuals alike would howl for my scalp and perhaps return of the $3 million or so they'd given to fund the case.

[65] U.S. Army slang for trash can.

CBS, the media, and opponents of the Vietnam War would pile on, looking for payback for my having brought the case. If I resigned, whatever my excuse short of stroke or death, I'd be excoriated as a cowardly quitter. The general would turn on me. No exit.

Had Westmoreland told me when we met what he'd blurted out a few minutes earlier, I'd have declined the case. But I didn't blame him; I knew clients lie, don't know what the truth is, or believe their friends will lie for them. There were warning signs before we sued: the general's inability to recall what he'd done with the cable, McChristian's steadfast accusation, my wife's *Why you?* I couldn't convincingly answer except with a reason I refused to address. I ignored them all; it was my fault I was about to charge the guns at Balaclava.

I told no one what the general had admitted, and on October 9, began to try the case. My heart was not in it, and it showed.

Manhattan, early February 1985. The general and I are riding uptown together to our pro tem lodgings after listening to McChristian testify for CBS. He swore that when he brought Westmoreland the draft cable with the new, doubled EOB numbers, the general had said he couldn't send the higher figures back to Washington because they would *create a political bombshell* and *embarrass my commander in chief,* pretty much what Westmoreland had shouted at me during trial prep. Seated to my left on the car's back seat, Westmoreland turned to me and said,

I don't know how much more of this I can take.

Do you want me to try and settle it?

His face lit up. *Do you think you can?*

I'll call CBS when I get to my hotel.

CBS is delighted to settle on the same terms they offered two and a half years earlier—a weak apology and no money. This time, the general accepts eagerly. He signs the settlement agreement next day, on Sunday afternoon, and CBS's general counsel signs for CBS when we meet in my hotel's lounge that evening.

The news we've settled leaks within minutes. When I pass my hotel's front desk after dinner sometime around 10 p.m. that night, the concierge hands me an envelope filled with perhaps one hundred pink message slips logging calls from reporters and says the hotel switchboard has been jammed for hours.

Westmoreland holds a morning press conference the next day, Monday, and declares victory. The night before, CBS had celebrated the settlement as a win with champagne at Regine's. The certain losers are onlookers across the right/left spectrum, feeling bilked of the resolution a verdict would have delivered.

Dan Burt leaving Federal District Court House, Manhattan. *New York Times*, 1985

As I leave the speaker's dais after the general's press conference, John Scanlon, a PR man working for CBS whom I'd never met, accosts me and says, *We're going to destroy you*. A few months before trial, Van Sauter, president of CBS News, believed *"Burt was going to eat us alive."* So *CBS News did something it had never done before. It hired an outside public relations expert to help save the public image of CBS News.*[66] I return to the hotel I've slept in during the trial's five months, pack, and fly home to DC.

* * *

Scanlon does his best to make good his threat. Newspaper articles, interviews, trade magazines, TV programs, colloquia, and soon books deriding how I tried the case seem everywhere. Hate mail arrives, some of it anti-Semitic; there are a few threatening phone calls.

In the middle of the brickbat deluge, an instance of grace. One morning, I open a hand-addressed letter containing a note with a single line of script—*Don't let the bastards get you down. David*, from David Boies, Cravath partner and CBS's lead counsel. We hadn't spoken or written after the case ended and haven't since, but thirty-five years later, I still value his gesture.

I stood down at CLF; the foundation paid its bills, gave away its files, and within a few months, had locked its doors for the last time. CLF's lawyers and staff found other jobs. Westmoreland headed parades, was interviewed, and accepted plaudits from believers nationwide. The day settlement was announced, Tony Murry, my number two at CLF, passed the best judgment on the case: *It was a classic struggle of wrong against wrong.*

---

[66] Boyer, *Who Killed CBS?*, 189.

Part V

Last Window

• • • • • • • • • • • • •

Cambridge, 2021

> For even life in exile . . . is not as bad as
> life alone in one's own country.
>
> **STEFAN ZWEIG**, *The World of Yesterday*

I left U.S. public life within weeks after the Westmoreland case ended and never saw or spoke with the general again or any of the CLF lawyers or anyone from CBS or Cravath. I declined all but two requests for interviews, which I gave within days of the settlement. In both, I refused to discuss it. For thirty-five years, I said nothing about the case to anyone, not to reporters, acquaintances, wives, nor lovers.

As always after deep disappointment, I left the field: shut up, holed up, took the hit, took stock. To disappoint someone often demands premeditation. What useful explanation or insight can you expect from someone who has just taken pains to screw you? You can know or deduce with some accuracy why someone disappointed you—insecurity (my father), self-interest (Tom Field; Westmoreland), greed and jealousy (the Partners at Burt & Taylor), the advent of a preferred lover (Cynthia). Inquiry merely prolongs the pain and gives cheats like the Partners satisfaction.

In childhood, I learned it's weak, shameful, and useless to reveal you've been cut to the quick. Better cauterize the wound and move on. Abandoning the field of loss forces and hastens reflection, analysis, acceptance, and recovery. If revenge is called for, hiding your reaction to disappointment facilitates it. It was not bravado but survival that stopped me whimpering after the Westmoreland case concluded.

The press pilloried me, as CBS's PR consultant John Scanlon had promised and almost certainly facilitated. The *Washington Post*, a leading national newspaper and my hometown broadsheet, devoted its Sunday features section, beginning on its front page, to reprinting an article from a legal gossip sheet saying I'd abandoned the general. Other than from Boies, there was no word of sympathy, comfort, or encouragement from my legal peers and none from former law school classmates.

I stayed *shtum*. What the general had blurted out that afternoon in my office lay buried beneath the attorney-client privilege,[1] his to assert till death. Even had it not bound me, I would have sat mute in the stocks, as befits a fool. There, pelted by garbage, I dwelt on the confluence of arrogance and rage that set me in them, the incompatibility that from youth unsettled my life in America, where my fists seemed always clenched, and what might free me.

In the late 1970s, I'd contemplated moving to England, the stated rationale to open a London office for Burt & Taylor. However, I viewed it as the first step in emigrating. I scouted offices in the Inns of Court and opened negotiations to buy land I'd found on the sea in Ireland to build a country house. The Partners' coup at Burt & Taylor and my consequent return to policy work in DC cashiered both plans. Now, at a slug's pace, I resurrected them.

I resumed practicing international tax law and soon founded my second law firm. It grew quickly, but with British, not U.S., clients, the heart of the practice international tax advice for FTSE 100 companies with U.S. subsidiaries. Significant U.S.-based clients were nonexistent. Things went better on the Atlantic's eastern than its western shores, both socially and commercially. Was it a coincidence that both law practices I'd built were rooted outside and east of the United States?

I'd been uneasy in America since returning from Cambridge twenty years earlier. The Westmoreland case taught me that it was more than

---

[1] The attorney-client privilege is a legal rule that forbids lawyers to tell others what their client has told them, unless the client gives their consent. The privilege is personal to the client and does not survive them.

unease that dogged me; it was anger. Elements of U.S. society were intolerable: the pressure to conform, the religiosity, the bigotry, the triumphal White Christian nationalism and smugness going under the rubric of *American exceptionalism*, the provinciality to be endured if I was to practice law for U.S. clients and rub along happily in Uncle Sam's society.

I began to appreciate that in the States, unconventionality rouses suspicion, whereas in Britain it's welcomed. More problematic than my origins, class, wealth, or ethnicity, my difference, irreverence, and atheism set American teeth grinding. The U.S. charge sheet listed unorthodoxy, eccentricity, and novelty as my crimes, character flaws too deep for extirpation.

America generally does not welcome eccentric or unorthodox views, especially in the practice of corporate law. Leading lawyers there practice in giant firms, and U.S. legal practice—unlike British—does not have barristers, who must practice alone. There is no cognate in American English for the British phrase *horses for courses*. American xenophobia, currently on prominent display, fears and shuns those who are out of sync in trade or lifestyle. The land of opportunity may be a melting pot, but it's outsiders who melt. There, I would always be out of step, hands balled for brawling.

I live in England now, exile by choice. Twenty-seven years ago, I moved here from DC, became a Brit, and sixteen years ago, renounced U.S. citizenship. Thomas Wolfe maintained you can't go home again—literally true in my case. I kept a seaside house in Maine when I left and visit it several times a year but, by law, cannot stay too long or return to live there. Entering America, I snake through the alien's channel at passport control like every other British citizen; leaving, I board a flight east, the right direction, to Heathrow. There, I use the U.K. passports channel and never clench my fist.

The author's set, St. John's College, Cambridge

Dan Burt, June 2021

Acknowledgments

Without the unflagging editing of John Kerrigan, Fellow of St. John's College and professor of English at Cambridge University, this book would not have appeared. He saved me from solecisms, confusions, inconsistencies, drivel, and liability. The faults remaining are mine.

Michael Schmidt, Carcanet Press' publisher, encouraged me to begin what became EWD, then published its U.K. edition. Peter Dougherty, Director Emeritus of Princeton University Press, led me to Micah Kleit, Director of Rutgers University Press, publisher of EWD's U.S. edition. Maren Meinhardt, a masterful copy editor, saw EWD into print; Harriet Griffey edited the first draft presented to publishers.

To the Master and Fellows of St. John's College, Cambridge, I'm indebted for the set, where I wrote substantial portions of EWD, and for listening patiently as I retold some of the events recounted in it.

But above all, I owe my wife, Yvonne, a debt I can never repay.

Index

About the Author

DAN BURT was born in 1942 in South Philadelphia, read English at St. John's College, Cambridge, and in 1969, graduated from Yale Law School. He has practiced commercial, government, and public-interest law in the United States, the United Kingdom, and Saudi Arabia; has been a businessman; and, since 2001, is an Honorary Fellow of St. John's. Carcanet Press published his first poetry collection in 2008 and his fourth in 2019. Marlborough Graphics / Lintott Press brought out a poetry and photography collaboration with Paul Hodgson (2010), and *You Think It Strange*, his brief childhood memoir, appeared in the United Kingdom and the United States (2014, 2015). U.K. and U.S. newspapers, periodicals, and anthologies have featured his poetry and prose—*The Financial Times*, *The Sunday Times*, *The New Statesman*, *Commonweal*, *TLS*, *Granta*, *PN Review*, and *Clutag Press*, among others—as has the BBC and Poetry Archive. He lives and writes in London, Cambridge, and Schooner Head, Maine.